1 MONTH OF
FREE
READING

at
www.ForgottenBooks.com

By purchasing this book you are eligible for one month membership to ForgottenBooks.com, giving you unlimited access to our entire collection of over 1,000,000 titles via our web site and mobile apps.

To claim your free month visit:
www.forgottenbooks.com/free1374626

ISBN 978-1-397-32152-7
PIBN 11374626

This book is a reproduction of an important historical work. Forgotten Books uses
state-of-the-art technology to digitally reconstruct the work, preserving the original format
whilst repairing imperfections present in the aged copy. In rare cases, an imperfection in
the original, such as a blemish or missing page, may be replicated in our edition. We do,
however, repair the vast majority of imperfections successfully; any imperfections that
remain are intentionally left to preserve the state of such historical works.

❧ 1897=1898 ❧

ANNOUNCEMENT

COLLEGE OF

Physicians and Surgeons

OF ONTARIO

And Report of Proceedings of Ontario Medical Council, July, 1897

FOR THE ACADEMIC YEAR, 1897-98.

BY AUTHORITY.

❧

REGISTRY OFFICE, COLLEGE OF PHYSICIANS AND SURGEONS OF ONTARIO,

South-East Corner Bay and Richmond Sts., Toronto.

JULY, 1897.

Published for the College of Physicians and Surgeons of Ontario by WILLIAM BRIGGS, Toronto.

MAIN BUILDING

Consulting Physicians and Surgeons.

General Diseases:
Drs. WM. E. QUINE,
· · · · Chicago
I. N. DANFORTH,
· · · · Chicago
FRANK BILLINGS,
· · · · Chicago
E. L. SHURLY,
· · · Detroit
G. H. FUERBRINGER,
· · · Saginaw
J. B. GRISWOLD,
· · · Grand Rapids

Surgery:
JOHN B. HAMILTON,
· · · · · Chicago
D. W. GRAHAM,
· · · · Chicago
THEO. A. McGRAW,
· · · · Detroit
G. K. JOHNSON,
· · · Grand Rapids

Gynæcology:
JAMES H. ETHERIDGE,
· · · · Chicago
HENRY T. BYFORD,
· · · · Chicago
H. W. LONGYEAR,
· · · Detroit
EUGENE BOISE,
· · · Grand Rapids

Nervous Disease:
H. M. LYMAN,
· · · · Chicago
D. R. BROWER,
· · · · Chicago
RICHARD DEWEY,
· · · Chicago
W. J. HERDMAN,
· · · Ann Arbor

Eye and Ear:
BOERNE BETTMAN,
· · · · · Chicago

Nose and Throat:
E. FLETCHER INGALS,
· · · Chicago

Pathology:
HENEAGE GIBBS,
· · · Ann Arbor

ELMORE S. PETTYJOHN, M.D.,
Medical Superintendent.

The ∙ ∙ Alma

A quiet, restful, modern, elegant
health-home free from
appearance of
invalidism

THE BUILDINGS are roomy, cheerful and commodious, erected for the purpose, and completely equipped. Every facility is present for the study and treatment of such chronic and convalescent conditions as are difficult to treat at home. Guests consult and are referred here by their own physicians. Every form of massage and scientific hydrotherapeutics is practiced, including Electric, Turkish, Russian, and the peculiar Alma-Bromo Mineral Bath. All treatments are prescribed by the physicians and administered by trained nurses. Static, Galvanic and Faradic electricity are skillfully applied.

A regulated, wholesome, nutritious dietary, with everything in season, is furnished. There are pure agreeable spring waters.

The climate is equable and delightful. Ample provision is made in the large private park and grounds for tennis, cycling, other amusements and out-door life. A liberal discount is accorded to the profession. Alma is on the tourist list the year round. A descriptive pamphlet will be sent on application, and all inquiries cheerfully answered.

Address—

Alma Sanitarium Co.,
ALMA, MICH.

ANNOUNCEMENT

OF THE

College of Physicians and Surgeons

OF ONTARIO.

FOR THE ACADEMIC YEAR, 1897-98.

BY AUTHORITY.

REGISTRY OFFICE:

COLLEGE OF PHYSICIANS AND SURGEONS OF ONTARIO

SOUTH-EAST COR. BAY AND RICHMOND STS., TORONTO.

JULY, 1897.

CONTENTS

AND

INDEX TO PROCEEDINGS.

THE COUNCIL

OF THE

College of Physicians and Surgeons of Ontario

TERRITORIAL REPRESENTATIVES.

DIVISION

J. L. Bray, M.D., Chatham, Ont....No. 1
J. A. Williams, M.D., Ingersoll, Ont. ɪɪ 2
W. F. Roome, M.D., London, Ont ... ɪɪ 3
W. Graham, M.D., Brussels, Ont.... ɪɪ 4
L. Brock, M.D., Guelph, Ont. ...... ɪɪ 5
J. Henry, M.D., Orangeville, Ont.... ɪɪ 6
G. Shaw, M.D., Hamilton, Ont....... ɪɪ 7
J. P. Armour, M.D., St. Catharines,
 Ont............................. ɪɪ 8
J. Hanly, M.D., Midland, Ont...... ɪɪ 9

DIVISION

E. J. Barrick, M.D., Toronto, Ont...No. 10
H. T. Machell, M.D., Toronto, Ont. ɪɪ 11
J. H. Sangster, M.D., Port Perry,
 Ont............................. ɪɪ 12
J. W. McLaughlin, M.D., Bowman-
 ville, Ont......................... ɪɪ 13
T. H. Thornton, M.D., Consecon, Ont. ɪɪ 14
W. W. Dickson, M.D., Pembroke, Ont. ɪɪ 15
R. Reddick, M.D., Winchester, Ont.. ɪɪ 16
A. F. Rogers, M.D., Ottawa, Ont.... ɪɪ 17

COLLEGIATE REPRESENTATIVES.

W. Britton, M.D., Toronto, Ont...................... University of Toronto.
H. S. Griffin, M.D., Hamilton, Ont.................. ɪɪ Victoria College.
V. H. Moore, M.D., Brockville, Ont................. ɪɪ Queen's College.
W. J. Douglas, M.D., Cobourg, Ont................. ɪɪ Trinity College.
J. Thorburn, M.D., Toronto, Ont .... Toronto School of Medicine.
F. Fowler, M.D., Kingston, Ont..................... { Royal College of Physicians and Surgeons, Kingston.
W. B. Geikie, M.D., Toronto, Ont.................... Trinity Medical College.
W. H. Moorhouse, M.D., London, Ont............... Western University, London.

HOMŒOPATHIC REPRESENTATIVES.

George Logan, M.D., Ottawa, Ont.
Cl. T. Campbell, M.D., London, Ont.
W. J. H. Emory, M.D., Toronto, Ont.

G. Henderson, M.D., Strathroy, Ont.
L. Luton, M.D., St. Thomas, Ont.

Medical Registration Office of the College of Physicians and Surgeons of Ontario, south-east corner Bay and Richmond Streets, Toronto.

Office Hours : 2 to 4 p.m.

ROBERT A. PYNE, M.D., M.C.P.S.O., Toronto, Ont., *Registrar.*

OFFICERS

OF THE

College of Physicians and Surgeons of Ontario

FOR 1897-98.

President.................J. THORBURN, M.D., Toronto, Ont.

Vice-President............J. HENRY, M.D., Orangeville, Ont.

Treasurer................H. WILBERFORCE AIKINS, M.D., Toronto, Ont.

Registrar................R. A. PYNE, M.D., Toronto, Ont.

BOARD OF EXAMINERS, 1897-98.

DR. F. LeM. GRASETT, Toronto, Ont.. *Anatomy, Descriptive.*

DR. D. E. MUNDELL, Kingston, Ont.. *Theory and Practice of Medicine.*

DR. H. HOWITT, Guelph, Ont........ { *Midwifery, Operative and other than Operative, and Puerperal and Infantile Diseases, Diseases of Women and Children.*

DR. A. S. FRASER, Sarnia, Ont...... *Physiology and Histology.*

DR. A. B. WELFORD, Woodstock, Ont. *Surgery, Operative and other than Operative.*

DR. H. WILLIAMS, London, Ont...... *Medical and Surgical Anatomy.*

DR. G. ACHESON, Galt, Ont.......... *Chemistry, Theoretical, Practical, and Toxicology.*

DR. H. B. SMALL, Ottawa, Ont....... *Materia Medica and Pharmacy.*

DR. C. V. EMORY, Hamilton, Ont.... *Medical Jurisprudence and Sanitary Science.*

DR. C. O'REILLY, Toronto, Ont...... *Assistant Examiner to the Examiner on Surgery.*

DR. J. THIRD, Kingston, Ont,........ *1st Assistant Examiner to Examiner on Medicine.*

DR. W. P. CAVEN, Toronto, Ont...... { *2nd Assistant to the Examiner on Medicine, Pathology, Therapeutics and Bacteriology.*

DR. E. T. ADAMS, Toronto, Ont...... *Homœopathic Examiner.*

STANDING COMMITTEES OF COUNCIL

OF THE

College of Physicians and Surgeons of Ontario

FOR 1897-98.

REGISTRATION COMMITTEE.

Dr. Fowler (*Chairman*).	Dr. Hanly.	Dr. Roome.
Dr. Campbell.	Dr. McLaughlin.	Dr. Shaw.
	Dr. Griffin.	

RULES AND REGULATIONS COMMITTEE.

Dr. Hanly (*Chairman*).	Dr. Douglass.	Dr. Reddick.
Dr. Armour.	Dr. Luton.	

FINANCE COMMITTEE.

Dr. Henderson (*Chairman*).	Dr. Bray.	Dr. Roome.
Dr. Armour.	Dr. Brock.	

PRINTING COMMITTEE.

Dr. Barrick (*Chairman*).	Dr. Luton.	Dr. McLaughlin.
Dr. Graham.	Dr. Machell.	

EDUCATION COMMITTEE.

Dr. Britton (*Chairman*).	Dr. Emory.	Dr. Rogers.
Dr. Bray.	Dr. Moore,	Dr. Sangster.
Dr. Dickson.	Dr. Moorhouse.	Dr. Williams.

PROPERTY COMMITTEE.

Dr. Machell (*Chairman*).	Dr. Emory.	Dr. Thornton.
Dr. Barrick.	Dr. Graham.	

COMPLAINTS COMMITTEE.

Dr. Geikie (*Chairman*).	Dr. Logan.	Dr. Shaw.
Dr. Fowler.	Dr. Reddick.	

EXECUTIVE COMMITTEE.

Dr. Thorburn (*Chairman*).	Dr. Henry.	Dr. Campbell.

DISCIPLINE COMMITTEE.

Dr. Bray (*Chairman*),	Dr. Moore,	Dr. Logan,
Chatham, Ont.	Brockville, Ont.	Ottawa, Ont.

The President and Vice-President are *ex officio* members of all Committees, excepting the Discipline Committee, and the Chairman of any Committee is *ex officio* a member of any Sub-Committee thereof.

OFFICERS

OF THE

College of Physicians and Surgeons of Ontario

FROM 1866 TO 1897-98.

[PRESIDENTS.

1. John R. Dickson...From 1866 to 1867	18. J. L. Bray.........From 1882 to 1883
2. John Turquand.... '' 1867 '' 1868	19. G. Logan .... '' 1883 '' 1884
3. James A. Grant.... '' 1868 '' 1869	20. H. W. Day .... '' 1884 '' 1885
4. William Clark..... '' 1869 '' 1870	21. D. Bergin.......... '' 1885 '' 1886
5. William H. Brouse. '' 1870 '' 1871	22. H. H. Wright...... '' 1886 '' 1887
6. Chas. W. Covernton.June to Dec., 1871	23. G. Henderson...... '' 1887 '' 1888
7. William Clark....Dec., †1871 '' 1872	24. J. H. Burns....... '' 1888 '' 1889
8. J. F. Dewar.......From 1872 '' 1873	25. J. G. Cranston .... '' 1889 '' 1890
9. William Clark .... '' 1873 '' 1874	26. V. H. Moore....... '' 1890 '' 1891
10. M. Lavell......... '' 1874 '' 1875	27. J. A. Williams..... '' 1891 '' 1892
11. E. G. Edwards.. .. '' 1875 '' 1876	28. F. Fowler .... '' 1892 '' 1893
12. Daniel Clark...:.. '' 1876 '' 1877	29. C. T. Campbell..... '' 1893 '' 1894
13. Daniel Clark...... '' 1877 '' 1878	30. D. L. Philip .... '' 1894 '' 1895
14. D. Campbell ...... '' 1878 '' 1879	31. W. T. Harris...... '' 1895 '' 1896
15. J. D. Macdonald... '' 1879 '' 1880	32. A. F. Rogers....... '' 1896 '' 1897
16. W. Allison .... '' 1880 '' 1881	33. J. Thorburn .,.... '' 1897 '' 1898
17. D. Bergin.......... '' 1881 '' 1882	

VICE-PRESIDENTS.

1. Wm. H. Brouse ....From 1866 to 1870	16. E. W. Spragge .....From 1884 to 1885
2. Chas. W. Covernton '' 1870 '' 1871	17. R. Douglas........ '' 1885 '' 1886
3. James Hamilton.... '' 1871 '' 1872	18. G. Henderson...... '' 1886 '' 1887
4. D. Campbell........ '' 1872 '' 1873	19. J. H. Burns....... '' 1887 '' 1888
5. John Muir......... '' 1873 '' 1874	20. J. G. Cranston..... '' 1888 '' 1889
6. E. G. Edwards ..... '' 1874 '' 1875	21. V. H. Moore....... '' 1889 '' 1890
7. E. M. Hodder ..... '' 1875 '' 1876	22. J. A. Williams..... '' 1890 '' 1891
8. D. Campbell .... '' 1876 '' 1877	23. F. Fowler......... '' 1891 '' 1892
9. D. Campbell .... '' 1877 '' 1878	24. C. T. Campbell..... '' 1892 '' 1893
10. W. Allison......... '' 1878 '' 1879	25. D. L. Philip .... '' 1893 '' 1894
11. G. Logan .... '' 1879 '' 1880	26. W. T. Harris...... '' 1894 '' 1895
12. D. Bergin.......... '' 1880 '' 1881	27. A. F. Rogers....... '' 1895 '' 1896
13. J. L. Bray......... '' 1881 '' 1882	28. J. Thorburn....... '' 1896 '' 1897
14. W. B. Geikie...... '' 1882 '' 1883	29. J. Henry.......... '' 1897 '' 1898
15. H. W. Day......... '' 1883 '' 1884	

TREASURER.

W. T. Aikins.....................................From 1866 to 1897
H. Wilberforce Aikins.......................... '' 1897

REGISTRARS AND SECRETARIES.

Henry Strange.........From May 3rd, 1866, to September 2nd, 1872.
Thomas Pyne........... '' September 2nd, 1872, to July 15th, 1880.
Robert A. Pyne .... '' July 15th, 1880.

---

* The President, Vice-President, Treasurer and Registrar of the College are elected at the Annual Meeting of the Council, and hold office until their successors are elected.

† Dr. William Clark was elected December 12th, 1871, at a special meeting of the Council, in consequence of the resignation of Dr. C. W. Covernton.

College of Physicians and Surgeons

OF ONTARIO.

ANNOUNCEMENT FOR THE ACADEMIC YEAR 1897-98.

"THE COLLEGE OF PHYSICIANS AND SURGEONS OF ONTARIO" is the name adopted by the Medical Profession of the Province of Ontario in its corporate capacity. As every legally qualified medical practitioner in the Province is a member of this College, it is not an institution for the teaching of medicine.

The Medical Profession of Ontario was first incorporated under this name by an Act of the Parliament of Canada, passed in 1866. This Act was subsequently repealed by the Legislature of Ontario in 1869, and now the affairs of the Profession in this Province are regulated by an Act passed in 1874 (37 Vic., Cap. 30), commonly known as the "Ontario Medical Act,' and further amended in 1887, 1891, 1893 and 1895.

By this Act, the "COUNCIL OF THE COLLEGE OF PHYSICIANS AND SURGEONS OF ONTARIO" is empowered and directed to enact by-laws for the regulation of all matters connected with medical education; for the admission and enrolment of students of medicine; for determining from time to time the curriculum of the studies to be pursued by them, and to appoint a Board of Examiners before whom all must pass a satisfactory examination before they can be enrolled as members of the College, and thus be legally qualified to practise their profession in the Province of Ontario.

The Council, moreover, has power and authority conferred upon it by this Act to fix the terms upon which practitioners of medicine, duly qualified in other countries, may be admitted as members of the College of Physicians and Surgeons of Ontario, this being the only mode in which they can become legally entitled to practise their profession in this Province.

For the information and guidance of students of medicine, the Profession, and the public generally, the Council, in conformity with the Ontario Medical Act, hereby promulgates for the year 1897-98 the REGULATIONS which herein follow, repealing all others heretofore in force.

Regulations for 1897-98.

SECTION I.—MATRICULATION.

Everyone desirous of being registered as a matriculated medical student in the Register of this College, except as hereinafter provided, shall be required to pay a fee of twenty dollars and to conform to the following regulations :

1. Any person who presents to the Registrar of the Medical Council a certificate that he has passed the examination conducted by the Education Department on the course prescribed for matriculation in arts, including chemistry and physics, and approved by the Lieutenant-Governor in Council, shall be entitled, on payment of the lawful fees in that behalf, to registration as a medical student within the meaning of Section 11 of the Ontario Medical Act.

2. Any person who before the 15th day of June, 1896, had not passed the examination in all the subjects prescribed for matriculation as aforesaid, shall be entitled to registration as a medical student on submitting to the Registrar a certificate that he has completed such examination by passing in the remaining subjects of such matriculation, including chemistry and physics.

3. Any student in medicine who submits to the Registrar certified tickets that he has attended not less than two courses of lectures at any chartered medical school or college in Canada, shall be entitled, on payment of the lawful fees in that behalf, to take the Primary examination, provided that the standing obtained at such examination may not be allowed until such student presents to the Registrar the matriculation certificate. But this privilege shall not be available on or after November 1st, 1898.

4. A certificate from the Registrar of any chartered university conducting a full arts course in Canada, that the holder thereof has passed the senior matriculation of such university or the examination conducted at the end of the first year in arts by such university, shall entitle such holder to registration. This provision shall remain in existence up to November 1st, 1899.

5. Any person who, on or before the 1st day of November, 1895, had passed the examination of any university in Canada for matri-

culation in arts, or the matriculation examination conducted by the Education Department entitling to registration in arts with any university in Canada—or an examination entitling to registration with the Medical Council subsequent to July 1st, 1888—shall be entitled to registration on submitting to the Registrar a certificate to that effect, signed by the proper officer in that behalf ; but these qualifications shall stand up to the 1st November, 1899.

6. Graduates in arts, in any university in Her Majesty's dominions, are not required to pass this examination, but may register their names with the Registrar of the College upon giving satisfactory evidence of their identity, the presentation of a certificate of qualifications and the payment of the fee of twenty dollars.

7. Excepting as provided for in Sub-section 3 of Section I. herein—every medical student after matriculation shall be registered in the manner prescribed by the Council, and this will be held to be preliminary to his medical studies which will not be considered to begin until after the date of such registration.

SECTION II.—MEDICAL CURRICULUM.

1. Every student must spend a period of five years in actual professional studies, except as hereinafter provided ; and the prescribed period of studies shall include four winter sessions of not less than eight months each. The fifth or final year shall be devoted to clinical work, six months of which may be spent with a registered practitioner in Ontario, and six months must be spent at one or more public hospitals, dispensaries or laboratories devoted to physiological or pathological research, Canadian, British or foreign, approved by the Council. The regulations relating to the eight months shall come into effect on the first of October, 1899.

2. Graduates in arts or science of any college or university recognized by the Council who shall have spent a year in the study of physics, chemistry and biology, and shall

have passed an examination in the subjects in their university course shall be held to have completed the first year of the five years of medical study ; after three years of attendance upon medical studies shall be eligible for the intermediate examination, and must thereafter comply with the requirements for the fifth or final year which is to be devoted to clinical work.

Homœopathic students who attend four sessions at any medical college where nine-month sessions are taught, to be held equal to four winter sessions of this College. This shall not in any way interfere with the practical and clinical work as prescribed by the Medical Council of Ontario for the fifth year.

No ticket for lectures will henceforward be accepted by the Council unless it is endorsed thereon that, as shown by teachers' roll, the pupil has at least attended seventy-five per cent. of the set number of lectures of each course—and it is enacted that said certificate shall specifically state that such attendance extended over a period of at least 75 per cent. of the eight-month course.

3. Application for every professional examination must be made to the Registrar of the College of Physicians and Surgeons of Ontario two weeks prior to examinations. No application will be received unless it is accompanied by the necessary tickets and certificates, and by the Treasurer's receipt showing that the fees have been paid.

4. Excepting as hereinafter specified each six or eight months' course shall consist of not less than fifty lectures, and each "three or four months' course" of not less than twenty-five lectures.

5. Every student must attend the under-mentioned courses of lectures in a university, college or school of medicine approved of by the Council, viz. :

Two courses of not less than six ·or eight months each (in the different years) upon—

Anatomy.

Practical Anatomy.

Physiology (including Histology).

Theoretical Chemistry.

Materia Medica and Therapeutics.

Principles and Practice of Medicine.

"   "   "   Surgery.

Midwifery and Diseases of Women.

Two courses of six or eight months consisting of not less than one hundred lectures and demonstrations in

Clinical Medicine.

Surgery.

One course of not less than six or eight months upon—

Medical Jurisprudence.

Medical, Surgical and Topographical Anatomy.

Two courses of not less than three or four months each (in different years) upon—

Diseases of Children.

Practical Chemistry (including Toxicology).

One course of three or four months upon—

Sanitary Science.

Practical Pharmacy.

The latter to be taken prior to candidate presenting himself for examination on Materia Medica and Pharmacy.

One course of ten lectures upon—

Mental Diseases.

One course of fifty demonstrations upon—

Physiological Histology.

Two courses of six or eight months each consisting of fifty lectures and demonstrations in Pathology.

One course of three or four months consisting of twenty-five lectures and demonstrations in Bacteriology.

A certificate of having attended five lectures, and five demonstrations upon the use of Anæsthetics.

6. Every candidate will be required to prove that he has carefully dissected the adult human body.

7. The following are the text-books recommended by the Council in the various branches :

GENERAL TEXT-BOOKS.

Anatomy—Gray, Quain, Cunningham's Practical Anatomy.

Physiology—Foster, Kirke, Yeo.

Chemistry—Roscoe, Attfield, Remsen and Jones, Richter, Simons.

Materia Medica—Ringer, Mitchell Bruce, Hare's Therapeutics, British Pharmacopœia and Therapeutics.

Surgery—Erichsen, Treves, Mansell Moulin, American System of Surgery.

Medicine—Hilton Fagge, Strumpell, Osler, Roberts.

Clinical Medicine—Gibson and Russel, Vierordt.

Midwifery and Gynæcology—Lusk, Thomas Munde, Playfair, Hart and Barber, American Text-Book of Obstetrics.

Medical Jurisprudence and Toxicology—Taylor, Reese.

Pathology—Ziegler, Green, Woodhead, Coates.

Sanitary Science—Wilson, Louis C. Parke.

Diseases of Children—Eustace Smith, Ashby and Wright, Goodhart.

HOMŒOPATHIC TEXT-BOOKS.

Materia Medica—Hahnemann, Hering.

Medicine and Therapeutics — Goodno, Arndt, Raue's Pathology and Diagnostics, Lilienthal.

Surgery—Fisher, Helmuth.

Midwifery—Guernsey, Ludlam.

8. Also must have attended the practice of a general hospital for twenty-four months during the first four years of study.

9. Also must have attended six cases of midwifery.

10. Also must, before being registered as a member of the College of Physicians and Surgeons of Ontario, have passed all the examinations herein prescribed, and attained the full age of twenty-one years.

11. Graduates in medicine from recognized colleges outside the Dominion of Canada, who desire to qualify themselves for registration, must pass the matriculation required by the Council; and must attend one or more full winter courses of lectures in one of the Ontario medical schools, and must complete fully the practical and clinical curriculum required by the Council after the fourth year, and shall pass before the examiners appointed by the Council all the examinations hereinafter prescribed, so as to complete fully the curriculum.

12. British registered medical practitioners, on paying all fees and passing the Intermediate and Final examinations shall be registered, provided they have been domiciled in Britain for five years after having been registered therein as practitioners.

SECTION III.—EXAMINATIONS.

1. The professional examinations are divided into three parts: A "Primary," "Intermediate" and "Final."

2. The Primary examination shall be undergone after the second winter session, and the Intermediate after the third or fourth winter session, the Final after the fifth year.

3. The following branches shall be embraced in the Primary examination:

a. Anatomy.

b. Physiology and Histology.

c. Chemistry (Theoretical and Practical).

d. Materia Medica and Pharmacy.

4. Every candidate for the Primary examination will be required to present, with his lecture tickets, a certificate of having undergone and passed an examination at the school he has attended at the close of his first winter session on Primary branches. Also a certificate of ability to make and mount microscopic specimens.

5. Each candidate for final examination must present a certificate of attendance at six post mortem examinations, a certificate of ability to draw up a report of a post mortem examination ; a certificate of having reported satisfactorily six cases of clinical medicine, and six cases of clinical surgery, and a certificate of having passed his Intermediate examination, the certificates to be signed by the teachers referred to upon these subjects, or the practitioner holding post mortem.

6. All candidates shall (excepting art graduates) present a certificate of having passed at the close of their third session in the college or school they may have attended, an examination in such parts of medicine, surgery and midwifery as may be thought advisable by the faculties of the respective colleges or schools. This examination is not in any way to interfere with any of the examinations of the Council. One year's attendance after the Intermediate examination as House Surgeon or Physician in any Hospital recognized by the Council shall be held to be equivalent to the fulfilling of the requirements for the fifth year of clinical work.

The following branches shall be embraced in the intermediate examination :

a. Medical, Surgical and Topographical Anatomy.

b. Principles and Practice of Medicine.

c. General Pathology and Bacteriology.

d. Surgery, other than Operative.

e. Surgery, Operative.

f. Midwifery, other than Operative.

g. Midwifery, Operative.

h. Medical Jurisprudence, including Toxicology and Mental Diseases.

i. Sanitary Science.

j. Diseases of Children.

k. Diseases of Women.

l. Therapeutics.

7. The Primary and Intermediate examinations shall be "written" and "oral." The Final "oral" and "clinical."

8. The following branches will be embraced in the Final examination :

a. Clinical Medicine.

b. Clinical Surgery.

c. Diseases of Women.

d. Diseases of Children, Medical and Surgical.

9. Candidates for the Primary who fail in all subjects but two, must make 60 per cent. in each of these subjects, or get no credit for any. Candidates for Intermediate who fail in all subjects save three, will be allowed those three if they pass 60 per cent. in each.

10. Candidates who intend to be examined by the Homœopathic Examiner in special subjects, shall signify their intention to the Registrar at least two weeks previous to the commencement of the examination, in order that he may provide means of preventing their identification by the other students, or by the Examiners.

11. In the event of any candidate signifying his intention to the Registrar to be examined and registered as a homœopathic practitioner, due notice of such must be submitted to the Registrar, so that the examinations may be conducted by the parties appointed for that purpose; prior to the acceptance of such notice from the candidate, the usual fees must be paid. In the event of any candidate presenting himself for such examination, due notice must be given by the Registrar to the special Examiner.

12. A professional examination will be held in Toronto on the second Tuesday in October, 1897. All candidates who have failed in a former examination will be required to pay a fee of twenty dollars for this examination. The next professional examination thereafter will be held at Toronto and Kingston on the third Tuesday in May, 1898.

SECTION IV.—FEES.

1. The following scale of fees has been established by the Council of the College of Physicians and Surgeons of Ontario :

a. Registration of matriculation...$20 00

b. Primary examination.......... 20 00

c. Final examination, including registration 30 00

These fees are to be paid to the Treasurer of the College before each examination.

d. Registration of persons duly qualified before 23rd day of July, 1870................. 10 00

e. Registration of persons duly qualified after 23rd day of July 1870 .... 25 00

f. Registration of additional degrees or titles $2 00

This fee is only payable when the additional titles are registered at different times, but any number of such titles as are allowed to be registered, may be put on record at the first registration, for the registration fee.

g. Diploma of membership of the College..................... 5 00

This diploma is granted free of charge to all those members of the College who attain their membership by passing the examinations of the College. All other members may obtain it on application to the Registrar, and paying the above named fee.

h. Annual assessment due by members of the College for the year
1892, payable to the Registrar. 2 00
1893   "   "   "   2 00
1894   "   "   "   2 00
1895   "   "   "   2 00
1896   "   "   "   2 00
1897   "   "   "   2 00

This fee is payable by every member of the College.

Fees after 1st of July, 1889 :

a. Registration of matriculation... 20 00

b. Primary examination......... 30 00

c. Intermediate and Final examination, including registration.... 50 00

This is not to affect any student who is registered as a matriculate prior to 1st July, 1889.

2. All fees must be paid in lawful money of Canada to the Treasurer of the College.

3. No candidate will be admitted to any examination until the fee for such examination is paid in full.

4. Candidates who have failed in any professional examination, shall pay a fee of twenty dollars for each subsequent examination.

SECTION V.—EXAMINATIONS.

RULES FOR THE GUIDANCE OF THE BOARD OF EXAMINERS.

1. The Registrar or Deputy Registrar must be present at every examination.

2. At the end of each written examination upon any subject, the answers to the ques-

tions are to be handed to the Registrar, who will open the envelopes, in which they are hereinafter directed to be enclosed, and to each set of papers affix a number by which the author will be known to the Examiners during the examination. The Registrar will then deliver the papers to the member of the Board of Examiners appointed by the Council to examine upon the subject.

3. The papers, when delivered to the member of the Board of Examiners appointed by the Council to examine upon the subject, are to be by him examined, and the relative value of answers marked by means of numbers in a schedule which will be furnished to him by the Registrar, ranging for the Primary subjects as follows :

4. That the percentage in the Primary branches be as follows, ranging from 0 to 100 on all subjects :

	Honors.	Pass.
Anatomy	75	50
Physiology and Histology	75	50
Chemistry — Theoretical and Practical	75	50
Materia Medica and Pharmacy	75	50

INTERMEDIATE.

Medical, Surgical and Topographical Anatomy	0 to 100
Principles and Practice of Medicine	0 to 100
General Pathology and Bacteriology	0 to 100
Surgery, other than Operative	0 to 100
Surgery, Operative	0 to 100
Midwifery, other than Operative	0 to 100
Widwifery. Operative	0 to 100
Medical Jurisprudence, Toxicology and Mental Diseases	0 to 100
Sanitary Science	0 to 100
Diseases of Children, Medical and Surgical	0 to 100
Diseases of Women	0 to 100
Therapeutics	0 to 100

Marks required for honors and pass :

	Honors	Pass
Medical, Surgical and Topographical Anatomy	75	50
Principles and Practice of Medicine	75	50
General Pathology and Bacteriology	75	50
Surgery, other than Operative	75	50
Surgery, Operative	75	50
Widwifery, other than Operative	75	50
Midwifery, Operative	75	50
Medical Jurisprudence, Toxicology and Mental Diseases	75	50
Sanitary Science	75	50
Diseases of Children, Medical and Surgical	75	50
Diseases of Women	75	50
Therapeutics	75	50

That the percentage in the Final branches be as follows : 0 to 100 on all subjects. Honors 75, pass 50.

5. The value awarded by the individual Examiners to the answers of candidates are not, to be subject to revision, except by an appeal by the candidate to the Council, when special cases of hardship may seem to have occurred.

6. The Examiners shall return the schedule to the Registrar, with values inserted, within seven days of notice to be sent by the Registrar. From these values a general schedule is to be prepared by the Registrar, and no change of value can be made after such schedules have been returned by the Examiners to the Registrar. The general schedule so prepared is to be examined as to its correctness by the President, and the results announced by the President.

7. Papers on the homœopathic subjects are to be finally submitted to the Examiner approved of for that purpose by the representatives of that system in the Council.

8. All oral examinations are henceforth to be as clinical, demonstrative and practical as possible, and the candidate shall be known to the Examiners by number only. It is recommended that the attention of the Examiners be specially directed to clause 9 for the guidance of Examiners.

9. That it be an instruction to the Examiners, in the questions in their respective subjects, to confine themselves to the text-books in ordinary use (see page x. of this Announcement), also that in referring to diseases or operations of any kind, the names of such diseases or operations most commonly in use should be employed.

The Examiners are instructed to attach to each question a printed number as the value of a full and correct answer thereof—the whole of such numbers to amount to 100— also that in reading the paper they mark in colored chalk what they regard as the numerical value of the answer given.

10. That it be an instruction to the President that he shall in no case report a candidate as having passed an examination when on any subject he makes less than the minimum of marks set by the Council for a pass on that subject. But in any case where he thinks there are special reasons for granting a license to such candidate, he shall report the same to the Council for its action.

RULES FOR CANDIDATES WHEN IN THE EXAMINATION HALL.

11. Each candidate shall receive from the Registrar a programme containing a list of subjects upon which the candidate is to be

examined, and it will admit him to the examination hall during the progress of the examinations upon such subject, but at no other time.

12. Candidates must write the answers to the questions given by the Examiners legibly and neatly upon one side only of each page of a book, which will be furnished to each candidate, and the number given with each question is to be put at the head of the answer to it, in such a manner as to have the first page facing outward to the view ; they are then to be folded once and enclosed in an envelope, on the outside of which each candidate is to write his name. The packet is then to be handed to the Registrar, or some one deputed by him. Neither signature, number or sign, by which the writer could be recognized by the Examiner, is to be written or marked upon any portion of the book to be enclosed in the envelope.

13. The questions of the Examiners in the homœopathic subjects will be handed in writing, at the beginning of the general examination on the same subject, by the Registrar, to such candidates as have given him notice in accordance with Section III., Sub-secs. 10, 11. They shall write the answers to these questions in the same hall with the other candidates, and hand their papers, when finished, to the Registrar in the same manner as provided for other candidates, to be by him given for examination to the homœopathic member of the Board of Examiners appointed to examine on that subject.

14. If any abbreviations are used in answering the questions, candidates must be careful that they are such as are generally understood, or which cannot be mistaken.

15. No candidate will be allowed to leave the hall after the questions are given out, until his answers have been handed in.

16. No candidate will be allowed in the hall during the hours of examination, except those who are actually undergoing examination.

17. Any candidate who may have brought any book or reference paper to the hall, must deposit it with the Registrar before the examination begins.

18. Candidates must not communicate with each other while examinations are going on, either by writing, signs, words, or in any manner whatever.

19. Candidates must at all times bear themselves toward the Registrar and Examiners with the utmost deference and respect ; and they will not be permitted in any manner to manifest approbation or disapprobation of any member of the Board of Examiners during the progress of the examination.

20. Candidates must not only conduct themselves with decorum while any examination is going on, but they will be held strictly responsible for any impropriety of conduct during the whole progress, both of the written and the oral examinations.

21. Any infraction of the above rules will lead to the exclusion of the candidate who is guilty of it from the remainder of the examination ; and he will not receive credit for any examination papers which he may have handed to the Registrar previous to his being detected in such misconduct.

22. And be debarred from further privileges, at the discretion of the Council.

MEMBERS

OF THE

College of Physicians and Surgeons of Ontario

WHO HAVE ATTAINED THEIR MEMBERSHIP
SINCE THE ISSUE OF

THE ONTARIO MEDICAL REGISTER,

On September 1st, 1892.

Addison, Wm. L. T..........Barrie 1895
Agnew, Thos....Belgrave, Co. Huron 1894
Aiken, Alex. Wallace........Chicago 1895
Alexander, William Henry....Bolton 1894
Alger, Harry Herbert......Colborne 1893
Allen, John Herbert..........Orono 1896
Allen, Mary E....Alameda, N.W.T. 1895
Allen, James Ross..........Napanee 1894
Alway, Robert Douglas......Grimsby 1893
Alway, W. R...............Vittoria 1897
Amyot, Herbert J........Belle River 1895
Anderson, Norman.Toronto, Church St 1893
Anderson, William John
    Winchester Springs, Co. Dundas 1894
Archer, Robert
    Milton, N. Dakota U.S.A. 1892
Argue, John Fenton............Carp 1896
Arkell, Herbert Edward..St. Thomas 1896
Armour, Donald John........Cobourg 1894
Armstrong, Henry Edward
    Orono, Co. Durham 1894
Armstrong, James Joseph
    Moore, Co. Lambton 1893
Armstrong, James Mitchell
    Walton, Co. Huron 1893
Arnott, William Joshua.......Berlin 1893
Arrell, William.............Cayuga 1894
Austin, James Herbert....Brampton 1893

Badgerow, Geo. W.........Toronto 1895
Baker, Milton...........Springfield 1894
Ball, Francis James
    Rugby, Co. Simcoe 1895
Ball, W. A................Toronto 1894
Barber, Geo. W.........St. George 1896
Barker, Alexander Norman
    Seeley's Bay, Co. Leeds 1893
Basken, John T...........Dunrobin 1896
Bean, Sidney B.........Elmwood 1895
Beasley, William Jas........Weston 1896
Beatty, Adam A. ....Toronto 1896

Beatty, Wm. John........Glencairn 1896
Beckett, James.........Thamesville 1895
Bedell, Thomas C...........Picton 1896
Bell, J. A...............Strathroy 1897
Bell, Thomas H..........Peterboro' 1896
Bentley, David B...........Forest 1892
Berry, Geo. H ....Gananoque 1896
Bier, Thomas H..........Brantford 1896
Bird, Charles Harold.........Barrie 1893
Blanchard, Fabian.....Sutton West 1893
Blow, Thos. H ... South Mountain 1896
Boileau, Francis X....Sturgeon Falls 1896
Boucher, Robert B........Peterboro 1895
Bouch, Chester W..Brinston's Corners 1895
Bourns, William Henry
    Frankville, Co. Leeds 1892
Bowie, Innes............Streetsville 1893
Boyd, William Brown .....Uxbridge 1894
Boyle, James F.............Toronto 1896
Bradley, John L....Airlie, Co. Simcoe 1894
Bradshaw, Katharine........Toronto 1897
Brander, Minnie May
    Priceville, Co. Grey 1893
Brereton, Cloudesley H....Schomberg 1896
Brien, John W........Essex Centre 1895
Brodie, Ralph...........Claremont 1892
Brown, George W......Aylmer West 1895
Brown, Peter McGregor
    Camlachie, Co. Lambton 1892
Brown, Wilber Franklin
    Medina, Co. Oxford 1893
Brown, William Ernest
    Rush, Munroe Co., N.Y., U.S.A. 1893
Bruce, Robert Frederick
    New Lothrop, Mich., U.S.A. 1893
Buchanan, Daniel.............Galt 1896
Bull, John Henry..........Weston 1894
Bulmer, Thomas Sanderson
    Soda Springs, Idaho, U.S.A. 1893
Burrows, Francis James.... Toronto 1893
Burrows, John George......Napanee 1892

Burt, Ellen A. A.
    West Valley, N.Y., U.S.A. 1894
Burt, George S............Hillsburg 1896
Butler, J. A................Toronto 1897
Byers, Wm. Gordon M....Gananoque 1896

Callander, C. N............Toronto 1897
Cameron, Donald A..........Dutton 1896
Cameron, Geo. S........Harrowsmith 1896
Campbell, Byron..Zurich, Co. Huron 1894
Campbell, G. L............Bellwood 1897
Campbell, Lewis Henry....Bradford 1893
Campbell, Neil...........Cookstown 1893
Campbell, Peter M..Forresters' Falls 1896
Carlaw, Thomas W......Warkworth 1893
Carron, Fred B...........Brockville 1896
Carter, Charles............Toronto 1893
Carveth, Annie E.........California 1893
Cavan, James G.... ......Toronto 1895
Chambers, William........Oakwood 1893
Chapin, Cecil D.........Brantford 1895
Chapman, Wm. J........Rat Portage 1895
Chevrier, Gustave Rodolph....Ottawa 1892
Clare, Harvey.............Lakefield 1896
Clark, David Andrew
    Agincourt, Co. York 1892
Clingan, George............Toronto 1892
Closson, John Hyland.......Toronto 1892
Colder, Robert Mortley
    Avon, Co. Middlesex 1893
Coleman, Frank...........Hamilton 1895
Connell, Walter Thomas
    Spencerville, Co. Grenville 1894
Connolly, Bernard G........Trenton 1896
Cooke, George Herbert......Chesley 1893
Corbett, Robert Thornley..Port Hope 1893
Cormack, John H...........Ottawa 1895
Coulthard, Walter L..Rossland, B.C. 1894
Countryman, John Edgar
    Tweed, Co. Hastings 1893
Cowper, James A..........Welland 1895
Craft, Robert A..........Chisholm 1895
Crain, William Eldridge....Brockville 1894
Cranston, James G.........Arnprior 1896
Crawford, Dan T.........Thedford 1896
Crawford, John..,..........Toronto 1894
Creighton, James Kelso....Nilestown 1893
Cummings, J. A..........Bond Head 1897
Currie, Morley.............Picton 1895
Curtis, James Davis......St. Thomas 1895
Cuthbertson, Hugh Alex.....Chicago, 1895

Dates, F. A.............Dunbarton 1897
Danard, Arthur Leslie
    Woodford, Co. Grey 1894
Darling, Robert Ellwood..Goodwood 1893
Davis, J. J................London 1897
Davidson, Allan..Swanton, Vt., U.S.A. 1895
Deacon, George R.........Stratford 1896
Deacon, John D..........Pembroke 1896
Delahey, Fred C..........Pembroke 1895
Devitt, Thomas G.
    Bobcaygeon, Co. Victoria 1895
Doan, Warren
    Harrietsville, Co. Middlesex 1893

Doig, Charles D...........Denbigh 1895
Douglas, Thomas..Moncton, Co. Perth 1893
Douglas, William..........Chatham 1895
Dow, Jeanie J..............Fergus 1895
Downey, Robert A.........Gormley 1895
Downing, Albert. McDonald's Corners 1895
Downing, Joseph J. B....... Chesley 1896
Drennan, Jennie G.........Kingston 1896
Drummond, Charles A. Highland Creek 1895
Drysdale, William F.........Perth 1894
Duncan Joseph Harrison
    Malton, Co. Peel 1895
Dunn, David James
    Beeton, Co. Simcoe 1893
Dyde, C. B................Kingston 1897
Dymond, Bertha............Toronto 1893

Earl William M.
    Bishop's Mills, Co. Grenville 1892
Elkington, John ....Ompah 1894
Elliott, Andrew F............Acton 1895
Elliott, Francis B.........Dorchester 1896
Elliott George ....Toronto 1895
Elliott, George A...........Ouvry 1896
Elliott, John J............Brantford 1896
Elliott, William............Mitchell 1893
Ellis, George A............Dundela 1896
Embury, Alex. T.........Belleville 1896

Farley, Frank Jones
    Smithfield, Co. Northumberland 1894
Farrell, Thos. H..........Kingston 1896
Farncomb, Thomas Stone
    Rednersville, Co. Prince Edward 1894
Feader Wm. A.............Iroquois 1895
Featherstone, Henry M.....Prescott 1895
Ferguson, Alex. K.
    Kirkton, Co. Perth 1894
Ferguson James Bruce .....Toronto 1893
Ferguson John H..........Toronto 1895
Ferris Geo. M.............Cobourg 1894
Field, Corelli Collard.......Cobourg 1894
Field Geo. Henry..........Cobourg 1894
Findlay, Charles ....Hamilton 1896
Flaherty, Thos. T.....Mount Carmel 1895
Fleming, Samuel E.....:...Webbwood 1895
Fletcher, Arthur Guy Ashton, Toronto 1894
Foley, Ignatius Joseph........Ottawa 1892
Ford, John Whitfield
    Thorndale, Co. Middlesex 1894
Forster F. J. R.........Palmerston 1897
Frank, Harry Robert......Brantford 1894
Futcher, Thomas Barnes..St. Thomas 1893

Galloway, Artemas .. Beaverton, Ont. 1894
Gallow, Wm. Forbes........Toronto 1896
Gardner, Albert E.........Belleville 1896
Gear, Henry...Marsville, Co. Dufferin 1892
Gibbs, Joseph............Meaford 1896
Gibson, Allen.............Hillsburg 1895
Gibson James C...........Kingston 1896
Gibson, James Cunningham
    New Haven, Mich., U.S.A 1892

xviii ANNUAL ANNOUNCEMENT.

Ludwig, A. G............Sebringville 1897
Lynch, Denis G............Almonte 1896
MacCallum, E. C. D.......Kingston 1897
MacCarthy, Geo. Stainstreet..Ottawa 1894
MacDonald,Albert Edgar....Stratford 1893
MacDonald, Walter S.......London 1893
Mackay, Alexander.......Creemore 1895
MacKay, Robert Burns.....Toronto 1893
Mackenzie, Wm. Graeme....Marmora 1895
Macklin, Alfred H.........Belmore 1896
Macklin, Daisy M.........Stratford 1895
MacKendrick, Harry F.........Galt 1893
MacKenzie, John Ross
           Cannington, Dak., U.S.A 1893
MacLaren, Peter S.........Trenton 1896
MacMillan, James A.......Strathroy 1893
Mair, Asa Wolverton
           Portage du Fort, Que 1892
Malloch, William J.........Toronto 1896
Malloy, Joseph A...........Preston 1896
Marquis, John A.........Brantford 1896
Marr, Delaski,..Ridgetown, Co. Kent 1893
Martin, Frank..Erin, Co. Wellington 1893
Marselis, Eathan H.....South Finch 1895
Maybury, W. F............Toronto 1897
Meikle, William F.......Morrisburg 1893
Mencke, John Richard.......Jarvis 1894
Metcalfe, Archie A.........Almonte 1896
Millen, William H
           Wheatley, Co. Kent 1894
Miller, Henry Wm
           Martelle, Mich., U.S.A. 1895
Millichamp, G. E...........Toronto 1897
Milligan, Arthur A.......U.S.A. 1895
Mills, Geo. B.Monticello, Wis., U.S.A. 1896
Minnes, Robert Stanley....Kingston 1893
Mitchell, John Alexander
           Caistorville, Co. Lincoln 1893
Moles, Edward B.........Arnprior 1895
Maloney, Paul J
           Ennismore, Co. Peterboro' 1893
Monteith, Joseph D.......Stratford 1895
Moore, John....Bath, Mich., U.S.A. 1893
Moore, Robert...............Maple 1896
Moore, George.............Kirkton 1896
Morris, Chas. E
           Delaware, Co. Middlesex 1892
Morris, James S...........Oshawa 1896
Morden, Fred Wilson.......Picton 1894
Morton, J. P.............Hamilton 1897
Moss, Frank Heyden
           Riverside, Cal., U.S.A. 1892
Mulligan, Fred Wm
           Millbrook, Co. Durham 1893
Mullin, J. H.............Hamilton 1897
Murphy, Arthur L
           Phelpston, Co. Simcoe 1892
Murphy, Joseph E
           Portland Co. Leeds 1893
Murphy, Stephen Henry....Renfrew 1894
Murray, Herbert G........Kingston 1896
Musson, George ....Toronto, 1896
McArthur, Wm. T ....Moorefield 1895
McBroom, James A........Washburn 1895
McCaig, Alex S.........Collingwood 1896
McCallum, Annie B.....Gananoque 1895

McCammon, Samuel H......Kingston 1896
McClenahan, Daniel Alex
           Tansley, Co. Halton 1894
McCallum, Wm. James.....Toronto 1894
McConaghy, Francis
           Midland, Co. York 1892
McConnel, John F
           La Cruees, New Mexico, U.S.A. 1896
McCrae, Thos...............Guelph 1895
McCrimmon, Alex. Addison
           St. Thomas 1894
McCullough, Edwin F
           Exeter, Co. Wellington 1892
McDonald, Hugh S.........Eganville 1895
McDonald, Wm..........Rothesay 1895
McEachern, J. S..........Cashtown 1897
McEwen, Duncan.........St. Elmo 1896
McGannon, A. V.........Brockville 1897
McGarry, James H......Niagara Falls 1893
McGinnis, John..Arva, Co. Middlesex 1892
McGrath, George
           Hamilton, Montana, U.S.A. 1893
McIlwraith, K. C..Carlton St., Toronto 1894
McInnes, N. W............Victoria 1897
McIntosh, John William....Gore Bay 1894
McIntosh, Lynden Young
           Apple Hill, Co. Glengarry 1894
McIntosh, Wilfred A........Simcoe 1896
McKay, Thos. W. G.........Oshawa 1895
McKechnie, Wm. B.
           Revelstoke, B.C. 1895
McKee, Chas. S..........Peterboro' 1896
McKee, Joseph Fennell......Petrolia 1894
McKenzie, David C... .....Durham 1896
McKenzie, William J
           Warwick, Co. Lambton 1893
McKeown, H..............Belleville 1897
McLennan, F..............Kintail 1895
McLennan, Kenneth
           North Lancaster, Co. Glen. 1893
McMaster, John............Toronto 1894
McMurrich, John B........Toronto, 1896
McNamara, A. T...........Toronto 1897
McNaughton, James Alex....Cornwall 1893
McNiven, James A........Alvinston 1895
McPhail. Malcolm..........Manilla 1895
McPherson, Charles F. S....Prescott 1896
McPherson, David W.........Toronto 1895
McPherson, Duncan A.....Toronto 1892
McRae, John R.........Dungannon 1896

New, Charles Frederick......London 1894
Nichol, Albert H. Listowel, Co. Perth 1893
Nichol, R.................Listowel 1897
Nichol, Wm. H..........Brantford 1896
Noble, Robert T.........Brampton 1895
Northwood, Alfred E.......Florence 1895

O'Connor, Edward J.........Ottawa 1894
Oliver, Joseph Henry....Sunderland 1896
Olmsted, William E........Caledonia 1893
Parfitt, Charles Daniel.......London 1894
Parker, Fred...........Bruce Mines 1895
Park, John............Bruce Mines 1894
Park, William Fred.......Chatham 1893

Parlow, Allan B.
Iroquois, Co. Dundas 1884
Partridge, Augustus W....Crown Hill 1896
Paterson, Hector M.........Rodney 1895
Pearson, Francis Geo. Ed.
Weston, Co. York 1893
Pearson, Henry C.....Demorestville 1895
Pease, Herbert D...........Toronto 1893
Perry, R. W..............Kirkfield 1897
Phillips, John R.
Northfield, Minn., U.S.A. 1896
Pickard, Henry G.............Glamis 1895
Pirritte, Fred W
New Haven, Conn., U.S.A. 1893
Porter, George Daniel......Brantford 1894
Pratt, John I.............Heathcote 1895
Pringle, Rose...............Fergus 1895
Pritchard, James
North Wakesfield, Quebec 1894
Proctor, Edgar Lovell....Niagra Falls 1894
Purvis, John W. F..............Lyn 1896

Quesnel, Eugene G.........Toronto, 1896

Rannie, John A............Chatham 1896
Ratz, John H..........New Dundee 1895
Reeves, James..Killaloe, Co. Renfrew 1894
Reynar, Albert F...........Palgrave 1896
Richardson, Edward K....Flesherton 1895
Rivers, John H..............Sarnia 1896
Roberts, Enoch L..........Lyndoch 1896
Robinson, Elmer L..........Toronto 1896
Robinson, John T.........Toronto 1893
Rogers, John M....Durham, Co. Grey 1893
Rorke, Robert F.........St. Thomas 1893
Rosebrugh, Frederick A....Hamilton 1892
Ross, Hugh H...............Clinton 1896
Rounthwaite, Frank S.....Thessalon 1895
Royce, G................Davenport 1897
Rudolf, Robert D...........Toronto, 1896
Ruppert, Andrew......New Hamburg 1896
Russell, John Parrington....Toronto, 1894
Rutledge, Henry Noble
Streetsville, Co. Peel 1894
Ruttan, Frank Sheldon
Sydenham, Co. Frontenac 1893
Ryan, Eva Jeanette..Toronto Junction 1893
Rykert, Arthur F.....St. Catharines 1893
Sagar, Daniel S............Brantford 1895
Sanderson, Herman H.
Sparta, Co. Elgin 1893
Sands, Wm. W............Sudbury 1896
Saulter, William W..........Ottawa 1892
Scott, F. A.................Clinton 1897
Scott, Walter H............Toronto, 1896
Seaborn, Edwin.............London 1895
Seager, James
South Monaghan, Co. Peterboro' 1894
Sharpe, William D.............Lyn 1895
Shaw, Robert W..........Springfield 1895
Shaw, Robert W.
Hudson, Mich., U.S.A. 1892
Sheahan, John..............Newark 1895
Shier, Daniel W............Lindsay 1895
Shillington, Adam T.........Ottawa 1894

Shouldice, James H.......Hamilton 1893
Shurie, Joseph S............Trenton 1894
Shuttleworth, Charles Buckingham
Toronto 1894
Silcox, Wm. L...............Boston 1896
Sills, Clarence H......... .....Picton 1896
Simpson, Geo. D. R.......Hamilton 1895
Sinclair, Christie ....Ottawa 1896
Sinclair, Herbert H ....Walkerton 1894
Sinclair, John Peter.......Toronto 1894
Singleton, Ambrose B.
Elgin, Co. Leeds 1893
Skinner, Emma L.........Davisville 1896
Skippen, Alfred
Hillsburg, Co. Wellington 1892
Sloane, John G. M......Owen Sound 1895
Small, Arthur A............Toronto 1895
Smith, Charles H..........Bradford 1896
Smith, David K...........Toronto 1897
Smith, Frank Ware
Sheffield, Co. Wentworth 1894
Smith, Israel G..........Hintonburg 1896
Smith, Melville B........Waubashene 1895
Smith, Ralph G., Oakland, Iowa, U.S.A. 1893
Smuck, James W........... Toronto 1893
Smyth, Charles Ernest ...... Toronto 1894
Sneath, Charles R.......... Toronto 1897
Sneath, Thomas H......... Midhurst 1895
Snider, Rufus O.......... Toronto 1896
Somerville, John T........... Essex 1894
South, Thomas E......... St. George 1893
Stafford, Ezra H........... Toronto 1893
Stammers, Chas., L.B........Milton 1895
Steele, Fred. C..............Orillia 1896
Stenhouse, John............Toronto, 1894
Stephens, William
Wallaceburg, Co. Kent 1894
Stevenson, Hugh A..........London 1895
Stevenson, Wm. J..........London 1896
Stinson, John G...........Brantford 1893
Stockton, Fred. W....... Beachville 1894
Story Simeon G..Blenheim, Co. Kent 1893
Sutherland, Jas. A.......... Toronto 1896
Switzer, Frank L.
Riceville, Co., Prescott 1892
Symington, Maggie P.......Brighton 1895

Tait, Nelson J................ Blyth 1896
Taylor, Charles J............Toronto 1893
Taylor, Walter H. ....Toronto, 1896
Taggart, Arthur H. F.
Lloydtown, Co. York 1893
Thomas, Chas. H............Toronto 1896
Thomas, Julia ....Toronto 1892
Thompson, Charles W..... St. Mary's 1893
Thomson, Walter Proudfoot....Orillia 1893
Thomson, David.............Annan 1894
Thomson, F. L............. Hanover 1897
Thorne, Joseph S............ Hilton 1896
Tomlinson, Edward........Brantford 1893
Tremayne, Henry E..Yarmouth, N.S. 1894
Tufford, Wm. H........... Toronto 1893
Turner, Adelaide .... Gananoque 1896
Tyerman, Peter D. ....Toronto 1893

Verth, Annie.................York 1896

Waddy, John P.... Rosseau, Muskoka 1892
Wade, Alfred S.... St. Lambert, Que. 1893
Wade, G. H................Brighton 1897
Wakefield, William T. B.
              San Diego, Cal., U.S.A. 1893
Walker, Robert J.
              Sangatuck, Mich., U.S.A. 1894
Walker, Wm. G............Stratford 1892
Wallace, Herbert E. ......Port Elgin 1895
Wallace, Norman, Clyde.
              Alma, Co. Wellington 1894
Wallbridge, Francis G...... Midland 1895
Wardell, Henry A........... Dundas 1893
Webb, Alfred............Newmarket 1896
Webster, Ben. E.......... Kingston 1896
Weeks, Ethridge C......... Glencoe 1896
Weir, William H......'... Brantford 1896
Wells, Robert Bruce .... Durham 1894
Wesley, W. J.............Newmarket 1897
Westman, Samuel H........Toronto, 1896
White, Edwin B.
              Oil City, Penn., U.S.A. 1896

White, Ernest A........... Toronto 1895
White, Frank A.....'...... Aylmer 1894
White, John Arthur
              Oakwood, Co. Victoria 1894
Whitelaw, Thos. Henderson .. Guelph 1894
White, Prosper Deming......Glencoe 1894
Whitteker, Walter C...... Avonmore 1895
Wickett, Thomas.. Crediton, Co. Huron 1894
Wickson, David D .... Toronto 1893
Wiley, Walter D...........Dresden 1895
Williams, Joseph J.. Gorrie, Co. Huron 1893
Windell, James Douglas
              Milton, North Dakota, U.S.A. 1894
Wilson, Jas. A. G.. Keewatin, Algoma 1893
Wilson, Thomas................ Elm 1894
Wood, Peter Burke...........London 1893
Woods, Ninian W. ....Toronto 1893

Young, George S...........Prescott 1895
Young, Thomas A........ Brougham 1897
Young, Thos. W. H.........Rosseau 1896

Zumstein, John M .... Smithville 1895

Examination Questions.

SEPTEMBER, 1896, AND APRIL, 1897.

SEPTEMBER EXAMINATIONS, 1896.

Primary.

ANATOMY.

Value 0 to 100.   Time 2½ hours.

Values.

18   1. Describe the upper extremity of the ulna, and lower extremity of radius.

12   2. Name the nerves supplying the following muscles : Pyriformis, peroneus longus, brachialis anticus, rhomboid minor, flexor brevis pollicis, latissimus dorsi.

18   3. Describe shortly the superficial lymphatic glands of the head and neck.

20   4. Give the relations of the left common iliac artery.

18   5. Describe the formation of the cardiac plexus, superficial and deep.

14   6. Dissection necessary to expose the 2nd portion of the axillary artery.

F. Le M. Grasett, F.R.C.S.E.,
Examiner.

PHYSIOLOGY AND HISTOLOGY.

Value 0 to 100.   Time 2½ hours.

Values.

20   1. Give the origin and termination of the fibres which constitute the internal capsule.

20   2. What circumstances determine the pressure and velocity of the blood current in the capilliaries ?

25   3. Prove that a normal temperature is maintained in the animal body by means of the nervous system.

35   4. Give the chemical composition of bile. Pancreatic juice, and succus entericus. Describe the nervous mechanism of vomiting.

A. S. Fraser, M.D., Examiner.

CHEMISTRY.

Value 0 to 100.   Time 2½ hours.

Values.

15   1. Enunciate the laws governing the variation of the volume of gases for changes of pressure and temperature. What volume of chlorine at 15°C. and 500 m.m. pressure can be got from 100 grammes of sodium chloride by manganese dioxide and sulphuric acid ?

15   2. Give the natural modes of occurrence, method of preparation, and principal chemical facts regarding mercury ; and from it how would you manufacture calomel ?

10   3. What is the general chemical composition of the following bodies :—Amethyst, bone-ash, clay, emery, flint, felspar, marble, plaster-of-paris, sand, white lead ?

7   4. Write constitutional formulæ for the following substances :—Thio-carbonic acid, calcium hypochlorite, pyro-phosphoric acid, di-methyl ketone, amido-acetic acid, potassium ferrocyanide, trimethyl-triethyl-ethane, triphosphonium-iodide.

10   5. What substances are formed when ethyl alcohol is acted on by each of the following :—Hydrochloric acid, potassium hydroxide, sodium, iodine and potassium carbonate, and phosphorus tri-iodide ? Give equations.

8   6. An organic acid on analysis gives the following percentage composition :—

Carbon 40.00
Hydrogen......... 6.67
Oxygen........... 53.33

Its vapor density is 3·12 (air=1). Calculate its molecular formula, and give the name of the acid.

15   7. How is benzoic acid artificaly prepared ? Show by formulæ its relation to salicylic acid, toluene and saccharin.

8. In the following analysis of a drinking water explain each item, and tell how it is determined :—

20

	parts per million
Total solids....................	95.00
Chlorine.....................	22.22
Nitrogen in nitrates and nitrites.	0.24
Free ammonia	0.03
Albuminoid ammonia.........	0.06
Oxygen absorbed in 15 minutes..	0.06
" " 4 hours....	0.14

ATOMIC WEIGHTS.

H.— 1   C.—12   Na. 23.
O.—16.   Cl.—35.5 Mn. 54.
S.—32.

Geo. Acheson, M.A., M.B. (Tor.)
Examiner.

TOXICOLOGY.

Value 0 to 100. Time 1 hour.

Values.

20 1. Describe chloroform poisoning, and the treatment.

20 2. In what ways may chronic lead poisoning arise? Describe the symptoms.

20 3. Describe the method of examining the body in cases of suspected death from arsenic.

20 4. What are the appearances after death due to (a) carbolic acid (b) phosphorus?

20 5. Describe and compare the poisonous effects of curare and conium.

Geo. Acheson, M.A., M.B. (Tor.)
Examiner.

MATERIA MEDICA AND PHARMACY.

Value 0 to 100. Time 2½ hours.

Values.

20 1. Describe the following :—
Phenacetinum,
Iodoformum,
Jalapa,
Acidum Boricum.

2. Give the pharmacopœial title and composition of the following :—

20 Strong solution of ammonia,
Soda water,
Sweet spirits of nitre,
Dovers powder.

20 3. Describe and explain the physiological action of strychnine.

20 4. Give the source and physiological action of hydrocyanic acid.

20 5. Compare the alkaloids — Morphine and Codeine, and give the official forms of each.

H. Beaumont Small, M.D.,
Examiner.

MATERIA MEDICA AND PHARMACY.

(Homœopathic).

Value 0 to 100. Time 2½ hours.

Values.

10 1. Give the source, natural order, parts used, and mode of preparing the following :—Tr. belladonna, pulsatilla nig., arsenicum alb. 3X trit., mer. cor. 3X trit.

10 2. Give the physiological action of belladonna. Differentiate the delirium of bell. hyotcyamus nig. and stramonium.

8. 3. In what respects do the metals as a class resemble each other in their action?

8 4. What are the distinguishing features in the action of mer. cor. from the other preparations of mercury?

14 5. Describe the action of colocynth on the intestinal tract. Describe lead colic and lead paralysis.

10 6. Give the action of arsenicum, kali bich., and tartar met. on the respiratory system.

10 7. Give three characteristic symptoms of the following :—Kali bich., apsis mel., bryonia, cham. rhus.

10 8. Name all the structures on which the following drugs act :—Aconite, bryonia, rhus, tox., and digitalis.

10 9. What is the minimum and maximum dose of the following :—Tr. aconite, hyos, digitalis, morphia, sulph., strychinia sulph., potas. bromide and chloral hydrate?

0 10. Describe the effects of arsenic and mer. cor. on gastro intestinal canal.

D. J. Sinclair, M.D.,
Examiner.

Intermediate and Final.

THEORY AND PRACTICE OF MEDICINE.

Value 0 to 100. Time 2½ hours.

Values.

20 1. Describe the condition of a patient during the second week of an attack of typhoid fever of moderate severity. What is the Brand method of treating this disease?

20 2. Distinguish briefly between :—
Hæmoptysis and hæmatemesis,
Gastric ulcer and gastric cancer.

20 3. What is the appearance of a patient the subject of myxœdema? What organ is at fault, and how would you treat the disease?

25 4. Bronchial asthma. Give etiology and symptoms including character of sputum and physical signs. Mention the conditions that may result from repeated attacks. What treatment would you employ during an attack?

15 5. Polio-myelitis anterior (acuta). Give symptoms, morbid anatomy and treatment of this disease.

D. E. Mundell, B.A., M.D.,
Examiner.

Intermediate and Final.

PATHOLOGY.

Value 0 to 100. Time 3 hours.

All questions equal.

1. What are the points of difference between the carcinomata and the sarcomata?

2. What are the different forms of blood-poisoning? Differentiate them.

3. Describe the pathological changes met with in the different organs as a consequence of long standing mitral leakage with failure of compensation.

BACTERIOLOGY.

1. How would you prove that a disease depends upon a specific organism as to causation ?

THERAPEUTICS.

1. Explain the action of the heart and blood vessel— digitalis, strophanthus, alcohol and caffeine.

2. Explain the terms : hypnotic, anodyne and narcotic. Give an example of each, with minimum and maximum dose.

W. P. CAVEN, M.B., L.R.C.P. (Lon.),
Examiner.

N.B.—Candidates on Final write on Pathology and Therapeutics only. Candidates for Intermediate write on Pathology and Bacteriology.

MIDWIFERY, OTHER THAN OPERATIVE.

PUERPERAL AND INFANTILE DISEASES.

Value 0 to 100. Time 2½ hours.

Values.
20 1. Mention the accidents to the soft parts which may occur during labor,
20 2. Give the functions of the liquor amnii, and state the usual amount of fluid at term.
10 3. State the cause of bleeding in placenta prævia.
30 4. Why is it, though we may have local pain, swelling, disturbance of temperature and pulse, and even a rigor, rare to have a mammary abscess when the mother does not nurse her infant ?
20 5. Give diagnosis and treatment of parasitic stomatitis.

H. HOWITT, M.D., Examiner.

Intermediate and Final.

MIDWIFERY, OPERATIVE.

Value 0 to '00· Time 2½ hours.

Values.
25 1. Outline a case in which you would employ the hydrostatic dilator.
25 2. Give causation, prognosis and treatment of complete inversion of uterus.
25 3. How would you treat a case of prolapsed funis after rupture of membranes ?
25 4. State your treatment of post-partum hemorrhage caused by severe laceration of cervix.

H. HOWITT, M.D., Examiner.

Intermediate and Final.

SURGERY, OTHER THAN OPERATIVE.

Value 0 to 100. Time 2½ hours.

Values.
25 1. What condition of injury to the extremities necessitate amputation ? Would

you apply the principles alike for upper and lower limbs ?
20 2. Enumerate the various situations of abscess of the breast.
20 3. What is the probable injury, resulting from a blow on the side, with extensive emphysema of the cellular tissue beneath the skin resulting ?
20 4. In severe injury to the pelvis, producing fracture of the pubic bone, what complications are most likely to result ? Give symptoms of one of the most important.
15 5. Enumerate the various causes producing entropion and ectropion.

A. BEVERLY WELFORD, M.B., Examiner.

Intermediate and Final.

SURGERY, OPERATIVE.

Value 0 to 100. Time 2½ hours.

Values.
15 1. Give causes, symptoms and treatment of acute abscess of the antrum. What diseases may it resemble ?
20 2. Describe the operative treatment of goitre. Mention some of the objections to the treatment, and how to avoid them.
15 3. (a) What is house maid's knee ? Give the radical treatment. (b) Describe the operation of circumcision.
20 4. Describe Pirogoff's amputation at the ankle. When would you perform it ?
30 5. Describe in detail the operation of trephining for a fracture of both plates of the skull, with depression.

A. BEVERLY WELFORD, M.B., Examiner.

Intermediate and Final.

MEDICAL AND SURGICAL ANATOMY.

Value 0 to 100. Time 2½ hours.

Values.
10 1. Locate tonsils.
10 2. Shape, size, position superior laryngeal opening.
10. 3. What enters into formation of wrist joint ?
10 4. Trace conjunctiva.
10 5. Attachments, size, usual location of vermiform appendix.
10 6. What structures form the pedicle of an ovarian tumor ?
10 7. Map out the heart.
10 8. What forms the anterior and posterior fontanelles ? When do they usually close ?
10 9. Trace round ligament uterus.
10 10. What bony connections are divided in excision of upper jaw ?

HADLEY WILLIAMS, M.D., Examiner.

MEDICAL JURISPRUDENCE.

Value 0 to 100.   Time 2½ hours.

All questions equal.

1. What are the signs of recent delivery?
(*a*) In the living. (*b*) In the dead.

2. What are the more common signs of
pregnancy ; and at what periods of gestation
may each sign be looked for ?

3. Describe minutely the post-mortem
conditions in deaths from " suffocation."

4. What are the " immediate " and " re-
mote " causes of death from wounds ?

5. Define legally the terms " born alive,"
" legitimacy," " murder " and " justifiable
homicide."

TOXICOLOGY AND MENTAL DISEASES.

1. Give the symptoms and treatment of a
case of poisoning by " corrosive sublimate."

2. Describe minutely the post-mortem
conditions where death has been caused by
acute arsenical poisoning.

3. What is the gauge of a person's legal
responsibility for a criminal act ; considering
simply the mental condition of the person
committing the act ?

4. Describe a case of " melancholia " and
also one of "hallucinations," giving the relative prognosis as to a favorable outcome in
each case.

C. VAN NORMAN EMORY, M.D., Examiner.

N.B.—Candidates for final write on Medical Jurisprudence only. Candidates for
Intermediate write on Medical Jurisprudence, Toxicology and Mental Diseases.

SANITARY SCIENCE.

Values 0 to 100.   Time 1½ hours.

Values.

25.   1. (*a*) Define the term " vital · statis-
tics." (*b*) What purposes are served by
their careful tabulation ?

25.   2. (*a*) Define " birth-rate," " death-
rate," and "natural increase." (*b*) Give
some causes that may influence the " birth ·
rate " and "death-rate."

25.   3. How would you examine air to determine the presence of "suspended matter," "ammonia " and " watery vapour ?'

15.   4. How would you proceed to test the
plumbing in a house where the presence of
" sewer-gas " was suspected ?"

10.   5. What kinds of soil are preferable as
building sites ? Give your reasons.

C. VAN NORMAN EMORY, M.D., Examiner.

THERAPEUTICS.

Value 0 to 100.   Time 2½ hours.

Values.

20.   1. Describe the stages of anæsthesia
from chloroform. What unfavorable symptoms may arise during its administration ?
and how would you deal with them.

20.   2. Give full directions as to the administration of cold baths to a patient suffering
from enteric fever. What is its physiological action ?

20.   3. What do you understand by drastic
cathartics. How do they act. What are the
indications for their use ? Name the drugs
which may be classified under this heading.

20.   4. What is the action on the intestine
of magnesia sulphate ; opium ; salol ; and
calomel.

20.   5. What are the indications for the use
of digitalis in diseases of the heart ? what
precautions are to be observed during its
administration ?

W. P. CAVEN, M.B., L.R.C.P., (Lon.)
Examiner.

DISEASES OF WOMEN.

Values 0 to 100.   Time 2½ hours.

Values.

25.   1. State the pathological changes that
may result from laceration of the cervix
uteri.

25.   2. State the causes of pruritis vulvæ.

25.   3. What conditions may be mistaken
for cancer of the body of the uterus ?

25.   4. Give the predisposing causes of fibrid
tumors of uterus.

H. HOWITT. M.D., Examiner.

DISEASES OF CHILDREN.

Values 0 to 100.   Time 2½ hours.

Values.

25.   1. Give the exciting causes and symptoms of laryngismus stridulus.

25.   2. Give the etiology and treatment of
acute gastroenteritis.

30.   3. Mention three kinds of spina bifida.
How would you treat a simple spinal men-
gocele ?

20.   4. In reference to rash and enlarge-
ment of cervical glands, how does rubella
differ from measles ?

H. HOWITT, Examiner.

MAY EXAMINATIONS, 1897.

Primary.

ANATOMY.

Value 0 to 100. Time 2½ hours.

Values.

10 1. Describe accurately the two main trunks of superficial veins in the lower extremity.

20 2. Describe as clearly yet as concisely as you can the nasal fossa.

20 3. Give the dissection necessary to expose the lingual artery in the whole of its course.

10 4. Trace the ulnar nerve from just above the wrist to its ultimate distribution.

20 5. Name in order the fissures and convolutions seen in a lateral view of the cerebrum.

20 6. Follow from origin to anastomosis giving their relations, the transversalis colli and transversalis humeri (supra scapular) arteries.

F. Le M. Grasett, F.R.C.S.E.,
Examiner.

PHYSIOLOGY AND HISTOLOGY.

Value 0 to 100. Time 2½ hours.

Values.

20 1. Describe the terminations of nerve fibres in the skin, spinal cord, and heart.

30 2. Describe the various methods by which it may be demonstrated that certain glands have an internal secretion.

25 3. Classify the proteids and give a distinguishing characteristic of each class.

25 4. Give an account of the nervous mechanisms concerned in the maintenance of a sense of equilibrium.

A. S. Fraser, M.D., Examiner.

Primary.

CHEMISTRY.

Value 0 to 100. Time 2½ hours.

All questions equal.

1. Enunciate the law of multiple proportions, and show how it may be deduced from the atomic theory.

2. Distinguish clearly between valence and affinity, and between atomic and molecular compounds.

3. Give proofs for the statement, that in most of the acids which contain oxygen the characteristic hydrogen is in combination with oxygen in the form of hydroxyl (OH.)

4. Describe the natural occurrence, metallurgy, and general physical and chemical properties of mercury.

5. Give the methods of preparation and general properties of the various acids that chlorine forms with oxygen and hydrogen.

6. How would you determine, (1) whether a particular body is an alcohol ; and (2) whether it is a primary, secondary, or tertiary alcohol ?

7. There are two series of compounds of the same composition, but of different constitution, both of which contain the group NO_2. Show how this is, and explain by formulæ the relationship of these two series.

8. Explain fully any method for the quantitative estimation of urea in urine.

9. What is the chemical constitution of the following substances :—Rochelle salt, fusel oil, kaolin, litharge, salol, copperas, gun-cotton, plaster-of-paris, smelling salt, solder.

10. Complete the following equations :—
(1) $2 KI + Mn O_2 + 2 H_2 SO_4 =$
(2) $C + 2 H_2 SO_4 =$
(3) $3 K_2 Mn O_4 + 2 H_2 O =$
(4) $C_2 H Cl_3 O + Na OH =$
(5) $C_6 H_5 O Na + CO_2 =$

Geo. Acheson, M.A., M.B., (Tor.)
Examiner.

Primary.

TOXICOLOGY.

Value 0 to 100. Time 1 hour.

Values.

25 1. Describe the symptoms, treatment, and *post-mortem* appearances of carbolic acid poisoning.

25 2. What are the symptoms, mode of action, and treatment of poisoning by illuminating gas ?

25 4. A medical man was called to see a woman, whom he found in a collapsed condition, cold and clammy, pulse 75, pupils contracted, no signs of injury, no typical smell from the breath, and nothing suspicious in the room. The day previous she had complained of abdominal pain, and had vomited three times. The morning of the day she was seen she had abdominal pain, vomiting, and diarrhœa. She had taken no food whatever that day. She was unconscious, could not be aroused, was breathing quietly, abdomen was not distended, and there was no rise of temperature. Next day the temperature rose to 101.6° F., and the pulse to 136. Coma persisted, and death occurred on the day following. It was found on inquiry that all the members of the family had been more or less ill at the same time.

Briefly discuss the above case, giving your treatment.

GEO. ACHESON, M.A., M.B., (Tor.)
Examiner.

MATERIA MEDICA AND PHARMACY.

Value 0 to 100. Time 2½ hours.

Values.

20 1. Give the pharmacopœial title and composition of the following :
Cream of tartar,
Lime water,
Chalk mixture,
Reduced iron,

20 2. Give the composition and strength of the following :
Liquor morphinas acetatis,
Linimentum belladonnæ.
Tinctura iodi,
Unguentum iodi,

20 3. Describe the following drugs, giving the physiological action and preparations of each :
Digitalis folia,
Strophanthus.

20 4. Give the doses and explain the physiological action of hydrargyrum subchloridum.

20 5. Compare and explain the physiological actions of hydrate of chloral and sulphonal.

H. BEAUMONT SMALL, M.D.,
Examiner.

MEDICINE.

Value 0 to 100. Time 2½ hours.

Values.

16 1. Describe the skin eruption peculiar to the following : Scarlet fever, measles, typhoid fever and varicella.

2. (a) Define (1) Icterus hepatogenous.
16   (2) Icterus haematogenous.
(b) Give the general symptoms of obstructive jaundice.

18 3. What are the physical signs corresponding to the different stages of lung involvement in acute lobar pneumonia.

20 4. Describe (a) the murmur peculiar to
(1) Aortic insufficiency
(2) Mitral incompetency
with reference to its nature, point of maximum intensity, direction of transmission and relation to heart's sounds.
(b) The management of valvular lesions
(1) During stage of compensation
(2) During state of broken compensation.

18 5. What treatment would you employ in acute Bright's disease ?
Compare the urine in case of
Chronic interstitial nephritis with that of
Chronic parenchymatous nephritis in regard to quantity, specific gravity and amount of albumen.

12 6. (a) Mention three leading features common to the different forms of eczema.
(b) Distinguish eczema squamosum from psoriasis. (c) Give general lines of treatment of the former condition.

D. E. MUNDELL, M.D., Examiner.

Intermediate and Final.

THEORY AND PRACTICE OF
MEDICINE.

HOMŒOPATHIC.

Value 0 to 100. Time 2½ hours.

Values.

20 1. Give causes, symptoms, diagnosis and prognosis of variola. Describe treatment under the following heads :

(*a*) Prophylactic,
(*b*) Hygienic,
(*c*) Dietetic,
(*d*) Medicinal.

15 2. What are the causes, symptoms and treatment of rheumatic fever? From what conditions would you have to diagnose it?

20 3. How would you diagnose between the following diseases: Acute gastritis, gastric ulcer?

20 4. What are the symptoms indicating complications in typhoid fever and what would be your treatment for each of the complications?

10 5. What is empyema? What are the causes, symptoms, and treatment?

15 6. What diseases give raise to pain and distress in the pericardial region? Diagnose between the different conditions.

D. J. SINCLAIR, M.D., Examiner.

Intermediate and Final.

PATHOLOGY.

Value 0 to 100.   Time 3 hours.

All questions equal.

1. Describe and give the life history of the tænia mediocanellata.

2. Given a case of advanced alcoholic cirrhosis of the liver; give a concise *post-mortem* (gross) report.

3. What are the characteristics of malignant growths as compared with begnign. What are the malignant growths of the stomach and intestines.

4. What is an aneurism. Describe the different forms anatomically.

THERAPEUTICS.

1. Describe the therapeutical management of a patient suffering with dyspnœa, consequent upon consolidated lung in pneumonia.

2. Describe in detail the action of opium on the stomach and intestines.

BACTERIOLOGY.

1. Gonococcus: Tell where found; describe and give ordinary process of determining presence in pus.

2. Given an infective material containing the diphtheria baccillus, streptococcus pyogenes, and staphylococcus pyogenes aureus; describe the process by which you isolate one from the other so as to get pure cultures.

W. P. CAVAN, M.B., L.R.C.P., (Lon.),
Examiner.

N.B.—Candidates for Final on four year course, write on Pathology and Therapeutics only. Candidates for Intermediate write on Pathology and Bacteriology.

Intermediate and Final.

MIDWIFERY, OTHER THAN OPERATIVE.

PUERPERAL AND INFANTILE DISEASES.

Value 0 to 100.   Time 2½ hours.

Values.
15 1. What is natural labor? Write a short definition of it.

15 2. Do you favor early or late rupture of membranes in pelvic presentations? Give your reasons.

15 3. State the abnormal conditions of the soft parts that may obstruct labor.

25 4. Mention the usual situations where septic absorption takes place in puerperul septicæmia, and state why the primiparæ are more liable to infection than multiparæ.

15 5. What accidents or injuries may occur in precipitate labor?

15 6. Define the forms of jaundice which come on a few days after birth.

H. HOWITT, M.D., Examiner.

Intermediate and Final.

MIDWIFERY, OTHER THAN OPERATIVE.

PUERPERAL AND INFANTILE DISEASES.
HOMŒOPATHIC.

Value 0 to 100.   Time 2½ hours.

Values.
15 1. What are the causes of delay in
(*a*) The first stage of labor.
(*b*) The second stage of labor.

15 2. Give the diet for an infant two weeks old in which from some cause you are unable to have the child nurse.

10 3. What are the causes, symptoms, prognosis and treatment of ophthalmia neonatorum ?

30 4. What are the different forms of ectopic gestation ? How would you diagnose such a condition and from what other conditions would you have to diagnose it ?

30 5. Name and diagnose the most frequent accidents or complications met with during the period of gestation and give an outline of your treatment in each case.

D. J. SINCLAIR, M.D., Examiner.

Intermediate and Final.

MIDWIFERY, OPERATIVE.

Value 0 to 100.   Time 2½ hours.

Values.
25 1. Under what circumstances during the puerperal period would you give an intra-uterine douche ? Specify the instruments and other agents you would require.

25 2. How would you manage incomplete abortion in which the placenta is not only retained but attached ?

25 3. How does Sanger's operation differ from Porro's. Outline a case in which you would advise Sanger's method.

25 4. In reference to the blunt hook :

(a) Describe it and give your opinion of its value in practice.

(b) State an obstetric complication in which you have good authority to use it, and mention to what part you would apply it.

(c) State what injuries are liable to result from its use and describe any substitutes for it of which you have knowledge.

H. HOWITT, M.D., Examiner.

Intermediate and Final.

SURGERY, OTHER THAN OPERA-TIVE.

Value 0 to 100.   Time 2½ Hours.

Values.
18 1. Give symptoms and treatment of fracture of the femur below the great trochanter. What are the dangers to aged people under such circumstances.

25 2. When is colostomy indicated ? Where would you perform it and why ?

15 3. How would you treat a compound comminuted fracture of the tibia.

12 4. Give cause, symptoms and treatment of acute teno-synovitis ?

30 5. How would you distinguish between hæmorrhage coming from the kidneys ? bladder ? urethra. Enumerate the surgical diseases of the testicles, with treatment of each ?

A. BEVERLY WELFORD, M.B., Examiner.

Intermediate and Final.

SURGERY, OTHER THAN OPERA-TIVE.

HOMŒOPATHIC.

Value 0 to 100.   Time 2½ Hours.

Values.
10 1. Describe floating kidney. Give symptoms and prognosis.

25 2. What are the different dislocations occurring at the shoulder joint ? Give symptoms of each and methods of reduction.

20 3. Describe acute osteo-myelitis. Give causes, pathology, symptoms, prognosis and treatment ?

15 4. What are the different forms of erysipelas, its symptoms and treatment ?

30 5. Name the different malignant growths giving a brief clinical history of each.

D. J. SINCLAIR, M.D., Examiner.

Intermediate and final.

SURGERY, OPERATIVE.

Value 0 to 100.   Time 2½ hours.

Values.
30 1. What are the three well recognized forms of appendicitis, with treatment of each form ?

15 2. Give the symptoms, physical signs and treatment of ileo-colic intussusception ?

15 3. Describe Wyeth's amputation at the hip joint.

MEDICAL AND SURGICAL ANATOMY.

Value 0 to 100.   Time 2½ hours.

All questions equal.

1. Locate gall bladder.

2. Description female urethra.

3. Composition spermatic cord.

4. Position arteries supplying scalp.

5. Nerve supply to eye-ball and muscles.

6. What enters into formation wrist joint.

7. Relations of a loop of intestine in inguinal canal.

8. Course and importance deep epigastric artery.

9. Of what use, as a landmark, is the cricoid cartilage to the surgeon?

10. How does the venous blood leave the rectum?

HADLEY WILLIAMS, M.D., Examiner.

———

Intermediate and Final.

MEDICAL JURISPRUDENCE.

Value 0 to 100.   Time 2½ hours.

All questions equal.

1. Give the signs of " live-birth " as found on examination of the " thoracic " and " abdominal " cavities.

2. Give the evidences of recent delivery at full term ; in the " living," and in the " dead."

3. What *post-mortem* conditions would enable you to decide that death had been caused (*a*) by "strangulation," (*b*) by "drowning." In the latter give external and internal conditions.

4. Distinguish between " self-inflicted " wounds and those inflicted by an " assailant."

5. Distinguish between " burns " inflicted before and after death.

legal responsibility in each case.

C. VAN NORMAN EMORY, M.D.,
Examiner.

N. B.—Candidates for final under 4 year course, write on Medical Jurisprudence only. Candidates for intermediate write on Medical Jurisprudence, Theology and Mental Diseases.

———

Intermediate and Final.

SANITARY SCIENCE.

Value 0 to 100.   Time 1½ hours.

Values.

25   1. Define the two great classes of foods ; the purposes served by each ; and the result of too great a preponderance of either.

25   2. Conduct a case of " diphtheria," the patient being treated at home. From a sanitary point of view give means to prevent its spread.

25   3. What are the various sources of " water" supply? Give the comparative purity of each. The most frequent impurities found in each.

25   4. Name and describe fully what you consider the best two modes of ventilation for public buildings.

C. VAN NORMAN EMORY, M.D.,
Examiner.

———

Intermediate.

THERAPEUTICS.

Value 0 to 100.   Time 2½ hours.

All questions equal.

1. Describe the action of nitrite of amyl on the circulatory system. What are the indications for its use therapeutically?

3. Write a prescription for a diuretic mixture and explain its action.

4. Describe in detail the action of salicylic acid both externally and internally. What are its specific uses?

5. Explain the action on the secretions of opium, belladonna, and mercury.

W. P. CAVEN, M.B., L.R.C.P. (Lon.), Examiner.

Intermediate.

DISEASES OF WOMEN.

Value 0 to 100.   Time 2½ hours.

Values.

20 1. Give symptoms and treatment of irritable urethal caruncle.

25 2. Give symptoms, diagnosis and treatment of fungoid degeneration of uterine mucous membrane.

25 3. In reference to fibroid tumors of the uterus, give

(a) Predisposing causes.

(b) Varieties as to situation.

(c) Your treatment of submucous form with frequent and severe hemorrhages.

H. HOWITT, M.D., Examiner.

Intermediate.

DISEASES OF CHILDREN.

Value 0 to 100.   Time 2½ hours.

Values.

25 I. Give the exciting causes of infantile convulsions and your treatment during an attack.

25 2. Write a prescription for whooping cough, and mention the complications which are liable to occur in the disease.

25 3. Mention at what age in the following congenital malformations you would advise operative measures, and give reasons:

(1) Hare lip.

(2) Cleft palate.

(3) Hypospadias.

25 4. Give the symptoms of Raynaud's disease and the etiology, and treatment of chorea.

H. HOWITT, M.D., Examiner

BY-LAWS OF THE MEDICAL COUNCIL

College of Physicians and Surgeons of Ontario

By-Law No. 39.

Rules and Regulations for conducting the proceedings of the Medical Council of the College of Physicians and Surgeons of Ontario.

MEETINGS.

1. The annual session of the Council shall take place on the first Tuesday of July in each year, at Toronto ; but special sessions may be called by the President whenever he may consider it advisable. And it shall be the duty of the President to call special sessions on a requisition signed ' by two-thirds of the members. No business shall be taken up at a special session except that for which the session has been called, and of which every-member has been notified.

2. At the annual session of the Council the President (or, in his absence, the Vice-President) shall take the chair and declare the Council organized, when the Council shall proceed to elect officers. In the absence of the President and Vice-President the Council shall appoint a Chairman, *provided* that at the first meeting of a new Council the Registrar shall call the Council to order, read over the names of the members, and shall call on the Council to elect a President.

3. The President and Vice-President shall be elected from among the members of the Council, after nomination by open vote and not by ballot ; that after nomination, when only one candidate is nominated, it shall be the duty of the presiding officer to declare such candidate duly elected, and a majority of the votes of the members present shall be necessary to an election ; *provided*, that in case of a tie, the election shall be decided by the member representing the greatest number of registered practitioners.

4. The first business after the organization of the Council and the election of officers, shall be the appointment of a Committee to Nominate the Standing Committees.

OFFICERS.

1. The officers of the Council shall be a President, Vice-President, Registrar, Treasurer and Solicitor, and such others as the Council may deem necessary.

2. The salaried officers shall be elected after nomination, and shall hold office during the pleasure of the Council.

RULES OF ORDER.

1. The President shall preside at all meetings, call the Council to order at the hour appointed, and cause the minutes of the preceding meeting to be read, confirmed and signed.

2. In the absence of the President, the Vice-President shall call the meeting to order, or a Chairman *pro tem.* may, in the absence of the latter, be chosen by the Council.

3. When the President or other presiding officer is called on to decide a point of order or practice, he shall state the rule applicable to the case without argument or comment, subject to an appeal to the Council.

4. The President shall declare all votes ; but if any member demands it, the President, in case of open vote, without further debate on the question, shall require the members voting in the affirmative and negative respectively to stand until they are counted, and he shall then declare the result. At the request of any member the yeas and nays shall be taken and recorded.

The President or other presiding officer may express his opinion on any subject under debate ; but in such case he shall leave the chair until the question is decided, appointing some other member to take it. But he shall decide points of order or practice without leaving his place.

6. When any member is about to speak in debate he shall rise in his place and address the presiding officer, confining himself to the

question under debate and avoiding personality.

7. When two or more members rise at the same time, the President or presiding officer shall name the member who is first to speak.

8. No member while speaking shall be interrupted by another, except upon a point of order, or for the purpose of explanation. The member so rising shall confine himself strictly to the point of order, or the explanation.

9. If any member, in speaking or otherwise, transgresses the rules, the President shall, or any member may, call him to order; in which case the member so called shall immediately sit down, unless permitted to explain ; and the Council, if appealed to, shall decide on the case, but without debate.

10. No member shall speak more than once upon any resolution or motion, except the proposer, who shall be permitted to reply; nor shall any member speak longer than a quarter of an hour on the same question without the leave of the Council, except in explanation, and then he must not introduce new matter.

11. Any member of the Council may require the question under discussion to be read at any time of the debate, but not so as to interrupt a speaker.

12. No member shall speak to any question after the same has been put by the President.

13. Notice shall be given of all motions for introducing new matter, other than matters of privilege and petitions, at a meeting previous to that at which it comes up for discussion, unless dispensed with by a three-fourths vote of the members present. Any matter when once decided by the Council shall not be re-introduced during the continuance of that session, unless by a two-thirds vote of the Council then present.

14. A motion must be put in writing and seconded before it is stated by the President, and then shall be disposed of only by a vote of the Council, unless the mover, by permission of the Council, withdraws it. Every member present shall vote unless excused by the Council.

15. At the close of the annual session the minutes of the last meeting shall be read over, adopted and signed by the President or other presiding officer.

16. The Registrar shall make a list of all resolutions and reports on the table, which shall be considered "The General Orders of the Day," the order of the same to be as follows:

(1) Calling names of members and marking them as present or absent.

(2) Reading of the minutes.

(3) Notices of motion.

(4) Reading of communications, petitions, etc,, to the Council.

(5) Motions of which notice has been given at a previous meeting.

(6) Inquiries.

(7) Reports of standing and special committees.

(9) Unfinished business from previous meetings.

(10) Miscellaneous business.

No variation in the foregoing order of business shall be permitted, except by the consent of the Council.

17. When a question is under debate, no motion shall be received unless—

(1) To adjourn.

(2) The previous question.

(3) To postpone.

(4) To lay on the table.

(5) To refer.

(6) To amend.

The Chairman shall put the previous question in this form : "Shall the main question be now put?" and its adoption shall end all debate and bring the Council to vote upon the main question.

18. The Chairman shall consider a motion to adjourn as always in order, and that motion and the motion to lay on the table shall be decided without debate.

19. Any member who has made a motion may withdraw the same by leave of the Council, or it may be allowed to stand, such leave being granted without a negative voice.

COMMITTEES.

1. The Standing Committees shall be the following :

(a) Registration, consisting of seven members.

(b) Education, consisting of nine members.

(c) Finance, consisting of five members.

(d) Rules and Regulations, consisting of five members.

(e) Printing, consisting of five members.

(f) On Complaints, consisting of five members.

(g) Executive, consisting of three members.

(h) On Property, consisting of five members.

(i) On Discipline, consisting of three or five members.

2. A majority of a committee shall constitute a quorum.

3. When a committee presents its reports, such report shall be received without motion or debate, On reading the Order of Business for the "Consideration of Reports," the reports previously received shall be taken up in the order of their reception, and may be acted on directly by the Council or referred to Committee of the Whole.

4. When the Council shall determine to go into Committee of the Whole, the Chairman shall name the member who will take the chair.

5. The rules of the Council shall be observed in Committee of the Whole, except the rules respecting the yeas and nays and limiting the number of times of speaking; and no motion for the previous question or for an adjournment can be received, but a member may at any time move that the chairman leave the chair or report progress, or ask leave to sit again ; and all original motions shall be put in the order in which they are proposed, and shall not require to be seconded.

6. On motion in committee to rise and report, the question shall be decided without debate.

7. Every member who shall introduce a petition or motion upon any subject which may be referred to a select committee appointed to consider such motion or petition, shall, during the sittings of the Council, be one of the committee without being named by the Council. Any member of the Council may be placed upon a committee, notwithstanding the absence of such member at the time of his being named to such committee.

8. Committees appointed to report on any subject referred to them by the Council shall report a statement of facts and also their opinion thereon in writing, and it shall be the duty of the chairman, or acting chairman, to sign and present the report.

9. All petitions or communications on any subject within the cognizance of a standing committee shall, on presentation, be referred by the chairman, or presiding officer, to the proper committee without any motion ; but it shall be competent for the Council, by a three-fourths vote, to enter on immediate consideration thereof.

10. The President and Vice-President shall be *ex-officio* members of all committees of the Council, standing and special, excepting " Committee on Discipline."

DUTIES OF THE COMMITTEES—COMMITTEE ON FINANCE.

1. The Committee on Finance shall have the supervision of the fiscal concerns of the Council, and report the condition of the various funds.

2. They shall prepare a detailed statement of the necessary estimates of money required by the Council for the year, and report the same for the consideration and action of the Council.

3. They shall consider and report on all matters referred to them by the Council.

EXECUTIVE COMMITTEE.

The Executive Committee shall take cognizance of and action upon all such matters as may be delegated to it by the Council, or such as may require immediate interference or attention between the adjournment of the Council and its next meeting.

DUTIES OF THE REGISTRAR.

1. The Registrar shall attend all meetings of the Council, and record minutes of the proceedings of such meetings.

2. He shall give notice to each member of all meetings of the Council or its committees twenty days before each meeting.

3. He shall conduct all correspondence.

4. He shall receive and submit all documents for the Council or standing committees, take charge of all reports, correspondence, accounts and other documents and fyle the same.

5. He shall make returns of all salaries, make out all orders for payment, and keep full accounts of all expenditure.

6. He shall examine the credentials of candidates for examination and make the necessary preparation for examinations, and every candidate shall fyle with his application a statutory declaration that the schedule he has signed and presented is correct.

7. He shall number all by-laws and affix the seal of the college thereto.

8. He shall, on the 31st day of October in each and every year, send to each member of the College of Physicians and Surgeons of Ontario who has up to that date failed to pay his dues and take out his annual certificate, a registered letter addressed to the registered address of such member, informing him that unless the said dues are paid by the 31st December of that year his name shall be erased from the register of the College of Physicians and Surgeons of Ontario, and the Registrar shall erase the names from the register of all persons who have not paid their dues for one year, counting such year from the 31st December in one year to the same date in the next.

DUTIES OF THE TREASURER.

1. The Treasurer shall keep a detailed statement of receipts and expenditure and submit annually a balance sheet, setting those forth fully, as well as a statement of sundries, and the particular accounts to which these belong, and pay out moneys in settlement of all accounts that have been certified correct and signed by the President, Chairman of the Executive Committee and Registrar.

SOLICITOR.

1. The Solicitor shall give to the Council, or its President, his advice or opinion upon any question of the law (properly) submitted to him for that purpose.

2. He shall also give, on requisition signed by the President, his opinion in the same way to any officer now appointed or who may be hereafter appointed by the Council.

3. It shall be the duty of all officers of the Council to furnish the Solicitor, upon request, with any documents, books or papers in the custody or possession of such officers, and to give to the said Solicitor such other aid and assistance as he may require in the performance of the duties of said office.

AUDITOR.

The Auditor shall audit all the accounts of the Council and present his annual report on the same on or before the first day of June in each year.

BY-LAWS.

1. After notice of motion given at a previous meeting, a proposed by-law may be introduced, read a first time, and referred to Committee of the Whole.

2. The second reading shall take place in Committee of the Whole, and shall be clause by clause.

3. When the Committee of the Whole report the proposed by-law, it shall be read a third time in Council, and if adopted on such third reading, the President shall declare the by-law passed, and shall sign the same.

AMENDMENTS.

No amendment or addition to any of the foregoing rules and regulations shall be made unless the notice, setting forth the proposed amendment or addition, shall have been given at a meeting previous to that at which the same comes up for discussion, and all resolutions of the Council inconsistent with the above rules and regulations are hereby repealed.

All of which is respectfully submitted.

(Signed) HENRY W. DAY, Chairman.

Adopted as amended.   J. L. BRAY,
Chairman Com. of Whole.

By-law read a third time and declared passed.   J. G. CRANSTON,
President.

Wednesday, June 12, 1889,

Toronto, Ont.   [SEAL.]

BY-LAW No. 47.

For fixing the salary of the Registrar.

Whereas power hath been granted to the Council of the College of Physicians and Surgeons to make by-laws, be it therefore and it is hereby enacted ; That the salary of the Registrar be fixed at $1,800.00 per annum, to be paid monthly or quarterly.

Adopted in Committee of the Whole.

R. B. ORR, Chairman.

Adopted and read a third time in Council,

V. H. MOORE, President.

BY-LAW No. 52.

Whereas power has been given to the College of Physicians and Surgeons of Ontario to make by-laws, be it therefore and it is hereby enacted : That the Treasurer and Registrar of the Medical Council of the College of Physicians and Surgeons of Ontario are hereby authorized to jointly borrow in their official capacity, as officers of the College, upon the security of the College, such sum and sums of money as may be required for the use of the College, not, however, to exceed in the aggregate at any one time $12,000.00, from the Imperial Bank of Canada, or other chartered banks in good standing, and that for such sums they are authorized to use promissory notes, each of such notes to be signed by the Treasurer and Registrar of the Council of the College of Physicians and Surgeons of Ontario. Such sums are to be placed to the credit of the College, subject, like other College funds, to the order or cheque of the Treasurer of the Medical Council of the College of Physicians and Surgeons of Ontario.

Read first, second and third time, and adopted.

G. HENDERSON,
Chairman Committee of Whole.

J. ARTHUR WILLIAMS,
President.

BY-LAW No, 53.

A By-law to amend By-law No. 39.

Whereas power has been given to the College of Physicians and Surgeons of Ontario, to make by-laws, be it therefore enacted : That the Registrar shall, on the 31st day of October in each and every year, send to each member of the College of Physicians and Surgeons of Ontario who has up to that date failed to pay his dues and to take out his annual certificate, a registered letter addressed to the registered address of such member, informing him that unless the said dues are paid by the 31st December of that year his name shall be erased from the Register of the College of Physicians and Surgeons of Ontario, and the Registrar shall erase the names from the Register of all persons who have not paid their dues for one year, counting such year from the 31st December in one year to the same date in the next.

Adopted. J. L. BRAY,
Chairman Committee of Whole.

Adopted in Council.

J. ARTHUR WILLIAMS,
President.

BY-LAW No. 58.

To amend By-law No. 39 as amended by By-law No. 50.

1. Clause (meetings) is amended by erasing the word "seven" (7) in the seventh line thereof, and substituting therefor the words "two-thirds of the."

2. Clause (committees) is amended by erasing the word "three" in line "h," and substituting therefor the word "five."

Adopted. D. L. PHILIP, President.

BY-LAW No. 59.

By-law to provide for the election of the territorial members of the Medical Council of the College of Physicians and Surgeons of Ontario.

Whereas power hath been granted to the Medical Council of the College of Physicians and Surgeons of Ontario to make by-laws to regulate the time and manner of holding the elections under the provisions of the Ontario Medical Act, R.S.O. 1887, C. 142, 56, 50 V., C. 24, S. I., and amendments thereto, be it therefore enacted as follows :

1. That this by-law shall only apply to the election of territorial representatives of the divisions named in schedule "A" and appended to the amended Medical Act of 1893, and for appointing returning officers for the ensuing elections of territorial representatives to serve in the Medical Council for the time allotted to them, in accordance with the amendments to the Medical Act as made in 1893 ; that is to say :

No. 1. For the counties of Essex, Kent and Lambton, Dr. J. P. Rutherford, Chatham, Ont.

No. 2. The counties of Elgin, Norfolk and Oxford, Dr. C. E. Duncombe, St. Thomas, Ont.

No. 3. County of Middlesex, Dr. B. Bayly, London, Ont.

No. 4. Counties of Huron and Perth, Dr. A. Taylor, Goderich, Ont.

No. 5. Counties of Waterloo and Wellington, Dr. A. MacKinnon, Guelph, Ont.

No. 6. Counties of Bruce, Grey and Dufferin, Dr. C. Barnhart, Owen Sound, Ont.

No. 7. Counties of Wentworth, Halton and Peel, Dr. F. E. Woolverton, Hamilton, Ont.

No. 8. Lincoln, Welland, Haldimand and Brant, Dr. U. M. Stanley, Brantford, Ont.

No. 9. Simcoe, districts of Muskoka, Parry Sound, Nipissing, Algoma, including Manitoulin, Thunder Bay and Rainy River, Dr. J. L. G. McCarthy, Barrie, Ont,

No. 10. The city of Toronto lying east of Yonge street, Dr. George Bingham, Toronto, Ont.

No. 11. The city of Toronto lying west of Yonge street, Dr. R. B. Orr, Toronto, Ont.

No. 12. Counties of Ontario, Victoria and York, exclusive of Toronto, Dr. J. F. Gilmour, Toronto Junction, Ont.

No. 13. Northumberland, Peterboro', Durham and Haliburton, Dr. R. P. Boucher, Peterboro', Ont.

No. 14. Counties of Prince Edward, Hastings and Lennox, Dr. H. W. Day, Belleville, Ont.

No. 15. Counties of Frontenac, Addington, Renfrew and Lanark, Dr. A. S. Oliver, Kingston, Ont.

No. 16. Counties of Leeds, Grenville and Dundas, Dr. W. P. Buckley, Prescott, Ont.

No. 17. Counties of Carleton, Russell, Prescott, Glengarry and Stormont, Dr. E. C. Malloch, Ottawa, Ont.

2. That any member of the College presenting himself for election as the representative to the Medical Council of the College of Physicians and Surgeons of Ontario for a territorial division, must receive a nomination of at least 20 (twenty) registered practitioners resident in such division, and that such nomination paper must be in the hands of the returning officer of the division not later than the hour of 2 o'clock p.m. on the 9th of October, the second Tuesday in October, 1894.

In the event of only one candidate receiving such nomination, it shall then be the duty of the returning officer to declare such candidate duly elected, and to notify the Registrar of the College by sending him such declaration in writing.

3. That the Registrar of the College shall send to every registered member of the College of Physicians and Surgeons of Ontario (excepting only those who are registered as the homœopathic members thereof), a voting paper (in accordance with the residence given on the Register) in form of

Schedule " A " attached to this by-law, and a circular directing the voter to write his or her name as the voter, and his or her place of residence, and the county in which his or her place of residence is situated, and to fill up said voting paper on form of Schedule " A " attached to this by-law, as directed in circular to be enclosed.

The Registrar shall, fifty (50) days before the time for receiving nominations for the elections, which time is second Tuesday (9th) of October, 1894, send a post card to every registered medical practitioner, excepting the homœopathic members, in the Province, in accordance with address in hands of Registrar, giving the dates up to which nominations for representatives to the Medical Council of the College of Physicians and Surgeons will be received.

The Registrar shall advertise in the medical journals published in Toronto, during August and September, 1894, the fact that elections for the Medical Council are to be held, stating the time that nominations will be received up till, and the time of holding the election.

Also a voting paper shall be sent to every registered practitioner entitled to receive the same, by the third Tuesday (16th) of October, 1894, and that every member of the College not having received a voting paper, when a candidate has been properly nominated for their division, shall send by post to the Registrar their name and address, and the Registrar will forward paper to member so applying.

The voter is to be directed in the circular, which is to accompany the voting paper, to send by post or mail the voting paper, properly filled up, giving the name and residence of the person for whom he or she votes, enclosed in an envelope, which shall be forwarded along with the circular and voting paper. The envelope in which the voter is to place his or her voting paper shall have the name and the address of the returning officer appointed to act in the territorial division in which the voter resides.

4. That the Registrar of the College shall mail the voting paper to the members of the College of Physicians and Surgeons of Ontario who are legally entitled to vote, according to their addresses in the possession of the Registrar on the third Tuesday (16th) of October, 1894, the postage, etc., all of which is to be paid by the College, and that the Registrar shall forward to any member making application a voting paper for his division after the 16th of October, upon application.

That the Registrar shall place a stamp upon each of the enclosed envelopes, which are to be used by the members of the College in sending their voting paper to the returning officer for the division. That the returning officer shall receive the votes sent to him up to the hour of 2 o'clock p.m., on the 30th of October, 1894.

5. That the returning officer in each division at the hour of two o'clock p.m., on the 30th of October, 1894, shall open the envelopes and carefully count and examine the voting papers, and make a record of the entire number of votes cast, together with the declaration of the name of the person and address who has recieved the greatest number of votes, who shall be declared elected as the representative of the division, and in case two or more candidates receive an equal number of votes, the returning officer shall give the casting vote for one of such candidates, which shall decide the election ; and then at the hour of 2 o'clock p.m., on the 30th of October, 1894, when the returning officer opens the envelopes he has received and counts the votes, all or any of the candidates in the division, or their agents, may be present if duly appointed and authorized to act in writing on behalf of any candidate, and see the envelopes opened and the votes counted, and they shall be permitted to examine all voting papers to satisfy themselves as to the voting papers being properly filled up, and that the persons signing the voting papers were duly registered members of the College of Physicians and Surgeons of Ontario, and entitled to vote at the election of territorial representatives in the Medical Council of the College of Physicians and Surgeons of Ontario.

6. The returning officer in each division shall not open any envelopes he may receive as returning officer until the hour of 2 o'clock p.m. arrives on the 30th of October, 1894, and that the returning officers, respectively, shall seal up and return all the voting papers connected with the election to the Registrar of the College within six (6) days from the time appointed for holding the election, which time is 2 o'clock p.m., on the 30th of October, 1894.

That the returning officer shall reject all voting papers that are not properly filled up in accordance with instructions contained in circular which is to be sent with each voting paper.

The returning officer shall return all envelopes received after 2 o'clock p.m., on the afternoon of the 30th of October, 1894, stamped as returning officer of the division, to the Registrar of the College, unopened and marked "too late."

7. That the Registrar, on receiving declaration from the returning officer, declaring a candidate has received the largest number of votes in the division, shall forthwith inform the candidate declared elected that he has been chosen to represent said division in the Medical Council of the College of Physicians and Surgeons of Ontario, and the Registrar shall inform each member so elected of the time and place of the first meeting of the

Council after the said election shall have taken place.

It shall be the duty of the Registrar to attend the said meeting of the Council and to have with him there and then all the papers and documents sent to him by the returning officers, in order that they may be submitted to the Council, and the representatives so named by the returning officers as duly elected shall form the territorial representatives to the Medical Council of the College of Physicians and Surgeons of Ontario.

8. It is hereby enacted that the returning officer of each division is to be named by the Council or Executive Committee and appointed by the Council, and in case any returning officer appointed either refuses to act or is incapacitated, that the Registrar shall fill such vacancy by appointing some member of the College residing in the territorial division on recommendation of the Executive Committee of the Council.

That the fee for acting as returning officer shall be ten dollars ($10.00) for each division.

9. The form of voting paper to be sent to each member of the College, and the form of circular to be used at election of territorial representatives to the Medical Council is to be the same as that on Schedules "A" and "B," appended to this by-law.

D. BERGIN,
Chairman Committee of the Whole.
June 14th, 1894.

SCHEDULE "A."

SCHEDULE "B."

COLLEGE OF PHYSICIANS AND SURGEONS OF ONTARIO.

Election for territorial representatives to the Medical Council of Ontario, 1894.

The voting paper herewith enclosed is to be filled up carefully and put into the enclosed envelope, which is directed to the returning officer, and mailed in time to reach him not later than 2 o'clock p.m. on Tuesday, October 30th, 1894.

Sign your name to voting paper.

R. A. PYNE, Registrar,
Coll. Phys. and Surgs. Ont.,
Toronto, Ont.

Adopted.   D. BERGIN.

BY-LAW No. 60.

To provide for the election of the homœopathic members of the Medical Council of the College of Physicians and Surgeons of Ontario:

Whereas power has been given to the College of Physicians and Surgeons of Ontario to regulate the time and manner of holding the election under the provisions of the Ontario Medical Act, R.S.O. 1877, C 142, 56, 50 V., C. 24, S.I., and amendments thereto, be it therefore enacted as follows :

1. This by-law shall only apply to the election of the homœopathic members to the Medical Council of Ontario.

2. That the Registrar shall send to every registered homœopathic member of the College of Physicians and Surgeons of Ontario a voting paper and circular, directing each to write his name, his residence, etc.

3. That on or before a certain time, to be named in the circular sent to each voter, the voter shall send by post or mail to the Registrar of the College, so that the Registrar shall receive the same on or before the 30th day of October, 1894, the said voting paper, enclosed in an envelope, which is to be sent to the voter, with the voting pap-r filled up properly with his name and residence, and the person or persons for whom he voted.

4. That R. A. Pyne, M.D., Registrar of the College of Physicians and Surgeons of Ontario, is hereby appointed returning officer for the said homœopathic elections to take place on the 30th day of October, 1894, at the hour of 2 o'clock p.m., and in case a tie occurs, the returning officer is to give the casting vote, which will decide the election.

5. The said returning officer shall carefully preserve the voting papers sent to him, and shall upon the day appointed, at the hour of 2 o'clock p.m. on the said day, open and examine the voting papers sent to him, and carefully count the votes, and make a record thereof of the votes cast, and shall inform by letter the five homœopathic candidates having the greatest number of votes that they are elected as the homœopathic representatives in the Medical Council of the College of Physicians and Surgeons of Ontario.

And the said returning officer shall, after counting carefully the votes contained in the envelopes, preserve the voting papers and all other documents, envelopes, etc., sent to him connected with the election of the homœopathic members of the College of Physicians and Surgeons of Ontario, and present the same to the Medical Council.

6. The returning officer shall not open any paper or document he may have received as returning officer for the homœopathic elections after 2 o'clock p.m. on the 30th day of October, 1894.

7. The returning officer shall not count any voting paper that is not properly filled out, in accordance with instructions contained in the circular which has accompanied the voting paper when sent to the voter.

8. The returning officer shall permit any candidate, and the agent of any candidate duly appointed and authorized in writing to act on behalf of any candidate, to be present at the counting of the votes, and who shall be permitted to satisfy himself as to the voting paper being properly filled up, and that the person signing the voting paper was a duly registered member of the College of Physicians and Surgeons of Ontario, and entitled to vote at the election of the homœopathic representatives in the Medical Council of the College of Physicians and Surgeons of Ontario, and who may examine any or all of the voting papers.

9. The form of voting paper and circular for the homœopathic elections is to be the same as that on Schedules "A" and "B," to this by-law appended.

10. It shall be the duty of the Registrar of the College of Physicians and Surgeons of Ontario to inform the said elected members of the time and place of the first meeting of the Medical Council of the College of Physicians and Surgeons of Ontario.

J. L. BRAY,

Chairman Committee of the Whole.

Adopted in Council.

D. L. PHILIP, President.

HOMŒOPATHIC ELECTIONS, 1894.

SCHEDULE "A."

COLL. PHYS. & SURG. OF ONT. OFFICE OF MEDICAL REGISTRATION

S. E. cor. Bay & Richmond Sts., Toronto.

SCHEDULE "B."

COLLEGE OF PHYSICIANS AND SURGEONS OF ONTARIO.

Election for Homœopathic representatives to the Medical Council of Ontario, 1894.

The voting paper herewith enclosed is to be filled up carefully and put into the enclosed envelope, which is directed to the returning officer, and mailed in time to reach him not later than 2 o'clock p.m. on Tuesday, October 30th, 1894.

Sign your name to voting paper.

R. A. PYNE, Registrar,

Coll. Phys. and Surg. Ont.,

Toronto, Ont.

BY-LAW No. 68.

Council of the College of Physicians and Surgeons of Ontario, to amend By-law No. 39 as amended by By-law No. 50.

Whereas power hath been granted to the Medical Council of the College of Physicians and Surgeons of Ontario to make by-laws under the Ontario Medical Act, be it enacted as follows:

1. That Article 3 of the duties of the Finance Committee, page lvii. be amended by striking out the whole clause and substituting therefor these words, "They shall consider and report on all matters referred to them by the Council."

Also,

2. That Clause 1 on duties of the Treasurer, page lvii, be amended by striking out all the words after "moneys" in the fourth line and inserting in lieu thereof the following words : " In settlement of all accounts that have been certified correct and signed by the President, Chairman of the Executive Committee and Registrar.

3. The Auditor shall audit all the accounts of the Council and present his annual report on the same on or before the first day of June in each year.

JAMES HENRY, Chairman of Com.

June 26th, 1895.

WILLIAM T. HARRIS, President.

BY-LAW No. 69.

Whereas by Section 6 of the Ontario Medical Amendment Act, 1893, 56 Vic., Chap. 27, Sec. 27 of the "Ontario Medical Act" (R.S.O., 1887, C. 148) and section 41a amending the same, enacted by the Act passed in the 54th year of Her Majesty's reign, Chap. 26, and entitled, "An Act to amend the Ontario Medical Act," were suspended, and it was by the said Act declared that the said section should continue suspended unless and until after the elections of 1894, a by-law should be passed by the Council of the college adopting the same in whole or in part.

And whereas this college has a floating debt which must be provided for and outstanding assessments which if made available would cover the same, it is therefore necessary and expedient that the same shall be adopted and put in force.

And whereas it is necessary and expedient that the same should be adopted.

Now therefore the Council of the College of Physicians and Surgeons of Ontario enacts as follows :

1. Section 27 of the Ontario Medical Act (R. S. O. 1887, C. 148) and Section 41a amending the same, enacted by the Act passed in the 54th year of Her Majesty's reign, Chapter 26, and entitled " An Act to amend the Ontario Medical Act," are hereby adopted.

2. Each member of the College shall pay to the Registrar towards the general expenses of the College an annual fee amounting to two dollars ($2.00) pursuant to the provisions of Section 27 of the Ontario Medical Act aforesaid for year 1895.

3. It is further hereby declared and enacted that the said suspended sections are adopted by the Council of the said college and the suspension thereof abrogated from

the day of the date when the same were by the Ontario Medical Amendment Act, 1893, suspended, and that each member of the college shall pay to the Registrar pursuant to the provisions of Section 27 aforesaid the annual fee of two dollars ($2.00) for each year during the time when the said sections were so suspended, viz.: for years 1893 and 1894.

4. The Registrar is hereby directed to collect the annual fee hereinbefore fixed and determined, together with all other fees and dues in arrear and owing by any member of the said college, and to enforce all provisions of the Ontario Medical Act as amended. Upon default, subject to the provisions of this by-law.

5. And be it further enacted, that part of Clause 1 known as 41a be suspended until the first of June, 1896, then to come into force in case a sufficient amount of dues is not paid over to the bank liability.

6. And be it further enacted, that the Registrar be required to send to each practitioner a registered letter, enclosing a copy of the by-law, together with a circular letter and account of dues, explaining the necessity of imposing the fee and calling special attention to the suspension of 41a until June 1st, 1896.

Adopted in committee of the whole as amended.

V. H. MOORE,

Chairman Committee of Whole.

Adopted in Council, June 28th, 1895.

WILLIAM T. HARRIS, President.

BY-LAW No. 70.

That this By-law shall apply to the payment of members of Council, members of committees, members of Board of Examiners;

Whereas power hath been granted to the Medical Council of the College of Physicians and Surgeons of Ontario to fix the amount to be paid its members and officers, under Sections 12 and 13 of the Ontario Medical Act, be it therefore and it is hereby enacted.

1. That each member of Council shall receive $12.50 per diem for days necessarily absent from home, with an allowance of four cents per mile for each mile travelled.

2. That each member of the Discipline Committee shall be paid the same and mileage per diem as is paid members of this Council at its meetings.

3. That members of committees other than Discipline Committee, when meeting during the recess of the Council shall be paid a per diem allowance of $8.00 and four cents per mile for each mile travelled.

4. That each Examiner shall receive the sum of $20.00, and in addition thereto he shall receive thirty-five cents for each paper he may have to read over the number of fifty. Each examiner shall also receive $12.50 per diem for each day's attendance at oral examinations and meetings, with the same allowance of four cents per mile for the distance travelled to and from the examinations to place of residence.

That the oral examinations shall continue for five hours each day until they are completed.

5. That an allowance of $50.00 be paid to the Examiner on Descriptive Anatomy for providing wet preparations and dissections upon Descriptive Anatomy.

6 That By-law No. 22, and reports dealing with payment of members of Council, committee members, and members of the Board of Examiners are hereby repealed.

H. T. MACHELL,
Chairman Committee of Whole.

Passed in Council, June 27th, 1895.

WILLIAM T. HARRIS, President.

———

BY-LAW No. 73.

Whereas by By-law No. 69, passed under the authority of Section 6 of Chapter 27 of the Ontario Medical Amendment Act, 1893, the Council of the College of Physicians and Surgeons of Ontario adopted Section 27 of the Ontario Medical Act, R.S.O. 1887, Cap. 148 and Section 41a amending the same of an Act passed in the 54th year of Her Majesty's reign, Chapter 26, entitled "An Act to amend the Ontario Medical Act;"

And whereas by the said Section 6 of the Ontario Medical Amendment Act, 1893, the Council have power from time to time to vary such by-law ;

And whereas it is expedient that any member of the College of Physicians and Surgeons of Ontario who may not practice in any year should be relieved of payment of the annual fee for such year ;

Now therefore the Council of the College of Physicians and Surgeons of Ontario enacts as follows :

1. By-law No. 69 above referred to is hereby varied as follows : The annual fee determined by by-law of the Council under the authority of Section 27 of the Ontario Medical Act shall not be due and payable by any member of the College who, by reason of absence from the Province, or for any other reason, shall in no way practise medicine, surgery and midwifery in Ontario during the year for which such annual fee may be imposed.

Any registered medical practitioner who shall apply to the Registrar for a certificate in accordance with Section 41a of the Ontario Medical Act, claiming to have been relieved by this by-law of payment of the annual fee for any year, shall prove to the satisfaction of the Registrar that he has not practised his profession during the year for which such fee has been imposed, and shall, if the Registrar so requires it, make a statutory declaration to that effect, and furnish such other evidence as may be required.

The decision of the Registrar upon such application as to the liability of the applicant for the fee in question shall be final and conclusive.

Adopted in Committee of the Whole.

R. REDDICK, Chairman.

Read a third time and adopted in Council.

A. F. ROGERS, President.

———

BY-LAW No. 74.

To amend By-Law No. 70.

That paragraph 2 of Section 4 is amended by erasing the word "seven" and substituting therefor the word "five."

J. H. SANGSTER,
Chairman Committee of Whole

Adopted in Council.

A. F. ROGERS, President.

———

BY-LAW No. 75.

Whereas it is necessary and expedient that an annual fee be paid by each member of the College of Physicians and Surgeons of Ontario towards the general expenses of the College ;

And whereas by By-law No. 69 of the Council of the said College it was enacted that Section 41a of the Ontario Medical Act be suspended until the 1st day of June, 1896, then to come into force in case a sufficient amount of dues is not paid to cover the bank liability ;

And whereas a sufficient amount of dues has not been paid and it is expedient to remove all doubts as to the coming into force of the said section ;

Now therefore the College of Physicians and Surgeons of Ontario enacts as follows :

1. Each member of the College shall pay to the Registrar, toward the general expenses of the College for the current year, an annual fee of the amount of two dollars ($2.00), pursuant to the provisions of Section 27 of the Ontario Medical Act.

2. And it is hereby declared and enacted that Clause 41a of the Ontario Medical Act has been in force from the 1st of June, 1896, and is now in full force and effect.

Adopted in Committee of the Whole.

G. M. SHAW,
Chairman Committee of Whole.

Adopted in Council.

A. F. ROGERS, President.

BY-LAW No. 76.

Whereas the Council of the College of Physicians and Surgeons of Ontario has power to make rules and regulations, or pass by-laws governing the Council in its proceedings and times of meeting ;

And whereas it is expedient that By-law No, 39 be amended ;

Therefore be it enacted, and it is hereby enacted, that the first clause be amended by striking out the words "second Tuesday in June," and substituting the words "first Tuesday in July."

Adopted. GEO. LOGAN,
Chairman Committee of Whole.

A. F. ROGERS, President.

BY-LAW No. 77.

Whereas the Council of the College of Physicians and Surgeons of Ontario has power to make rules and regulations, or pass by-laws governing the Council in its proceedings and times of meeting ;

And whereas it is expedient that By-law No. 39 be amended ;

Therefore be it enacted, and it is hereby enacted ;

Section No. 3 under the head of meetings is altered by striking out the words "By ballot" in the third line thereof, and substituting therefor the words "By open vote, and not by ballot ;"

That after nomination, when only one candidate is nominated, it shall be the duty of the presiding officer to declare such candidate duly elected.

All by-laws inconsistent with this by-law be and are hereby repealed.

J. P. ARMOUR,
Chairman Committee of Whole.

Adopted in Council, July 8th, 1897.

J. THORBURN, President.

[Seal.] R. A. PYNE, Registrar.

BY-LAW No. 78.

Under and by virtue of the powers and directions given by Sub-section 2 of Section 36 of the Ontario Medical Act, Revised Statutes of Ontario, 1887, Chapter 148, the Council of the College of Physicians and Surgeons of Ontario enacts as follows :

1. The committee appointed under the provisions and for the purposes of the said sub-section shall consist of three members, three of whom shall form a quorum for the transaction of business.

2. The said committees shall hold office for one year, and until their successors are appointed, *provided* that any member of such committee appointed in any year shall continue to be a member of such committee notwithstanding anything to the contrary herein, until all business brought before them during the year of office has been reported upon to the Council.

3. The committee under said section shall be known as the Committee on Discipline.

4. Dr. J. L. Bray, of Chatham, Ont. ; Dr. Geo. Logan, of Ottawa, Ont.; Dr. V. H. Moore, of Brockville, Ont., are hereby appointed the committee for the purpose of said section for the ensuing year.

Adopted. H. S. GRIFFIN,
Chairman Committee of Whole.

Adopted in Council July 9th, 1897.

J. THORBURN, President.

[Seal.] R. A. PYNE, Registrar.

BY-LAW No. 79.

For fixing the salary of the Treasurer.

Whereas power hath been granted to the Council of the College of Physicians and Surgeons of Ontario under Section 13 of the Ontario Medical Act (R. S. O. 1887, C. 142), to make By-laws to fix the salaries of officers. Be it therefore enacted as follows :

1. That the salary of the Treasurer of this Council be, and is hereby fixed at $400 per annum, to be paid monthly.

JOHN HANLY,
Chairman Committee of the Whole.

Adopted in Council July 10th, 1897.

J. THORBURN, President.

[Seal.] R. A. PYNE, Registrar.

BY-LAW No. 80.

For appointing an Auditor and fixing his salary.

Whereas power hath been granted to the Medical Council of the College of Physicians and Surgeons of Ontario under Section 13 of the Ontario Medical Act, R. S. O. 1887, C. 148, to make By-laws—be it therefore enacted as follows :

1. This Council hereby appoints Dr. James Carlyle, Toronto, as Auditor for the purpose of auditing the accounts of the Council.

2. The salary or fees to be paid to the Auditor by the Council for his services as Auditor be, and are hereby fixed at $40.

G. HENDERSON,
Chairman Committee of Whole.

Adopted July 10th 1897.

JAS. THORBURN, President.
[Seal.]   R. A. PYNE, Registrar.

BY-LAW NO. 81.

By-law to levy the annual fee.

Whereas it is necessary and expedient that an annual fee be paid by each member of the College of Physicians and Surgeons of Ontario towards the general expenses of the College ; and

Whereas the Council is authorized by statute to pass By-laws for this purpose. Now, therefore, the Council of the College of Physicians and Surgeons of Ontario enacts as follows :

1. That each member of the College shall pay to the Registrar, toward the general expenses of the College for the current year, an annual fee of two dollars ($2.00), pursuant to the provisions of Section 27 of the Ontario Medical Act.

G. HENDERSON,
Chairman Committee of Whole.

Adopted July 10th, 1897.

J. THORBURN, President.
[Seal.]   R. A. PYNE, Registrar.

BY-LAW NO. 82.

For fixing the salary of the Council's Prosecutor.

Whereas power hath been granted to the Council of the College of Physicians and Surgeons of Ontario under Section 13 of the Ontario Medical Act (to make By-Laws to fix the salaries of officers [R.S.O. 1887, C. 142]), be it therefore enacted as follows :

1. That the salary of the Prosecutor of this Council be and is hereby fixed at $600 per annum, to be paid monthly.

H. T. MACHELL,
Chairman Com. of Whole.

Adopted July 10, 1897.

J. THORBURN, President.
[Seal]   R. A. PYNE, Registrar.

BY-LAW NO. 83.

By-Law to fix the time, manner and places for holding Examinations and appointing Examiners.

Whereas power hath been granted to the Medical Council of the College of Physicians and Surgeons of Ontario under the Ontario Medical Act, to make By-Laws, be it therefore enacted, and it is hereby enacted, as follows :

That a fall examination be held in the College Building, in the City of Toronto, on the second Tuesday of October, 1897, and it is further enacted that examinations be conducted in the College Building, in Toronto, and in the City Hall, in the City of Kingston, on the third Tuesday of May, 1898, in the manner and form prescribed in the annual Announcement of the College of Physicians and Surgeons of Ontario, and the Examiners for the same be as follows :

BOARD OF EXAMINERS, 1897-98.—Dr. F. LeM. Grassett, Toronto, Ont., Anatomy, Descriptive ; Dr. D. E. Mundell, Kingston, Ont., Theory and Practice of Medicine ; Dr. H. Howitt, Guelph, Ont., Midwifery, Operative and other than Operative, and Puerperal and Infantile Diseases, etc. ; Dr. A. S. Fraser, Sarnia, Ont., Physiology and Histology ; Dr. A. B. Welford, Woodstock, Ont., Surgery, Operative and other than Operative ; Dr. H. Williams, London, Ont., Medical and Surgical Anatomy ; Dr. G. Acheson, Galt, Ont., Chemistry, Theoretical, Practical and Toxicology ; Dr. H. B. Small, Ottawa, Ont., Materia Medica and Pharmacy ; Dr. C. V. Emory, Hamilton, Ont., Medical Jurisprudence and Sanitary Science ; Dr. C. O'Reilly, Toronto, Ont., Assistant Examiner to the Examiner on Surgery ; Dr. J. Third, Kingston, Ont., 1st Assistant Examiner to Examiner on Medicine ; Dr. W. P. Caven, Toronto, Ont. ; 2nd Assistant Examiner on Medicine, Pathology, and Therapeutics ; Dr. E. T. Adams, Toronto, Ont., Homœopathic Examiner.

V. H. MOORE,
Chairman Com. of Whole.

Adopted July 10, 1897.

J. THORBURN, President.
[Seal.]   R. A. PYNE, Registrar.

PROCEEDINGS AT THE MEETING

OF THE

MEDICAL COUNCIL OF ONTARIO

JULY, 1897.

MEDICAL COUNCIL BUILDING,

TORONTO, July 6th, 1897.

The Medical Council of the College of Physicians and Surgeons of Ontario met this day, Tuesday, July 6th, 1897, at two o'clock p.m., in accordance with the by-laws of the Council.

The President, Dr. ROGERS, in the chair, called the Council to order.

The REGISTRAR called the roll, and the following members of the Council answered to their names :

Drs. Armour, Barrick, Bray, Britton, Brock, Campbell, Dickson, Douglas, Emory, Fowler, Geikie, Graham, Griffin, Hanly, Henderson, Henry, Logan, Luton, Machell, Moore, Moorehouse, McLaughlin, Reddick, Rogers, Roome, Sangster, Shaw, Thorburn, Thornton, Williams.

Dr. ROGERS then addressed the Council as follows :

Gentlemen of the Council : Before we proceed with the business of the meeting, it has been customary in the past for the retiring President to either give an address or make such recommendations as he feels inclined in regard to the work which he has been engaged in as President of the Council during the previous year. It was my intention to have written out an address, or a series of recommendations to bring before you to-day. I found that was not possible, from the fact that I was very busy, and, consequently, I have simply arranged a few headings, with the idea of briefly discussing them now as the President retiring.

At the outset, I may say that it affords me a very great deal of pleasure to see the members of the Medical Council once more together, and, as President, to welcome you here again. Whilst I rejoice with you in our mutual greeting, we have to deplore the fact that there is a break in our ranks to-day owing to the death of two important and well-known members—I refer to the loss the Council has sustained in the death of Drs. Harris and Rosebrugh. I know full well that we are all saddened by the absence of these members from our meeting. They were associated with the work here for many years, they proved by their devotion and by their loyalty to the Council that they were worthy representatives of a noble profession ; and while to-day we can only feel the deepest possible sorrow that we miss their friendly greeting, that we miss them from amongst us; still, after all, it is only the lot of all of us ; we have to meet that grim monster which they have met, and pass over, as they have, to the great majority. The Council also to-day mourn the death of a highly esteemed and worthy officer, the late Treasurer, Dr. W. T. Aikins. The late Dr. Aikins was one of the founders of this Council, and was Treasurer since the foundation of the Council, in 1866, and remained in that position until his death, this year. By his faithfulness and devotion in this office he rendered splendid service to the medical profession, and during the early years by his financial assistance, with that of another member of the present Council, carried the Council over many difficulties. He has gone to his well-earned rest. While we mourn to-day the loss of these worthy men we also are in a position to bid a hearty welcome to those members, Drs. Griffin and Douglas, who have come to replace the two deceased members. I know they come here for the first time, but I am sure they come prepared to take their part in the work of this

Council, and to do their best to promote the interests of the profession and of this Council. I am sure I voice the sentiments of all here when I bid both a hearty welcome to-day. One of the first things which it will be incumbent upon me to mention is the petition of the Legislature, which you ordered to be prepared at the last meeting of the Council. I found early that it was probably a very large contract on my hands, or the hands of the Executive Committee ; that is, the preparation of the petition, and of a circular to be sent to the whole profession of Ontario. The Executive Committee did the best they could. They prepared a petition, which you have all seen, and prepared an explanatory circular to accompany that. It affords me, let me assure you, a great deal of pleasure, as President of this Council, to express the feelings of gratitute I had and have, and always will have, to the medical men of this Province who responded so well and promptly to that petition. It was a matter of some surprise to me to find that inside of a week we got back something like 1,500 names on that petition, and the whole of the 1,821 names responded within a very short time. It proved one thing, to my mind at least, that there was an amount of attention being paid to Council matters which was very gratifying indeed. It proved also that there was an unanimity—it showed to me that there was a large amount of unanimity—in the profession of medicine in Ontario. The fact that that petition to the Legislature was signed by such a large number as 1,821, out of a possible 2,250, or so, shows that the medical practitioners of this Province are prepared to stand together to uphold this Council, and to uphold the honor and dignity of the profession. I can safely say this, that never before in the history of medicine in Canada was there known such a large petition as that to be presented to any legislative body. When we succeeded in getting such a large petition signed, when our circular was so quickly and promptly responded to, we felt it incumbent upon us to ask the Legislative Committee to meet and to consider this matter. The Executive Committee came to Toronto, and called a meeting of the Legislative Committee, but prior to that they proceeded to the House, to interview those members of the Legislature who are medical men—the medical members, who have always proven by their conduct in the Legislature to be the strongest and warmest friends of the medical profession in Ontario. The medical members of the House have invariably worked, and worked hard, to get such amendments to the Medical Act as the Council wished or required. Therefore, we believed it was judicious, that it was prudent, to interview the medical members of the House in the first instance, in order to find out whether they considered it was wise at that time to ask for legislation or not. We therefore requested a meeting of all the medical men in the House, and their unanimous verdict was that, while it would be beneficial to present the petition to the Government at the present time, that element in the House, without giving it a name, which was antagonistic to the profession of medicine throughout the country, was still there ; and it was thought by the medical men who are members of the Legislative Assembly that it would be unwise to press for legislation at that time, they were of the opinion the petition would keep for a period, and that inasmuch as in all probability there would be an election this year, or if not this year certainly next year, and the complexion of the House might be changed, and that element which was antagonistic would probably be away from there ; therefore, it was thought advisable by our friends, the medical members of the Legislative Assembly, that we should postpone attempting to get legislation until such time as that adverse element was at least reduced. Acting on this opinion, and we believed we were doing what was best, because the doctors in the House strongly objected not only to fighting that element I have spoken of, but they thought it would probably end in our not getting as good an Act as if we waited for another year, we concluded that although we were not going to press for the Act we wanted, although we were not going to press the House to give us an amendment to the Medical Act just then, there was no reason why we could not present this petition to the Government, and ask in the name of the medical men of this Province that the Government should do certain things. Accordingly, the Legislative Committee and the Executive Committee met the members of the Government and the Premier of this Province, and presented the petition and asked them two things : First, that the Government would respond to the first prayer in the petition ; that prayer, as you know, is that the Legislature, or the Honourable Body, would extend to the medical profession of this Province the courtesy of not changing or amending the Ontario Medical Act until any proposed change or amendment had been placed before the Ontario Medical Council for consideration.

In regard to that, while no response was made or remark passed from the Premier, it was thought we had gained a certain amount of attention, at least, in presenting this petition before the Premier and the members of the Government in that way. It is certain that no Government could afford to ignore such a large medical petition as that which I have spoken of. I am glad to tell you one thing, that is that we were at least assured in a private way that it was not likely that any amendmends would be brought up, or allowed to be brought up, during the last session or the next session. That being the case we felt assured that the tinkering or attempted tinkering with the Medical Act which has been going on for the last two or three years would be stopped, and I believe there is no doubt that stoppage was the result of our petition.

We also succeeded by this petition in gaining another point, and a very important point I think it is. You remember, in 1895, the Hon. G. W. Ross brought forward a proposed Medical Act which would compel this Council to accept certain matriculations; that is, we would have to accept the matriculations which he mentioned in his proposed Act. This last winter when we presented this enormous petition of medical men of this Province to the Government, the Hon. G. W. Ross then declared that the reason he introduced the bill in 1895 was because he wanted to "clean the slate," as he termed it, of a large number of students who could not get through their matriculations; that it was not his wish, and that it was not his intention in the future to interfere with the matriculation of the Council, that the Council should have full power and authority over the standard of medical matriculation in the future. I think you will agree with me that Mr. Ross having admitted such a thing as that, and having admitted that the Council had, notwithstanding his bill of 1895, the full and absolute control of matriculation, we are repaid for all the trouble and expense we went to in formulating and having signed this magnificent petition.

Although this matter, of course, will come before you again in the report from the Executive Committee, I thought it was advisable in making my remarks here to mention it now. In regard to the standard of matriculation to be adopted this year I would strongly urge on this Council the importance of taking up the matriculation we had adopted in 1895 just as if Mr. Ross had never brought in his bill. Another point is the fact of having legislation for the future. One reason why I, and I know other members of the Legislative and Executive Committees, considered the worthy suggestion of the doctors in the House this last winter of acceptance was the fact that we had not had time to fully consider all the legislation which might be necessary in the interests of this Council. I mean to say that from the time the petition was received until the time we were forced to go before the Government we did not have time to consider what legislation we ought to have. I consider to-day it would be in the interests of the Council and profession if you appointed now a Legislative Committee to take into consideration not only the bill which we had drafted last winter, but any other legislation which you might think advisable, not necessarily to go to the Legislature next session, but to go as soon as may be after a new election has been held of the Legislative Assembly. I think we ought to prepare, or have prepared, a memorandum of such things as we want changed in the Medical Act and have it ready so that as soon as the session of the new Legislative Assembly will be held we can go to the Legislature with this petition and ask for such amendments as we consider necessary to the Medical Act. Passing those points, I have a great deal of pleasure in briefly bringing before you the financial position of the Council. I know you nearly all have seen the financial report which is printed and published and placed before you to-day. By that report you are able to see at a glance the financial position we are in to-day. I am very glad to tell you that we have received from the annual dues something like $6,000.00 and that the $6,000.00 has been paid by 1,538 members; that is to say, that 1,538 members of the profession have responded to the call and have paid up their dues in full and there is a balance due from 750 members who have yet to pay, all of whom, I have not the slightest doubt, within the next six months will pay up in full. Then another thing which is of great importance is that we have succeeded, thanks to the work, the great work, the almost invaluable work of the Property Committee, in having the interest on the loan on this building reduced from five to three and a half per cent., making a saving annually of something like $900.00. In this connection it might be of interest to refer to the fact that with the interest now, at this time, of $2,550.00, and with the cost of maintenance of the building of $4,785.55, the total cost of maintaining this building is $7,335.55. Deducting from that amount $4,622.03, received from rents, we have a cost of $2,713.52 for the accommodation which is had in this building. In other words we have a large examining hall, we have a large Registrar's office, large committee rooms, a Council Chamber and the full and ample accommodation which this building gives this Council, and we have paid in that amount which I speak of as maintenance, all the taxes, water rates, gas, fuel and everything else, and paid for our caretaker and elevator man, and after all that, it costs us the sum of $2,713.52 for our own part of the building. I think if you consider the fact that we have such ample and splendid accommodation in this building, and if you consider the fact that the whole amount is only some $2,700.00 odd, it cannot be said that we are paying a very large amount for the accommodation we get. At the same time I admit I would, and I know you all would, like to see that cost reduced. But if we reduce the cost of maintaining our building and conducting our affairs we must look out that we do not reduce the cost of maintenance at the expense of efficiency. We have to-day a series of machinery carrying on the affairs of this Council and the profession which I think is second to none in any Province of Canada, perhaps in the world. We have machinery, such as an able Registrar, an able Board of Examiners, and splendid accommodation for examinations, and I think in paying such a sum of money as we are paying, we are paying nothing but what we get a good return for.

Another subject to which I would like to refer to is the subject of interprovincial reciprocity. This topic came up before the Canada Medical Association at its last meeting in August in Montreal. ' It is a matter of the greatest interest to the profession all over the Province of Ontario, and other medical men outside are interested in this subject of reciprocity in medical registration between the provinces. I am quite satisfied it is important, and it requires serious consideration, but I am equally certain that the resolution passed at the last meeting of the Canada Medical Association would not carry in this Council, that is, for instance, that we accept the registration from the Province of Quebec, where the examinations, as you know, are conducted by the colleges and overlooked by censors appointed by the Quebec Medical Council.

After my experience in this position as President this year, I have two or three recommendations which I would like the Council to consider. The first is, I recommend that each year the Registrar shall bring 'in a report giving the names of all the students who have registered as matriculants since the last meeting of the Council, and the qualifications under which they registered ; also the names of all students who have passed the primary examination ; also a list of all persons who have been admitted to registration, and also a list of those who have become registered on account of being domiciled in Great Britain for five years and passing the intermediate and final examinations.

I think this report would be of great importance. In the first place it would be, under the by-laws, referred to the Registration Committee who should examine it and compare it with the original register. I do not mean to say for a single instant I doubt, I am sure no one doubts, the entire honor of our worthy and esteemed Registrar, but I think it would be something that would help us to have before us for the use of the Council, a list in tabulated form of the students under those various headings and it would compel the Registration Committee to examine and compare it with the original register. I am not so sure that the register is examined by the Registration Committee. I might say, as President I made the request, and Dr. Pyne has kindly responded to it, and he says he will bring in a report of that kind this year, and if you think it is worthy of consideration you can continue it in the future.

Another recommendation which I would like to bring before you is in regard to students taking the primary and final examinations at one time. I find a great many students go up for both primary and final, and sometimes they fail in their primary and get through in their final.

I have strong objections to our allowing students who are deficient in the primary branches to get through in their final. I would recommend that where a student fails in three subjects of his primary examination, he should not be allowed anything on his final. I do not think it is the correct thing to allow students to go through in this piece-meal manner. However, it is only my opinion, but given to you to-day after some serious consideration.

Another recommendation which I am sure will be met with some difference of opinion, and it is the final recommendation I have here, is that the five-year course shall be continued and the session be nine months instead of six ; also that the fifth-year students be compelled to devote the entire twelve months in clinical work in some large hospital, a hospital where there are not less than 150 beds in constant occupation by patients. From the report of various medical men in the city of Toronto and others, I find that great objection has been raised by students that they are not compelled to put in a pure clinical year during their fifth year. I think that should be met. We should have a clinical year after the four years. The student should be forced to take a full year—his fifth year—in clinical work at some large hospital, designated, as I say, by having an average bed occupation of 150. In that way I think we would get a better clinical year than we do now. In regard to four sessions of nine months each, in Great Britain they require from all students before registration five full years, not academical years, but five calendar years of actual study in medicine, and they require that every student shall take five sessions of nine months each. That being the case, I think that we can fairly require our students to take four sessions of nine months each, and then one year devoted to actual clinical work.

In conclusion I have again to thank you for the kindness with which you have received my remarks and also to once again thank you for the honor you have conferred upon me in making me President of the Council. (Applause).

The PRESIDENT called for nominations for the office of President.

Dr. BRAY—I have great pleasure in nominating Dr. Thorburn for the position of President of this Council for the ensuing year. It is not necessary to make any introductory remarks ; he is one of the best known practitioners and members of the profession in the Province of Ontario ; he has held honorable positions ; he has been President of the Dominion Medical Association, and I am sure he will acquit himself as creditably and honorably in the office of President of this council, should he be elected, as he did in that office while he held it.

Dr. ROOME—I have great pleasure in seconding that motion ; I am confident if elected to the position he will do honor to himself and be a credit to the Council.

The PRESIDENT called for other nominations.

Dr. SANGSTER—There appears to be no other nomination and, in my opinion, there is not likely to be. I cannot allow that matter to go to a vote without expressing my views upon it. I presume I am in order in making remarks upon the matter. Personally to Dr. Thorburn I have no objections whatever ; I esteem him very highly. He has won the respect of everybody acquainted with him. Officially I have some objections to make and I claim the privilege of stating them. I object to the election of Dr. Thorburn as President of this Council on two or three grounds. Your habit, your usage of deciding in caucus who shall be President of this Council and merely submitting it to the Council as a matter of form, precludes the possibility of making any other nomination. No member of this Council will permit himself to be nominated to that office with the certainty of having to suffer the humiliation of rejection, so that I cannot make the remarks I would in support of another candidate. My objection to Dr. Thorburn I will state in the baldest possible manner, because I do not wish to occupy the time of the Council. I object to Dr. Thorburn in the first place as a protest, so far as my vote and voice go, against the continuance of this system of electing the President of this Council which, in my opinion, precludes the possibility of the best man being placed in that chair, and renders it certain that if the best man in this Council should, by a chance, find himself occupying that upholstered chair his occupancy thereof is limited to one year. I object to that. I object to Dr. Thorburn, but I am quite sure that Dr. Thorburn will understand, that while I have to state myself emphatically in this matter, I do it with no unkindly motive ; it is a matter of official onus with me. I object to Dr. Thorburn because, in my opinion, and in the opinion of a very large section of the profession, Dr. Thorburn, as nominee of a defunct educational institution, has neither a moral nor a legal right to a seat in this Council, and therefore inferentially he has no right to sit in the President's chair. And I object in the third place because on a matter last year in which I think, if Dr. Thorburn had been a law-abiding citizen, he would have felt that his mouth was closed by statute—I refer to the re-institution of the assessment clause of the Medical Act—he saw fit to interfere, and in reference to the action of a large number, of over one-half the members of the profession, in refusing to pay that, which according to the law of their judgment was unjust, which they deemed unnecessary and which they deemed unconstitutional, many of whom are as respectable and quite as self-respecting as Dr. Thorburn himself, he was injudicious enough to apply to their action the term "contemptible." On those three grounds I object to Dr. Thorburn's election to the Chair at present, and I should say, sir, that I claim the right of crystalizing my objections by casting my ballot.

The PRESIDENT—Are there any other nominations? There not being any other nominations I will ask some member to cast a ballot for Dr. Thorburn.

Dr. BRITTON—I move, seconded by Dr. BROCK, that Dr. Bray cast a ballot for Dr. Thorburn.

The PRESIDENT—I might say before that is discussed, that last year the same thing was done and has been done for many years past. In order to prevent the trouble of taking a ballot from everybody the custom has been, and it is the custom carried out in other bodies, to have a ballot cast by the nominator of the nominee ; that is, that where there is only one nominee, the ballot is cast by the nominator, the reason being that there could be nothing else but the one nominee's name put on the ballot paper ; that is to say, if Dr. Bray put any other name on the ballot paper than Dr. Thorburn's name, I would throw the ballot out, and if it was a blank I would merely pass it back.

Dr. MCLAUGHLIN—You have no right to discuss this matter.

The PRESIDENT—I am not discussing it, I am only explaining it. We have two members here who were not here last year and I thought it would be only courtesy to explain what was done last year. Last year, as you are aware, and as our two new members are probably not aware, this very question came up in my own election, this same objection was raised then and very much more vehemently, and the whole by-law was referred to the Committee on Rules and Regulations, and after they had discussed the thing for a long time, the Committee on Rules and Regulations brought in a report which was not in favor of any change in the by-law. Dr. Reddick was a member of that Committee. Therefore, I see no harm.

Dr. MCLAUGHLIN—Dr. Sangster called our attention last year to the by-law under which we are now purporting to proceed ; the by-law reads as follows :—"The President and Vice-President shall be elected from among the members of the Council, after nomination, by ballot, and a majority of the votes of the members present shall be necessary to an election ; *provided*, that in the case of a tie, the election shall be decided by the member representing the greatest number of registered practitioners." Our by-law says, as clearly as the English language can say it, that the President must be elected by ballot, and that a majority of the votes of the members present shall be necessary to an election. There is no provision for the election of a President by a single ballot. I hold that our election of the President last year was illegal. Now, sir, not to be dictatorial, or to ask the Council to attach too much importance to my own opinion, I obtained the opinion of a man who, in Canada, stands foremost amongst all the interpreters of constitutional law and practice in bodies such as this. I refer to Dr. Bourinot, the Clerk of the House of Commons. You will notice, gentlemen, the section to which I have referred, and from which I have quoted, is on page xlviii. of the Announcement of last year. I sent Dr. Bourinot the Announcement of last year and I wrote him as follows :—" On page xlviii. of the ANNOUNCEMENT OF THE COLLEGE OF PHYSICIANS AND SURGEONS OF ONTARIO," is the section governing the election of the President and Vice-President of the Council. First, by that section, what is the proper method of electing the President ?" The answer is :—" Clearly by ballot. A majority of the members present is necessary to an election ‚by ballot, with the limitation only in case of a tie. (Signed) J. G. BOURINOT."

I then submitted another question as follows : " In the case of only one nomination for either the office of President or Vice-President and A. moves, seconded by B., that C. cast a ballot, and this motion is carried, and C. casts one ballot for the candidate, does that fulfill that law, is the election proper ?" His answer is "No, the law of the constitution requires a vote by ballot and a majority of the votes of the members present is necessary to an election. The practice stated in these two questions is not uncommon in some bodies but it is irregular and clearly so here." Then again, I put another question in the next above case, that is, where A. moves, seconded by B. that C. " cast a ballot." " In the next above case the motion by A. and B. being opposed but carrried by a majority and C. casts one ballot, is the election lawful ?" And his answer is the same as that given to question No. 2, " Not correct. (Signed) J. G. BOURINOT."

Mr. President, we appealed last year from the decision of the chair to the Council and if you propose to say that that is the correct method and the method we are to adopt to-day we will have to do so again. We stood last year clearly upon the best authority in Canada, and perhaps the best in the world, and I object to any one gentleman casting a ballot. If you give me the power to cast a ballot and I chose to cast it for any person I say that person would be elected, but you say no. I say there is nothing in your by-law to contradict that. But, the law demands that the election shall be by ballot and by a majority of the votes of the members present, and Dr. Bourinot, the best authority in Canada, says that is the correct method.

The PRESIDENT—I will go so far as to say that if Dr. McLaughlin or Dr. Sangster has a nominee, although the nominations were practically closed, we will accept the nomination now, and we will have an election, but when there is only one. nominee before the Council, to waste the time taking a ballot in order to please one or two objectors, it seems to me it would not be exactly polite to the Council in former years. If Dr. McLaughlin or Dr. Sangster will nominate a member—

Dr. McLAUGHLIN— I submit.that the members on the floor of this Council can discuss that question, but you have no right to do so.

Dr. SANGSTER—It is not very courteous either to Dr. McLaughlin or myself to ask us to follow a course that is impracticable, because you know that no gentleman would accept a nomination with the certainty of having to stand the humiliation of rejection.

The PRESIDENT stated the motion.

Dr. REDDICK—As a member of that Committee I might say that very same question was referred to us and the law itself seemed so plain to the Committee to whom it was referred that we could see no reason to change it. That is, the law seemed to say plainly that there must be a majority, no President could be elected without a majority, and that majority must be obtained by a ballot. That is what the law means and that is what is there, and as one of your Committee we. recommend no change. If heretofore the Council has been doing what is not exactly right in the eyes of this body it is time we were making a change, but it does seem that there is a power in this Council which will permit no suggestion or change especially if it comes from a certain section.

Dr. GEIKIE—-Wouldn't it be simplier just to have everybody supplied with the papers so that a ballot could be taken ? I suggest this for this reason that I do not want it to be in anybody's power to say that the Council objected to a vote being taken. Not that I have any objection to Dr. Thornburn because if he is elected here he has a right to the place if a majority of the Council say so. I have a great deal of esteem for Dr. Thorburn. Nobody can object if everybody has a ballot and votes upon it.

Dr. ARMOUR—Mr. President, I object to the motion of Drs. Britton and Brock asking that a single ballot be cast, on account of it being irregular and out of order, and I ask for your ruling.

Dr. WILLIAMS—Mr. President, last year I believe this subject was objected to and I moved to have an amendment made and I think that an amendment could have been put there that would have placed it beyond dispute as to what was really intended. My own conviction is, and was then, that the intention of the by-law when it passed was that a full vote be taken in the Council, and that the majority of the full vote should prevail. But as long back almost as I have known the other method was considered a legal and proper one, and upon that ground it was carried out. Now, personally, I would prefer the other method, that is, that the full vote be taken. It would take up very little time and I believe it is the best method and would do away with the possibility of any disputes in the matter. Person-ally I prefer doing that, although I cannot see that any harm comes to anybody in the method that has been followed, yet, I believe the intention of the by-law was in the other direction.

Dr. DICKSON—I think we should not differ on matters of such little consequence as this. What Dr. McLaughlin has stated to us is perhaps in the handwriting of Dr. Bourinot, which is an authority that I think we should not doubt, and to my own mind the wise thing for this Council to do now is to accept this opinion and follow the course suggested.

Dr. BRAY—While I quite agree with what has been said it seems to me that it is a reflec-tion upon the previous course of this Council. However, if we were wrong we should be put right, but there is a vote taken, I think it has been lost sight of ; it was moved and seconded that a ballot be cast ; that is a vote and anybody who objects to that can ask that the yeas and nays be taken and a majority of the Council will elect the President in that way. If they do not like that way they can move an amendment. A gentleman comes up here and says it is a foregone conclusion, there is no use nominating anybody. I would like to know if he knows the feelings of every man in this Council, or is he speaking for himself alone ? I say he has no right to make such a statement that it is no use nominating anyone else ; I take exception to that, but I think, this discussion is wasting time and I will say no more ; I am perfectly willing the ballots should be passed and I think perhaps it is the best and quickest way to do it.

The PRESIDENT—Before coming to the Council yesterday I saw Mr. Osler. I might also inform you that Mr. Bourinot is not a lawyer, he is simply an authority on parliamentary pro-cedure ; he is not a legal interpreter. Mr. Osler I think is ; Mr. Osler told me that this was not only quite in accordance with our by-law but that it was quite legal and regular, therefore, I propose to carry it out because Mr. Osler told me it was correct. I have got one motion be-fore me and Dr. Armour has asked for a ruling.

Dr. ARMOUR—I asked you to rule that motion was irregular and not in order, not com-plying with the rules and regulations of the Council.

The PRESIDENT—The motion before the chair is, that Dr. Bray has nominated, seconded by Dr. Roome, that Dr. Thorburn be President of the Council for the ensuing year. It was then moved by Dr. Britton, seconded by Dr. Brock, that Dr. Bray cast a ballot for the Council. Now, gentlemen, I have been asked for a ruling and in view of the fact that I am acting under the advice of our solicitor on this question and in view of the fact that this has been the rule for years in this Council and in view of the fact that we carried it out last year and to prevent any suspicion that we had not a President last year, I am forced to decide that this motion is in order.

Dr. SANGSTER—I appeal to this Council.

The PRESIDENT—You have heard the ruling. Is the chair sustained? (Cries of yes, yes.)

The PRESIDENT—I declare the ruling of the chair sustained.

Dr. SANGSTER—I call for the yeas and nays.

The PRESIDENT—Instructed the Registrar to take the yeas and nays.

The REGISTRAR—Took the yeas and nays as follows :

Yeas—Drs. Barrick, Bray, Britton, Brock, Campbell, Douglas, Emory, Graham, Griffin, Henderson, Logan, Luton, Machell, Moore, Moorhouse, Rogers, Roome, Thorburn—18.

Nays—Drs. Armour, Dickson, Fowler, Geikie, Hanly, Henry, McLaughlin, Reddick, Sangster, Shaw, Thornton and Williams—12.

The PRESIDENT—The chair is sustained and I therefore declare that the motion of Dr. Britton, seconded by Dr. Brock, is carried and Dr. Bray will now cast a ballot for Dr. Thorburn.

Dr. BRAY—I think it is not well to antagonize this Council. I voted to sustain the chair; I did it because I think as a general thing the chair should be sustained when this is and has been the custom in this Council for years.

The PRESIDENT—There is nothing before the chair. Dr. Bray, you have been ordered to cast a ballot. Will you cast the ballot ?

Dr. BRAY cast the ballot.

The PRESIDENT—I have the ballot cast by Dr. Bray for the Council and I find written on it " Dr. Thorburn for President." I therefore declare Dr. Thorburn elected President of this Council for the ensuing year.

Dr. SANGSTER—Do I understand you to say that the ballot was cast for the Council, that the Council takes this high-handed manner and asks every member of this Council to adopt that ?

The PRESIDENT—You are out of order. There is nothing before the chair.

Amid very hearty applause Dr. Thorburn, the President-elect, took the chair and addressed the Council as follows :

Gentlemen of the College of Physicians and Surgeons of Ontario: I do not like to make use of the old hackneyed saying "the happiest moment of my life," but it is one of the happiest moments of my life. It is a position that anybody might be proud of occupying and I hope that when my term of office is up that my record will be such that at all events I shall receive commendation rather than censure. I like everyone to have freedom of speech so long as he confines himself to the subject matter and I ask the same indulgence for myself that you have given to my predecessors. I thank you gentlemen for the high honor I have received. (Applause).

Dr. ROGERS—Allow me to rise to the question of privilege. As to why I did not allow a ballot to be passed in this case I would like to say as a matter of privilege to myself——

Dr. McLAUGHLIN—I rise to a point of order. Dr. Rogers has already told us why he objected to that. He cannot repeat what he has already stated, as a matter of privilege.

Dr. ROGERS—A question of privilege is always in order. The reason why I did not allow a general ballot to be passed was that my election was objected to on the very same grounds that yours was, sir ; and therefore if I had admitted for a moment the contention that was advanced I would have admitted that my election was somewhat irregular, and the election of my predecessors was also irregular. In the face of that I maintain I could not have allowed any departure from the usual method of voting : I could not have permitted it, although I would have been quite willing to have had a general vote taken and I am quite satisfied that you would have been elected, sir, by a very large majority. I am satisfied also I would have been elected last year by a large majority but at the same time to have admitted a departure from the custom would have been, to say the least, admitting that we probably had some doubt about our having a President during the past several years and for the sake of the Council I could not admit that. I took care to arm myself with the opinion of one whom I believed to be the best legal authority in this country, who told me that the practice which we carried out last session was perfectly regular and therefore I think I was President and regularly and properly elected, I am quite satisfied, by a vast majority of the members of this Council.

The PRESIDENT—Dr. Rogers' contention is quite right. He was not going to ignore his position last year ; he could not possibly do it ; it is only right to uphold the same position he held last year. I feel I am legally entitled to this chair.

Dr. McLAUGHLIN—The explanation given by you, sir, and by Dr. Rogers, is simply this, because he was wrong last year, he has to be wrong now.

The PRESIDENT—Oh, no. There is no call for this discussion ; let us proceed to business. I call for nominations for the office of Vice-President.

Dr. MOORE—I take great pleasure in nominating for this office a gentleman who, as a member of this Council, has done his duty ably and well for many years, and I am satisfied he will fill the office with dignity to himself and with honor to the Council. I have great pleasure in nominating Dr. Luton as Vice-President for the ensuing year.

Dr. ROGERS—I have great pleasure in seconding that. I do so with a great deal of warm feeling towards the doctor personally and also as an old member of the Council. He has been here for many years and has worked hard ; he has always been on hand and done his duty faithfully and well, and he has found favor, I hope, with every member of this Council.

Dr. DICKSON—I rather expected the gentleman whose name was before this Council last year, to whom no objection could be taken, so far as I know, would likely be nominated. I have reference to Dr. Henry. He has been an old and efficient member of this Council, and I would be very sorry indeed, if on this occasion his name should be passed over, and he should be nominated for the office of Vice-President, and, therefore, I take pleasure in nominating Dr. Henry.

Dr. McLAUGHLIN—I beg leave to second the nomination of Dr. Henry ; he was prominently before the Council last year. I think now, sir, it would be only an act of grace and an act of justice that Dr. Henry would receive the nomination of this Council. I second this because I would like to see one of the two leading officers of this Council a representative of the general profession. I enter my protest here to-day that the chief officer of this organization should be a school man, and that the other officer should represent a section of the profession, while nine-tenths of the profession at large is to be unrepresented. I therefore second the nomination of Dr. Henry with much pleasure.

Dr. SANGSTER—May I ask, instead of having a ballot cast as it was last year and read by the Registrar and the President, which practically renders it no ballot at all, because the handwriting of the members in the room—

The PRESIDENT—You will excuses me. Your remarks are not relevant to this matter. We are now asking for nominations for Vice-President, and nothing else. You have heard the first proposition ; it has been moved by Dr. Moore, seconded by Dr. Rogers, that Dr. Luton, of St. Thomas, be Vice-President of this Council for the ensuing year ; the second is on motion of Dr. Dickson, seconded by Dr. McLaughlin, that Dr. Henry be elected to the office. Are there any further nominations ? If not, I will ask the ballots to be taken.

Dr. SANGSTER—I asked you, as President, whether it was intended to a have *pro forma* ballot, as it was last year, the ballots to be read by the Registrar and by the President instead of being read, as is the usual custom, by scrutineers appointed? I object to the former loose manner of conducting our business. I have no confidence in a ballot cast in that manner, and I claim to have the right of having scrutineers appointed from the members of the Council to examine the ballots and declare who is elected.

Dr. CAMPBELL—I think that might be done without any trouble, and I would move that Drs. Sangster and McLaughlin be the scrutineers, and that Dr. Armour collect the ballots.

Dr. BRITTON—I second that.

Dr. BRAY—I think in that case all the question of any wrong-doing in the counting of ballots or the reading of handwriting or knowing who marked these ballots would be done away with.

The PRESIDENT—I don't think we ought to attribute motives.

Dr. BRAY—I rose to endorse that, and in doing so I say that there cannot be any wrong done if these three gentlemen take charge of the vote.

Dr. ARMOUR—I am not accustomed to be assigned duties of this kind. I understand in the past it has been the duty of the Registrar to collect the ballots.

Dr. ROGERS—It is the scrutineers' business to collect the ballots.

Dr. REDDICK—That is the practice, but it casts a certain amount of reflection on Dr. Armour.

Dr. CAMPBELL—I am not casting reflections on anybody, but certain members of the Council have clearly expressed their opinion that other members of the Council cannot be trusted, and to show I have no doubts I have suggested the names of these parties.

Dr. McLAUGHLIN—I object to such remarks as have fallen from Dr. Campbell ; we have questioned no man's honesty here, and he has no right to make such a remark as that.

Dr. BRITTON—I seconded a motion introduced by Dr. Campbell, and if I had taken a few minutes longer to think I would have seconded no such motion, because the suggestion that was thrown out by one or two members of this Council was equivalent to a reflection upon the credibility, the honor and the integrity of the President and Registrar of this Council. I know it is a frequent custom to have scrutineers to look over the ballots. We have never required heretofore, so far as I know, that we should have scrutineers, and I am going to withdraw, so far as I am concerned, any connection with that motion. To allow such a motion to pass would be equivalent to recognizing that there was a certain amount of truth in the dirty insinuations that were thrown out, that you, sir, and our honorable Registrar who has served us so faithfully for so many years, would be sufficiently guilty to spread abroad incorrect reports.

The PRESIDENT—I do not think Dr. Sangster threw out any insinuations ; he said it was usual to have scrutineers appointed, and I know that is the case.

Dr. BRITTON—You will pardon me for taking a different ground from you in the matter. My recollection of it is very distinct ; Dr. Sangster made the statement that such a ballot would not be a ballot in truth, it would be simply a ballot *pro forma*, inasmuch as the ballots would come before the attention of the President and Registrar of this College, and the handwriting of the members of this College would be well known to the Registrar ; if this is not insinuating something I do not know what an insinuation is. I withdraw so far as being the seconder of that motion.

Dr. DICKSON—I think it would be desirable that Dr. Sangster should withdraw his remarks. I must agree with Dr. Britton in his remarks. I did feel Dr. Sangster was casting a reflection upon the President and Registrar, and we must be conscientious on both sides of this house if we are to have unanimity. I think it would not have been too much for Dr. Sangster to have allowed the matter to have proceeded as in the past.

Dr. SANGSTER—I cannot agree with my friend Dr. Dickson, or with the remarks made by Dr. Britton. There are only two ways of electing officers, by an open vote or by a secret one. My objection was to allowing the Registrar and yourself, an old member of this Council, to act as scrutineers ; I think the more righteous course in that case would be to have it by open vote ; yet if you have to ballot the only proper course to preserve the secrecy of voting is to have scrutineers appointed. That was the position I took, and I intended to cast no reflection upon the personal honor of yourself and the Registrar.

The PRESIDENT—I am so obtuse it never occurred to me to take offence, and I think with Dr. Sangster's explanation that he did not mean anything personal or offensive, that we had better follow out the suggestion that he made and have a ballot taken and scrutineers appointed to see that the ballot is all right.   Drs. Sangster and McLaughlin are named as scrutineers.   I hope they will act.

Dr. McLaughlin—There should be no motion in regard to that.   It is customary for the presiding officer to name the scrutineers.

Dr. Moore—I would ask you to appoint two gentlemen as scrutineers who do not know the handwriting of anybody.   We have two members here that I am satisfied we all have confidence in.   If we are to have a ballot and we are afraid of each other's handwriting let us get the ballot-box, get the marbles and go playing marbles again like boys, and I would now suggest that the two new members, Drs. Douglas and Griffin, be the scrutineers.

Dr. Rogers—I second that.

The President—If you wish I will name those gentlemen as the scrutineers.

Dr. McLaughlin—I certainly rise to a point of regularity ; I submit it is neither customary or right for the members on the floor to name the scrutineers, it is the prerogative of the presiding officer.

The President—I will name Drs. Douglas and Griffin as the scrutineers. (Applause). The ballots were collected and examined by the scrutineers, who reported that 30 votes were cast, of which Dr. Henry had received 16 and Dr. Luton 14.

The President—I declare Dr. Henry Vice-President of this Council for the ensuing year. (Applause).

Dr. Henry—I must return thanks to the Council for electing me to the position of Vice-President ; I appreciate this honor ; I had no caucus, nor I asked no man to vote for me ; I think that is the true principle that ought to govern in this Council ; I think a man should come here untrammeled, free to do what he thinks is right ; and I have always opposed the principle of a few men getting together in a room and dictating to this Council, as has been done in the past, and I am pleased to-day that the Council has placed me in this position without anything of that kind on my part.   I think, gentlemen, that there will be no doubt to-day about the election of your vice-president.   You have had a proper vote taken to-day. It has been the custom that has prevailed to-day, and has prevailed for years past, to elect our officers by the casting of one ballot ; and while I do not object to that, I think from the verdict we have had to-day that it is quite evident we should have a vote taken.   With our worthy President, who is an old hand at the business, I know my duties will be light, but be they light or heavy I will do my best to discharge them.   In conclusion, I feel very much pleased indeed at my election.   I am sorry my friend Dr. Luton did not get there.   I had no intention of being, and I did not know that I was going to be a candidate, and I am sorry I had to run for it against my friend from St. Thomas.

Dr. Luton—I just wish to return my sincere thanks to those who supported me in this election, and to say that I have asked no one and never was approached by anyone, as every-one can testify, but I simply thank you for the unsolicited support you have given me. (Applause).

The President called for nominations for the office of Registrar.

Dr. Logan—I take much pleasure in moving that Dr. R. A. Pyne be Registrar of this College for the ensuing year.

Dr. Graham—I have much pleasure in seconding that.   It is not necessary for me to say anything about Dr. Pyne.

The President called for further nominations and there being none he stated the motion which on a vote being taken was declared carried.

The President—The next appointment is that of Treasurer.

Dr. Britton—I beg to move, seconded by Dr. Moorhouse, that Dr. H. Wilberforce Aikins be appointed Treasurer for the ensuing year.

Dr. Brock—I move, seconded by————,that instead of appointing a Treasurer the Registrar shall in future be known as the Registrar-Treasurer, and that he shall perform all the duties of the said office for the salary which he now receives as Registrar.   I thought it would be a matter of economy to nominate the same gentleman to fill both offices.

The President—You could not do that unless you had a by-law to that effect ; a by-law might be introduced to that effect.

Dr. Sangster—I have one question to ask in regard to that ; I understand that the Finance Committee has certain recommendations to make in regard to the Registrar and the Treasurer, and if you appoint a Treasurer now by name how can you give effect to the recommendations of the Finance Committee ?   It seems to me the matter should be deferred until the Finance Committee's report is in.

Dr. Bray—How does the gentleman know what the Finance Committee are going to report ?   There may be nothing of the kind in it.   The Committee was ordered to make some recommendations as to reducing the expenses of this College, and I think it is premature for any gentleman to get up here and say, how could they do an act in face of the Committee's report.   We are voting now on the appointment of a Treasurer, and if it is thought best not to appoint a Treasurer a motion to that effect can be made ; if it is thought

best that the appointment be deferred that can be done, but I think it is not well to anticipate what will be in the report of the Committee.

Dr. BRITTON—It has been mentioned by some one that the report from the Finance
Committee will have in view or will recommend retrenchments in various directions; that
is right, that is commendabi <olong as it is not carried too ft ar, so long as it does not interfere with the constitution of this College. I would call your attention to page xvi. of the
Medical Register and I think the wording of paragraph 13 is as plain as English can express
intention. I shall read the paragraph with your permission. "The Council shall annually
appoint a President, Vice-President, Registrar Treasurer, and such other officers as may
from time to time be necessary for the working of the Act." I need not read the remainder
of that paragraph. If I can interpret English, I submit that any of us can interpret that
but in the one way, it means that a Treasurer shall be appointed and that a Registrar shall
also be appointed. It does not say if the Council deem it wise they may unite or combine
the functions of two of these offices in one man. It does not say that the President may
discharge the duties of both President and Vice-President, or that only one office shall be
filled. Dr. Pyne has been, I may say, a devoted servant of this Council for a great many
years, ever since the death of his lamented father, who had preceded him in the occupancy
of that position. Dr. Pyne has been an ardent worker, and I do not remember any instance
when anyone connected with this Council or outside of it was in a position to call his actions
to account. I do not know of an occasion when any Finance Committee, or any member of
the Finance Committee, no matter how carping his tendency might be, was able to find a
mistake or discrepancy in anything he has done. We have named from year to year a salary
that we thought was due to Dr. Pyne. I believe he has earned every dollar that he has
received. He has to devote a great deal of his time to this Council work; from his connection in this city of Toronto, and from the fact that he has so many friends in the community
he would be able to work up an extensive practice were it not for the work he has to do here.
And I say he is, if anything, imperfectly remunerated for his services. If we are going to
combine the offices in one, as some one has suggested, as probably the Finance Committee,
would recommend, in order to save, Dr. Pyne must not only do the work that he does at
present but the additional work for the same salary; that is equivalent to either imposing
upon Dr. Pyne that which should not be imposed upon him, or equivalent to acknowledging
to the profession at large that we heretofore have paid him a few hundred dollars too much
and that now we exact from him a *quid pro quo* in the shape of additional work, in order to
satisfy ourselves that we are at any rate acting conscientiously. I might also say—

Dr. ROGERS—We are not questioning the desirability of combining them.

Dr. BRITTON—I am giving you reasons why I am speaking to my motion and I claim
the right within my limit of time; I have confined myself strictly to the line mapped out in
that motion. I am giving reasons why a Treasurer should be appointed and why I think
Dr. Aikins should receive the position. I am speaking upon the hypothetic combining of
the two offices, as has been spoken of to me by different persons, or a possible combining of
the—

Dr. ARMOUR—The question of amalgamating these offices is not before the Council.
I rise to a point of order. My point of order is this, the propriety or not of uniting the
offices of Treasurer and Registrar is not before the Council and it should not be discussed.

The PRESIDENT—Dr. Brock withdrew his amendment.

Dr. BROCK—I had no seconder.

Dr. BRITTON—I would like to say why I think we should have a Treasurer. We are
not empowered by the statute to pass a by-law contrary to anything that is stated in the
by-law.

The PRESIDENT—Certainly not. We can change the law.

Dr. BRITTON—We cannot change that statute without proceeding to the Legislature and
asking for such an amendment as we require.

Dr. HENRY—This discussion is out of order altogether. This cannot be done unless
you get the law altered; and the very fact of trying to combine the two positions seems to
me monstrous.

Dr. BRITTON—As to why I nominate Dr. Aikins—

The PRESIDNET—Keep to that.

Dr. BRITTON—I spoke of the other because the suggestion as to change had been made
to me by private individuals. and again here. I suppose a matter of sympathy is no argument; however, I think it is not out of place for me to refer to the late lamented Dr. W. T.
Aikins; the Council and the profession both have a great deal to thank him or his memory
for; in times of distress, when it seemed almost as though the Council was going to fall to
pieces and the profession go back into the condition of chaos that it had formerly occupied,
Dr. Aikins financially carried us through. That is an actual fact. Dr. Aikins has gone over
to the great majority; he has left behind him a worthy son, and I apprehend that Dr. Wilberforce Aikins will be glad to accept the position, and he deserves it. He has for the past

couple of years done his work faithfully as acting Treasurer during his father's illness. He has done well, the Finance Committee have had no fault to find with the statement made by him, they have found every voucher and paper necessary in its proper place and everything correct. Personally I would esteem it as a great favour to myself for any member of this Council to vote for Dr. Aikins.

The PRESIDENT called for further nominations, there being none, he stated the motion which, on a vote being taken, was declared carried.

Dr. ROGERS—I move, seconded by Dr. WILLIAMS, that Mr. Alexander Downey, C.S.R., be appointed official Stenographer of the Council for the ensuing year.

Dr. McLAUGHLIN—I would like to know if there have been any applications for this position, and if there are any now in the hands of the Registrar ?

Dr. PYNE—No sir, none.

Dr. BARRICK—In this connection I would just like to state a few facts. As Chairman of the Printing Committee, I would say we were instructed to get out as speedily as possible the announcement for last year, and at the least possible expense; and we find that we have reduced the expense of this announcemant to $1.32 per page. Now, the cost of preparing the stenographic report, that is, a type-written copy of the verbatim report is about ninety cents per page. I am not prepared to say whether ninety cents per page for preparing that report is enough, is too much, or is too little, and to put myself in a position to judge I asked several stenographers to give me a price per printed page of this announcement for that work. I communicated with our stenographer yesterday, stating that it cost us last year about ninety cents, and I wished him to give me a sealed tender for the price per page for this year, in order that it might be compared with tenders from others for the same work. I have a sealed tender from another very capable gentleman I have received none from our stenographer, and I asked Mr. Angus, who is acting to-day for Mr. Downey, if he was prepared to give us an estimate, and he did not wish to do so. So that we are unable to judge whether the cost of ninety cents per page is too much or too little. That is the position of things now. I have a sealed tender from another capable person, which tender will not be opened unless the Council wish it to be, but the present stenographer has so far declined to submit a tender for the work. We know exactly what the printing costs per page, and I would like, for my own satisfaction to say to those who say, "you are extravagant in this work," that we had received tenders from competent persons, and that we had selected the—

Dr. GEIKIE—Is there a motion in regard to the appointment of a stenographer ?

The PRESIDENT—Yes.

Dr. GEIKIE—It seems to me that it is a thousand pities to take up so much valuable space ; this Announcement is an encyclopædia, and when you look at the amount of information that is in it, and the diarrhœa of words that the rest of it is taken up with, I confess I do not like it ; and it has occurred to me a thousand times during the year, not that I have any animus towards our friend, the phonographer, because he has done admirably, but I think it better that we should dispense with that altogether, and simply have a synopsis.

The PRESIDENT—That is a matter of detail for the Printing Committee. I have a letter here from Mr. Downey, which has been put into my hands, in which he states, "that he was confined to his house as the result of an accident.

Dr. BARRICK—Does that appointment carry with it the remuneration ?

The PRESIDENT—No.

Dr. BARRICK—What is done to-day fixes it for this session of the Council.

The PRESIDENT—He is appointed, and you ask for his terms, and if not agreeable, he must either conform to your suggestion or resign.

Dr. BARRICK—The Printing Committee has no power to deal with his prices.

Dr. ROGERS—Put the motion. (Cries of "Question, question.")

Dr. SANGSTER—I claim that the only way to appoint a stenographer to this Council is to take tenders for that position, and to see that we appoint a stenographer who is not only competent to give a verbatim report, but who will do it without mutilating it in any manner, and who will give a report in grammar that is at least presentable in a public school. I claim Dr. Geikie was quite right in bringing up the question, whether it was necessary to appoint a stenographer at all in the way we have appointed one in the past. I claim it would be the right and proper way for this Council to advertise for tenders for that position, so that we might have some guarantee that the work was done at the lowest possible remuneration, or the least sufficient remuneration. I object to acting blindfold in the manner we are doing in regard to a stenographer now.

The PRESIDENT—We have a stenographer. Mr. Downey's representative has been with us until the present. We can submit to Mr. Downey, or whoever it is, what we require and then if he does not carry out our suggestions that means his resignation.

Dr. McLAUGHLIN—We are bound to get our work done efficiently, and at the least possible expense, and if by the election of Mr. Downey we are bound to accept his terms. I think Mr. Downey should have given Dr. Barrick a statement such as was asked for by Dr. Barrick, and then we would be in a position to know what we wanted.

By permission of the Council, Mr. Angus stated, on behalf of Mr. Downey, that he had not received Dr. Barrick's letter until the evening before at a late hour, that he had been engaged almost continuously until the opening of the Council, and had not had an opportunity to reply to Dr. Barrick, but that, on behalf of Mr. Downey, he would say that the work would be done at as reasonable a rate as was consistent with a correct and accurate report of the proceedings.

Dr. MACHELL—In regard to this point, Mr. Pres: lent, I do not see how we can do anything else than appoint Mr. Downey for this session ; his representative is here, and has done part of the work of the Council now, and that has to be paid for ; and to get in another, an outsider, would mix up matters very much, and it would not be to the interests of the College or the profession, but I think Dr. Sangster is quite right when he says tenders should be asked for for this position ; and while the talking has been going on, in a hurried way I have dotted down a motion which is something as follows : "That tenders be asked for at this session for the stenographic work of the Council for the next session of the Council." You can impose whatever conditions you like ; have all the tenders for the same kind of work, and then we will know exactly where we stand. A man can be appointed at this session of the Council, and he will be here when the Council opens next year.

Dr. GEIKIE—I have not a word to say against our stenographer, I am in favor of paying every farthing that is due to him, but I would like to move, seconded by ——, that in the view of this Council, it is necessary to employ a stenographer, or to have more than a good synopsis of its proceedings furnished. That motion is made in the interests of economy.

The PRESIDENT—This is entirely out of order ; that is for the Council to decide afterwards. The question is now the election of this officer, and I must insist upon putting this motion.

The President stated the motion as follows : "Moved by Dr. Rogers, seconded by Dr. Williams, that Mr. Alexander Downey, C.S.R., be appointed official stenographer of the Council for the ensuing year, which, on a vote being taken, was declared carried.

Dr. MOORE—I move that Mr. B B. Osler, Q.C., be the solicitor of this Council for the ensuing year.

Dr. ROGERS—I have great pleasure in seconding that motion.

The PRESIDENT called for further nominations ; there being none, he stated the motion, which, on a vote being taken, was declared carried.

Moved by Dr. BRAY, seconded by Dr. BRITTON, that Drs. Logan, Williams, Moore, Dickson, Machell, Moorhouse, Brock, Sangster, Barrick, Henry, Rogers, Graham, Reddick, Roome and the mover be a Committee to strike the Standing Committees.

The PRESIDENT put the motion, which, on a vote having been taken, was declared carried.

Dr. BRITTON—I beg to move, seconded by Dr. BRAY, that the Council do now adjourn for half an hour, or longer, as may be necessary in order to allow time for the Committee to bring in its report.

The PRESIDENT put the motion, which, on a vote having been taken was declared carried.

The Council adjourned.

The PRESIDENT called the Council to order.

The PRESIDENT—I would ask the Chairman of the Committee appointed to name the Standing Committees to read the report.

Dr. MOORE—As Chairman of the Committee appointed to strike the Standing Committees, I beg to report as follows :

Registration Committee—Drs. Fowler, Campbell, Griffin, McLaughlin, Hanly, Roome, Shaw.

Rules and Regulations Committee—Drs. Reddick, Douglas, Hanly, Luton and Armour.

Finance Committee—Drs. Henderson, Armour, Roome, Brock and Bray.

Printing Committee—Drs. Barrick, Machell, Graham, Luton and McLaughlin.

Education Committee—Drs. Britton, Dickson, Bray, Rogers, Emory, Moore, Moorhouse, Sangster and Williams.

Property Committee—Drs Machell, Barrick, Emory, Graham and Thornton.

Complaints Committee.—Drs. Logan, Fowler, Geikie, Reddick and Shaw,

All of which is respectfully submitted.

(Signed) V. H. MOORE, Chairman.

Dr. MOORE—I move, seconded by Dr. ROGERS, that the report be received and adopted.

Dr. FOWLER—I rise to object to the withdrawal of my name from the Education Committee and including me on two committees in which I have no interest. I have made education my study and I am sorry to object so publicly on an occasion of this kind, but I certainly object to being struck off the Committee upon which I have worked so long and in which I take such an interest and being put upon committees in which I have no interest whatever.

Dr. GEIKIE—I object in the same way. I am the oldest member of this Council and that I should, as the representative of our largest college, be left off is a matter of nothing to me ; it means less work for me, but it is not a good thing for the Council and therefore cannot be justifiable.

Dr. WILLIAMS—In looking at the rules and regulations, if I understand it, I haven't read them over just now very carefully, I do not think they positively state you shall not have more than a definite number on a committee. I admit that I sympathize with Dr. Fowler in this case and I think with Dr. Geikie ; they are gentlemen who take an interest in educational matters, and if the by-laws do not positively say that committee shall not exceed nine, then I see no reason why we should not enlarge that committee, keeping the quorum down as we did at a former period. There was a time when we had a large committee and there was a difficulty in carrying on the work, because there was a large quorum and we were obliged to reduce it to five in order to facilitate the work. I see no objection, if the rules do not positively say we shall not, why we should not enlarge the committee and allow those gentlemen who have taken an interest in educational matters to have a seat on it.

Dr. ROGERS—You cannot enlarge a committee by notice of motion.

The PRESIDENT—They are all fixed by by-law. The Education Committee shall consist of nine members.

Dr. SANGSTER—You cannot over-ride your by-law by a motion, and the Striking Committee gave that the best attention. There are four representatives of schools and colleges including yourself, on that committee, a committee of eleven in all and I think it is a pretty fair distribution.

The PRESIDENT—What is your pleasure, gentlemen ? The motion before the Chair is that the report of the committee be received and adopted and Drs. Fowler and Geikie protest against this but they have not put in an amendment.

Dr. GEIKIE—When the late Dr. Harris was put on it was explained to me it was supposed he represented us in our interests ; it was stated that he did and that that was the reason why he was put on and there was not room for us both. Now, I see that he is dead ; a non-educationalist takes his place, so that neither the college that I have the honor to preside over, nor the university is represented.

The PRESIDENT stated the motion which, on a vote being taken, was declared carried and the report received and adopted.

NOTICES OF MOTION.

1. Dr. ARMOUR—To introduce a by-law to amend by-law No. 39 in regard to the introduction of bills and proceedings thereon.

2. Dr. GEIKIE, seconded by Dr. MOORHOUSE, that the sincere sympathy of this Council be hereby expressed with the relatives of our late Treasurer, Dr. W. T. Aikins, who for so many years discharged the responsible duties of his office satisfactorily ; also with those of the late Dr. W. T. Harris, Ex-President of this Council, and the late Dr. J. W. Rosebrugh, one of its members, and that the Registrar be requested to send a letter to the proper parties in each of these cases expressing on behalf of this Council its sense of the great loss sustained through the death of each of these gentlemen, and also the sympathy of this Council be and is hereby expressed with the relatives of the late Dr. Bergin, Surgeon-General of the Canadian Militia, who, although not a member of the present Council, was an Ex-President and for a great many years an active member of this Council ; also that a similar letter of sympathy be sent to Mrs. Miller, Hamilton, widow of the late Dr. Miller, a former member of this Council recently deceased.

3. Dr. GEIKIE, seconded by Dr. CAMPBELL, that in the interests of economy it is unnecessary to have verbatim reports of the proceedings of the Council at its various sittings ; that the correct reports kept always for years by the Registrar are and are hereby deemed all that shall be required and are more likely to be read by the profession than the very lengthy and costly reports sent out for some time past.

4. Dr. BROCK gave notice of motion, seconded by Dr. ROOME, that the Medical Council of the Province of Ontario, at this their annual meeting, desire to express for themselves and the profession at large their sense of the just and wise legislation enacted by the Dominion Parliament in exempting medical works and surgical instruments from custom duties.

5. Dr. SANGSTER—That the Council advertise for tenders for the work done by the official stenographer, such tenders to be for the work of the next and future sessions.

6. Dr. ROGERS—To amend by-law 39, Section 3, under the heading "Meetings."

7. Dr. BRAY—That the first order of business on Friday, the ninth of July, at two o'clock p.m., will be the Discipline Committee's report *re.* Dr. Charles John Parsons.

Dr. BRAY—It was necessary for our Committee to meet yesterday to arrange when this report would be brought before the Council in order to notify Dr. Parsons to be here, and we fixed two o'clock on Friday afternoon, and the Registrar was instructed yesterday to notify Dr. Parsons to that effect.

COMMUNICATIONS, PETITIONS, ETC.

The REGISTRAR presented petitions from Dr. F. L. Johnson, Dr. T. Gibson and W. R. Thomas, British Licentiates, the Registrar's report, the Treasurer's report and the Solicitor's account which were referred to the respective committees, also the Solicitor's opinion upon matters referred to him by the Council and committees.

Dr. WILLIAMS—Should not that be read now?

Dr. BRAY—That is a matter for the Council as a whole to deal with.

The PRESIDENT—Do you wish to have this communication from the Solicitor read at the present?

Dr. ROGERS—Yes.

Dr. ROOME—What is it in regard to?

Dr. PYNE—Matters submitted to the Solicitor for his opinion.

Dr. CAMPBELL—That should certainly be read.

The PRESIDENT—If it is your pleasure we will read it. I will ask the Registrar to read it.

The REGISTRAR read communication from Solicitor dated June 23rd, 1897, as follows :

R. A. Pyne, Esq., M.D., Medical Council Building, Toronto.

DEAR SIR,—In reply to your letter of the 11th inst., asking my opinion upon various matters therein stated, I beg to say as follows :

THE EXECUTIVE COMMITTEE.

As to the constitution of the Executive Committee upon referring to by-law No. 39, passed at the session of June, 1896, it appears that the Executive Committee for the current year was duly constituted in accordance with Section 14 of the Ontario Medical Act, and I am of opinion that this committee was properly constituted by the appointment of three members, two of whom to be the President and Vice-President respectively. I understand that the provision that the President and Vice-President should be ex-officio members of the Committee is re-enacted each year, so that the provisions of Section 14 to the effect that the members of this committee should be appointed annually are complied with.

PAYMENT OF MEMBERS OF EXECUTIVE COMMITTEE.

It is possible that objection might be raised to the payment of per diem allowances to cover fees and travelling expenses of members of Executive Committee upon the ground that the Act does not specifically mention the Executive Committee in authorizing payment of fees and travelling expenses. Upon the other hand Section 12 does not limit the right to pay fees and expenses to members of the Council for attending the general session of the Council, and Section 13 authorizes payment of salaries and fees of all officers necessary for the working of this Act. After carefully considering the matter, I am of opinion that whatever doubt there may be as to the right to pay a per diem allowance to cover fees and travelling expenses under Section 12, that members' of the Executive Committee are officers of the Council necessary for the working of the Act within the meaning of Section 13, and that any reasonable allowance may therefore be paid to them in the discretion of the Council.

PAYMENT OF SALARY TO OFFICAL PROSECUTOR.

I am of opinion that under the provisions of Section 13 of the Ontario Medical Act the Council has power to appoint an official prosecutor as an officer necessary for the working of the Act, and to provide for payment to such official prosecutor of a reasonable salary out of the funds in the hands of the Treasurer in accordance with Section 58 of the Act.

EXAMINATION. TIME. PLACE.

I am of opinion that Section 28 of the Ontario Medical Act confers upon the Council an absolute discretion to provide for the holding of examinations at Toronto or at Kingston or at both places at any time or times, subject only to the provision that such examinations must be held at least once in each year.

The above are all the points that occurred to me under the heading's of your letter. If there are any other questions upon which an opinion is desired I shall be pleased to consider them at your request.

Yours truly,

(Signed)   B. B. Osler.

Toronto, June 23rd, 1897.

The REGISTRAR—I again wrote Mr. Osler and he sent me this :

R. A. Pyne, Esq., M.D., College of Physicians and Surgeons of Ontario, Toronto.

DEAR SIR,—Your memorandum asking further explanation of some of the points considered in my opinion of June 23rd ult., has been handed to me.

With regard to the payment of fees and expenses to members of Committees other than the Executive Committee, I am of opinion that members of such other Committees are not officers to whom the Council can pay salaries or fees under Section 13 of the Act, and while, as pointed out in my former opinion, there would seem to be some doubt as to whether payment for attendance at committee meetings is provided for by Section 12, I am upon the whole of opinion that in so far as the work of Standing Committees is necessary for carrying the Act into effect, the Council may in their discretion under this section provide for the payment of fees and reasonable travelling expenses to members attending such committee meetings.

The right to pay salaries and fees to the Board of Examiners is expressly provided for by Section 13 of the Act.   •

It is expressly provided by Section 13 of the Act that the Council must direct by by-law the time and manner of holding examinations at either Toronto or at Kingston.

Yours truly,

(Signed)   B. B. Osler.

July 5th, 1897.

Dr. WILLIAMS—Might we ask to have those two clauses in the two letters with reference to the examinations read over ; as it strikes me, one goes one way and the other the other.

The PRESIDENT—That would be a discussion of the matter.

Dr. WILLIAMS—I would not wish it discussed.

The REGISTRAR read from two communications as requested.

Dr. CAMPBELL—Is it a fact that the Council does direct by by-law or resolution the holding of an examination.

The PRESIDENT—It is by regulation laid down in the curriculum.

Dr. CAMPBELL—Had not that better be referred to the Rules and Regulations Committee to see if there is any change required ; I am not sure from the reading of those communications, but as you have to dispose of that communication in some way, it strikes me it would be well to refer it to the Rules and Regulations Committee, and I would make a motion to that effect.

Dr. SANGSTER—I have no objection to that being referred to the Rules and Regulations Committee, but Mr. Osler's language is as explicit as can be selected in the English tongue. We have no question raised as to the power of the Council to appoint a place and time for the holding of examinations, so that the answer that was first read does not cover the point raised in the least.   The answer that was read last goes to the pith of the whole matter, and Mr. Osler gives as his official opinion that that specific section of the Act explicitly demands that the time and place of holding the examination shall be settled by this Council on a by-law and only on a by-law.

Dr. BRAY—It is pretty late now, and some of the gentlemen might wish to discuss this matter, and I think it would be well to lay it over for future consideration ; we can receive it and have a motion made to discuss it at some future time.   There may be some things in it that we would all like to look into a little and I think it would be a good thing to have this matter laid over for future discussion.   It can be referred to a committee to report upon, and I would second Dr. Campbell's motion.

The REGISTRAR also read a communication from Mr. B. B. Osler giving his opinion with regard to practitioners who allow their names to be used or have personally aided in promoting the sale of secret proprietary medicines by companies, etc., which was referred to the Discipline Committee.

The REGISTRAR presented the credentials of the new members, Drs. Douglas and Griffin.

Dr. BRAY—It is hardly necessary to move a committee on credentials ; these gentlemen have already taken part in the proceedings.

Dr. SANGSTER—What is the rule of procedure ?

Dr. Bray—The rule I think is to refer those things to a Credential Committee and I would move that they be referred to a Committee on Credentials to be named by the President.

The President—I suggest the names of Drs. Bray, McLaughlin and Barrick as a Committee on Credentials.

Dr. Bray—I think that committee should meet at once.

Dr. Sangster—They can meet the first thing after the Council adjourns.

The Registrar read communication from Dr. H. Cooper asking permission to practice ; the Prosecutors Annual Report ; W. A. McCarthy asking to be allowed to take the final examination in the fall ; Edward B. Oliver asking to be permitted to take the final examination in the fall ; W. B. Carter asking permission to practice ; as to Dr. Carter, now in the Central Prison ; from Dr. Mallock asking for permit to practice ; D. G. Ruthven asking permit to practice, which were referred to the respective committees.

The Registrar read communication from H. E. Allen thanking the Council for the report made last year.

Dr. Campbell—That might be filed. That as I understand is a communication of thanks for something this Council has done. I move that it be filed.

Dr. Rogers—I second that.

Dr Williams—I suggest it be read that we may know what is in it.

The Registrar read communication from H. E. Allen.

Dr. Campbell—I renew my motion that this be filed.

The President put the motion which, on a vote being taken, was declared carried.

The Registrar read a number of other communications which were referred to the respective committees.

ENQUIRIES.

Dr. Armour—I desire to know if the by-laws in the Annual Announcement are a correct transcript of the original copies.

Dr. Pyne—I believe they are, as far as I know. I think they are exact.

Dr. Armour—I desire also to know why the sub-clauses of the Finance Committee's Report of last year are not numbered as passed by the Council, and why the clauses of the report referring to the Auditor's remuneration struck out by the Council is still in the report of the Committee ? It will be found on pages 140 and 141 of the proceedings of last year.

The President—The Printing Committee will be responsible for that.

Dr. Armour—The Printing Committee are not responsible for the correctness of these reports. I think Dr. Pyne has the supervision of them.

Dr. Pyne—I think the members of the Council will bear me out how difficult it is, when last year this report was run through in a few minutes, to do this, and something may have got in perhaps improperly but it is the transcript of what I have got and what I believed to be passed.

Dr. Armour—That clause referring to the remuneration of the Auditor that we threw out is still in the Committee's Report. You will find the resolution near the bottom of page 141.

Dr. Pyne—I suppose the Chairman of the Committee of the Whole did not strike it out. I have the report of the Committee of the Whole and I can look it up.

Dr. Armour—I called attention to this for the purpose of holding some one responsible for the correctness of the reports. I also desire to know how many of the medical practitioners have taken out the annual certificates during the past year as required by Section 41a, clause 1, which reads as follows : " Every registered practitioner shall obtain from the Registrar annually before the last day of December in each year a certificate under the seal of the College that he is a duly registered medical practitioner.

The President—We are able to answer that question. There are 1,537 in Ontario who have.

Dr. Sangster—Might I suggest that I think it is hardly fair to do otherwise than follow the parliamentary practice. I feel that Dr. Pyne should not be required at a moment's notice to answer a question of that kind ; that a notice of inquiry in a case of that kind should be given so as to let the officers of the Council prepare their replies to them.

The President—I have looked over the matter myself and I know for a fact that that number have paid their fees.

Dr. Bray—Dr. Sangster's contention is the correct one. I have no doubt that in parliament a member will give notice of what he requires. It is impossible to answer a member off-hand, and I think that matter might be taken into consideration by the Rules and Regulations Committee and have a clause put in to that effect.

Dr. Campbell—That can be easily gotten over. If an officer of the Council is not prepared at the moment to answer he can simply say; I cannot answer it now. I will answer at the next session or at the session following.

Dr. Logan—Our Registrar is a very extraordinary person; he is able to answer any question almost instantly.

Dr. Williams—On page 36 of the Announcement at the bottom you will find a resolution was carried giving instruction to the Educational Committee to leave out the names of those persons who had matriculated, those who have passed first, second and third year examinations and those who had obtained their membership through examination and substitute therefor the names of the registered practitioners who have become registered since the publication of the last Register; that was an instruction which has not been carried out. Was there any good and sufficient reason why it was not carried out?

The President—I am not able to answer that question.

Dr. Williams—The Printing Committee was to carry it out.

Dr. Rogers—I ask you, further down on the page, why it was not referred directly to the Printing Committee?

Dr. Williams—Yes; and you will find the Chairman of the Printing Committee says, "This motion appears to me to be so reasonable that we ought to pass it without any further discussion," and it was understood the Printing Committee was to carry the matter out.

Dr. Pyne—When the Printing Committee met, I brought that matter before them, and I asked Dr. Britton. as Chairman of the Educational Committee to come down and meet with them, which was done, and the doctor said it had not been sufficiently considered by the Council, although you sent the resolution passed by the Council on to the Education Committee, and he said the lists must appear, and I will take the responsibility of it.

Dr. Britton—That is correct; so much work had come before the Education Committee. You will find about the middle of page 36, which has been referred to, that that was one of the matters referred to the Education Committee, so that while it had come before that Committee it was really impossible to discharge the work in full or even this part of it; it would have taken some time to go over the Announcement and remove the names coming under these classes, so that in conference with the Printing Committee I did state what Dr. Pyne has stated now.

On motion of Dr. Bray, seconded by Dr. Moorhouse, the Council adjourned to meet on Wednesday, at ten o'clock, a.m.

SECOND DAY.

Wednesday, July 7th, 1897.

The Council met at ten o'clock a.m., according to motion for adjournment.

President Thorburn in the chair.

The Registrar called the roll and the following members answered to their names : Drs. Armour, Barrick, Brock, Campbell, Dickson, Douglas, Emory, Fowler, Geikie, Graham, Hanly, Henderson, Luton, Machell, Moorhouse, McLaughlin, Reddick, Rogers, Roome, Sangster, Thorburn, Thornton and Williams.

The minutes of the previous meeting were read by the Registrar, confirmed and signed by the-Presi lent.

NOTICES OF MOTION.

No. 1. Dr. Brock—That he would move at the next regular meeting of the Council regarding the conducting of examinations.

COMMUNICATIONS, PETITIONS, ETC.

None.

MOTIONS OF WHICH NOTICE HAS BEEN GIVEN AT A PREVIOUS MEETING.

Dr. Rogers—I gave notice yesterday of a motion to amend By-Law No. 39. With your permission I now beg leave to move, seconded by Dr. Logan, that By-Law —, to amend By-Law No. 39, be now read for a first time.

Dr. Armour—You are introducing a by-law?

Dr. Rogers—Certainly.

Dr. Armour—The orders of the day must be followed in the regular order. My notice of motion was given before yours, and therefore it comes first.

Dr. Rogers—What rule is that?

Dr. Armour—That is a common rule.

Dr. McLaughlin – There is a point of order involved just now, if Dr. Rogers is allowed to proceed. I submit that the proper method of proceeding with notices of motion is to take them as they are handed in. That is unquestionably the rule under such circumstances that the first notice of motion be given precedence.

Dr. Rogers—The President called for motions of which notice has been given ; I happened to catch the eye of the President first, and consequently I went ahead. I am quite willing to allow Dr. Armour to precede me.

Dr. Armour—I withdraw my objection.

Dr. Rogers—I make a motion, which you have in your hands, that By-Law No. —, to amend By-Law No. 39, be now read a first time.

Dr. McLaughlin—I still rise to a point of order. I think this ought to be determined. Are we to take up notices of motion in the order in which they have been handed in, or not ?

The President—Take them up in their proper order. I think, gentlemen, we should not dwell on technicalities and little things of no vital importance. It is only wasting the time of the Council, and, therefore, even if it is not altogether in form you should not try to retard the meeting beyond what is necessary. I rule you are right, Dr. McLaughlin.

Dr. McLaughlin—I would not have raised the point, only another gentleman put in a notice to amend this same by-law before Dr. Rogers did. I think the gentleman who put in the first notice of motion to amend that by-law should have the priority. Certainly, it is right.

Dr. Rogers—When was the notice of motion given ?

The Registrar—The first, Dr. Armour ; Dr. Geikie, No. 2 ; Dr. Geikie, No. 3 ; Dr. Brock, No. 4 ; Dr. Sangster, No. 5, and Dr. Rogers, No. 6.

Dr. Rogers—I would like to know on what ground that is the ruling ?

The President—The different general orders of the day are to be considered in the order in which they are handed in.

Dr. Rogers—Where is the rule that the person who gives the first notice shall have his notice of motion considered first ?

The President—I think that is common practice.

Dr. Rogers—There is no rule in our by-laws to that effect. There never has been a rule to that effect. I have been in this Council a good many years, and I have always seen tha the man who got to his feet first got the hearing.

Dr. Sangster—May I ask whether you have passed the order of reading of notices of motion ?

Dr. Rogers –Yes.

Dr. Sangster—I thought you took up some other business.

The President—I called for them before.

Dr Rogers—We have a certain set of rules, therefore I would like to have the ruling.

The President—I don't know that there is any particular rule bearing on it ; but I think it is parliamentary that they should be taken in the order of presentation, if the parties are present.

Dr. Rogers—I don't think so. There is no parliamentary rule—

The President—Common usage.

Dr. Sangster—I rise to a point of order. If the gentleman is not satisfied, let him ask the ruling of the Council without further discussion.

Dr. Rogers—Well, go on.

The President—You do not ask for it ?

Dr. Rogers—No.

Dr. Armour—I move, seconded by Dr. Williams, that leave be given to introduce a by-law entitled a by-law to amend By-Law No. 39, with regard to the reading of bills and proceedings thereon, and that the same be now read a first time.

The President put the motion, and on a vote having been taken, declared it carried.

Dr. Armour read the by-law a first time. By-law No. —, a by-law to amend By-Law No. 39 with regard to the reading of bills and proceedings thereon.

Whereas it is necessary and expedient to amend By-Law No. 39, therefore be it enacted that Sections 1, 2 and 3, under "By-Laws," of By-Law No. 39 be and are hereby appealed and the following substituted therefor :

1. Every bill shall be introduced upon motion for leave specifying the title of the bill, or upon motion of a committee to prepare and bring in a bill.

2. No bill shall be introduced either in blank or in an imperfect shape.

3. Every bill shall receive three several readings.

4. The question that this bill be now read a first time shall be decided without amendment or debate and every bill after receiving a second reading shall be considered in committee of the whole, each clause in its proper order, then the preamble and then the title and shall be read a third time before it is signed by the President.

5. The Registrar shall endorse on all bills the dates of the several readings and be responsible for their correctness should they be amended.
6. All by-laws adopted by the Council shall, immediately after being sealed by the seal of the College and signed by the President and Registrar, be deposited by the Registrar for security in the safe connected with his office.
7. Every by-law which has passed the Council shall be published in the next annual Announcement.

Dr. ARMOUR—I move, seconded by Dr. WILLIAMS, that the by-law just read a first time, entitled a by-law to amend By-Law No. 39 in regard to the reading of bills and proceedings thereon be now referred to the Committee of the Whole for a second reading.

The PRESIDENT—Is that your pleasure?

Dr. WILLIAMS—Before we get a second reading or refer it to Committee of the Whole it would be wise to see if the Council adopt this as the first reading of the by-law.

The PRESIDENT—It has been read a first time.

Dr. WILLIAMS—I don't understand that it has been put to the Council. The motion should be : Shall this constitute the first reading of the by-law? If the Council adopt that then the by-law has been considered to be read a first time.

Dr. ARMOUR—I think, Mr. President, I moved the motion that is placed in your hands. I understood that leave was given to read it a first time ; then I read it a first time ; then the next practice is to move that it be read the second time.

Dr. WILLIAMS—When it is read the first time it should be put to the Council. Shall this constitute the first reading? If that is carried then it is marked as having been read a first time.

Dr. BRAY—Dr. Williams is right, but I do not see any use in wasting time over these little quibbles, one is just as good as the other. I am perfectly willing it should be taken either way, but the way Dr. Williams has described is the practice. What I am objecting to is taking exception to every one of these little things ; let them go and let us go on with the regular business of the Council.

The PRESIDENT put the question and the Council consented that this should constitute the first reading of the by-law.

Dr. ARMOUR moved, seconded by Dr. WILLIAMS, that the by-law just read a first time be now referred to the Committee of the Whole for a second reading.

The PRESIDENT stated the motion which, on a vote being taken, was declared carried.

COUNCIL IN COMMITTEE OF THE WHOLE.

Dr. BARRICK in the chair.

Dr. ROGERS—I will ask that the by-law be read.

The CHAIRMAN—Is it your pleasure that we should proceed with the second reading this by-law.

Dr. ROOME—I don't think that this is customary at all. I never saw it. I don't think it is customary to have the second reading immediately after the first reading. I don't think there is any parliamentary practice in regard to that.

Dr. ROGERS—Let Dr. Barrick read the by-law for our information.

The CHAIRMAN—The Council is now in Committee of the Whole for the purpose of considering this by-law.

The CHAIRMAN read the by-law.

Dr. BRAY—I would like to ask Dr. Armour what this by-law is.

Dr. ARMOUR—It is shown at page li. under "By-Laws."

The CHAIRMAN—Is it your pleasure that this by-law be taken up clause by clause. ?

Dr. ROOME—I think this would be a very important amendment to our by-laws and I think that it should be typewritten and placed in the hands of the members and left over until another meeting of the Council. We are going at this hurriedly and we may pass it through and then want to vary it subsequently. As you have read it, and as it has been read to us I do not comprehend it fully. I would move that this be left over, typewritten, and placed in the hands of the members so that they may peruse it.

Dr. BRAY—I second that.

Dr. ARMOUR—The question that has just now arisen shows the necessity for this by-law. The rules and regulations we have been proceeding under with regard to by-laws here are such that I have not had the proper opportunity to discuss the general details of this by-law until we come here in Committee of the Whole, and then the custom is to discuss it clause by clause. Every by-law brought in should be read a first time so that the members will be possessed of the nature of the by-law ; that should be read without debate or amendment ; you may vote it down on its first reading but you should not debate it. After you have its first reading then it should be moved to be read a second time, and the general nature of the by-law should be discussed during that second reading ; the general discussion should then proceed, when amendments may be made at that stage ; After it has a second reading and it is amended, if so desired, then it will be referred to Committee of the Whole and considered more particularly clause by clause.

Dr. EMORY—I rise to a point of order. I would call your attention to what immediately follows the by-laws ; it says : " No amendment or addition to any of the foregoing rules and regulations shall be made unless the notice, setting forth the proposed amendment or addition, shall have been given at a meeting previous to that at which the same comes up for discussion, and all resolutions of the Council inconsistent with the above rules and regulations are hereby repealed." That was not set forth in the notice of motion, consequently we are discussing matter contrary to that regulation.

Dr. ARMOUR—I think the notice of motion was quite sufficient.

The CHAIRMAN—Do you object to the motion of Dr. Roome ?

Dr. ARMOUR—I am objecting qualifiedly ; I think the members will agree with me regarding the matter.

Dr. EMORY—I call for the ruling of the chair as to whether this is in order. It was simply said that this was a by-law to amend By-Law No. 39 and the proposed amendments or additions were not set forth in the notice of motion.

Dr. ARMOUR—It was set forth in these particulars, " A by-law to amend by-law No. 39, with regard to the reading of bills and proceedings thereon." That covers the whole matter.

Dr. EMORY—This section I have read tells you that it shall contain the proposed amendments or additions.

The CHAIRMAN—If we can take Dr. Roome's motion it will settle the whole business. According to the strict reading of this, no amendment or addition to any of the foregoing rules and regulations shall be made unless the notice setting forth the proposed amendment or addition shall have been given at a meeting previous to that at which the same comes up for discussion, and all resolutions of the Council inconsistent with the above rules and regulations are hereby repealed. It is just a question whether the members of this Council were seized of the form of the changes proposed by Dr. Armour. If there is any doubt upon it I think we should not proceed, and there seems to me—

Dr. ARMOUR—You cannot discuss it from the chair. I will have to call you to order.

Dr. WILLIAMS—We have accepted the bill, and we have read it a first time, and we have gone into Committee of the Whole to discuss it ; then some one commences to complain that it is out of order and ought to be thrown out altogether—it looks to me very much like child's play and I have no sympathy with that kind of work at all. The by-law which is before the Council is to amend this procedure. My conviction is, that this By-law No. 39, needs amending very materially from first to last, and this part that is brought in to-day is just simply to get it before the Council and to get that discussed and considered, and when that is done, so far as I am concerned, I want it referred to the Committee on Rules and Regulations, or some other committee, together with Dr. Rogers' amendment and all other amendments, so that by another year we may have a thoroughly digested and complete set of rules to take the place of No. 39 from first to last. The object of getting this into Committee of the Whole is, that the Council may become seized of the whole questions of facts in it. I think it is child's play to go on and carp and keep the business back in this way. I think I understand it now, the proposition is to change the method of introducing a by-law in the Council. Any of you who have had business to do with the Council in the past know they are old regulations and are not in harmony with those of Parliament, or municipal councils or anything else, they are simply a set of rules that were adopted here, and they are obsolete and put every member of the Council at cross purposes when they come to carry through a by-law. The object of this by-law is to get them in harmony with the adopted system in the country, so that a man who comes here knowing something about a by-law knows how to take it up and proceed, and does not have to go in and learn his A B C's over again.

Dr. BARRICK—I must rule that we are perfectly in order in discussing this matter in Committee of the Whole. There was no objection taken when it was proposed to go into Committee of the Whole to discuss this matter, and the Council decided we should go into Committee of the Whole, and clearly we are now in order to proceed.

Dr. BRAY rose as if to speak.

Dr. McLAUGHLIN—Dr. Armour was proceeding in his speech when this point of order was raised, therefore Dr. Armour has the floor.

Dr. BRAY—I was going to compliment Dr. Armour. I was just going to say to avoid discussion, if Dr. Armour will make his remarks short and agree with the motion Dr. Roome has made, that this be printed and given to all the members of the Council so that all the members can discuss it, then I would be glad to have Dr. Armour go on. But I do not wish to take up the time now when we will have lots of time to discuss it.

Dr. Armour—I only wanted to conclude that I do not disapprove of having this by-law typewritten and placed before the members before it is finally adopted, but I think the better procedure would be to go on and consider it first, in Committee of the Whole, and then have it typewritten and presented to the members before it gets the third reading. Our rules and regulations are such now that we cannot proceed very well with the by-law in any other way. I think Dr. Roome should withdraw his motion and allow it to be discussed in Committee of the Whole, and then we can have it typewritten, and perhaps referred to some other committee for consideration.

Dr. Roome—I am not prepared to discuss this until we know what we are discussing. On the second reading of any matter coming before any body they should know what they are reading. I am not prepared to say what changes should be made. By passing my resolution we can soon have it in form and then we could vote intelligently and assist in discussing it. I think we all should have a voice in the discussion before the Committee of the whole house.

Dr. Geikie—I think that view is quite correct. People who are making speeches understand everything, but the general members of the Council require to have a thing of that kind so that they can look it over.

Dr. McLaughlin—The proper way to dispose of this is that it should go to the Committtee on Rules and Regulations, then, if that Committee thinks it wise that it should go over for another year, or if the Council, after it comes back, thinks it should go over then is the time to do it. But we will make progress by taking that by-law before the Committee on Rules and Regulations, then it will come back to us properly crystalized and in a way that we can deal with it.

Dr. Roome—I am obliged to Dr. McLaughlin. I think Dr. Rogers' motion, and Dr. Armour's, and every other motion should be printed, and in that way we can discuss it and understand it.

Dr. Rogers—I quite agree with Dr. Roome. I think the whole procedure of putting through a by-law of such importance as to change the system under which we have done the business of this Council for years, is one which ought to be very carefully considered. It seems to me where there is a radical change to be made in our procedure, such as is proposed by Dr.·Armour, he should have at least asked for a special committee in order to discuss the whole subject of By-law No. 39 ; inasmuch as he has not done that I quite agree with Dr. Roome's resolution which is to have typewritten copies made of Dr. Armour's proposition and give them to the members ; then, if necessary, the by-law which I have brought in could also be included, and the members could have a copy of each, and it could be discussed intelligently. I think Dr. Roome's motion to have this proposed by-law tpyewritten and a copy given to each member is not only a proper one, but one which we ought all to support.

The Chairman—Are you ready for the motion ?

Dr. McLaughlin—I move in amendment that the Committee rise and report progress to the Council, so that the Council can refer it to the Committee on Rules and Regulations.

Dr. Rogers—Your motion would be correct and proper after Dr. Roome's motion has been carried.

Dr. McLaughlin—No ; if that motion is carried the whole thing is killed.

Dr. Roome—After deciding whether we shall do this we will rise and report progress and ask leave to sit again.

Dr. Williams—The objection I take to Dr. Roome's motion, and the only objection is that I think this should go to the Rules and Regulations Committee first, then Dr. Rogers amendment goes there and all other amendments, and when they have crystalized something into shape and put the whole thing in typewritten form, it can then come before the Council. That is the way in which I think Dr. Roome is rather blocking up our progress. In the way I suggest the matter could be dealt with intelligently.

Dr. Bray—What I object to is this, Dr. Armour brings in a by-law, he wants it discussed now though nobody but himself knows the exact wording of the by-law he is going to introduce. I say I may be obtuse, but I don't think there is anybody who can give it an intelligent consideration unless he has something before him and can follow Dr. Armour as he goes along, and the only way to do that is to have it typewritten as is proposed in the motion of Dr. Roome. Why should we go into committee of the whole now to discuss this by-law if it has to be referred to a committee ? I do not know that this Council ever passed a by-law and then referred it to a committee. Not at all. The by-law may be referred to a committee and afterwards to the Council. I am sorry I have to take up so much time to press my views upon the members, but I say we want to have it under our notice so that we can discuss it intelligently, or at least understand it. I may say I don't understand it at all the way it has been put.

Dr. Sangster—We are wasting needlessly a good deal of time ; there is no intention of passing the by-law and then having it typewritten. Before that subject comes up for final discussion this and other amendments will be typewritten and submitted to the Council, and only after full discussion thereupon will the by-law or the changes in the by-law eventually be made. It looks to me like a childish way of wasting time.

Dr. ROGERS -- I think that is not altogether correct, but one thing I would say, that if this by-law or the proposed by-law is ever referred to the Committee on Rules and Regulations we have no guarantee, judging from the past, that it will ever be resurrected. We referred several by-laws last year to that committee ; one was to amend this very section of by-law No. 39 ; the committee brought in a report, but never said anything about the proposed amendment. If Dr. Armour wishes to have his proposed by-law ever become law, and if that by-law has virtue in it, the proposal of Dr. Roome is one that ought to have received his approval at the very beginning, but he objects to it. Dr. Williams says, it should be referred to the Committee on Rules and Regulations. Everybody who has had any experience knows that the rules and regulations committee have so much to do that they will not be able to discuss it. I think what Dr. Roome says should be done and then if necessary we can refer it to a special committee.

Dr. ARMOUR—I don't propose to cut off the full discussion of this by-law after it is printed and in the hands of the members ; it is only the first consideration of the by-law that comes up in this Committee of the Whole. We have, by motion of the Council, resolved ourselves into committee of the whole for the purpose of reading this by-law a second time. I think we should read this by-law a second time and then go out of committee of the whole and move that the by-law be printed and referred to the Committee on Rules and Regulations for further consideration ; it will then come up again at a subsequent stage in this Council for the third time, and at that time every member will have an opportunity to criticise the by-law and propose such amendments as he desires.

Dr. MOORE—I quite agree with Dr. Williams. I think this very committee is the committee in which we should have a printed or typewritten copy of this by-law before us. It is only in committee of the whole that a man has an opportunity of speaking more than once, and when we get into a third reading it will be shut off in a few minutes ; this is the place where all explanations should be given, and this is the only place where full discussion can take place. Why should not this Council desire to have every member acquainted with the changes in the by-law ? These by-laws we are now about to amend were under consideration for three years, and for two years under the consideration of the committee ; and when a typewritten copy was laid upon the desk of every member they were then relegated back for another year. I felt then when they came up they were imperfect, and I feel now it would be a great injustice to push forward anything in a hurry. Let us have full time to discuss it and understand it, and give it the best judgment we have.

It was moved by Dr. ROOME, seconded by Dr. BRAY, that the proposed by-law be typewritten and a copy placed in the hands of each member of the Council, which, on a vote being taken, was declared carried.

Dr. ROGERS—I move that the Committee rise.

Dr. ARMOUR—I move that we proceed with the consideration of the by-law.

Dr. ROGERS—I moved before that that the Committee rise and report.

The CHAIRMAN stated Dr. Rogers' motion, which on a vote having been taken, was declared carried.

The Committee of the Whole rose.

President THORBURN in the chair.

Dr. GEIKIE—I have great pleasure in moving, seconded by Dr. MOORHOUSE, that a letter of condolence be sent to the relatives of each of the gentlemen named in my motion. As to the late Dr. Aikins, the Treasurer, I do not need to say anything whatever in regard to his services to this Council during many years ; the Council lay very near his heart, and a more faithful servant than Dr. Aikins nobody ever had, and it well becomes us to express our sympathy with his family in their loss by his recent death. I may say perhaps here what a good many members of this Council are not aware of, that for years Dr. Aikins, from his feeling of attachment to this Council and his devotion to its interests, had his own name down on notes, was involved in personal responsibility for thousands of dollars, without which the business of this Council at that time could not have been successfully carried on ; and I have pleasure in saying, and it is only just to say, that the President's own name and the name of at least another member of the Council, was down in the same way. To Dr. Aikins for his services we are greatly indebted, and his memory deserves this tribute as the very least we can do. With regard to the late Dr. Rosebrugh we sympathise with his friends, and we all grieve over his loss ; and Dr. Harris, of course, is fresh in your memory. With regard to Drs. Bergin and Miller, whom I have taken in my motion, although they were not members of this Council ; of course Dr. Bergin's memory is fresh in everybody's recollection ; he was indefatigable in his work, whether he agreed with us always or whether he did not. The sympathy of this body should also be expressed in the case of the late Dr. Miller, not long a member of this Council, who by his gentlemanliness and gentlemanly bearing, won the affection of everybody. I have great pleasure, seconded by Dr. Moorhouse, in moving the adoption of this motion.

Dr. Moorhouse—As seconder of this motion, I quite heartily endorse all that Dr. Geikie has stated. Dr. Aikins was Treasurer, I believe, ever since the first inception of this Council, in 1866, and it involved a very great responsibility, not only the responsibility of labor, but a pecuniary responsibility, in which he many times very ably helped the Council, and I think that it is nothing but right that we should forward to his family our expression of condolence. Also, to the family of our ex-President, the late Dr. Harris ; he was an old fellow-student of my own ; I have known him very intimately for nearly thirty years, and I can quite truly speak of his sterling worth ; he also was, for a long time, a member of this Council, and I think every man that has come in contact with him cannot but bear out the very glowing remarks that the mover, Dr. Geikie, has made respecting his name. Although every member of the Council may not have seen eye to eye with him, neither can we all with one another, but I am sure Dr. Harris always worked with a true eye for the good of the profession in general.

The President—There cannot be two opinions as to the remarks that have been made in reference to our departed friends. All these different gentlemen distinguished themselves, not only in the Council but in the country generally ; they were men of note. I take it for granted that there cannot be any objection to the motion. Let us approve of this resolution by a standing vote.

The members of the Council arose in a body.

The President—I declare the motion carried unanimously.

Dr. Geikie—I move, seconded by Dr. Campbell, that in the interests of economy, it is unnecessary to have verbatim reports of the proceedings of the Council at its various sittings ; that the correct reports kept always for years past by the Registrar are and shall hereafter be deemed all that is required, and will be more likely to be read by the profession than the very lengthy and costly reports sent out for some time past. My motion is not aimed at the stenographer ; he will of course know that there is no ill-feeling at all with regard to anybody, but it is simply and solely, as the motion states, in the interests of economy. It is not merely the cost of the stenographic report, but the cost of printing ; think of the cost of postage for this large quantity of matter. I think a synopsis, such as the Registrar has always given—they are correct enough for the Council—is enough to tell the public everything that has been done, and is easier read, and when read they will take a deep interest in the proceeings of the Council. The rest of that report frightens everybody. Each gentleman who figures here reads what he said over very carefully, and is able, years afterwards, to quote from his own speeches, but I suppose if he could not do that there would be no great loss sustained, and there would be a great saving of the Council's funds effected. I don't know that I need detain you ; it is not aimed at anybody, it is aimed at cutting down the expenses of the printing more than half, and making the report look a good deal more common sense than it does. Imagine stenographic reports of such small talk as we have been indulging in ; it is not necessary to report it. A synopsis is all that we need, and it is in the interests of economy ; and the profession will look to our advocating and carrying out economy when it can be done without a sacrifice of efficiency ; and efficiency will be promoted by the motion, if adopted, and economy as well.

Dr. Moorhouse—I would suggest that it would be a very excellent motion for us to pass as it might perhaps repress some of these very rhetorical efforts that we have had.

Dr. Sangster—I would like to know to whom the formation of the synopsis Dr. Geikie refers to is to be entrusted ? I thoroughly am in accord with him as to the non-necessity of the printing and publishing of a necessarily long diarrhœtic, I think was the term our friends applied to those reports of our proceedings, but I would like to have some guarantee that if they are epitomized that those epitomies should be entrusted either to a printing committee or to somebody whom we could hold responsible for supplying a correct and fair synopsis of the remarks made. If a guarantee can be given in that direction I will support that motion.

Dr. Geikie—Dr. Sangster's remarks are already answered ; the Registrar makes a synopsis and reads it at every sitting of the Council, and if it does not suit the Council, and the report is not correct, then is the time to correct it ; and surely when we listen to our synopsis the entire Council are good judges and it is moreover satisfactory.

Dr. Sangster—You should have discussions on discussions, and the reading of the synopsis by the Registrar would occupy more time than the discussions in the Council.

Dr. McLaughlin—It is an impossibility that that motion can be carried out. The Registrar has all he can do to follow the proceedings of the Council and get the motions into his hands and put them in place. It would be impossible for the Registrar to listen to anyone speaking and put down a synopsis of what is said. We must either have a hansard or have nothing, or else we must appoint a stenographer or some other person to make a synopsis of the remarks made.

Dr. BRITTON—A number of years ago when the late lamented Dr. Bergin introduced a by-law bearing upon the curriculum, the matter was thought of so much importance that a resolution was carried to the effect that a stenographic report be prepared and sent to the profession. I thought then, and, as years go by, the more I am convinced, that that was a proper course to take. Up to that time there had been but a very short synopsis in the shape of a report of the proceedings of this Council appearing in one or other of the medical journals, and, really, I think it would be safe to venture in the statement that nine out of ten of the medical profession throughout the country knew scarcely anything about the proceedinge here. I think there is a duty that every member of the profession owes to himself, as well as to the profession of which he is a member, that is, not only to be a well cultivated man himself and capable of discharging his duties from a professional standpoint, but to know what the polity of his position is. We, ourselves, cannot make rapid advance in the elevation of the profession, except through conversation and communication with our constituents ; we are not men so brainy that we require no advice. I think it behooves every member here to consult with his constituents to know what the views of the members may be ; what is the use of conferring with constituents if they have no opportunity of following the course that has been taken in this Council, excepting to read a resolution moved by so and so, seconded by so and so, and declared carried or lost. They know nothing of what has been said for and against it. Also, looking at it from the standpoint of parliamentary usage, year after year we have to refer at times in our controversies, in our discussions, to what has been said or done in the past. If we have no verbatim report, if we have a synopsis simply, such as has been suggested, why one member will get up and say, "that is not correct," another will say, "I believe it is correct, such and such was said, such and such was done." It has been mentioned that the "postage on this announcement amounts to a great deal." Let us reduce that Announcement to just one-tenth of its present compass and the postage would be just the same. So that, so far as that part of the argument is concerned it must fall to the ground. The only additional expense is the getting up of this announcement in its present form. A large part of the Announcement would have to be in it at any rate, the by-laws, regulations, and so forth. But, I must oppose any resolution which would have the effect of abridging even to the extent of one word, the report that is given of our proceedings here.

Dr. WILLIAMS –Mr. President, this subject is largely, not entirely, with the Council. Our custom was to follow the plan of simply publishing the ordinary minutes, and as Dr. Britton has stated, the verbatim report was made but a few years since, and I for one at that time thought it was a too expensive course to pursue. I admit to having entirely changed my opinion since that time. I agree with Dr. Geikie that there is, perhaps, too much froth, too many words in our reports, but I think if you take the reports of any similar body in the country you will find that this is largely proven, and we do not need to go past the Parliament at Ottawa to find that they publish four times as many words as are necessary. Supposing they could sit down and condense properly the material they wished to use so that there would be no excessive words used they would have an exceptional body. The reason for changing my mind has been this : we had no means of getting the profession acquainted with the work that was being done, the steps that were being taken and the reason for those steps by the Council ; the profession were largely at sea as to whether the Council were doing anything or not ; they had no means of becoming acquainted with the reasons for any part of the work, and because of that a great deal of dissatisfaction grew up in the country. I just have in my mind at present a gentleman in the town of Simcoe, when I called upon him one time and had a conversation on this subject, he berated me and the balance of the Council in good round terms, notwithstanding he was a personal friend of my own and had been since my student days ; he was very strongly opposed to paying the fee or anything in connection with it. In 1895 I was laid off, as many of you know, through illness, and was away in Nova Scotia, and when I came home one of the first letters I got was from this very gentleman, complimenting me on the production of our Annual Announcement, with the verbatim report, and intimating he had been so pleased on reading it that he willingly contributed his fee and had sent it in and felt it to be an honour to belong to a profession of that kind, and intimating that he had no idea that there were any body of men doing so much and so important work as he had found to be the fact when he came to read that report. I have met some other men, who, while not being so strong termed as that, have still felt that getting that information and knowing what was going on was worth a good deal. For these reasons I changed my mind entirely and I believe that while it does cost money that it is a good investment inasmuch as each number of the profession has it placed within his power to acquaint himself with exactly what is being done and the reason therefor. That the reports might be improved there is no question ; if we could go over our remarks ourselves and reconsider them there is no doubt we could cut them down, improve their form and all that, but, gentlemen, it is not done in any of the similar bodies in the country and they too, as well as we, use a superfluity of words. Under these circumstances I cannot, for one, support Dr. Geikie's resolution. I do think it would be difficult to get a synoysis that would be satisfactory and under the circumstances I think there is vantage ganied ; that acquainting the profession fully with what is done, or giving them an opportunity of becoming acquainted with what is done, more than compensates for the cost and trouble of that report.

Dr. DICKSON—Dr. Williams has covered the ground and said very much that I proposed to take up ; however, I might add with reference to the matter of a condensed report being acceptable to or read by the profession, I think the opposite would be the case ; I think if we sent out simply a bald synopsis, such as our minutes, the result would be that they would be thrown in the waste paper basket. When it is known that the report is given as a verbatim report and all that transpired is there it becomes a matter of interest. I know that to be a fact from some things that my own constituents have stated to me. With reference to the postage, the Annual Announcement is delivered, and it must be remembered it would cost as much to send the Announcement alone as to send our verbatim report with it ; I must therefore oppose the motion.

Dr. THORNTON—I could not agree with Dr. Geikie's motion for several reasons. In the first place, the point that he mentioned, the reading of a synopsis by the Registrar appears to my mind to be entirely out of place, and in the next place if he is prepared to read such a synopsis I, as one member of this Council, am not prepared to listen to it. Now, some of us have said a great deal about reforms in this Council. If. we are going to get reforms in this Council by any kind of a report we will never get it by a synopsis. The questions that have been brought up here from time to time have been threshed out, and those who gave utterance to them have been held accountable for the last words they uttered. I am well aware that there is a little force in the old doctrine that every evil has its good and every good its evil ; probably a verbatim report leads some of us to say a little more than is wise, or a little more than we would say if it was put in the form of a synopsis. With regard to a synopsis, I think that there are many in this Council, and myself for one, who would not be willing to be held accountable for their utterances by any synopsis that might be given. It is very easy to misconstrue a man's meaning, and in that way I would only be willing to be judged by every word that was uttered or else by nothing at all. If we are to adopt any way of publishing our proceedings here it appears to me that there can only be one of two ways, that is, to publish the measures we adopt and the procedure we go through and drop every discussion, or publish everything verbatim.

Dr. CAMPBELL—The proposition of Dr. Geikie is simply to place this body in line with every organization, municipal, legislative and everything else in the country, except the Dominion Parliament ; I am not aware of a single organization that publishes a verbatim report of all the varied remarks that are made by the members on every conceivable occasion, except the Dominion Parliament ; I am not aware of any, I do not know of any ; they publish a journal of the proceedings as the old parliament used to do, and that is what Dr. Geikie refers to when he speaks of a synopsis ; he does not mean that the Registrar shall make a synopsis of the debate ; he means that the report that we shall publish in our Annual Announcement shall be the official minutes of the meetings of the Council as they are read by the Registrar at the opening of every sitting ; that is an official record, and that, as far as I know, is the only record that is published by any association of men in the Province or in the Dominion, except the Dominion Parliament, which publishes a hansard, and in which it buries a vast amount of glowing eloquence and simply excretary material as we bury in our Annual Announcement. I am glad to hear from the remarks that have been made by some of the members here that the reading of these debates have had the good effect of impressing upon some members of the profession the good that is being done by this institution, and the great benefits that accrue to the profession. I candidly confess that so far as my personal experience is concerned I have not met very many members of the profession who have read that journal of proceedings. I do not know whether any members in my own town have read it or not, I never have found out. As Dr. Geikie intimates, I am able to read over my own speeches, probably Dr. Moorhouse and Dr. Roome do the same. I don't know as you read the other people's speeches and I don't know that the other members of the profession read very much of that book, and I don't know that a great many of those throughout the country do ; that some few do appreciate the full verbatim report of our speeches I have no doubt whatever. It is a grave question in my mind whether the benefits accruing from a few appreciating it are such as will compensate us for the expense that is incurred every year, not only in the printing bill, but in the per diem bill ; because I think human nature is the same here as everywhere else—there is no doubt if our speeches were not going on record they would be considerably shorter than they are. For these reasons I second Dr. Geikie's motion.

Dr. MOORE—I was in favor at the very beginning of having a verbatim report, and I have the very opposite view from that which my friend Dr. Campbell has expressed ; I thought if every word we said was reported that it would cut our speeches down very materially; I thought a lot of us would be very much afraid of being reported verbatim, but probably that is not so. However, I think I am right yet. I think if we had not this verbatim report we would probably have more squabbles than we now have. It is a beautiful thing to be put on record sometimes, especially if you are put on record well. Do we look to see how well we look in print? I admit I have looked, and I have not been pleased with myself, and probably that keeps my tongue from wagging. We must have a complete report or it is an incorrect report. I submit that one of the reasons this Council met with the opposition that it did some years ago was simply because half the profession were not aware of what we were doing. This complete report is the only means of communication we have with the profession. The public press did not report us at all. We were simply reported, as someone has said, "moved by so and so, seconded by so and so," and finally winding up by saying "carried" or "lost." Many of us have had similar experiences to that which Dr. Williams has given us. The profession now knows what we are doing, and they think a great deal more of the work this Council is doing. The very reason we are getting that annual fee in is very largely due to the verbatim report.

Dr. BARRICK—I shall just speak from the financial side of this question; we have this year (1896-7) 150 pages of proceedings, costing us for printing and binding, $1.32 per page, amounting to $189.00; that is for the proceedings printed. One hundred and fifty pages of stenographic report costing us about ninety cents, and as I said before, I am not sure whether we are not paying too much for that; however, that comes to $135.00, and that makes a total of $324.00 for publishing the proceedings of the Council. Now, if Dr. Geikie's resolution can reduce it to half that or two-thirds, making say fifty pages, that would save us about $200.00. The postage, as has been explained by Dr. Dickson, would be about the same; so. it whittles down to this, it would cost us now $324.00, and the Printing Committee will do their utmost this year to try and cut it lower still. As to the postage, as Dr. Dickson explained, the Announcement has to be sent anyway, and on an Announcement containing one hundred pages less, the postage would be very little less.

Dr. ROOME—You have not figured on shortening the time of the Council.

Dr. BARRICK—If you take the publishing of the minutes as explained by someone—I think Dr. Geikie intends to go a little further—then the reading of those minutes extended would take up more time, and if it took up two-thirds of say any whole session, and our days cost about $300.00 a day, we would wipe out all we would save, and, therefore, from a financial point of view, I say it would not be any saving. Again, if you are so particular about the financial side of the question, we find that there are 150 pages of the proceedings and there are thirty members, that is about five pages to each member, then I say put a tax upon every member who uses up more than five pages; I think in that way we would have a wholesome effect upon the speeches, and we would have perhaps only one hundred pages in the report. But, so far as the other side is concerned, I think it is of great value that we do have a verbatim report of the proceedings of this Council. I am satisfied of this, that there is a gain apart from the financial side of the question. I thank you, gentlemen.

Dr. MOORHOUSE—I think the arguments adduced by Dr. Barrick are unanswerable. I was somewhat half inclined to vote for Dr. Geikie's motion, but, having heard this very unanswerable argument of our friend, Dr. Barrick, I must say that we would be retrograde should we decide to abolish the stenographer's report, therefore I will heartily vote against the motion.

The PRESIDENT read the motion, which, on a vote being taken, was declared lost.

Dr. BARRICK moved, seconded by Dr. LOGAN, that the Medical Council of the Province of Ontario, at this their annual meeting, desire to express for themselves and the profession generally their sense of the just and wise legislation enacted by the Dominion Parliament in exempting medical works and surgical instruments from customs duties.

The PRESIDENT read the motion, which, on a vote being taken, was declared carried.

Dr. SANGSTER moved, seconded by Dr. McLAUGHLIN, that the Council ask, during the present session, for tenders for the work done by the official stenographer, said tenders to apply to the next and future sessions of the Council.

Dr. SANGSTER—If I may be permitted to add to that, I would add "and report of the Discipline Committee trials." I suppose one includes the other, really.

The PRESIDENT—I think so.

Dr. BRAY—Couldn't tenders be advertised for now, and the tenders be brought before this Council before we adjourn?

Dr. BRITTON—Might I be allowed to ask Dr. Sangster for information. He uses the expression at the latter end of his resolution, "such tenders to relate to the next and future sessions of the Council." I would like to know whether or not these tenders are for the work for a number of years to come or simply for next year's?

Dr. SANGSTER—The reason I put in that, I was told that the matter was largely settled for the present session, that the official stenographer had already done some work, and was daily doing work, and was supposed to be under the agreement in the past, and that the Council would naturally object to allowing that resolution to apply to the present session.

Dr. BRITTON—I understand that perfectly, but you use the expression "next and future sessions."

Dr SANGSTER—We can strike out the words "and future sessions."

Dr. BRAY—Will you add to your motion that tenders be advertised for to-morrow, and to be in here by Friday. I suppose the stenographers all live in the city, and the tenders can be settled by this Council.

The PRESIDENT—The tenders for the next session ?

Dr. BRAY—Precisely. But you will have to have the man here.

The PRESIDENT—I think somebody will have to move the method of advertising.

Dr. MACHELL—That can be left to the Printing Committee.

The PRESIDENT read the motion as amended : Moved by Dr. Sangster, seconded by Dr. McLaughlin, that the Printing Committee of the Council ask, during the present session, for tenders for the work done by the official stenographer, said tenders to apply to the next session of the Council and reports of the Discipline Committee trials ; and that the Printing Committee be requested to ask for such tenders to-day or to-morrow, and report at once.

The PRESIDENT—You have heard the motion.

Dr. WILLIAMS—I think in that advertisement it is well to have it understood that it shall not be a mere amateur reporter ; we want a regular standard official reporter.

The PRESIDENT—You would not entertain a tender from an amateur ?

Dr. SANGSTER—I will make my remarks very short. Of course, it is understood that amateurs are not brought into the matter. We want the best official stenographer to make our reports that is procurable, and we want some guarantee that the reports will be correct, that there can be no possible tampering with them by the omission or addition of words as there has been in the past, and sometimes by the addition of clauses. If these stenographic reports are to carry any weight with the profession they must either give the *ipsissima verba* of the debate, or they must be regarded as a merely good synopsis of what was said. I think the very strongest guarantee should be required of any gentleman tendering for that work, a guarantee almost approaching to a declaration, that he would give a perfect, clean and clear transcript of the debates of the Council ; and unless it is the intention of the Medical Council to appoint also an official grammarian, to correct the report after it comes out of the stenographer's hands, it is important that it should be the duty of somebody to look through those reports to bring them more in accord with the principles of Murray and other grammarians. I myself have the strongest possible objections to being reported, as I am in those reports, as using the plural verb with a singular noun, and saying, "The Council do this," "The Council decided that it was their duty"—using plural pronouns and using plural verbs with a noun that is singular in its meaning. To me it is just as objecionable as it would be to say "that the Legislature decided to amend their proceedings," "that the Synod of the Church of England decided that they had nothing to do with the matter," and so throughout that form of false grammar is used, from the first page to the last. I maintain that the gentlemen who get up and speak in this chamber are not guilty of such lapses of grammar, and it should be somebody's duty to attend to it and correct it. When I brought this matter up last session in the Council and complained of it, and complained especially of the manner in which my own remarks had been rendered incomprehensible, I was told I could appeal to nobody but Dr. Orr ; and I object to leaving myself at the mercy of any man outside this Council, and I think it should be the duty of the stenographer, or the Printing Committee, to see that the reports are exact reports of what is said, or, otherwise, that the report should be submitted to the gentleman making the speech, and he should be suffered not to make any material change, but to correct it so as to make it a fair transcript of what he said. I think it is material that that matter should be done. I believe the matter should be done by tender ; I believe the matter is really covered by a resolution of the past, that all work done by this Council in the future should be tendered for, but in order to bring it specifically before the Council, I moved that resolution.

Dr. BRAY—Dr. Sangster asks for a verbatim report. He says that there is to be a guarantee that the stenographer is to give a verbatim report, and then he wants to appoint a professor of grammar to correct it. How can you have a verbatim report if it is corrected ? This is inconsistent. It doesn't amount to very much, but we are not all grammarians possibly ; we are not all grammarians such as our friend, Dr. Sangster, who spent a good part of his life in the honorable calling of teaching. A man makes little slips occasionally, and I think those should be corrected ; but, at the same time, you cannot have a verbatim report if you correct it.

Dr. BARRICK—With regard to what Dr. Sangster says with regard to the printing, when we got the tenders last year we made it a condition that the persons getting the contract must do their own proof-reading ; had we not done that, they would have charged us for proof-reading. Now, we will either have to leave it just in that same way, and let the tender be that the successful tenderer does his own proof-reading, or we will have to appoint a proof-reader. I am very much in sympathy with Dr. Sangster's resolution, and I would just like to add one thing to it. The financial side of the question is still fresh; it cost us last year 90 cents per page for preparing a typewritten copy of a verbatim report of the proceedings. Now, we don't know this year what it is going to cost. Now, I would like this to be added "That the remuneration for the preparation of a typewritten copy of a verbatim report of the proceedings of the Council for this year be the same as that fixed by tender for next year." A stenographer has been appointed, his pay has not been fixed, but he has said he will do it as cheaply as anybody else. If that then is the case, and we get tenders for next year, and the tender for the next year fixes the price, then I wish this added, "that the remuneration for the preparation of a typewritten copy of a verbatim report of the proceedings of the Council for this year be the same as that fixed by tender for next year."

The PRESIDENT—Do you move this as an amendment?

Dr. BARRICK—Or to be added as an amendment.

The PRESIDENT—I think the stenographer said he would do the reporting as cheaply as any other competent man.

Dr. BARRICK—Do you think the Committee are going to appoint an incompetent man to do the work for next year? We ask for tenders and when we get them we shall decide then who shall do the work, if they do not give us that privilege—

Dr. ROGERS—That is out of order. I am going to ask for a ruling. You are discussing the payment of the stenographer now, whereas the motion is a tender for the future, a totally different question; your question will be decided by the Printing or Finance Committee; leave it there for the time being. But Dr. Sangster's motion is for the future.

Dr. BARRICK—You wish to get away from the expenses of this year.

Dr. ROGERS—No, we don't.

Dr. BARRICK—Every attempt that has been made to diminish the expenses of this Council, anything that interferes with what has been done before is looked upon as a reflection on what has been done; the sooner we get away from that the better. I am as conservative as any member of this Council and I will not allow any changes to be made that should not be made, but I am not going to fossilize. This is no reflection, gentlemen, it is just to fix the price for this year the same as what we are getting tenders for for next year.

Dr. MACHELL—Mr. Chairman, I think the motion of Dr. Sangster is a move in the right direction; it is in line with one read yesterday when we were discussing the appointment of the stenographer; unless we have some such motion of this kind it seems to me it will be impossible to ever make a change in our stenographer. I thing the motion is quite right and it is a business-like way of doing business.

Dr. ROOME—I think the amendment which has been made is out of order and does not apply to the resolution at all. If this resolution is passed which Dr. Sangster has moved, then Dr. Barrick can move his resolution. An amendment must be in accord with the resolution or else it is no amendment.

Dr. BARRICK—I merely asked that Dr. Sangster add this to his resolution.

Dr. ROGERS—Before this goes to a vote I would like to make one remark in answer to a reflection that Dr. Sangster has made on our official stenographer, Mr. Downey. I beg to protest against the assumption and the assertion on his part that the stenographer has added words and sentences in his report; I am satisfied that that report has not only been as near a verbatim report as it is possible for any stenographer to make, but I am satisfied it has been a thoroughly honest one. As I have been your President during the past year and Vice-President the year before I have some reason to know whether the stenographer's report has been fair.

Dr. SANGSTER—I rise to a point of order. I stated I was misrepresented, I state so still. I said I was systematically misrepresented, I state so still; and if the Council chooses to doubt me and gives me a committee, for the past two years, I will establish that fact beyond a doubt. I stated I did not know where the responsibility rested; I stated I asked last year and I was told it rested with Dr. Orr. Wherever it rests I want in future the irregularity corrected. I complimented Mr. Downey last year on the impartiality of his work; and I stated then, as I state now, that I have very strong doubts that it originates with him. I repeat my statement, whether Mr. Downey is reappointed or not, this Council shall have some guarantee.

Dr. ROGERS—Is this an explanation or a speech? I don't see how a gentleman can get up and interrupt a speaker and then make a speech.

Dr. SANGSTER—My point of order was that he was deliberately misrepresenting.

Dr. ROGERS—I will ask the stenographer to read his notes. I say Dr. Sangster has stated in his remarks that the stenographer put in words and sentences in his report.

The PRESIDENT—I think this is out of place.

Dr. ROGERS—I will ask the stenographer to read his notes.

As requested, the stenographer read from his notes as follows : "We want the best official stenographer to make our reports that is procurable, and we want some guarantee that the reports will be correct, that there can be no possible tampering with them by the omission or addition of words as there has been in the past, and sometimes by the addition of clauses."

Dr. ROGERS—The information must be drawn by any person who reads that, that the reference is to the stenographer.

Dr. SANGSTER—That casts no reflection upon the stenographer.

Dr. ROGERS—If it does not mean that I do not know what it means, and I am capable of understanding English. I want to state another thing, although perhaps Dr. Sangster considers he is well-known as an educationalist, and perhaps he is, perhaps he has had many years experience in teaching, but I think the form he used, and the very words he used as to grammatical construction of sentences is not correct. I think that both rules are open to doubt. He referred to the use of the singular noun with the plural verb or pronoun where plurality was understood in the context. Mr. Downey preferred to use the plural form ; both forms are correct in certain cases. I think Mr. Downey would be perfectly correct in regard to such a phrase as "the Church of England Synod' in using the plural verb. I maintain that the report has not only been a well made report but it has been a good report and a truthful report and has been in every sense a verbatim report, and I congratulate Mr. Downey and I congratulate this Council in having one of the best reports that has ever been made.

Dr. SANGSTER—I have no reflection to make on Mr. Downey, but I do say if Dr. Rogers is to be an authority on grammar and that if our daily press in the city of Toronto were to repeat in their daily issues the grammar that is found from one page to the other of those official proceedings, we would cry shame on them.

The PRESIDENT stated the motion which, on a vote being taken, was declared carried.

Dr. GEIKIE—I move that we adjourn.

Dr. BRAY—There is a lot of business to do and I think we should go through the order of business before we adjourn.

Dr. ROGERS—My motion may stand.

On consent of the Council, Dr. Rogers' motion was allowed to stand.

ENQUIRIES.

Dr. ARMOUR—I would like to ask that a copy of the opinion of Mr. Osler be laid on the table on the questions as indicated in the motion I moved last session (at page 38) as follows : 1st. Had the Medical Council, at the annual session of 1895, the legal right to assess an annual tax on the medical profession for the years 1893 and 1894, as enacted in Clause 3 of By-law 69. 2nd. To what proportion of the arrearages of the annual tax which are outstanding at various dates from 1874 to the present time, Section 41a of the Medical Act, can be legally applied for their collection. I desire that be laid on the table.

On motion of Dr. ROGERS, seconded by Dr. BRITTON, the Council adjourned to meet at two o'clock p.m.

AFTERNOON SESSION.

The Council met at two o'clock p.m., in accordance with the motion for adjournment.

The PRESIDENT in the chair.

The REGISTRAR called the roll and the following members answered to their names : Drs. Armour, Barrick, Brock, Campbell, Dickson, Douglas, Emory, Fowler. Geikie, Graham, Griffin, Hanley, Henderson. Henry, Logan, Luton, Moorhouse, McLaughlin, Reddick, Rogers, Roome, Sangster, Shaw and Thorburn.

The minutes of the previous meeting were read by the Registrar.

Dr. PYNE—I do not know that there is an opinion of Mr. Osler on all these matters referred to by Dr. Armour.

Dr. WILLIAMS—That part with reference to the collection of back fees was submitted to Mr. Osler and he prepared a by-law and the by-law was brought to the Council and put through.

The PRESIDENT—That was done to my recollection.

Dr. PYNE—But whether there was any written opinion of Mr. Osler I don't remember.

Dr. WILLIAMS—He said that was our course to pursue.

Dr. ARMOUR—I have raised the question because it ought to be within the knowledge of every member of the Council that Mr. Osler had given an opinion. I have not seen the opinion, but I would like to have it to peruse it.

Dr. ROGERS—That opinion was given a year ago last summer. I think you will find it in the proceedings of the Council of 1895-96.

Dr. ARMOUR—There is no opinion in the proceedings of the Council referring to the matter in that way.

The PRESIDENT—If we have not got it, you can move that it be procured by giving notice of motion.

The minutes were confirmed as read, and signed by the President.

NOTICE OF MOTION.

Dr. ARMOUR—I desire to put in the question asked this morning as a notice of motion as it is now in the hands of the Registrar.

Dr. SANGSTER—I gave notice of motion, asking that a return be granted showing by what authority, and in what year, the fourth particular in the declaration appended to the candidates' printed form of application for admission to the Council's examinations was first inserted therein.

· Dr. BRITTON—Will it be in order to ask now that that clause be read, because if notice of motion means anything, it means time is to be given us to consider the matter before it comes up for discuss on here. I do know what that clause is.

Dr. SANGSTER—The clause is of the nature of a cast-iron oath, that every student shall abide by the by-laws of the Medical Act and the amendments thereto by this Council. The declaration is as follows:

Province of Ontario, County of——————to wit : etc.

1. That I am the person named in the above written application.
2. That the answers to the questions therein above contained are of my own proper handwriting.
3. That the said answers are true in substance and in fact.
4. That I promise to comply with the Ontario Medical Act and amendments thereto.

And I made this solemn declaration conscientiously believing the same to be true and knowing that it is of the same force and effect as if made under oath and by virtue of The Canada Evidence Act, 1893.

(Signed) etc., etc.

It is since 1893, because it refers to the Act of 1893, and I want particulars as to how and by what authority that was inserted. I also give notice of motion asking that a return be granted showing every case in which the arrearage of assessment dues has been commuted to a partial payment, the commutation accepted and the authority upon which such commutation was agreed to by the officers of the Council.

READING OF COMMUNICATIONS, PETITIONS, ETC.

The REGISTRAR read communications from Charles H. Stewart, asking for registration as a matriculant ; from C. D. Cowan, re an appeal, he having failed at the recent examination ; from J. T. Clarke, asking that he be granted a license as he has passed the intermediate examination, which were referred to the respective committees.

Dr. CAMPBELL—It is evident that in order to facilitate the business of the Council the various committees should have an opportunity to consider the matters that have been referred to them ; for that purpose I would move that the Council adjourn till to-morrow morning at ten o'clock.

Dr. ROGERS—I beg to move in amendment that the Council adjourn until to-night at half-past eight, otherwise it will be difficult to get the members of the committees together.

Dr. WILLIAMS—The notice of motion I sent up this morning has not been read.

Dr. SANGSTER—If Dr. Campbell's motion means that the committees will work all afternoon and into the night, I think Dr. Rogers' difficulty will be overcome.

Dr. ROGERS—I think so too, but I think the most of the members will bear me out that the difficulty is to get the committees together. I think if the Council adjourns until half-past eight, the members will come back and then we can adjourn immediately afterwards. I think it is a far better way to get the committees together and then adjourn until to-morrow morning. If we adjourn the Council until half-past eight and then re-adjourn at once, you will have all the members here.

Dr. CAMPBELL—You occupy time in the evening while the committees might be at work, and something may crop up then that will cause discussion.

Dr. BRITTON—I think I can vouch for the members of the Education Committee ; that committee has a lot of work on hand, and if we adjourn and they are told to assemble again at eight o'clock or half-past, they will be here.

Dr. MOORE—Don't you think it would be better to run through the order of business and complete the meeting and then adjourn.

Dr. CAMPBELL—If you once start that you do not know when you will get through.

Dr. LUTON—I second Dr. Campbell's motion.

The PRESIDENT—Is it your pleasure that we adjourn until to-morrow morning at ten o'clock ?

Dr. ROGERS—I moved in amendment that we adjourn until to-night at eight o'clock.

Dr. HENRY—I second that, if there is an assurance that there will be no business taken up.

Dr. ROGERS—I am satisfied there will be a better scheme of business carried out if you adjourn till to-night at half past eight.   To adjourn till to-morrow morning from two o'clock to-day means a long adjournment.   I would strongly urge the members to adjourn until eight o'clock, and then re-adjourn at once.

Dr. ARMOUR—As a member of an important committee, the Finance Committee, I would prefer that the Council adjourn until to-morrow morning to allow the committee to spend all the available time between now and then at their work.

Dr. SANGSTER—If you would adjourn until eight o'clock just to re-adjourn, you would not have the effect of bringing the members to the building at all.   I do not see any force in the objection.

The PRESIDENT put the amendment, which, on a vote been taken, was declared lost.

The PRESIDENT put the main motion which, on a vote been taken, was declared carried, and the Council adjourned until Thursday, July 8th, 1897, at ten o'clock a.m.

THIRD DAY.

THURSDAY, July 8th, 1897.

The Council met at ten o'clock a.m., in accordance with motion for adjournment.

President THORBURN in the chair.

The REGISTRAR called the roll, and the following members answered to their names : Drs. Armour, Barrick, Bray, Brock, Campbell, Dickson, Douglas, Emory, Fowler, Geikie, Graham, Griffin, Hanly, Henderson, Logan, Luton, Machell, Moore, Moorhouse, Mc-Laughlin, Reddick, Rogers, Roome, Sangster, Thorburn, Thornton and Williams.

The REGISTRAR read the minutes of the last meeting which were confirmed and signed by the President.

NOTICES OF MOTION.

Dr. WILLIAMS—I give notice that I will move at the next meeting of the Council to have a special committee appointed to prepare a new set of rules of order and have them ready for submission to the Council at its next meeting in 1898.

COMMUNICATIONS, PETITIONS, ETC.   .

Dr. PYNE—These are the diplomas of the gentleman whose application has been already referred to the Education Committee.

Dr. BRITTON—I might say that the case has been dealt with already on its merits, and these diplomas are simply proof of the statements made, therefore I think they do not require to be shewn to the Education Committee ; they will be in custody of the Registrar. I might also say that there were some testimonials forwarded which I have amongst my papers and I will hand these to the Registrar and he will dispose of them in the same way.

MOTIONS OF WHICH NOTICE HAS BEEN GIVEN AT A PREVIOUS MEETING.

Dr. ROGERS—I move, seconded by Dr. LOGAN, that the By-law No. — , to amend By-law No. 39. be now read a first time.

The PRESIDENT put the motion which, on a vote having been taken, was declared carried.

Dr. ROGERS read the by-law as follows :

Whereas power has been given to the College of Physicians and Surgeons of Ontario to make by-laws, be it therefore and it is hereby enacted : By-law No. 39 of the Council of the College of Physicians and Surgeons of Ontario is hereby altered as follows :

First.   Section No. 1, under the heading of "Meetings," is altered by striking out the words in the second line thereof, "first Tuesday in July," and substituting therefor the words, "first Tuesday in November."

Second. Section No. 3, under the heading of "Meetings," is altered by striking out the words "by ballot" in the third line thereof, and substituting therefor the words "by open vote and not by ballot."

Third. That all by-laws inconsistent with this by-law be, and are hereby repealed.

Dr. ROGERS—I now move, seconded by Dr. LOGAN, That By-law No. —, to amend By-law No. 39, be referred to the Committee of the Whole and read a second time. I would prefer, if the Council would allow me, that it carry without debate and go into Committee of the Whole rather than discuss it now ; it would take up less time.

The PRESIDENT put the motion which, on a vote being taken, was declared carried.

Dr. ARMOUR in the chair.

Dr. ROGERS—Mr. Chairman, this by-law which is put before you is one that is necessary to-day in order to overcome difficulties which have arisen during the last two sessions of this Council. In the first place, the first section is one which provides for our holding our annual session of the Council on the first Tuesday in November rather than on the first Tuesday of July. Now, I am prepared te admit that there may be a difference of opinion about that. I understand from my friend, Dr. Britton, and I would not willingly offend Dr. Britton about an important matter like this, that we ought to meet in July in order to hear the appeals of the students who have been rejected, or otherwise, in the late examinations. While that may be so, it seems to me that the dog-days, or July weather, is not a proper time to hold a meeting of men who wish to do a fair amount of work. I think it is unfair to this Council, it is unfair to the profession, and it is unfair to our officers to ask them to come to a meeting in such weather as we have had lately, and, therefore, I think we ought to alter the time. I therefore beg to move that this by-law be taken up clause by clause and that the first clause be carried.

The CHAIRMAN—Is it your wish that this clause carry?

Dr. BRITTON—For my part I do not see any special necessity. I do not not see any necessity for changing it from July to November. I have not heard yet a sufficient reason for it. We have not merely to consider our interests and our comfort and our convenience, but we have also to consider the comfort and convenience of the larger number of students who come before us annually for examination. I think it would be the greatest hardship in the world that students who are placed in the position of making appeals to this Council for the re-reading of papers, should receive no answer to their appeals until after the proposed meeting in November ; that would be from May until November, four or five months ; that I think would be unfair to any student placed in such a position. It may be said that it is a trivial matter, considering the inlerests of the student who asks for the rereading of his papers, but, gentlemen, we are here to do justice, as far as we possibly can, and if there is any provision made in our regulations for the possibility of re-reading of papers, then I say we ought to conrider the interests of those who may be placed in such a position. • This is the strong objection I have to changing it. I do not see any necessity for it ; I think it would be injurious to the students, and I think that students as a whole would take exception to it ; I think that the faculty of every school would take exception to it. There is no demand on the part of the profession at large that we should hold our meetings at so late a period of the year ; I think the profession at large is perfectly satisfied with the time of meeting as set at present. It would be very unwise, I think, to make the change.

Dr. BRAY—The motion Dr. Williams brought in a few minutes ago commands itself to me strongly. I think these matters ought all to be relegated to a special committee. While I have a good deal of sympathy with the mover, the gentleman who introduced this by-law, on account of the hot weather, I think there is a good deal of force in what Dr. Britton has said ; we should not consider our own comfort altogether to the exclusion of that of others. I would like if we could meet in a cooler time, and I think these things require due consideration, but I believe all these matters had better be referred to that special committee who would meet during the interim and bring in a report at the next meeting of the Council. As to revising all these rules—they all want revising. The by-law Dr. Armour brought in yesterday shows the necessity in his opinion that these things should be revised, and I think we all agree that the rules are imperfect. I believe that would be the better way ; that committee could give it due consideration during the months before we meet again and have a well digested report brought in, and I think it would shorten up the discussion very materially and would probably be the means of getting a better set of rules than we have ever had before.

Dr. SANGSTER I sympathize with the object of Dr. Rogers Hot weather is apt to produce hot temper, and hot temper hot words, and I think if we met in November we should be cooler and perhaps more select in our references. I only rise to point out the fact that this Council ceases to exist by lapse of time on the 30th October, and we could hardly hold a meeting in November.

Dr. MOORHOUSE—I quite sympathise with the remarks Dr. Britton made regarding the grievances of the students ; at least, they would have good grounds. It would be five, nearly six months before their cases could be looked into, especially as cases of grievances are cropping up from time to time ; though that might be overcome by referring their grievances to a committee appointed by the Council There are a number of school-men here, myself amongst the rest, and it would be very difficult for us to absent ourselves for a week from lectures. Dr. Fowler would also find it difficult, and probably it would interfere with Dr. Geikie's teaching hours ; it would with mine ; and, therefore, I must object to holding the meeting at any time during the session of the schools. I must emphatically oppose it on that ground.

Dr. McLAUGHLIN—It seems to me of supreme importance when we revise our rules and regulations in regard to the procedure of this chamber, that they should be revised with great maturity of thought and care. I think we ought not, in the hurried manner in which we do things in this Council, and in which we are necessitated to do them because of our brevity of time, to take up a matter of such great importance, and I think that we should adopt the suggestion of Dr. Williams, the referring of all these by-laws to a committee that would con- sider them during the interim between our sessions and then come to us with something we could stand by. I think the work is of such great importance that it would be well for the Council to adopt this course and not waste any further time in discussing the sections or particular amendments that are brought before us now, because it is practically a waste of time, if the Council will take this view. Whatever procedure is necessary to lead to this result, I hope it will be adopted without further discussion.

Dr. ROGERS—I beg to withdraw clause one. I am not prepared to express an opinion as to whether it is really a fact that appeals of students could not be received in November, but if there is a doubt about it we ought not to have the meeting in November. I desire to state also, that with the greatest deference I look upon the expressions Dr. Britton and Dr. Moor- house have made in regard to this matter, and I think in that respect we might better, perhaps, meet next year in July. I would therefore beg to withdraw that section of the by-law, with the consent of my seconder.

Dr. GEIKIE—Would it not be wise for the members of the Council to make it September ? Not only the school-men, but a good many, perhaps, would like in July to take a holiday, whether they live in Toronto or elsewhere. This July meeting just stops them, and it is excessively uncomfortable, and if it was about the 15th September it would answer every purpose with very much more comfort, and would not interfere with any school or anything else.

On consent of the committee Dr. Rogers withdrew clause one of the by-law.

The CHAIRMAN read section 2 of the by-law.

Dr. ROGERS—I would like to explain that section. We have a cause for quarrel, or a cause for disturbance, if you like, in the by-law as it stands now, and although I do not care how the Council shall choose their officers, whether it is by open vote or by ballot, it seems there are certain members here who do not read the by-laws now the same as others of us do and in order to drive away this source of quarrelling at the beginning of every session I would ask the members of this Council to change the mode of electing the President and Vice-President. In the first place, I am strongly opposed to this Council, a Council of Pro- fessional men, a Council of educated men, having an election of their officers by means of a ballot ; I think we ought to be able to get up and say who we vote for, without resort to the ballot. I know in electing the Chairman of the Law Society there is no ballot used and in other bodies I am acquainted with, where the members are all educated and intelligent pro- fessional men, they do not have a ballot ; but if we are going to have a ballot we ought to do away with the word "nomination." I am not prepared to accept Dr. McLaughlin's conten- tion. I am satisfied that my contention is absolutely correct, but in order to wipe away this source of irritation let us have an election every year by a full vote of the whole Council. If I nominate Dr. Fowler or Dr. Logan, I simply do so in the same way as any ordinary motion is made and you will hold your hands up the same as in any other motion before the Council, or the yeas and nays may be called for. I think it is the most open, the most manly and the most straightforward method of electing our officers and therefore, after a great deal of con- sideration, I urge this change. I have considered it for a good many years and I have al- ways thought that open voting was the right way and therefore I beg to move that the clause now before the committee be passed.

Dr. McLAUGHLIN—As I said before, if it is the intention of the Council to appoint a committee to consider all these by-laws and revise our mode of procedure, I think we are wasting time in taking up this by-law clause by clause. My friend, Dr. Rogers, I hope will understand that I am not in any way trying to choke off his by-law, because with some of his motions I agree, but if we are to do that surely it would be better for us to proceed at once and appoint that committee in the proper way. I move that the committee rise and re- port progress.

Dr. Bray—Perhaps Dr. Rogers will withdraw.

Dr. Rogers—No. I think the motion under ordinary circumstances would be quite correct, but next year we will have a repetition of the same row we had last year and this year. Surely there is not a man here but can say, I would rather have the election by open vote or by ballot ; surely this matter is so simple that we ought to be able to decide it now without waiting for a committee to bring in a report next year. If you do not change it to-day then the same trouble will occur next year, under the present arrangement, which we have had for the last two years. I maintain we ought to stop that.

Dr. Britton—I am quite in sympathy with Dr. Bray and Dr. McLaughlin in their expression of the opinion that it would be well for us to refer this to a special committee appointed to consider the rules and regulations during the interim and to report to us thereon at the next session of this Council, next July, but we must bear in mind that the first duty to be performed by this Council when we meet next time will be to elect a President, Vice-President and other officers of the Council ; that must take place before we can receive a report from any committee ; that must occur before there can be any revision of this by-law, or of this clause of the by-law, and therefore the matter seems plain to me, I think it is plain enough to everybody, that it is a fair course to pursue, that is, that everybody should be above board and give his vote for whoever he thinks best. There is no reason why we should not now adopt that clause of the by-law. Next year there will be a different opinion regarding the interpretation of that clause, as this year ; everyone is consistent in holding his own opinion.

Dr. Bray—I did not wish to have it understood that I was opposed to the proposition in Dr. Rogers' by-law, because I think all the members in this Council who were in it at the time those regulations were adopted will remember I firmly opposed the election by ballot; I believe, in a society of gentlemen as we are all presumed to be here, that a manly and proper way is to vote openly ; I am not ashamed at any time to cast my vote openly. I think it is a different thing where there are a large number of laborers under the control of a contractor or a manufacturer, or something of that kind, in a political election where they are not free to express their opinion ; in that case I think the ballot is all right. But I say for a sooiesy of gentlemen, as we are here, intelligent men and men who should have the courage of their convictions, the open vote is the proper thing. But, I did not want to take up the time discussing this by-law ; I think that perhaps it could be obviated that there be no trouble next year at the elections, and then all these matters could be considered.

Dr. McLaughlin—There is going to be a lot of candidates for all the offices next year so that we probably will not have the trouble we have had this year. I am going to run for President. (Laughter.)

Dr. Williams —I fully sympathise with the motives that have induced Dr. Rogers to introduce that part of the by-law, but while I sympathise with that, I think that with just a very little conference with one another all around the members can agree on what they will adopt as to the method next year ; they can do that and then refer this until the rules are gone over next year. If it is determined to go on with this by-law, then I shall move an amendment. Of course, I like to hear men talk with a great deal of bravado as to how intelligent men can get up and give their votes, but, gentlemen, when we come down to solid facts there is not a single man here who does not have qualms of conscience about expressing his reasons why he cannot vote for a certain member as President, or Vice-President, or some other office. If there is such a man here, I would like to see him. My own conviction is, the better way is to withdraw that by-law for the present year, let the rules be gone over and matured and then let us agree upon a system and try and put it so plain that there may be no misunderstanding.

Dr. Moore—I am much in sympathy with the proposition, I believe of Dr. McLaughlin; that these by-laws and rules and regulations be relegated to a committee to report next year, and I would suggest also that we have a copy of their report in the hands of every member a week or ten days before we get here, then we will be ready to discuss them intelligently, but if it will obviate a little difficulty next year by putting this patch on let us not waste time, but let us put it on and then we will be out of the difficulty. I will support this clause and let it drop at that.

Dr. Rogers—I hope it is not in any sense of bravado as my friend Dr. Williams has suggested that I have spoken. I did not mean that in an offensive way, but I simply thought every man should have the courage to record his vote openly and above board. It is not a sense of bravado, it is simply an ordinary sense of manliness which would compel us all to do this. I feel we ought not to have this ballot in this way and in order to get rid of the difficulty let us " put this little patch on " as Dr. Moore suggests.

The Chairman—Dr. Rogers has moved that section two of the by-law be adopted.

Dr. McLaughlin—I move in amendment that the committee rise and report.

The Chairman put the amendment, which, on a vote being taken, was declared lost.

Dr. Rogers—I withdrew section one.

The CHAIRMAN—I have written "withdrawn" and my initials on it.

Dr. WILLIAMS—Then that covers it.

Dr. ROOME—I might say a few words with regard to this. I think as the proposition is to appoint a committee for the purpose of revising or consolidating the by-laws or changing the procedure of this Council, it would be well to leave all these matters to that committee. You, Mr. Chairman, have brought down a series of resolutions which will be placed in our hands shortly, making some changes, which shows clearly that changes should be made, which I agree to. If we are going to make these changes why not let that committee take charge of all these matters? For my own part, I am not afraid to vote openly, still, I extend to others the same privilege I might ask for myself; I might have a warm personal friend whom I might not wish to record my vote against; I may not have the same manliness that others have, but still I think we have all that feeling at times. That clause could be worded "after nomination, where only one candidate is nominated he shall be declared elected by the chair." You can put that in if that is necessary. Still, there seems to be some difference of opinion as to whether that is correct or not. That could be included in it and, as it is becoming optional with all bodies in Canada to vote by ballot, I do not think anybody could find fault with a member if he wished to cast his vote for any particular party by ballot. Therefore if you put those words in, which I have suggested, amending that particular clause, I am willing to support it. As to the other clause, I think we should lay it aside and leave the whole matter in the hands of the committee and, as Dr. Moore has stated, let that committee make their report at least two weeks before the Council meets so that we may come prepared to vote, knowing what we are doing.

Dr. DOUGLAS—Mr. Chairman, I quite sympathize with, and I believe that Dr. Roome has touched the matter in the right spot just now, and I like the sentiments he has uttered on the floor of this chamber. I believe that the ballot is the better way, if a vote must be taken, and I believe if but one candidate is nominated that the rule should be so amended that without any ballot the presiding officer, whether he be the Registrar or the retiring President, shall simply declare that nominee, whether it be by acclamation or any other way, elected. I think there is a pretty general feeling in the Council that the rules, as we have them here before us, are defective, that they are not up to date, and that it is necessary that a thorough revision should take place. And, sir, while that feeling is existing in the Council I sympathize with the motion that has been introduced by Dr. Williams, that a committee should be appointed to revise all these rules, and next year, a week or ten days or two weeks prior to the meeting of this Council, a copy should be transmitted to every member, that he may be in a position to speak and act intelligently in revising the various rules. Apparently for the last two years there has been a source of irritation with regard to the election of officers where only one candidate was nominated. For that reason I sympathize strongly with Dr. Rogers in endeavoring to set aside that source of irritation; and, if that clause can be so amended that, where but one candidate is in nomination, it shall be the duty of the presiding officer then and there to declare that nominee elected President or other officer of this Council, I think it would be well.

Dr. WILLIAMS moved that it be resolved that the section be amended by striking out the words "by open vote" in the fifth line and substituting therefor the words "by ballot without nomination."

Dr. WILLIAMS—I will not devote any time to discussing the question of an open vote and a vote by ballot. Years ago it used to be contended that it was a non-British method to vote by ballot, but that has been set aside entirely. The country and the leading institutions in the country racognize the ballot system, and I will, therefore, not discuss that at all. Then, everybody knowing the difference between ballot and open vote, the only question for discussion is, the "ballot without nomination." I have had some considerable experience in Councils where they vote by that method and my preference is strongly in favor of that method. The only objection I have heard urged against it is, that there is no end to the amount of balloting that may take place. As a matter of experience, I think that is not so; for instance, we will assume that slips are passed around the Council here, each man fixes in his mind who would be a good man for President, and he puts his name down; they are all collected, and when they come up the scrutineer or the clerk, as it is in the county councils, counts over the names and he reads them out, and the next vote is almost sure to bring the man that the Council wants to the front, and rarely do they go over three ballots till they have the whole matter completed. That has been my experience in the past; I believe it has the effect of bringing the best man to the front without any previous canvassing, the man who has impressed himself upon the Council as being a suitable man for that position. Each man, when he writes his ballot, writes the name of the man that he believes the most suitable for the office, and it brings that man to the front. Sometimes they adopt the method of dropping the last man; but sometimes a man who is the lowest at first becomes the top man after a few votes are taken. I do not think it is necessary to drop the last man, for, in two or three votes you have the man that commands the respect of the Council, and I believe that is the best plan, and one that can be followed without hurting anybody's feelings.

Dr. SANGSTER—I strongly approve of Dr. Williams' proposition; I believe it is the only one that will meet the requirements of this Council and stop the perpetual wrangling over the appointment of the officers. I think it is just what we want and I hope it will be adopted.

Dr. BRAY—The objection I take to it is the one Dr. Williams touched upon, the length of time occupied, which he answers by saying, "three ballots decide the question." I, like Dr. Williams, have had some municipal experience; I have been in the county council, and I remember consuming two whole days in electing a warden in that way; there was ballot after ballot. He says "It will decrease the canvassing"; it only increases it, and makes more wire-pulling, a man will go there and promise to vote for so and so, and you are not sure he will do so. Another thing, Dr. Williams spoke with regard to "feeling qualms of conscience." A man may feel regret at having to vote against a friend, but how is a ballot going to remove those "qualms of conscience?" It cannot remove them if he has any conscience at all, because his conscience will surely prick him for doing secretly what he did not want to do openly. If you are going to have a ballot at all, have it so that the last man will drop out. If you are going to have a ballot without any restrictions at all it may take us a week to elect a President.

Dr. ROOME—I move an amendment to the amendment, that all the words after the word "ballot," in the third line of Clause 3 be struck out, and that the following be added after the word "ballot": "that, after nomination, where only one candidate is nominated, it shall be the duty of the President to declare that candidate elected.' I think that will get over all the difficulty, I approve of what Dr. Williams has said, but the danger is, we might be detained here for days; we might ballot here continuously for two or three days before we strike a candidate, but when we have a nomination we know the candidate is before the Council, and by placing the privilege in the hands of the President or Registrar to decide where only one candidate is nominated, I think no one in this room would object to his declaring that candidate elected. I contend that anyone who does not feel in favor of the candidate who is nominated for President should propose some one in opposition to that man, and in that way a vote can be taken. But, where only one man is proposed, as was the case in this session, it seems ridiculous to me that we should cast a ballot around this room to say whether we ought to elect him or not. It is the duty of the President to declare that candidate elected, and, therefore, this amendment to the amendment will cover all that difficulty.

Dr. SANGSTER—I don't think Dr. Roome's amendment will stop one iota of the wrangling over the election of officers, and I am sure the members of the Council who have witnessed the proceedings in the past year will agree that we have done just what he proposes to do, except that there was the formality present of casting a single ballot, which was equivalent to the President determining that that man should be elected. That has been the whole bone of contention during the past year, and I do not conceive that there is much force in the objection raised against Dr. Williams' proposition that it is going to produce an endless series of ballots. I cannot conceive that in the Council, in any one year, there will be more than three or four nominations, and in a small batch of thirty members there cannot be more than three or four names on the first ballot, and it certainly will not require long to throw all those out but one. I am strongly in favor of Dr. William's proposition as the only one that will produce quiet and accord in the Council.

The CHAIRMAN—It has been moved by Dr. Roome, in amendment to the amendment, seconded by Dr. Douglas, that the words "by open vote" be struck out after the word "ballot" in the third line and the following inserted: "where only one candidate is nominated it shall be the duty of the President or Registrar to declare such candidate elected."

Dr. CAMPBELL—If you are going to look upon those two additional propositions that have been made before the Committee of the Whole as an amendment and an amendment to the amendment in the ordinary sense of the word, I shall be placed in rather an embarrassing position. I am in favor of the proposition in the proposed by-law to have the election by open vote, but if we cannot have it by open vote, if it is the desire of the majority of the members of the Council to retain the ballot, then I am unquestionably in favor of Dr. William's proposition, because that is the proposition which I submitted myself last year, which went to the Committee on Rules and Regulations and there received decent sepulchre; I don't know whether it was ever resurrected that session or not. Dr. Roome has kindly tried to remedy it under our present system of voting by ballot, and I am in favor of Dr. Roome's amendment. I would prefer that we strike out the word "ballot" and have an open vote. I have had to vote for people in municipal councils where it was an extreme advantage in having a ballot, but this is a very different matter here with us, and it seems to me, judging from my own experience, that there ought not to be much difficulty in voting for whom I want to. I have had, in this Council, to vote against personal friends for particular reasons and I have had the courage to go to my friend and tell him I had voted against him ; I am sorry to have to do it, but my conscience always approved me. I think we can manage to get along with the open vote for the election of officers without a very great deal of trouble. Occasionally, no doubt, cases will arise when there will be unpleasantness, but in the vast majority of cases it can be managed without any difficulty and the evils that may come from the ballot are greater than the temporary personal inconvenience that may result sometimes from the open ballot, for that reason I am in favor of Dr. Roger's proposition, if I have to vote according to our order of procedure. I think those two propositions ought to be taken as two separate amendments and be taken in the order in which they are submitted. If you rule they are to be taken as an amendment and an amendment to an amendment, and Dr. Roome's proposition comes first, I cannot vote for that because I am voting against the proposition which first came in and which I am in favor of. If we have the vote as to whether we will continue to ballot, or whether we will have an open vote settled first then we can go into details, as if it is decided to continue the ballot, then we have the two propositions to choose between, namely Dr. William's and Dr. Roome's.

Dr. WILLIAMS—I feel myself placed in the same position as Dr. Campbell, the difference is that while he prefers the original proposition I prefer to vote by ballot. When it comes to a question of whether Dr. Roome's proposition shall prevail or Dr. Rogers' I am unquestionably in favor of Dr. Roome's ; I am in favor of having a ballot taken. If we take the vote first on Dr. Roome's proposition as an amendment I am of necessity compelled to vote against him, even though I would prefer that to the other, because I want to have my own amendment carried, and I believe my proposition to be the best method. I think it would be well if Dr. Roome would withdraw his amendment and let us decide the question of the vote by ballot first, as Dr. Campbell has suggested, and then Dr. Roome's motion to amend what is carried can be put. I think that can be done, and that will help us out of what we feel to be a somewhat awkward position.

Dr. BRAY—It is hardly fair to ask Dr. Roome to withdraw his and you not withdraw yours. Why not withdraw them both for the present ?

Dr. WILLIAMS—I will do that. I move that the vote be taken by ballot and not by open vote.

Dr. BARRICK—Without nomination.

Dr. WILLIAMS—No ; I am leaving that. I am moving now the question as to whether it shall be an open vote or by ballot.

Dr. THORBURN—The tendency of the present day is to have elections by ballot ; that is, in a general public way, but our's is not similar to a general public election ; we all appear here together and we have not any client who is looking for our favor or disfavor and therefore the ballot, although very excellent in many cases of election, is not applicable to this. I cannot see any objection in the world to an open vote in a body like this. I have no qualms of conscience about it ; I am not troubled in that way ; I like to strike out from the shoulder every time and then you understand where your man is.

The CHAIRMAN—It has been suggested that Dr. Williams' amendment to the motion, and Dr. Roome's amendment to the amendment be withdrawn, and that we substitute therefor an amendment to the original motion by Dr. Williams, that the sense of the meeting be taken on whether there shall be a ballot or not. Are you agreeable to it being put in that position at the present time ? On a vote being taken Dr. Williams' suggestion was approved of.

The CHAIRMAN—A ballot or no ballot is the question before the members.

Dr. LOGAN—I will not detain you very long. I could not sit quietly here without at least repeating to some degree the expression I made use of on a previous occasion in reference to the taking of the ballot. I have always been opposed in this Council to the ballot, and I have always been in favor of an open vote. I cannot see why the members of this Council, constituted as it is, as my friend Dr. Bray says, supposed to be friends, at least, should make use of the ballot. I have not the slightest doubt that it is absolutely necessary among politicians and some other bodies, because there is a large number of our population dependent upon their employer, and if the manner of their voting should become known it might be the means of their losing their positions. I think in cases of that kind, and under those conditions, the ballot is absolutely necessary. But is that the condition of affairs in this Council ? If it is, I am very sorry to learn it ; and I think if any man's mental equilibrium is so uncertain that he cannot give open expression to his conviction he had better have it improved. It strikes me that the honest way is to state positively what your opinion may be upon any matter of that kind ; and in a case of that kind I think your conscience is not likely to give you any disturbance, and for that reason I am happy to have this opportunity of expressing my views in favor of the open vote.

Dr. SANGSTER—In the dilemma in which I am placed I shall have to vote in favor of an open vote. I would vote for the ballot in the sense Dr. Williams has suggested, but if it involves the danger of practically introducing into this Council at the commencement of each session the wrangling we have had in the past two sessions, as I know it would, I would vote in favor of the open vote.

Dr. HENRY—In the selection of our officers I think the difficulty of the past has been that the ballot is not properly passed, and in that way I strongly approve of Dr. Williams' amendment, taking away the words "after nomination" and having the ballot cast by the whole Council. I think if those words were removed from that section we would have no difficulty. I would strongly support Dr. Williams' amendment to the amendment.

Dr. McLAUGHLIN—I don't think there should be any difficulty as Dr. Sangster expresses it ; the question now is, a ballot or no ballot. If we say it shall be by ballot we can adopt either Dr. Williams' or Dr. Roome's modification.

Dr. REDDICK—We are here contending for a ballot or no ballot. My own conviction is that the best method, and what I would personally like best, is the ballot. We are all elected to this Council by ballot, a ballot which is practically an open vote, and we are now in this Council trying to have a ballot that is a secret ballot. The question is, how will it do for us to have a secret ballot here when we are elected ourselves by an open vote?

Dr. GEIKIE—I am going to support Dr. Williams' motion ; and to amend it by saying that all caucusing hereafter in connection with this Council be and is hereby done away with. (Applause.)

Dr. THORNTON—I think if the outside profession could hear our discussions this morning they would think we were more anxious for official position than the welfare of the profession, and I think for that reason we should have an open vote.

Dr. THORBURN—I know of one very important body in this Province where they commenced to vote that way and the present ruling officer had one vote only cast in his favor at first out of some two hundred, but he worked and worked away and the result was the man with one vote was elected.

Dr. BARRICK—If we can spend one minute now right, we will save in our next meeting. If you could just strike out of that third clause the words "after nomination," it would bring it straight in line with Dr. Williams' resolution, and we would not have a bit of trouble next year. All that has been said with regard to the prolonged time in electing officers is visionary.

Dr. BRAY—Not at all ; I have had experience.

Dr. BARRICK—Take some of the large Councils in this country, with perhaps some three or four hundred members and they do not go beyond three or four ballots. In our own city here they have not gone beyond the second ballot ; usually the result is obtained on the first ballot ; so that so far as that is concerned a vote by ballot without nomination leaves every member of this Council perfectly free, and it completely puts an end in that way to what Dr. Geikie has spoken of, any caucuses, and the profession will crystallize upon some one and he will come to the front. I am strongly in favor of the ballot, and if, as was stated, a person has any qualms of conscience, and if after voting by ballot he feels he must let it be known how he voted, we could give him the privilege.

Dr. BRITTON—Dr. Barrick has referred to the Board of Control, and to the great advantage that would be derived from voting by ballot in electing our officers, that it would prevent caucuses. I don't want to see any caucuses, but I might say it is the impression of the reading public in the city of Toronto, as expressed in the leading papers in the city of Toronto, that there is more caucusing by men who want to occupy positions on that Board of Control than perhaps by any other body of men resident in the city, of the same number.

Dr. LUTON—It is not very often I speak, but now I would like to say a few words. I want to say something as to the practical results that follow an election by ballot. Some ten years ago in the County of Elgin, a body of men, about the same number as ourselves, met at two o'clock in the afternoon for the purpose of electing a warden. How much caucusing took place previous to the hour of two o'clock I do not know. However, the ballot was passed around and around and around until six o'clock in the evening without a warden being elected. They repaired to the various hotels, caucusing was rife all night and on into the small hours of the morning ; the next morning at ten o'clock when the Council resumed business to elect a warden the ballot was passed around and around and around till noon ; they adjourned for dinner, the caucusing went on again, and in the afternoon they went at it again and spent the whole afternoon, and the caucusing was only successful in electing a warden on the morning of the third day. (Laughter.)

Dr. SANGSTER—In the city of London last January the same process began with the open vote, and they met and they met, and they did not elect their chief officer by open vote. There is nothing in the ballot that necessitates that any more than the open vote.

Dr. WILLIAMS—That is purely a matter of party. At Hamilton, where the Council is divided politically between Reformers and Conservatives, they vote and vote and re-vote, each one standing to his own party, but that cannot possibly occur in the Medical Council.

Dr. HENRY—I have had experience in civic affairs, and I have never seen anything of this kind occur ; I don't think we ever spent more than half an hour at it.

6

The CHAIRMAN—The original motion, which was formerly number two of the by-law, which now becomes number one, is that Section No. 3 under the heading "Meetings" is altered by striking out the words "by ballot" in the third line thereof and substituting therefor the words "by open vote and not by ballot;" Dr. Williams' amendment is that the section be amended to read "vote by ballot."

The CHAIRMAN put the amendment, which, on a vote being taken, was declared lost.

Dr. ROOME—I would beg to move in amendment that after the word "nomination" the the following words be added : "Where only one candidate is nominated it shall be the duty of the President or Registrar to declare that candidate elected."

Dr. DOUGLAS—I am in sympathy with the amendment which has been proposed by Dr. Roome just now, and if Dr. Williams will simply leave his amendment out until next year, until the committee that is to be appointed to revise the rules of this Council brings in a report, I then am in sympathy with Dr. Williams' idea of electing our officers without nomination, and will support a by-law to that effect, if it is recommended by the committee to be appointed.

Dr. SANGSTER—I am in sympathy very much with what Dr. Douglas says. If Dr. Roome's amendment is pushed, I wish to point out that it abrogates Section No. 3, because subsequently in Section No. 3 it declares—I presume that proviso was put in for a good cause—"and a majority of the votes of the members present shall be necessary to an election." If that is left there it is absurd to say it shall not be by a vote of the entire Council. If it is understood that Dr. Rogers' motion is only to apply to next session, that the matter will then be submitted to the Committee, and that Dr. Williams will be at liberty to bring up his proposition, I shall be glad to support that.

Dr. ROOME—In reference to that, that is the case where there are two candidates ; it then requires a majority. Where there is only one candidate it is not necessary for a ballot or division at all ; where there are two candidates it requires a vote.

The CHAIRMAN stated Dr. Roome's amendment.

Dr. SANGSTER—I rise to a point of order. It would satisfy a great many of us if you would declare whether what we are doing now is for the next session only.

Dr. DICKSON—I think it would be well to alter the words, "president or registrar" to "presiding officer" in Dr. Roome's amendment, because a chairman might be presiding.

The CHAIRMAN put the amendment, as altered in accordance with Dr. Dickson's suggestion, which, on a vote being taken, was declared carried.

Dr. BRAY moved, seconded by Dr. WILLIAMS, that the Committee of the Whole rise and report progress. which, on a vote having been taken, was declared carried.

The Committee rose.

The PRESIDENT in the chair.

Dr. ARMOUR—I beg leave to report the by-law as amended.

Dr. ROGERS moved, seconded by Dr. LOGAN, that the report of the Committee of the Whole be adopted.

The PRESIDENT put the motion, which, on a vote having been taken, was declared carried.

Dr. ROGERS moved, seconded by Dr. LOGAN, that By-law No. —, to amend By-law No. 39, be now read a third time, passed, numbered, signed by the President, and sealed with the seal of the College of Physicians and Surgeons of Ontario.

The PRESIDENT put the motion, which, on a vote having been taken, was declared carried.

The PRESIDENT—Are there any other motions ?

Dr. ARMOUR—In accordance with a notice of motion, given yesterday, I move, seconded by Dr. McLAUGHLIN, that the advice of Mr. B. B. Osler be had on the following : 1st. Had the Medical Council, at the annual session of 1895, a legal right to assess an annual tax on the medical profession for the years 1893 and 1894, as enacted in Clause 3 of By-law 69 ? 2nd. To what part of the arrearages of the annual tax, which are outstanding at various dates from 1874 to the present time, can Section 41a of the Medical Act, passed in 1891, be legally applied for their collection ; also that the President, Vice-President and the mover be a delegation to wait on Mr. Osler, to secure the above advice.

Dr. BROCK—I think that my motion should come up first ; I gave notice of motion yesterday.

Dr. ARMOUR—Mr. President, I think mine has precedence ; the day before it was in another form, and yesterday you allowed me to put it in as a notice of motion.

Dr. BROCK—I think as Dr. Armour's notice of motion will cause a good deal of discussion that it will be well to take my motion up first.

Dr. ARMOUR—I do not think it will cause any discussion at all. I asked that the opinion be brought down, and the Registrar wasn't able to obtain it.

The PRESIDENT—I think we should have this.

Dr. ROOME—We have collected that fee from a great many of the medical practitioners in Ontario, and if we had no right to do so they can sue us ; therefore I must oppose the motion. We have had trouble enough without it. Let some one else hunt it up.

Dr. WILLIAMS—I am perfectly satisfied that it is not cultivating any lawsuits, and I have no objection to it whatever.

Dr. DICKSON—It is simply to get rid of the difference of opinion that exists in this Council, and to enable us without any indecision to carry out Section 41a.

Dr. BRAY—There is just a question here as to which of these two motions has precedence. Dr. Armour's was an enquiry in the first place, and it was allowed to be changed yesterday to a notice of motion ; if that is the case, I presume it has precedence.

The PRESIDENT stated Dr. Armour's motion.

Dr. MCLAUGHLIN—Will you pardon my saying a word about these verbal opinions that have been given by Mr. Osler. I hold that this Council should have no more of them. A gentleman goes to Mr. Osler, and asks for his opinion, and he comes back and he says his opinion is so and so. I say that sort of thing ought to be at an end, because we do not know how that gentleman has presented the case to Mr. Osler, and therefore we are utterly at sea, and we are called upon to accept opinions in this Council without having them properly before us. I say, if any opinion is expressed by Mr. Osler viva voce in this Council we have a right to have that opinion at Mr. Osler's pen.

Dr. ROOME—I do not wish you to understand that I am opposed to getting opinions, but the time this opinion should have been gotten was before this Council took action upon this particular question ; it is late in the day to take an opinion on an action that has passed by for two years, and it may cultivate a lawsuit to have an opinion on this. If Dr. Armour or Dr. McLaughlin or anybody else had applied for it at that time I would have stood up for it very strongly, but they have taken action, and it has gone on for two years, and now they are asking an opinion as to whether they did right two years ago. I think any question like that should come up at the time, and we would have the opinion. I do not believe myself in a verbal opinion ; we should have a written opinion, and that written opinion should be placed before this Council on all questions where there is any doubt.

Dr. BRAY—I was just going to ask to have that motion read, but if it is asking for an opinion on the statute that governs it, I think there is no lawyer's opinion which will go beyond the statute ; if there is a question about it, it will have to come before a court of law for decision. If it conflicts with the statute, or if it is only confirming something that is already in the statute there is no necessity for it, because we have the opinion of the law advisers of the Crown.

The PRESIDENT, on request, read the motion.

Dr. MOORE—I see you, sir, and the Vice-President and Dr. Armour are the gentlemen who are to go and give Mr. Osler this information. Now, sir, according to Dr. McLaughlin's contention, we cannot meet his views because we do not know, nor have we any right to believe that you and these gentlemen know all about the law, and all about the proper way to present this case ; the only way we can meet Dr. McLaughlin's views is to bring Mr. Osler here, and then state the case to him, and then—

Dr. MCLAUGHLIN—My statement was this, that when Mr. Osler has stated so and so upon a question we should have it in black and white.

Dr. MOORE—You stated you didn't know how the case was put to him.

Dr. SANGSTER—I rise to a point of order ; the gentleman is simply misrepresenting matters.

Dr. MOORE—I am simply stating that, in order to meet the views of Dr. McLaughlin, the only way is to bring Mr. Osler here—

Dr. MCLAUGHLIN—I said, we do not know what may have been said to Mr. Osler when his opinion was asked, and we ought to have it in black and white.

Dr. MOORE—That is just exactly what I am stating, that you didn't know how the questions were put to him. The only way we can have Dr. McLaughlin's views met with is to bring Mr. Osler here and have somebody state the facts and then we will know how it is put and we will get his answer.

The PRESIDENT—I don't think it is necessary for a deputation at all to wait on him ; I will just instruct the Registrar.

The PRESIDENT put the motion, which, on a vote being taken was declared lost.

Dr. DROCK moved, seconded by Dr. CAMPBELL, that it be an instruction to the Examiners to meet after the oral examinations are held, and then and there decide who have received a sufficient number of marks and are entitled to registration ; and that in no case shall the Registrar insert any person's name in the register who is not so qualified by the Board of Examiners That it also be an instruction to the Registrar that in all oral examinations the students undergoing such examination shall be placed in a room or rooms and detained therein, until such time as each one of them shall have been examined, and that a student who passes from said room to be examined, shall not be permitted to return to said room until all the students have been examined.

Dr. Brock—In explanation of this motion I will read the following letter from an Examiner :

A little more than a week ago I had a short conversation with you regarding matters relating to the examinations of the Medical Council. I stated then that in my opinion considerable improvement could easily be made in the method of conducting the oral. As now held students who have had their oral are allowed to see and converse with those who are waiting their turn to enter the examination hall. Owing to this some obtain information which gives them an advantage of an unfair nature. In England, and I believe in all European countries, communication between those examined and those awaiting examination is always rendered impossible. If you bring the matter to the notice of the Council the defect will probably be removed, for, in justice to the students themselves, it requires attention. Besides it would render it less difficult for examiners to ascertain the attainments of each applicant, while at the same time the test would be alike to all. Would it not be well for the examiners to meet after they have finished their duties in order to make a report giving the names of the students who, in their opinion, are qualified? Probably this would prevent a good man's rejection by reason of being a few marks behind in one subject. Yours sincerely,

(Signed)   H. Howitt.

Guelph, July 6th, 1897.

Dr. Sangster—I would move that that be placed in the hands of the Education Committee.

Dr Williams moved, seconded by Dr. Shaw and resolved, that the Printing Committee be instructed to omit from the Annual Announcement the names of all matriculants, of those who have a first or second or third year standing, and also the names of those who have obtained their membership through examination, and to substitute therefor the names of all who have become registered since the last register was published.

Dr. Roome—I was of the opinion, and intended moving that the time had come when it , was necessary to have a new register published. In 1887 the last one was published and many names are there of persons who are dead and gone. Dr. Williams' motion, if adopted, would do away with the necessity for a new register.

Dr. Williams—We had a register published in 1892.

Dr. Roome—I was under the impression it was 1887.

The President put the motion, which, on a vote having been taken, was declared carried.

Dr. Bray presented and read the report of the Committee on Credentials, as follows : Your Committee on Credentials beg leave to report that they find that Dr. Douglas and Dr. Griffin have been regularly appointed to represent Trinity and Victoria Universities in the College of Physicians and Surgeons af Ontario.

All of which is respectfully submitted.

(Signed)   Jno. L. Bray, Chairman.

Dr. Bray moved, seconded by Dr. Rogers, that the report of the Committee on Credentials be received and adopted.

The President put the motion which, on a vote having been taken, was declared carried.

Dr. Bray presented and read Report No. 1 of the Committee on Discipline.

Dr. Campbell—You will have to leave this on the table and follow the usual order, which requires a report to be presented and a subsequent order takes up the report for consideration.

Dr. Moore moved, seconded by Dr. Rogers, that this report No. 1 of the Discipline Committee be taken up as the first order of business on re-assembling after the adjournment, which, on a vote being taken, was declared carried.

Dr. Henderson presented and read the Special Report of the Committee on Finance as follows :

To the President and Members of the Medical Council of the College of Physicians and Surgeons of Ontario :

Gentlemen,—In compliance with a resolution of last meeting of Council regarding retrenchment, the Finance Committee met and have considered the matter and report for your consideration :

There are several sources of expenditure in which a reduction might be made, if, after your deliberation thereon, they would be considered in the interest of the Council.

1st.   One examination each year would save, we are informed by the Registrar, about six hundred dollars.

2nd.   If the examinations were held in one place it would be a further saving of four hundred dollars.

3rd.   If the time of the Oral Examinations were increased from five, to six hours each day—say three hours in the forenoon and three in the afternoon—which could not be considered excessive labor, there would also be a saving of two hundred dollars.

4th.   Regarding the examinations, we are also informed that by the withholding of the retainer of twenty dollars now paid the examiners who conduct no written examinations, a saving of forty dollars would be effected.

5th.   If ten minutes' Oral Examinations were considered sufficient, instead of fifteen as now required, a saving of two hundred dollars would be thereby effected.

6th.   We have also been informed that the Examiner on Anatomy has been using for five years, the same wet specimens continuously, and for which he has been allowed one hundred dollars per year.   Your Committee consider twenty-five dollars to be sufficient when the same specimens are used.

7th.   The reduction of Treasurer's salary, or the amalgamation of the offices of Registrar and Treasurer.

8th.   As regards the maintenance of the building, the expense might possibly be somewhat lessened by making it part of the Registrar's work, to let the apartments and collect the rents without being allowed a commission thereon as has been the custom in the past.   We consider, however, now that it is the most cheaply managed building in the city of Toronto. There has been an annual saving of $983.00 effected on the carrying of the building by the reduction of interest and amount of insurance carried, which will be referred to by the Property Committee in their report, and on temporary loans, interest reduced from seven per cent. to 6½ per cent.   If this clause meets with your approval we recommend that the Council pay the Registrar's stenographer.

9th.   The reduction of interest and amount of insurance carried was largely brought about by the efforts of your Registrar.

10th.   The reduction of expenses connected with the Annual Meeting of the Council. With regard to the indemnity of members, we do not consider it judicious to open up a fresh discussion of this matter again, as the by-law fixing the sessional allowance has been thoroughly considered at previous sessions and no change is recommended.

11th.   Discussions might at times be shortened and expenditure lessened in this way.

All of which is respectfully submitted.

(Signed)   G. HENDERSON, Chairman.

MEDICAL COUNCIL CHAMBER, July 7th, 1897.

On motion of Dr. HENDERSON, the Special Report of the Committee on Finance was received.

On motion of Dr. ARMOUR, seconded by Dr. BRAY, the Council adjourned to meet at two o'clock p.m.

AFTERNOON SESSION.

The Council met at two o'clock p.m., in accordance with the motion for adjournment.

The REGISTRAR called the roll and the following members answered to their names : Drs. Armour, Barrick, Bray, Britton, Brock, Campbell, Dickson, Douglas, Emory, Geikie, Graham, Hanly, Henderson, Logan, Luton, Machell, McLaughlin, Reddick, Rogers, Roome, Sangster, Shaw, Thorburn, Thornton and Williams.

The REGISTRAR read the minutes of the last session, which were confirmed and signed by the President.

NOTICES OF MOTION.

Dr. DICKSON—To re-consider the motion by Dr. Armour relative to the obtaining of Mr. B. B. Osler's opinion.

Dr. ROGERS—In regard to the procuring by the Council of certain appliances for the conducting of examinations in Anatomy.

COMMUNICATIONS, PETITIONS, ETC.

The REGISTRAR read a number of communications which were referred to the respective Committees.

Dr. ARMOUR—The by-law which was spoken of yesterday will now come in order. I move, seconded by Dr. WILLIAMS, that the Council do now go into Committee of the Whole on the by-law entitled, "A by-law to amend by-law No. 39, with regard to the reading of bills and proceedings thereon."

Dr. MOORE—Didn't we agree to consider the report of the Discipline Committee first ?

The PRESIDENT—We did agree to that.

Dr. BRAY—I move, seconded by Dr. MOORE, that the Council go into Committee of the Whole to consider the report of the Discipline Committee.

The PRESIDENT put the motion which, on a vote having been taken, was delared carried.

COUNCIL IN COMMITTEE OF THE WHOLE.

Dr. BROCK in the chair.

Dr. BRAY—I move that this report of the Discipline Committee be read clause by clause. Carried.

Dr. BRAY read Clause No. 1.

Dr. BRAY—I move the adoption of that clause of the report. I may tell you that this is a little quarrel between two doctors ; Dr. Carruthers complains that Dr. MacDonald, while drunk, went in and visited his patient. It is something that should never have come before this Council at all.

On motion, Clause No. 1 of the report was adopted as read.

Dr. BRAY read Clause No. 2.

Dr. BRAY—These people travel in the western portion of the Province with a band, and all that kind of thing, and this Kamama, Jr., dressed up as a Hindoo or something of that kind ; and they have this registered practitioner, Dr. Sovereen, working for them. They were in my own county, and I took it upon myself to personally investigate the matter a little. I brought the detective up there and he interviewed Dr. Sovereen, and Dr. Sovereen acknowledged he was working for these men. They scoop up any quantity of money and just rob the people right and left. We recommend that the Discipline Committee take action on Dr. Sovereen's conduct, and that the Council give us instructions to do so. I move the adoption of Clause 2 of the report.

On motion, Clause 2 of the report was adopted as read.

Dr. BRAY—Read Clause No. 3.

Dr. BRAY—It is not necessary for me to say much about the Munyon Company ; it is all over the country. You see signs in drug stores and all that kind of thing. In order to protect themselves they have to engage a registered practioner. I think any registered practitioner who will allow himself to help people of that kind deserves investigation, to say the least of it. I move the adoption of Clause 3 of the report.

On motion, Clause 3 of the report was adopted as read.

Dr. BRAY—Read Clause No. 4.

Dr. BRAY—It appears that this Dr. Fisher has been working for the Viavi Company and they have had a falling out. We do not recommend that there be any investigation of her conduct, but we want to find out their method of conducting business for the information of the Council, so that in future if anybody else takes the position which she has occupied it may be reported to the Council. The Committee are not acting in this case, but only wish the Council to give instructions to the prosecutor to find out all about it.

Dr. McLAUGHLIN—Is it necessary on the part of the Discipline Committee to ask the Council for permission in order that the detective may go and look up evidence of that kind ? It is an extraordinary think if this committee cannot during the year instruct Detective Wasson to go and look up evidence.

Dr. BRAY—I am not so sure about that. We want to make it certain. I am not sure they have that power ; I do not think they have. We have not had an opportunity to investigate this case because it was only reported to us during this meeting and we thought we would ask for this permission at any rate. I think we should have the power to investigate, if we have not.

Dr. McLAUGHLIN—I think that committee ought to have power to look up evidence on all those cases without asking the Council for permission in each individual case.

Dr. MOORE—You are quite right, Dr. McLaughlin.

On motion, Clause No. 4 of the report was adopted as read.

Dr. BRAY, read case No. 5.

Dr. BRAY—I think most of you know of this man. He styles himself an "orificial surgeon," and in many towns he has obtained money—I hardly like to say by false pretences, but pretty near that—by promising to do what nobody could do. I move the adoption of this clause of the report.

On motion, Clause 5 of the report was adopted as read.

Dr. BRAY, read Clause No. 6.

On motion, Clause 6 of the report was adopted as read.

Dr. BRAY, read Clause No. 7.

Dr. BRAY—You all know these Doctors of Refraction ; they are in every town and village and it is very hard to get at them as illegal practitioners, and we thought we would bring this recommendation before the Council so that if we have to go to the Legislature, the Council might appoint a committee to obtain such legislation as might be necessary.

Dr. DICKSON—What is the difficulty in the way of dealing with them ?

Dr. BRAY—I do not mean to say the difficulty is with the practitioners ; it is not the practitioner, it is those opticians, as they call themselves. This is not a matter for our committee, but it was referred to us and we just make this recommendation to the Council. We have no power to deal with them, but for the information of the Council, we report back, in order that the Council as a whole should deal with the matter by going to the Legislature to get some power to act at some future time

Dr. WILLIAMS—Are they the persons who go to the United States and get degrees as Doctors of Optics, and then come back and travel through the country ?

Dr. BRAY—Yes, some of them.

Dr. WILLIAMS—If that is so, is it wise that we should go to the Legislature ? Will we not be snubbed ?

Dr. McLAUGHLIN—I think the law is that if any man claims to be a medical doctor when he is not, he makes himself liable. If these men go around and examine people's eyes, they certainly come under that heading.

Dr. WILLIAMS—They put up their signs as Doctors of Optics. I have seen one, or two, or three of them, Doctor So and So, on the first line, and " Optician," perhaps, on the second line.

Dr. MACHELL—While it may not be in order to take any action against these so-called Doctors of Refraction, it may be in order to investigate the conduct of a regular practitioner who assists these men to obtain this degree of Doctor of Refraction. It is a well understood thing here, Mr. Chairman, that a legalized practitioner who is acting in the interests of a firm which makes spectacles in Montreal, is given $100 for every class he turns out from the community. He gives them from two to four or six lectures and then he gives them a certificate and they forward that to Montreal and become Doctors of Refraction. I think we are commencing at the wrong end to take any notice of Doctors of Refraction ; we ought to commence to take some notice of our own licentiate who allows himself to be made a tool of for the paltry sum of $100 for every class of graduates.

Dr. BRAY—I quite agree with Dr. Machell. As I have stated here, the Discipline Committee have no power to act in this case, but we ask that the Council consider this report with a view to procuring the necessary legislation to enable them to be dealt with ; or, I could add a clause to that :—" Or in any other way that may be deemed proper by this Council."

Dr. BRITTON —I would move that the Council instruct the prosecutor to secure all the evidence required in the case of the licentiate referred to who professes to teach, or who has classes of men to whom he issues certificates as Doctor of Optics ; and when the evidence has been furnished, that the Discipline Committee proceed to make proper investigation.

Dr. MOORE—There was no charge before us against this doctor. I am well aware of all that Dr. Machell has said, and I smart under it just the same as the rest of the members. In the town where I live the people go down and get their eyes tested free, and every jeweller in the town is a Doctor of Refraction. We brought this recommendation in for the purpose of having a discussion and having this matter brought up. We would not bring in a recommendation against the man when we had no charge laid.

Dr. MACHELL—Since I spoke Dr. McLaughlin has just told me of a case of this very kind which came up for consideration at Kingston, and the Council there had the benefit of the advice of the County Attorney. That particular case cost the present Council some $60.00, and the County Attorney gave it as his opinion that it wasn't worth while dealing with the case, that we would certainly lose.

Dr. BRITTON—My resolution does not apply to those who are graduated, so-called, by this licentiate to whom Dr. Machell has referred, it applies particularly to that individual. I do not know his name, but I have specified who it is sufficiently to enable our prosecutor to investigate the case ; then, after having received information from him, I would like the Discipline Committee to take the matter in hand and use their best judgment as to what course to pursue.

Dr. LUTON—In the vicinity in which I live there is a man that every month or two puts in an appearance as a Doctor of Optics, a graduate of some Philadelphia college and with a strong intimation that he also holds some degree from some institution in Toronto, and I ave known patients to go to him to have their eyes tested, and upon examination he would tell them that they required glasses of a certain kind ; but, in addition to that, he would tell them, "now, glasses is only part of your treatment ; I think it is necessary that you should take some medicine internally," probably containing strychnine, to give tone or something else to some of the muscles connected with the eye ; and he would write out a prescription and they would get it filled at the drug store. He would treat them as a Doctor of Optics and as a medical man at the same time, and sometimes would request the physician of the person asking him for his assistance to suggest to them the propriety of giving this, that, or the other medicine.

Dr. McLAUGHLIN—I think we might pass that clause with the omission of the suggestion that we get legislation. It is a matter for serious consideration whether we can get that legislation in view of the state of public opinion. I think we had better not pass that part of the clause which asks for permission to seek legislation in regard to the matter.

Dr. SANGSTER—I think something ought to be done in the direction which Dr. Machell indicates. I know in my region the public has been fleeced largely by these men. I know one individual that sold two pair of spectacles to a man and his wife at $5.00 a pair; the day after they went back and complained that they didn't suit, and he told them they cost him nearly $5.00, but finally he took $1.50 for the two pairs.

Dr. BROCK—These suggestions of Dr. Britton and Dr. Sangster come under the ordinary prosecutions over which the Discipline Committee of last year had power.

Dr. BRAY—I think it would be well to adopt the suggestion made by Dr. McLaughlin. There is nothing in the clause binding the Council if we strike that out.

Dr. ROGERS—Still, you might put in something.

Dr. BRAY—Dr. Britton has already made a motion.

Dr. BRITTON—Perhaps I am a little out of order in having made a motion ; I presume the proper way would be to wait until we are in Council again, and then move a resolution in order that we might dispose of it in the right way without being forced to give notice of motion.

Dr. ROGERS—Why not add it to that report ?

Dr. McLAUGHLIN—My suggestion does not interfere with that at all ; it is just with reference to that part of the clause asking permission to go to the Legislature.

On motion, Clause 7 of the report as amended was adopted.

Dr. BRITTON—I am sure you will pardon me asking for permission to interrupt the proceedings for a few moments. I have great pleasure in introducing to you Dr. Osler, of Johns Hopkins University, a Canadian boy, who stands at the head of his profession, and is one of the most eminent men in the land.

Dr. OSLER was received with applause, and addressed the Council as follows : Mr. Chairman, I am here accidentally ; I did not know that the meeting was going on ; I simply came up to consult something in the library. But I assure you it gives me very great pleasure indeed to be here and seeing this representative gathering, for I might say that this and the other representative bodies in the Dominion of Canada, represent in reality the only democratic body of men in the profession throughout the world. The Canadian Provinces are the only provinces in which the medical men control their own affairs ; it does not occur in any single one of the States of the Union, and this condition does not prevail in Great Britain, nor, so far as I know, does it prevail in any one of the Australian or New Zealand Provinces. The Canadian system, as it will be ultimately known, will, I think, prevail everywhere in English speaking countries before long, the system under which the medical profession will control their own affairs in a representative parliament such as that which I have the pleasure of looking upon at present.

Dr. BRAY—To this report we append the opinion of Mr. B. B. Osler as follows :

R. A. Pyne, Esq,, M.D., College Physicians and Surgeons of Ontario :

DEAR SIR,—In reply to your request for my opinion as to the application of the disciplinary sections of the Ontario Medical Act to cases in which practitioners allowed their names to be used, or have personally aided in promoting the sale of secret proprietary medicines by companies or individuals, such, for example, as the Munyon and Viavi remedies, I have to advise you as follows :—In my opinion, whether such conduct constitutes infamous or disgraceful conduct in a professional respect so as to render such practitioners liable to have their names erased from the register is entirely a matter of fact and not a question of law. It will be for the prosecutor to establish by the evidence of men of standing in the profession that such conduct is, from a professional point of view, infamous and disgraceful. If the accused can procure the evidence of reputable physicians, justifying such conduct, the matter will then have to be decided by the committee in the same manner as any other disputed question of fact which may come before them for adjudication. If a strong case is made out, and there is no considerable contradiction by reputable members of the profession, I am of opinion that a decision of the committee that the case under discussion constitutes infamous and disgraceful conduct in a professional respect, and directing the erasure of the names of the offending practitioners from the register can be upheld before the Courts. Yours truly,

(Signed.)   B. B. OSLER.

TORONTO, June 28th, 1897.

I read this opinion, which is appended, to this report to show that in regard to two or three of these cases Mr. Osler's opinion is that the committee have full power to investigate the parties who lend themselves to these companies, and, as he says here, "if reputable physicians throughout the Province say, 'such conduct is disgraceful and infamous,' the Court will uphold the action of the Discipline Committee."

DR. BRAY read case No. 8.

The Stenographer was instructed not to report the discussion on this clause of the report.

Dr. MCLAUGHLIN moved, that the Registrar be instructed to erase the name of Dr. Samuel Arthur Carter from the register as soon as he shall obtain a certificate from the Court having jurisdiction in the case of his conviction. Carried.

Dr. BRITTON moved, seconded by Dr. WILLIAMS, that Clause 7 of the report of the Discipline Committee be amended by the addition of the following words : "We recommend that the Discipline Committee be instructed to investigate the case, or cases, of any members of the College who may have issued certificates of 'Doctor of Optics,' or "Doctor of Refraction.' and that it be understood that the committee have power to order Mr. Wasson, or others, to secure all the necessary information." Carried.

Dr. BRAY—I move the adoption of this report of the Discipline Committee as a whole, as amended. Carried.

Dr. BRAY—I move the Committee rise and report. Carried.

The Committee rose. The President in the chair.

Dr. ROGERS—I beg to move, seconded by Dr. ARMOUR, that the report of the Committee on Discipline, as amended, be adopted, and that the said committee be, and is, hereby instructed to proceed in the investigation of the cases referred to in the said report.

Dr. MCLAUGHLIN—I think it would be better to strike out that last clause. I think all that is necessary is to move that the report be adopted. That is practically amending the report, and I submit in this way it cannot be done ; if you want to amend that report by adding those instructions, you must refer it back to Committee of the Whole. The only thing you can do now is to move the adoption of the report.

The PRESIDENT—It has been adopted.

Dr. MOORE—The report has been adopted. This was simply to give instructions.

Dr. ROGERS—The adoption of the report does not give instructions.

Dr. BRITTON—I think if you reproduce the wording of my resolution it will appear that, technically speaking, the instructions have not been given. The clause reads somewhat in this way : "it is advised, or we advise, that the Council give instructions to the Discipline Committee to do so and so." That is the report, and we have adopted the report. We believe it is correct ; we believe it is right to act upon it, but we have not yet given those instructions that that report advises us to give, so that I think it must be in order that those instructions should be given to the Discipline Committee before they can act.

Dr. BRAY—I think, perhaps, all has been done that is really necessary, but, in every case Mr. Osler has advised the Council to give the instructions to the Discipline Committee to carry on these investigations.

Dr. WILLIAMS—I believe that in all the cases where names have been stricken from the register in the past, it has been the custom to act, and, I think, under the advice of the solicitor, that it should be done in that way, when we are in Council in a formal way. We have carried the resolution to that effect in Committee of the Whole, will that answer the same purpose ? The solicitor was very particular, if I remember correctly, in the past, to have it done in the Council ; and the yeas and nays were invariably taken and reported upon the question considered. If that is the better way, we should carry that resolution in the Council, and take the yeas and nays, and make it beyond any question.

Dr. MCLAUGHLIN—What I understand is this, that as to any motion adopted in Committee of the Whole in a report, when that report is adopted by the Council, the Council formally adopts it.

The PRESIDENT—That is my reading of it.

Dr. BRITTON—I remember, in connection with the erasure of certain names, that Mr. Osler was here and he gave instructions as to the method of procedure, and there was a great deal of red tape about it. I suppose it was all necessary. I remember, very distinctly, the resolution was moved in the Council, after discussion in Committee of the Whole, and the yeas and nays were taken and recorded; I suppose that was done in case of any appeal being taken.

The PRESIDENT read Dr. Rogers' motion which, on a vote having been taken, was declared carried, and the report was adopted as amended, as follows:

To the President and members of the Council of the College of Physicians and Surgeons of Ontario:

Your Committee on Discipline, composed of Drs. Bray, Logan and Moore, beg to report as follows:

Your Committee met on Tuesday, the 6th July, 1897, at two o'clock p.m.

There were laid before your Committee letters (Nos. 1, 2 and 3) from one Dr. J. Carruthers of Little Current, Manitoulin Island, which contained charges against Dr. Y. J. McDonald. After fully considering these letters your Committee find that neither the Council nor the Committee have any jurisdiction, as it is clearly a case for civil action.

CASE NO. 2.—*Re* Dr. Albert Sovereen, in connection with the "Kamama" Hindoo Remedy Company of Windsor, Bombay and London. Kamama Junior, the Indian Scientist and Lecturer, etc." After considering Detective Wasson's report, also the letter of Dr. Sovereen of date the 23rd November, 1896, your Committee consider this a case for investigation and we recommend that the Council do so direct the Committee.

CASE NO. 3.—In the case of Dr. Robert Allen Clark of Ridgetown, Ontario and Dr. John Kirkpatrick, formerly of Chippawa, now of Montreal, who were employed by the Munyon's Homœopathic Remedy Company, after reading Detective Wasson's report your Committee consider that they are fit and proper cases for investigation, and they would recommend the Council to direct the Committee to take whatever action is necessary.

CASE NO. 4.—*Re* Dr. Eva Ryan Fisher, of Toronto Junction, who was employed by the Viavi Remedy Company, your Committee recommend that the Prosecutor be directed to investigate the methods of the Viavi Company and also Dr. Eva Ryan Fisher's connection with the said company.

CASE NO. 5.—*Re* Dr. William E. Bessey, your Committee recommend that the Committee be instructed to investigate the charges reported upon by Detective Wasson:

CASE NO. 6.—*Re* Dr. Walter Hamilton, your Committee recommend that no action be taken in this case until the matter is finally disposed of by the courts.

CASE NO. 7.—The report of Detective Wasson *re* Doctors of Refraction has been before your Committee and we would recommend that, while the Discipline Committee have no power to act in this case, the Council as a Council consider this report.

CASE NO. 8.—*Re* Dr. Samuel Arthur Carter of the County of Halton, your Committee report that they had before them a certificate of T. G. Matheson, Clerk of the Peace of the said County showing that the said Samuel Arthur Carter was convicted of a felony on the 15th day of December, 1896, and is now serving a year in the Central Prison. Your Committee consider that this is a matter to be dealt with by the Council as a whole.

To this report we append the opinion from Mr. B. B. Osler, Q.C., in regard to practitioners who allow their names to be used, or have personally aided in promoting the sale of secret proprietary medicines by companies, etc.

All of which is respectfully submitted.

Signed on behalf of the Discipline Committee.

JOHN L. BRAY, Chairman.

MOTIONS OF WHICH NOTICE HAS BEEN GIVEN AT PREVIOUS MEETINGS.

Dr. ARMOUR moved, seconded by Dr. WILLIAMS, that the Council do now go into Committee of the Whole on a by-law entitled a by-law to amend by-law No. 39 with regard to the reading of bills and proceedings thereon.

Dr. WILLIAMS—I think, Mr. President, that Dr. Armour has got under the wrong order. We are now on motions of which notice has been given. Dr. Armour's motion is some unfinished business; we commenced with it and went a certain distance and it remained there and that does not come up until a couple of orders lower down. I think Dr. Armour is just ahead of the order.

The PRESIDENT—I think you are right.

Dr. WILLIAMS—It would come up under No. 9; we are now at No. 5.

Dr. ARMOUR—That is the regular procedure but I thought there would be no objection to going on at the present time.

Dr. WILLIAMS moved, seconded by Dr. BRITTON and resolved, that Drs. Campbell, Bray, Armour, Moore, McLaughlin, Roome and the mover be and are hereby elected a special committee to take into consideration and to prepare a set of rules of order for the guidance of the Council in its proceedings and to have the same in readiness for submission to that body at its meeting in 1898.

The PRESIDENT—This is hardly comprehensive enough ; it was stated that this was to be ready and sent to the different members of the Council a fortnight before the meeting of the Council.

Dr. WILLIAMS—I wish to make a few remarks on it. On looking over the list I have tried to get at the names of persons who were somewhat familiar with the rules in municipal matters, parliamentary matters or Council matters and in looking over that list I find that the difficulty is that there are too many of that class of men and I found when I come to mark off a list of those who were familiar with that class of matter that we would have too many. Now, I have proposed seven names and I think if it were only three it would perhaps be a more successful committee. My supposition or my intention was that when the committee was appointed a chairman should be elected and that the proposition should then be made that each one of the committee should draft a set of rules and they could transfer these by mail from one to the other, review them, and out of the lot get in form what they thought would be a satisfactory set, and then have those that they finally agreed upon typewritten and send a copy to each member of the Council sometime before its meeting; it could be proceeded with that far probably without incurring any expense ; then, when the Council would meet the rules would be in proper form and they would be ready to deal with them.

The only objection I have to the Committee is that there are too many on it and there are so many more members present who are equally familiar with the same class of procedure that it is difficult to tell who to leave off and who to put on. I have made a selection which is subject to amendment.

Dr. BARRICK—I think that could be got over very easily ; if this committee would meet and appoint a sub-committte of three it would answer every purpose.

. Dr. SANGSTER—I do not think in the way Dr. Williams suggests that seven will be found an unwieldy number ; it does not involve a meeting and discussion but merely communication with one another. I think no one present would like to see any one of the names Dr. Williams has given omitted from that committee.

The PRESIDENT—I think there is force in what Dr. Sangster says ; it is a very important affair, and especially as they are not to meet but merely to correspond, they ought to be able to formulate a good set of by-laws and have it ready for consideration for the whole Council so that we may have an intelligent knowledge of it when it is brought before us. It is not a final thing at all, it is merely a preliminary investigation and I think seven is better than three.

The PRESIDENT read the motion, which on a vote having been taken, was declared carried.

It was moved by Dr. McLAUGHLIN, seconded by Dr. DOUGLAS, that whereas the following certificate has been received by the Council of the College of Physicians and Surgeons of Ontario, viz.: " These are to certify that at the County Court Judges Criminal Court for the County of Halton, held at the town of Milton in the County of Halton, on the fifteenth day of December, in the year of our Lord one thousand eight hundred and ninety-six, Samuel Arthur Carter (in the indictment and proceedings named Arthur Carter) then lately of the Township of Nassagaweya in said county, Doctor of Medicine, was in due form of law indicted, tried and convicted for that he, the said Samuel Arthur Carter, on the fifteenth day of September, in the year of our Lord one thousand eight hundred and ninety-six, at the town of Milton in the County of Halton, did unlawfully use a certain instrument called a catheter upon the person of one Hattie Wilkie, with the intent then and thereby to cause the miscarriage of the said Hattie Wilkie ; and the said Samuel Arthur Carter was thereupon ordered and adjudged by the said Court to be imprisoned in the Central Prison for the Province of Ontario for the term of one year. Given under my hand and the seal of the said Court at the town of Milton aforesaid this seventh day of January, A.D. 1897.

"(Signed)   T. G. MATHESON,

[Seal.]   " Clerk of the Peace, Co. Halton."

And whereas by Section 34 of the Ontario Medical Act power is given to the Council to erase from the register the names of medical practitioners found guilty of the crime of which Samuel Arthur Carter was convicted, therefore be it resolved that the Registrar be instructed to erase the name of the said Samuel Arthur Carter from the Register of the College of Physicians and Surgeons of Ontario.

Dr. ROOME—I understand it was the opinion of all the members that the yeas and nays should be taken. That is the decision of the Solicitor and I think it is necessary that that should be done.

Dr. BRITTON—That has always been done.

Dr. ROGERS—Will there be any objection to putting in the word "forthwith."

Dr. McLAUGHLIN—By all means put it in.

The REGISTRAR took the yeas and nays on Dr. McLaughlin's motion as follows :

Yeas—Drs. Armour, Barrick, Bray, Britton, Brock, Campbell, Dickson, Douglas, Emory, Fowler, Geikie, Graham, Hanly, Henderson, Henry, Logan, Luton, Machell, Moore, Moorhouse, McLaughlin, Reddick, Rogers, Roome, Sangster, Shaw, Thorburn, Thornton and Williams—29.

Nays—None

The PRESIDENT declared the motion as amended by Dr. Rogers' suggestion carried.

Dr. SANGSTER moved, seconded by Dr. THORNTON, that a return be granted showing by what authority and in what year the fourth particular in the declaration appended to the candidates' printed form of application for admission to the Council examinations was first inserted therein.

Dr. SANGSTER—As some one may not have been in the room when I gave notice of that motion it might, perhaps, be proper that I should state it refers to the declaration made before admission to examination of candidates. Particular four of this declaration is of the nature of an oath. That appears to me to be a peculiarly strong declaration to require students to make and I ask for information as to when it obtained insertion in that application and by what authority it was there inserted.

Dr. PYNE—It came about owing to the investigations before the Discipline Committee. Any of the old members of the Discipline Committee will bear me out in this. The question would be asked, when a man was before the Discipline Committee, is there no code of ethics he has to sign when he receives his license? Is there anything that is binding upon him? That is how that matter came about; and it was, I think, by the direction of the Discipline Committee it was first exacted, but it was not in the declaration until the year 1893 and then it was prepared by the Solicitor. But for some years before that I had the candidates, when they were leaving, sign a book that I have used in the examination hall. I have the book here going back as far as 1890 and I have always written at the top of the page, "We, the undersigned candidates for the license of the College of Physicians and Surgeons of Ontario, hereby agree, in the event of becoming members of the College, to comply with the Ontario Medical Act and amendments thereto and all by-laws, rules and regulations of the Medical Council of Ontario." That is how it came about; it was a direction from the Discipline Committee because there was nothing at all binding on the members until that was done and that application was revised and prepared by the Solicitor.

Dr. SANGSTER—I can understand readily now the insertion of an agreement of that kind, but this is of the nature of a solemn oath. I do not think it would be so objectionable if this Council were an homogeneous body, but I claim that to swear every man who enters this profession, that no matter how or by whom or when amendments are procured to the Medical Act, he is bound to abide thereby, that he is sworn to abide thereby, would be a very dangerous contention to make on his appearance before the Registrar and I think it would break up our own Medical Act.

Dr. BRITTON—Don't you think the interpretation of that is evidently until such amendmends are nullified by legislation?

The PRESIDENT—A declaration or a promise of that kind is exacted, so far as I know, by every teaching body in our land and outside of it. I know when I got my degree in Edinburgh, I swore to shed blood, if necessary, to defend the university in every respect. We take the oath of allegiance and we make the same declaration. It does not interfere with our opinion at all, and if we think the law is unjust, it does not prevent our agitating against it.

Dr. CAMPBELL—It simply means a man swears he will obey the law.

Dr. McLAUGHLIN—I quite agree that there should be some bond, some statement of that kind to leave medical students, graduating, upon their honor to be faithful and loyal to their profession, but I do not think we should have gone to the extent of a solemn oath. I am not prepared to take that oath to-day, and I doubt if there is a man in this Council to-day who is prepared to take that oath, that he will stand loyally by the law as it stands.

The PRESIDENT—That is not the meaning of it a whit more than it is the meaning of an oath of allegiance or anything else.

Dr. McLAUGHLIN—It says :—"And I make this solemn declaration, conscientiously believing the same to be true, and knowing that it is of the same force and effect as if made under oath and by virtue of the Canada Evidence Act, 1893." I could not swear to that; I would not take that oath. Now, sir, it is not correct that students in other institutions take such a declaration. I will give you the declaration made in the Law Society :—"Your petitioner, therefore, most respectfully prays that his qualifications being first examined and found sufficient, according to the Rules of the Society and Standing Orders of Convocation in that behalf, he may be admitted and entered accordingly; and he doth hereby undertake and promise that he will well and truly pay, or cause to be paid, to the Law Society of Upper Canada aforesaid, all such fees and dues of what nature or kind soever as now are due and payable by or from him to the said Society by or under any Rule, Resolution, Order, By-law or Regulation of the said Society, passed by the said Society or by the Benchers thereof, with the approbation of the Judges of the Province, as Visitors of the said Society, or which shall or may hereafter become due or payable by or from him to the said Society under the same, or under any other Rule, Resolution, Order, By-law or Regulation, to be passed by the Benchers of the said Society in Convocation, with such approbation as aforesaid ; and also, that he will moreover well, faithfully and truly submit and conform himself to obey, observe, perform, fulfil and keep all the Rules, Resolutions, Orders, By-laws and Regulations of the said Society, passed as aforesaid and now in force, or hereafter to be passed as aforesaid during such time as he shall continue on the books of the said Society as a member thereof." Now a declaration, a simple signing of a statement of that kind, is as far as we ought to go I think, and I do not think we ought to go so far as to make a man swear he will obey that law.

Dr. DOUGLAS—It is a declaration, but it is as binding as an oath.

Dr. McLAUGHLIN—It is as binding as an oath, and if he makes a false oath he is liable for perjury.

The PRESIDENT—That declaration of the Law Society is as binding as the other.

Dr. GEIKIE—This committee that has been appointed can go into that, and if that were modified it would be a splendid thing for our members ; if it had been in existence years ago there would have been no difficulty about the collection of dues.

Dr. ARMOUR—That is just exactly the difficulty which Dr. Geikie has referred to. He says, if it had been in existence years ago these things might have been different. I presume he means that those who have taken an active part in the past in amending the Medical Act would have been in such a position that they could not have done what they have done. I did not fully understand the question asked. What was the authority for the establishing of this requirement ?

The PRESIDENT—The Discipline Committee.

Dr. PYNE—What I read was their direction too, and they went further and added the other. The Discipline Committee was the authority for it.

Dr. MOORHOUSE—I think the oath, or declaration which is equivalent to an oath, that Dr. McLaughlin has just read, is quite as binding on the members of the Law Society as this. It is regarded by the law just as binding, according to the interpretation of the Act.

Dr. McLAUGHLIN—You have got to say it is a declaration under the statute so and so ; if you do not say that, it is not.

Dr. MOORHOUSE—Is not this College of Physicians and Surgeons the highest legal authority on medical matters in the land ? and surely we would not expect men to join us unless they expected to follow our rules and regulations. The Law Society, as is always characteristic of the law, is after the dollars and cents, and they have dived into that matter more stringently than we have done, and as Dr. Geikie has wisely said, perhaps if we had taken pattern after their declaration we might have been spared a great deal of trouble in the collection of fees, and I would suggest that that be referred to the committee.

Dr. MOORE—Has a large number of young men signed that declaration ?

Dr. GEIKIE—All have signed it.

Dr. MOORE—Has any harm been done ?

The PRESIDENT—No.

Dr. MOORE—Then, it must have had a good effect.

Dr. SANGSTER moved, seconded by Dr. THORNTON, that the return be granted, showing every case in which arrearage of assessment dues on the part of the members of the College has been commuted by the acceptance of a part thereof as payment in full, the amount in each case thus accepted and the authority on which the officers of the Council accepted such commutation.

Dr. SANGSTER—I would like to have that return placed in the hands of the Council as soon as possible,

The PRESIDENT read the motion which, on a vote being taken, was declared carried.

Dr. GEIKIE read the report of the Committee on Complaints.

Dr. GEIKIE moved that the Council go into Committee of the Whole to consider the report of the Committee on Complaints. Carried,

COUNCIL IN COMMITTEE OF THE WHOLE.

Dr. CAMPBELL in the chair.

It was moved by Dr. SHAW that the stenographer is hereby instructed to omit the discussion on the report of the Committee on Complaints while in Committee of the Whole from the Annual Announcement.

The CHAIRMAN put the motion which, on a vote being taken, was declared carried.

Dr. GEIKIE moved that the Committee rise and report.

The Committee rose. The President in the chair.

Dr. GEIKIE moved the adoption of the report as amended.

Dr. SANGSTER—I am in favor of its adoption. I wish to express my feeling that there ought to be some change in the mode of conducting the final decisions as to the passing of these gentlemen. It is a most painful thing to think that when matters are brought up individually before us here we may be doing an injustice to some ; and we are doing it, I think, illegally, in the face of the solicitor's opinion to the contrary. Now, it appears to me that there shuold be some means by which it could be remedied ; perhaps the Chairman of the Board of Examiners could acquaint himself with the feeling of the examiners as to shaky students ; and by having a meeting and having the President and Registrar present, when these papers are gone over, so as to represent the Board of Examiners, we should feel we were not flying in the face of our own examiners in changing any of their decisions and I think there would be a guarantee to the Council and students and the public that things were being more regularly done than they are at present. I would like to see the adoption of some such system as that, some system that will insure our carrying our Board of Examiners with us.

The PRESIDENT—I think that is a fit subject for the committee appointed to review our rules and regulations to consider.

Dr. SANGSTER—The Board of Examiners could hold one meeting and appoint a chairman and give the committee a synopsis of the result.

The PRESIDENT—I think that had better be left.

The PRESIDENT put the motion which, on a vote having been taken was declared carried, and the report adopted as amended, as follows :

REPORT OF COMMITTEE ON COMPLAINTS.

The Committee on Complaints met as soon as the Council adjourned yesterday (Wednesday) afternoon. All the business handed in for consideration was gone very carefully over, and the following report on the different items is respectfully submitted.

1. A letter from Dr. D. A. Coon of Elgin, Ont., dated June 21st, 1897, notifying the Council that he would hold it responsible for allowing G. S. McGhie, said to be an unlicensed practitioner, to continue to practice there.

The committee recommended that Dr. Coon be informed by the Registrar that the Council has taken every legal means in its power to in all such cases, and continues to do so, with the view of suppressing such illegal practice as is complained of.

2. A letter from Miss Jean M. Wilson stating that she had gone up for her examination as a final student and had been obliged to leave town at once before the oral part of the examination was held. And asking the Council's permission to be allowed to take the orals at a subsequent examination without extra expense. Her request is recommended to be granted on condition of her going up at the next examination which is held.

3. A. W. Bell requests his papers to be re-read and that he be allowed to practice till the results of the examinations of 1898 are published. It is recommended that this request shall not be granted.

4. W. S. Burd, applied for a pass on his examination in Materia Medica in which he recently failed. It is recommended that his request be not granted.

5. S. R. Clemes applied that his paper on Medicine, in which subject he failed at the last examination, be re-read. It is recommended that the request be not granted.

6. J. A. M. Clarke asks that a higher standing be allowed him than he obtained at the late Primary Examination, on account of ill-health and for other reasons. It is recommended that his request be not granted.

7. Chas. B. Cowan requests that a standing be allowed him in his primary examination. Recommended that the request be not granted.

8. J. A. Ferguson applies for a reconsideration of his paper at the late primary examination. Recommended that the request be not granted.

9. G. A. Hassard asked that he be allowed his intermediate examination. After very full examination of his record, which is very good, the committee recommended that his request be granted.

10. R. E. Hawken asks to be allowed his primary examination. It is recommended that the request be not granted.

11. J. W. Lennox asks a reconsideration of his marks on the primary examination. It is recommended that the request be not granted.

12. A. G. Ludwig asks to be allowed his final examination as he failed only in Sanitary Science. On careful examination of his record, he was one-half per cent. below passing on

that subject and had a good standing on all the others. It is recommended that his request be granted.

13. J. TenEyck asks to be allowed his Materia Medica in which he failed. It is recommended that his request be not granted.

14. J. C. McGuire asks to be allowed his examination on Operative Surgery. It is recommended that his request be not granted.

15. John H. Peters asks that his standing in Chemistry be reconsidered. Recommended that his request be not granted.

16. John P. Morton asks to be allowed his Operative Midwifery. As he was within a fraction of the required standing and had passed in every other subject, it is recommended that the request be granted.

17. S. Moore requests registration to be allowed him without taking the final examination, on presenting to the Registrar·evidence of his having taken a registerable qualification in Great Britain. He has passed the Council's intermediate. The recommendation is that the request be not granted.

18. H. Maw requests to be allowed his Chemistry, and that he be allowed his intermediate examination. It is recommended that the request as to Chemistry be not granted. But that as his average standing on the subjects of the intermediate examination was high, being short three marks only on Operative Surgery, and also on the ground that the answers to some of the questions in Surgery were not to be found in most of the text-books laid down by the Council, it is recommended that he be allowed his intermediate examination.

All of which is respectfully submitted.

W. B. GEIKIE, Chairman.

The PRESIDENT here left the Council Chamber, and Vice-President Henry took the Chair.

Dr. MACHELL—I have the report of the Special Committee on Prosecutions to present, if this is the proper time.

The VICE-PRESIDENT—The reception of reports is in order.

Dr. MACHELL moved, seconded by Dr. ROGERS, that the report of the Committee on Prosecutions be received, which on a vote being taken, was declared carried.

Dr. MACHELL read the report of the Committee on Prosecutions, together with letter from Mr. B. B. Osler, Q.C., and report of Detective Wasson respectively as follows :

To the President and Members of the Medical Council of the College of Physicians and Surgeons of Ontario.

GENTLEMEN,—Your Special Committee appointed to deal with infringements of the Medical Act and to instruct the Prosecutor, beg leave to report as follows :

Some five meetings were held and sixty-nine cases brought before the Committee, which were duly considered, and the Prosecutor directed in each case by the Committee, one being referred to the Committee on Discipline. The Prosecutor's report regarding the work done is appended hereto.

The Viavi Company, the Munyon's and Medical Companies generally were thoroughly considered. Last year almost immediately after the meeting of the Council the Munyon Company began operating here. Mr. Osler was consulted and advised against any action being taken without the direction of the Council.

It was ascertained that registered physicians, members of the College of Physicians and Surgeons of Ontario, were employed by such companies to shield them with their licenses and thus evade the Act. Your Committee directed the Prosecutor to procure all the evidence possible upon these matters, which he has done, as you will see by his appended report.

Your Committee beg leave to suggest that all members of the College of Physicians and Surgeons of Ontario who hire themselves to these companies, thus enabling them to impose upon the public, should have their conduct investigated by the Discipline Committee of the Council, with a view to bringing such physicians under the section of the Medal Act dealing with those who are guilty of infamous or disgraceful conduct in a professional respect.

Your Committee requested the President to place this matter before Mr. Osler, the Council's Solicitor, for his opinion under the Act. Said opinion has been obtained, and is appended hereto.

Your Committee believe that immediate action should be taken in regard to these cases with a view to protecting the public.

Your Committee received anonymous letters concerning infringement in certain localities. Such letters, of course, could not be considered. Your Committee now would urgently call the attention of the Council, and those of the profession generally, to the fact that all communications from medical men throughout the Province regarding the infringement of the Medical Act received by the Registrar or any by members of the Committee, have been and always will be, treated perfectly confidentially.

Inasmuch as your Committee believes that its functions are of a very important character, the discharging of which will prove beneficial to the profession, as well as the public, it is advised that a Special Committee of the same nature be appointed for the ensuing year.

All of which is respectfully submitted.

(Signed)   HENRY T. MACHELL, Chairman.

JULY 8th, 1897.

R. A. Pyne, Esq., M.D., College Physicians and Surgeons of Ontario, Toronto.

DEAR SIR,—In reply to your request for my opinion as to the application of the disciplinary sections of the Ontario Act to cases in which practitioners allowed their names to be used or have personally aided in promoting the sale of secret proprietary medicines by companies or individuals, such for example as the Munyon and Viavi remedies, I have to advise you as follows : In my opinion whether such conduct constitutes infamous or disgraceful conduct in a professional respect so as to render such practitioners liable to have their names erased from the register, is entirely a matter of fact and not a question of law.   It will be for the posecutor to establish by the evidence of men of standing in the profession that such conduct is, from a professional point of view, infamous and disgraceful.   If the accused can procure the evidence of reputable physicians justifying such conduct, the matter will then have to be decided by the Committee in the same manner as any other disputed question of fact which may come before them for adjudication.   If a strong case is made out and there is no considerable contradiction by reputable members of the profession, I am of opinion that a decision of the Committee that the case under discussion constitutes infamous and disgraceful conduct in a professional respect and directing the erasure of the name of the offending practitioners from the register, can be upheld before the Courts.

Yours truly,

(Signed)   B. B. OSLER.

TORONTO, June 28th, 1897.

Dr. H. T. Machell, Chairman of Infraction Committee.

DEAR SIR,—I beg leave to submit to you the list of prosecutions and investigations of unlicensed practitioners for violations of the Ontario Medical Act, in which all cases were considered by your committee with instructions to me as to their disposal.   I remain yours,

THOMAS WASSON, Detective C. P. and S. O.

PROSECUTIONS.

Prof. Prevost	Ottawa	Not disposed of.
Midwives	South Casselman	No case.
E. P. Zehr	Wellesley	Prosecuted, fined $50.00, paid.
Lavoie	Fort Francis	No action.
Druggist	Hillsburg	Referred to Crown Attorney.
Lloyd	Mount Albert	No case.
Prof. Bennett	Trenton	Prosc'ted, fined $25.00, went to jail.
Dr. Jebb	Kingston	Prosecuted, case dismissed.
Dr. Pratt	Lombardy	No case.
Mrs. Currie	Lion's Head	No case.
Dr. J. A. Pattie	Powassan	No case.
McKay	Napanee	No case.
Dr. High	Prescott	Prosecuted, skipped.
Mr. Wright	Victoria Harbor	No case.
Prof. Wesley	Sarnia	Prosecuted, fined $40.00, appealed and dismissed.
Kikapoos	Port Perry	Prosecuted, fined $25.00, paid.
Viavi	Toronto	No case.
Cancer Doctor	Windsor	No case.
Dr. McLeod	Penetang	Skipped.
Midwives		Got them to stop practising.
T. Pine	Flinton	Prosecuted, fined $25.00, paid.
Dr. Syleston	Galt	No action taken.
J. Y. Egan	Sarnia	No case.
E. A. Ball	Hamilton	Prosecuted and skipped.
Dr. Jebb	Kingston	Prosecuted and appeal dismissed.

M. D. Irvington	Ottawa	No case.
Viavi	Orangeville	Information laid. Party gone.
Dr. McLeod	Orillia	Left the place.
D. L. Thompson	Toronto	To prosecute.
Kikapoos	Westwood	Left the place.
Dr. Krausman	Clinton	Not disposed of yet.
Mathieson	Wiarton	Prosecuted, fined $25.00, paid.
Scotch Herbalist	Penetang	Left the place.
Prof. Chamberlain	Guelph	No case.
Dr. Shaw	Queensboro'	Stopped practising.
Dr. Gon	Plantagenet	To investigate.
Dr. Sovereen	Leamington	Discipline Committee.
Viavi	Brussels	To prosecute.
Prof. Bennett	Trenton	Prosecuted, 2nd case, went to jail.
Dr. H. H. Crippen (Munyon's)	Toronto	Prosecuted, case dismissed.
Dr. W. C. James	Toronto	Prosecuted and skipped.
D. Beadreau	Ottawa	To prosecute.
Midwives	Ottawa	Stopped practising.
Medicine Man	Port Perry	No case.
Miss Neff	Hamilton	To prosecute.
M. J. Maloney	Eganville	Will be attended to.
Medicine Tramp	Centralia	Referred to Registrar.
Viavi	Walkerton	To prosecute.
F. X. Toney	Oxden	No case.
Prof. Stewart	Delaware	To prosecute.
Viavi	Darnoch	To prosecute.
Viavi	Colborne	To prosecute. Have left.
Mrs. Frechette	Beaudette	To prosecute.
Kikapoos	Mapleton	To prosecute.
J. L. Thompson	Hanona	No case.
L. W. Fish	Tilsonburg	Referred to Pharmacy College.
Dr. Cooper Younge	Everett	Skipped.
Edwards	Komoka	To prosecute.
Mrs. Hafling	Walkerton	Prosecuted. Case dismissed.
D. McCarthy	Paris	Prosecuted, fined $71.99.
Medicine Co	London	No case.
Kikapoos	Merlin	Skipped.
L. V. Aube	Oregon	Prosecuted, went to jail.
Mrs. Plunkett	Bancroft	Prosecuted, fined $16.00.

Sixty-four cases prosecuted, investigated and considered.

Total amount of costs paid by Council for prosecuting illegal practitioners, in cases where no fines were received, parties going to jail, skipping, etc., $262.71.

Total amount of fines collected and paid to prosecutor which covered the expenses in each case, he paying all costs from the said fines, $213.49.

I remain yours,

THOMAS WASSON, Detective, C. P. and S.O.

TORONTO, June 30th, 1897.

Dr. MACHELL moved the adoption of the report.

Dr. ROGERS—I must say the Council must feel indebted to the members of that committee for the trouble they have taken in this matter, and I do not think we ought to allow this report to pass without in some way recording a vote of thanks to them for the more than ordinary trouble they have taken throughout the past year. They have done a great deal of good work and I presume they have done more work then probably all the committees put together since our last meeting. I have much pleasure in seconding the motion to adopt the report, and also in recording my personal vote of thanks as ex-President, for the trouble they have taken, and I am sure all the members of the Council will re-echo that.

Dr. ARMOUR—I would ask that Dr. Machell add to his motion, that it be adopted and referred to the Finance Committee.

Dr. WILLIAMS—You cannot adopt it and at the same time refer it to the Finance Committee. If you adopt the report the Finance Committee can apply to the Registrar and get it.

The VICE-PRESIDENT put the motion which, on a vote having been taken, was declared carried.

Dr. ARMOUR—I beg leave to move, seconded by Dr. WILLIAMS, that the by-law entitled a by-law to amend By-law 39, in regard to the reading of bills and proceedings thereon be referred to the Special Committee.

The VICE-PRESIDENT put the motion which, on a vote being taken, was declared carried.

Dr. ROGERS asked leave to give notice of motion. Leave was granted.

Dr. ROGERS gave notice to introduce a by-law appointing a Committee on Discipline.

Dr. THORBURN in the chair.

Dr. BRITTON read the first report of the Committee on Education.

Dr. BRITTON—If any gentleman should request any information regarding any one of these clauses I will be in a position to give it to him. I might also say I believe every conclusion arrived at was a unanimous conclusion. If I am in error, some member of the committee will kindly correct me. That being the case, it will obviate the necessity of asking for particulars in individual cases. I beg leave to move the adoption of this first report of the Committee on Education.

Dr. FOWLER—Before this report is adopted, I would like to ask as to the case of Carr-Harris, who is a graduate of the Royal Military College of Kingston. It may be that all the subjects for matriculation may not be taught there, but undoubtedly the standard is very high and it would be greatly to be regretted if a graduate of the Royal Military College who has been trained so carefully both mentally and physically could not be accepted as a matriculant in medicine.

Dr. BRITTON read the petition of Carr-Harris, dated 30th of June, 1897, as follows :

Dr. Pyne, Secretary College of Physicians and Surgeons, Toronto.

DEAR SIR,—Enclosed please find certificate of my graduation at the Royal Military College of Canada after a four years' course given to me by Colonel McGill. I also mail to-day to you a copy of the syllabus of the course of instruction of the Royal Military College.

He asked to be registered because he graduated at the Royal Military College.

This is the certificate :

DEAR PROFESSOR,—Your son, Carr-Harris, graduated with honors on the 24th of June, 1897, and stands second in the class. Yours very sincerely,

S. C. McGILL.

Dr. BRITTON read list of subjects taught at the Royal Military College. There is no Latin whatever. It may be a high training but it is not such as we require.

Dr. MOORHOUSE—Is there any Latin in the entrance examination ?

Dr. ROGERS—I do not think so.

Dr. FOWLER—A medical training can be acquired in different directions ; some are better adapted for being trained in one way and some in another. Undoubtedly this does not come within our requirements, but I think it would be within our power and it would be a very prudent course for us to accept a man who has undergone the training that they undergo at the Royal Military College. It is fully equal as a mental training or bodily discipline to any training that can be got at any college.

The PRESIDENT—I know this, that every year one or more boys leave the Upper Canada College to enter this college, and they are generally sixth form boys and they have to pass an examination before they enter the college, so that this gentleman must have a certain amount of knowledge of Latin and Greek ; his matriculation requires that.

Dr. ROGERS—I do not think there is any proof of that. Is there any proof he ever was an Upper Canada College boy ?

The PRESIDENT—No.

Dr. SANGSTER—I wrote and obtained the syllabus from the Royal Military College, o Kingston, and I ascertained what the preliminary requirements are on entrance. They are not of a very advanced character, and a gentleman can get through in that college without knowing more Latin than would qualify him for promotion from the first or second form in our high schools.

Dr. MOORHOUSE—It would be imperative that he should have more Latin than that would indicate. I suppose his knowledge of English would be quite assured. That is something in which I am sorry to say the great bulk of practitioners are deficient.

Dr. CAMPBELL—If there is no amendment to anything in regard to that clause I would like to ask for information as to the case of Mr. Thomas Gibson, of Ottawa.

Dr. BRITTON—I think I can give you that information. Dr. Thomas Gibson, of Ottawa, who is the private or family physician to His Excellency the Governor-General, obtained the degree of M.A. in Edinburgh—I cannot give you the exact date— but at any rate, after having obtained that degree of M.A., he entered upon the study of medicine in the medical school of the University of Edinburgh. He pursued the course for five years, when he took the degree of M.B.C.M. He then spent some time as resident physician in such wards of the Royal Infirmary of Edinburgh as were in the care of Dr. Athley. Then he made application for the house surgeonship of a Children's Hospital, I think in Edinburgh ; also, he received a number of testimonials which he had printed. These testimonials were from the teachers in the medical college of the University of Edinburgh, and some of them from physicians and surgeons to the Royal Infirmary, one from Cheyne, one from Athley, one from Duncan and a number of others—there are twelve, I think, in all—all of which speak very highly of his attainments. It seems that his object in getting these recommendations or certificates was to assist him in getting this position which he sought. It is not stated whether or not he secured the position. I do not think he did. He then, I think, was on board one of the trans-Atlantic steamers or one of the Pacific steamers. He returned then to Scotland, and when the Governor General was coming to this country he appointed him as his private physician.

The PRESIDENT—He was not the first one.

Dr. BRITTON—Well, between one and two years ago he appointed him as his private physician. He is a registered practitioner of three years' standing. He was registered in September of 1894, and in September of this year he would have completed three years, not resident of course in Great Britain, but it is three years since he was so registered.

Dr. CAMPBELL—The only thing in it that is required is the domiciliary condition in Great Britain.

Dr. BRITTON—He asks for a special examination, and in a letter he addressed to Dr. Pyne—he evidently asked for this special examination prior to the meeting of this Council—he said : "In case I be not allowed to pass a formal examintion, then it will be necessary for me to wait until the September examination." I suppose, in order to brush up on some of the work ; and he mentions the September examination on the supposition that we would have a supplementary examination then. So that, he was willing to pass a special examination and asks for it. In that case he would be exempted from passing the primary examination.

Dr. DICKSON—He would be exempted from passing the matriculation examination ; he would have to pass the primary.

Dr. BRITTON—He asks to be put on the same ground as British practitioners, only that he be granted a special examination.

Dr. CAMPBELL—He would not come under the provisions of our regulations because he had not been domiciled in Great Britian for five years after becoming registered. I think, in view of the circumstances, that he has not come out here directly to practice, but comes out with a private appointment, the Council might concede that clause regarding the five years' domicile in England ; we might allow him that, and allow him to come as a British registered practitioner, passing the intermediate and primary examinations. On his paying the annual fees, I think the Council might allow that.

Dr. ROGERS—Why ?

Dr. CAMPBELL—He is evidently an able and worthy man, and will be a credit to the profession and no harm can come from waiving this five-year clause. I think that five-year clause was put there for the express purpose of preventing people going from this country over to England and being registered and coming right back. I should be disposed to allow him that much, which is not of course what he asks, and I do not know whether it would be acceptable to him or not, but I think it would be a matter of fairness, and it would do no harm, and I would move, that Dr. Gibson be registered on passing the intermediate and final examinations and paying the usual fee.

Dr. SANGSTER—I object to our establishing any precedent of that kind. We should have to make the same precedent in other cases. If we have a regulation that can be amended with advantage to the public, and the public amend it, we can't help it, but while it remains a regulation in our Announcement we are bound to adhere to it.

Dr. MOORE—Dr. Campbell has stated, he thinks that clause was put in to prevent young men going from Canada to Great Britain, getting registered, and then coming back. If it was for that purpose, that is a mistaken point to view it from ; our men ought to have more rights than men on the other side. I think this young man, if he is so bright and intelligent, and only a short time out of the mill, would have no difficulty whatever in passing the primary examination, and, as Dr. Sangster says, "we are only opening the door to make trouble for ourselves." If we open the door to anybody at all, let us open the door to our own.

Dr. MOORHOUSE—I quite agree with the remarks of Dr. Moore. Having been on this committee, I know we all came to that conclusion. Dr. Gibson is not over-worked ; the Governor-General kindly allows him to practice amongst the poor in the district which is immediately surrounding his dwelling, but that is all, and he has plenty of time to prepare his work and come before our body in the usual way. I think if it was so represented to him he would hardly ask any such concession as that. If any of our young men went over to England and came back here we would not allow them any such privilege, for I remember when I came back the Council would not allow me to register, and forced me to remain over, and threatened me, "if I started to practice for even a day, that they would prosecute me," and the consequence was, that I remained six months before I could come up for examination—this is twenty-three years ago ; I had to remain from the spring until the fall idle, just waiting for the fall examinations.

Dr. DICKSON—This would manifestly be a case of class legislation ; I think our own young men would take umbrage at it.

Dr. CAMPBELL—In view of the manifest feeling of the Council I withdraw my motion.

Dr. BRITTON—I beg leave to move, seconded by Dr. ROGERS, that the report be adopted.

The PRESIDENT put the motion which, on a vote having been taken, was declared carried, and the report adopted as follows :

To the President and Members of the Medical Council of the College of Physicians and Surgeons of Ontario:

GENTLEMEN,—Your Committee on Education beg leave to report as follows :

The communications indicated below, and referred to us from the Council, were fully considered, and in the case of each the conclusion arrived at is stated in this report.

1st. Dr. G. W. Palmer, asking for Matriculation. His request be not granted.

2nd. Carr-Harris, asking for Matriculation. His request be not granted.

3rd. Mr. Allan, asking for Matriculation. His request be not granted.

4th. H. O. Boyd. As he has no legal status in the medical profession, his request be not granted.

5th. Dr. W. R. Thomas. He must comply with the regulations of the Council.

6th. Dr. Thomas Gibson. His request cannot be granted. He must comply with the regulations of the Council.

7th. Dr. F. L. Johnson. His request cannot be granted. He must comply with the regulations of the Council.

8th. W. A. McCarthy. His request not to be granted. He must comply with the regulations of the Council.

9th. Ed. B. Oliver. His request granted.

10th. W. B. Kaylee. His request cannot be granted.

11th. Dr. N. Mallock. His request cannot be granted.

12th. Mrs. G. D. Ruthven. Her request cannot be granted.

13th. The communication from H. E. Allen, Assistant Registrar Medical Council, Great Britain, was considered. Said circular requested the Council of the College of Physicians and Surgeons of Ontario to make an effort to elevate the standard of matriculation now in existence.

It is advised by your committee that the Registrar be instructed to reply that our present standard compares not unfavorably with that of Great Britain, and, in order to bear out this assertion, that a copy of our regulations be forwarded:

14th. John McCrae. No action taken, case not considered.

15th. T. McDonald. His request to be granted on his furnishing necessary credentials.

16th. T. Ferguson. His request be not granted. He must comply with the regulations.

17th. C. A. Stewart. His request be not granted.

18th. W. H. Wood. He must comply with the regulations.

19th. D. E. Winter. His request cannot be granted. He must conform to the regulations regarding matriculation.

20th. R. A. Caldwell. His request be granted.

21st. S. L. Gray. His request cannot be granted ; and Dr. E. A. Merkley. His request cannot be granted.

TORONTO, July 8th, 1897.

Dr. ROGERS gave notice of motion to appoint an Executive Committee.

Dr. WILLIAMS gave notice of motion to introduce a by-law dealing with the annual fee and the levying of the same.

On motion of Dr. Rogers, seconded by Dr. Armour, the Council adjourned, to meet at eight o'clock p.m.

EVENING SESSION.

The Council met at eight o'clock p.m., in accordance with the motion for adjournment. The PRESIDENT in the chair.

The REGISTRAR called the roll, and the following members answered to their names : Drs. Armour, Bray, Britton, Brock, Campbell, Dickson, Emory, Fowler, Geikie, Graham, Griffin, Hanly, Henderson, Henry, Logan, Luton, Machell, Moore, Moorhouse, McLaughlin, Reddick, Rogers, Roome, Sangster, Shaw, Thorburn and Thornton.

The REGISTRAR read the minutes of the last session, which were confirmed and signed by the President.

NOTICES OF MOTION.

Dr. ARMOUR—To introduce a by-law to amend By-law No. 69 and By-law No. 75, by placing in suspension Section 41a of Medical Act, commonly known as the penal clause.

Dr. HENRY—To introduce a by-law to amend By-law No. 70.

Dr. CAMPBELL—There was some special order of business fixed for to-night.

The PRESIDENT—That was Dr. Henderson's special report of finance.

ENQUIRIES.

Dr. HENRY—What became of a letter that was sent down from the Bruce Medical Association directed to the Council ?

Dr. PYNE—It was referred to the Finance Committee.

Dr. SANGSTER—I notice in the report of the Finance Committee, which was adopted last year, there is a clause authorizing the Registrar to make it a matter of discretion whether he supplies the Announcement to others than members of the Council. It strikes me there must be some mistake, that probably members of the College was meant there instead of members of the Council.

Dr. PYNE—The Announcement was certainly sent to the members of the College.

Dr. SANGSTER—If you look at that I think you will find it is members of the Council.

The PRESIDENT—I think, if I recollect right, it was intended for all the profession generally.

Dr. SANGSTER—I make another inquiry, in order to put ourselves right in the matter of the legality of our proceedings. There was a recommendation of the Finance Committee last year authorizing the increase in the Treasurer's salary to $500.00 ; I think that was a righteous increase, as far as Dr. Aikins is concerned ; I do not think that any member of the Council, either then or now, for one instant disputes the rightness and the righteousness of this increase, but I wish to enquire whether the payment of the $500.00 for last year was made to Dr. Aikins, and to point out, if it was, that it was not done as it ought to have been done, on the authority of a by-law.

Dr. PYNE—It certainly has been paid, but there was no by-law passed.

Dr. SANGSTER—I only call attention to it in order that we may not proceed in the future to do by resolutions or by adoption of reports what I maintain can only be done by by-law in a legal and proper way.

The PRESIDENT—I suppose we are all guilty in the respect that we ought to have called attention to the fact at the time.

Dr. BRITTON—I am still in the dark as to the necessity for that. I suppose Dr. Sangster has looked into the matter, and I would like to know where it occurs in the regulations or in the Act that we must fix a salary by by-law.

The PRESIDENT—I think the salaries are fixed by by-law.

Dr. PYNE—It is under Section 13 of the Act.

Dr. BRITTON—I do not think that is the meaning of the clause or sub-section. On page xvi. of the register at Section 13, it states, "The Council shall annually appoint a President, Vice-President, Registrar, Treasurer, and such other officers as may from time to time be necessary for the working of this Act, who shall hold office during the pleasure of the Council ; and the said Council shall have power to fix by by-law, or from time to time, the salaries or fees to be paid to such officers, and to the Board of Examiners hereinafter appointed." Now, I would say that those two expressions "fix by by-law," or "from time to time," do not mean exactly the same thing. I think the intention of that is that if we want to fix the salary for a longer period of time than a year or for a continued period we must introduce a by-law. But, if we wish to fix the salary from time to time, say from year to year, I would think the interpretation of that clause is, that a by-law is not required.

The PRESIDENT—I know in the expenditure of money it is always well understood as a parliamentary rule that there shall be a by-law.

Dr. GEIKIE—Dr. Henderson gives me permission to ask through you, Mr. President, the permission of the Council to put in a supplementary report.

The permission of the Council was granted.

Dr. GEIKIE presented and read supplementary report of the Committee on Complaints as follows :

To the President and Members of the Council of the College of Physicians and Surgeons of Ontario:

GENTLEMEN,—This supplemental report of the Committee on Complaints is hereby presented. The Committee met to-day, July 8th, 1897. The request of T. Bradley was considered. He desired to be allowed the subject of physiology to complete his primary. His record on this subject having been carefully examined, the Committee recommended that his request be not granted.

All of which is respectfully submitted.

(Signed)   W. B. GEIKIE, Chairman.

Dr. HENDERSON—As this special report of the Committee on Finance has been read, I move that the Council go into Committee of the Whole to consider the report.

Dr. BRAY—I second that.

The PRESIDENT put the motion, which, on a vote having been taken, was declared carried.

COUNCIL IN COMMITTEE OF THE WHOLE.

Dr. DICKSON in the chair.

Dr. HENDERSON read Clause 1 of the report.

Dr. HENDERSON—It seems that the fall examination has never been a paying institution, and we were a great number of years without a fall examination, and we seemed to get along quite as well without it. Probably it would be as well to do away with that.

Dr. ARMOUR—I move that Clause 1 of the report be adopted as read.

Dr. FOWLER—Does the adoption of this clause do away with the fall examination, or will the question come up again.

Dr. BRAY—This will dispose of it ; it will not come up again.

Dr. ROOME—I understand this is merely a report to the Council. I think we should consider that very carefully before we pass those clauses. If for one examination it will cost $600.00, it will put the students to considerably more expense if we hold two examinations. The money has been raised from the students to pay the expenses of the examinations, and if it will save the students $600.00, I think we should only have an examination once a year ; but by having one examination a student would have to go a year before he could have a second examination. I think it is something we ought to consider very carefully before we adopt it. I think it is very well for the Finance Committee to offer this as a suggestion.

Dr. ARMOUR—Dr. Roome is not right in saying that it would save the students $600.00 if there was only one examination. It would save the Council. The students would have one examination in the year instead of two, as at present, but they would pay the same amount of fees as at present.

Dr. BRITTON—Is this a recommendation from the Committee?

Dr. HENDERSON—It is a recommendation from the Committee, it is for the Council to consider and say whether it shall be adopted or not.

Dr. BRITTON—Mr. Chairman, I am quite well aware of the fact that, in the long run, a certain amount of loss is sustained by holding a fall examination, inasmuch as certain persons may go up for the fall examination, if such is conducted ; whereas if we did not have that fall examination they would go up in the spring, which simply means the gathering together of the examiners on one occasion only during the year, and that would save a certain amount ; but I have now to repeat what I once said this afternoon, we are here, not only in the interests of the profession, and in the interests of the public, but I think we are here also to look after the interests of those who are sure or likely to become part and parcel of the College of Physicians and Surgeons of Ontario. Our rules are almost as stringent as the laws of the Mèdes and Persians, regarding the conditions on which an applicant shall be admitted to the College ; on failing in certain subjects, we know perfectly well that he has to take a high percentage in other subjects before they be allowed him, the very high percentage of sixty per cent. I don't say it is too high, but, compared with many teaching bodies, it is a very high percentage ; hs has in the minimum percentages a high percentage—fifty ; in many of the best institutions it is only thirthy-three and a third. I do not complain of it being fifty, I do not want to see it any less, but I do claim that we ask from students, perhaps all that we should. They are subjected to a rigid examination ; it is an examination that is conducted fairly ; there is no favoritism shown to anyone, and it is a very rare thing for us in Council or in Committee to reverse any order of things, or rather, to revoke anything that has been 'stated by an examiner regarding a candidate ; his marks usually stand for law, and, as I said before, it is a rare thing for his finding to be changed in any respect by the Council or by the Committee of Complaints or the Committee on Education. That goes to show that in the spring examination, or at any examination a first class student may through accident, may through having an unlucky paper—no student knows everything—fail in a certain subject, only one out of, perhaps, ten or twelve subjects ; he may fail but by two marks. His other subjects are above the minimum fifty per cent., possibly largely above, and as I said before, that is a high percentage, still we think, and we in our judgment believe that he scarcely deserves to be accorded a license. He has failed but by two marks, has been an ambitious student, has worked hard all through his four or five years, has made all his arrangements to enter the profession ; or he has arranged to go to the Old Country, to pursue a post-graduate course there, or to one of the larger cities in the United States ; do you think it would be fair in such a case to compel him to wait for a whole year before he be examined in that one subject, and that, perhaps, a minor one, such as sanitary science ? I, for one, cannot agree with doing away with the fall examination ; there is no reason for it, except so far as economy is concerned, and I say that what is sometimes called " economy " might almost be designated stinginess ; at any rate it is very often the case, and when carried to extremes does not bring with it the best results. I think it is far better for the profession, for us, and for the army of students, small or large as it may be, and only fair to them that we should hold a supplemental examination in the fall for those that are worthy of having a supplemental examination. I have no sympathy for certain students who would go up for a fall examination, in the supposition that it would be easier to get through in the fall than the spring ; that is a fallacious supposition. I have been told that there are certain students who believe that, and if there are any such I have no sympathy with them. But, I say, we ought to do right, whether it be one student or twenty whose interests we are considering, and certainly no spring examination will occur without probably a dozen or more cases arising worthy of our consideration, cases that should not be put off until the next year's examination. For these reasons I could not myself vote for the adoption of that clause, and I would beg to move, if a resolution has not already been introduced, that the clause be struck out.

Dr. FOWLER—In supporting Dr. Britton to uphold the fall examination, I, on behalf of the College, have no selfish interest to serve, inasmuch as for some time on account of the fewness of numbers a fall examination has not been held at Kingston, but, I think we have a duty to perform to our students, and undoubtedly the receipts from them are sufficient to pay for the expense of a spring and fall examination, the one to be held at Toronto and the other at Kingston. I think, then, it would be very selfish on our part to oppose the holding of a fall examination. I know deserving students, who from accident or from some other cause, are often prevented either from going up for the spring examination or from being able to pass and it is an extreme hardship to these students to remain a whole year waiting, at considerable expense to themselves, until a year elapses before they can pass. This never occurs in England ; in the Royal College of Surgeons in England there are frequent opportunities for students to pass this examination which qualifies them to practice in Great Britain and I think we should afford our students an opportunity twice a year of being admitted into the profession.

Dr. ROGERS—How many qualifying examinations does Queen's College hold in medicine yearly ?

Dr. FOWLER—We hold an examination at the end of each year.

Dr. ROGERS—You only hold one examination each year.

Dr. FOWLER—Yes, and sometimes supplementaries in the spring.

Dr. ROGERS—Why is it you do not have two examinations ?

Dr. FOWLER—If there was necessity for it we would. If there are a sufficient number going up, and if they may be rejected in the spring of the year, they can have a supplementary in the fall

Dr. GEIKIE—I strongly support what Dr. Britton and Dr. Fowler have said ; their view of the case I think is the right one. Universities or medical schools may do as they like, but so far as licensing is concerned they have no power. I like the idea that the Council as a licensing body should be straight in its determination to do what is right ; it has a good effect ; it makes men work and makes better men of them than it would if they felt that there was laxity in the licensing board, which I am happy to say, there is not. In regard to what has been said. that there are students who think they will slip easily through the fall examination, I have not found anything of the kind ; they often come to me and I have said, if you are going up in the fall, gentlemen, you must work just as hard as at any other time because one examination is just as strict as another. I do not think there is any such impression abroad. It would be a very impolitic step, even to save $600.00 to take away the fall examination.

Dr. MOORHOUSE—I believe it is the practice of the Royal College of Surgeons to give four examinations annually ; but I believe when a man is rejected in his examination he is given what is called the six months' hoist : he is not allowed to come up for examination inside of six months. That would be the same as our examinations and forthe small amount of $600.00 I think it would be rather a retrograde movement to abolish the fall examination. I am happy to hear that Kingston men never require to come up for a fall examination and I compliment Dr. Fowler on giving them such capable teaching, but if they happen at some time in the future to be not so fortunate, let them come to Toronto. I would support the fall examination. With regard to the supplementary examinations, I know the impression is abroad that they are never so rigid. Dr. Geikie said he never heard that. They are always regarded as second class examinations ; a man that graduates or gets his license in the fall is never regarded so favorably by the public as a man who gets it in the spring ; even I myself look upon it in that way.

Dr. ROGERS—Do you oppose the examination ?

Dr. MOORHOUSE—No.

The CHAIRMAN put the motion that the clause be struck out, which, on a standing vote being taken, was declared carried ; fourteen members voting for and twelve against the motion.

Dr. SANGSTER—I take it for granted that there will be an opportunity of taking the yeas and nays on each of these items when discussed in the Council.

The CHAIRMAN—Dr. Britton's motion is carried.

Dr. SANGSTER—I would like a little information before we proceed further. That is a resolution in which the profession is vitally interested and if the omission of that clause now shuts me out of afterwards moving that that clause should be restored I shall be put in the position of having to give notice of a substantive motion.

Dr. McLAUGHLIN—When that report comes in the Council Dr. Sangster can move that it be referred back to the Committee of the Whole to insert such and such a clause.

Dr. CAMPBELL—It can be done a great deal better than that. This report is only a series of reommendations and the adoption of each one of them would not commit the Council to anything ; it would only show the feeling of the Council. This question of having a fall examination will come up again when we have the report of the Education Committee on the Announcement for next year.

Dr. HENDERSON read Clause 2 of the report.

Dr. ROOME—I am opposed to having only one examination, but I think we should hold the examinations in one place, and that in Toronto, because that is a central place. Kingston may have a claim for it, and if that is so, we claim for the Western University that it be held in London ; London would be just as much entitled to it as Kingston. My idea is, that where ambitious young men who have not got the means to lay idle for a year are willing to pay, they should have the chance. Therefore I am in favor of that clause being carried.

Dr. FOWLER—I hope I will be excused for speaking again upon this important educational point, inasmuch as I have been altogether silent and have not taken up much of your time during the previous part of the session. This is a resolution which vitally affects the medical college at Kingston, and I think carrying it out would be most unjust, most unfair and contrary to the agreement that was entered into with Kingston when the Act was first passed. I have nothing to say against London, I should be pleased to have an examination held there also, and no doubt the time will come when it will be held there. I am, perhaps, the only one conversant with the establishment of the Medical Council ; I do not know about my friend Dr. Geikie ; but I was present at the origin of it, and we in Kingston heartily upheld the formation of the Medical Council ; we felt while it might, to a certain extent, diminish our college, the passage of this Act would be a benefit to the profession at large, and, consequently while our charters, that of Queen's College and the Royal College, entitled us to grant degrees which enabled those holding them to practise both in Ontario and Quebec, we surrendered these powers in order to aid in the formation of the Medical Council ; but there was a distinct understanding, and there was in the Act until the very last moment, when it was smuggled through, a clause that the examinations should be held at Kingston and Toronto. But the word " or " was smuggled into the Act at the very last stages of it. I maintain then that we have a right to it, and it would be a gross injustice to deprive us of it ; and the fact would be that it would not only deprive our students of the privilege of having an examination in their own neighborhood but it would bring on them additional expense, and it is an act of meanness, I think, in the Council to attempt to save money which will result in an expense being thrown on the students. I think this would be most unjust, most unfair, and would be an act of meanness on the part of the Medical Council, and I trust that they will never perpetrate such an act as to pass a resolution of this kind. I trust what I have said will be sufficient to satisfy you that it is but an act of justice that the examination should be continued at Kingston as well as at Toronto. The expenses I believe are greatly exaggerated; all that will be required will be the additional expense of the examiners' railway fare coming from and to Toronto. They would require to devote the same amount of time to the work if the students were up at Toronto as they would at Kingston. I trust I have said enough to convince you of the impropriety of sustaining this clause.

Dr. MOORE—I am satisfied you have listened with a great deal of attention to the remarks that have fallen from Dr. Fowler. Certainly he was in earnest, and he told you what was true. When this Council was formed there was an earnest, compact entered into on the part of the originators of this Council that the examinations should be held at Toronto and Kingston, and three years ago I read here from the Act furnished me by Dr. Pyne, which unfortunately I cannot lay my hands on just now, "Toronto and Kingston," but when the Acts were consolidated, by some manner of means the word "or" crept in. We claim that the examinations must be held at Kingston still. If you do not hold them there every year, you must hold them there every alternate year, and hold the whole of them there. I do not think there is a gentleman on the floor of this chamber who desires to break up the compact that was made years ago, or who wishes to break up the method that has been carried on so successfully and so well. So far as the expenses are concerned, Dr. Fowler has told you plainly that all the increase in expense is simply the travelling fare of the examiners from Toronto to Kingston and return. Now, that is a trifling amount. One hundred or two hundred dollars to this incorporated body is nothing in comparison to one dollar, probably, in a poor student's pocket. If we do not do this, if we deprive Eastern Ontario of the rights that belong to them, there will be trouble. We may not make it probably, but you must remember that this Medical Council has enemies that are just waiting for another weapon to be put in their hands to go to the Legislature with, because they will not see their sons and daughters put to an unnecessary expense in order to please a corporation like this. We might better be careful, and conduct our examinations just as we have done before, rather than stir up a hornet's nest about our ears. It is only right and fair and just that we should have this, and I move that that clause of the report be struck out.

Dr. SANGSTER—I protest against the threats in the last speaker's remarks being uttered within the walls of this chamber. I think that threat of the Patrons has done all the service it is destined to do in this Council chamber. We have nothing to do with the Patrons ; we have nothing to do with the individual educational bodies; we have to do what is right. A demand is made on this Council on the part of the profession that it shall show some evidence of a desire to retrench its expenses. You have thrown out one suggestion that involved a saving of six or seven hundred dollars ; and I have gone over it carefully, and it is an average saving of $700.00. You are now asked to throw out another suggestion that proposes a further saving of $400.00. I take it for granted that this Committee has gone into the matter carefully and they have not exaggerated the saving they are proposing to make. Against that you are asked to continue a system in favor of an institution in the far east. I was on the Board of Examiners the first session that there was a Board of Examiners instituted, and we examined that year in Kingston, the next year the examination was held in Toronto, so that I know from the outset that the Act provided that the examinations should be held alternately in Toronto and Kingston, and not in Toronto and Kingston annually. You can do nothing in the way of legislation that does not pinch the fingers of somebody or some class of people. I think the small pinch given to the fingers of the students to the extent of requiring them to come to Toronto for examination is a very small pinch indeed, and I think it should not be taken into consideration. I do not propose to take up your time, I do not propose to enter here at large into these questions, but I simply state that you are asked, and that you have professed in this room a desire to economize. We have seen nothing, the profession has seen nothing heretofore in that direction, except a desire expressed in words ; it is about time this Council should crystallize its words into facts.

Dr. BROCK—I wish to make a few remarks upon this resolution ; this is the third time this resolution has been brought up in this Council on the question of economy ; I think the whole of this follows from a resolution moved by myself last year ; and feeling I have a duty to perform to my constituency, I have a desire that we should show some economy, and we have been looking in every direction to find some means of reducing the expenses of this Council. I am sure that not one member of that Committee desires to hurt the feelings of Professor Fowler, whom we all respect ; no one desires to injure a University which is so well known as Queen's, but it seems to me it is only a question of time when the examinations will have to be held in Toronto. I do not like to say the reason why, but it seems to me it is coming to that point where it will necessitate the examinations being held in Toronto. I think it would be a very good thing if Professor Fowler could see his way to accede to the desires of the territorial members in this Council, and permit us to have one examination in this city.

Dr. ROGERS.—As a territorial member and one interested quite as much as any member in economy, I would like to say something in regard to this. It is quite true that possibly we would have saved $600.00 had we adopted the first clause of this report, but if by saving $600.00 we would antagonize the great body of students we would lose a great deal more than $600.00. And I also say if we can have $400.00 by passing this resolution with regard to the second section of this report, and at the same time antagonize a large body, an influential body like Queen's University and the alumni of that body, and its graduates throughout the length and breadth of this Province, I cannot help but think we are saving the $400.00 very, very badly. I am a territorial member, I have to depend, it is true, upon the votes of a large section of the medical fraternity, but I am quite willing to risk my return, if need be, in that or any-thing else ; and I am going to do what I think is my duty irrespective of anything else. I think this Council has existed for a quarter of a century and over, and why ? Because a compact was entered into at the beginning by the Universities, by the Homœopaths and by the pro-fession. You can doubt it, but it is nevertheless true. I used to doubt it, I admit, until I took the trouble to investigate the matter, but I found it to be an actual fact that this Council would never have been in existence had it not been for the compact entered into by the Universities—Queen's University was one—and by the Homœopaths ; and one of the con-ditions of that compact was that there should be, if possible, always an examination in Kingston and Toronto, or alternately, if it was not possible to hold them in both places, once in Toronto and then in Kingston. There is no doubt that is the compact, just as much a compact as that the Homœopaths should have five representatives. Because we, the terri-torial members, are strong here, are we to say, we are strong, we will take the weak ones and shake them ? I say no, let us be at least generous. Not only would we break our compact, but I think we would make many enemies all over. When the time comes that Queen's University will voluntarily say, we will give up our examinations, I will be very glad, but we do not want to break faith with them.

Dr. MOORHOUSE—I would like to see the examinations consolidated and all held in Toronto. While I must confess I have that strong desire. I do not believe we have any right to take the examinations away from Kingston ; I think what Dr. Rogers has stated was a part of the original agreement, just as much as the Homœopaths came with us on condition that we would give them so many representatives. I think Queen's College sur-rendered her rights to license to the Council upon condition that the Council would give her an annual examination. I do not think we ought to have any fall supplementary examina-tion in Kingston.

Dr. ROGERS—We do not ask for it.

Dr. MOORHOUSE—I think probably we are wasting time about something we have no power to do ; it is all wind and words. At the same time I would like if we could have an examination in London, and I think it is a right we should have, too. I think we will fight for it and we will ask for it, and our men will demand it in time, and we will get it probably.

Dr. ROGERS—It is foolish to talk that way.

Dr. MOORHOUSE—Dr. Rogers says it is foolish to talk that way. I don't think I am foolish, I think I have just as much right to stand up for the west as Dr. Rogers has for the east ; he is ready to stand up for the east, and I am quite ready to stand up for the west.

Dr. SANGSTER—Did I understand you to say, Dr. Moorhouse, that we were shut out from the matter legally ?

Dr. MOORHOUSE—Yes.

Dr. SANGSTER—The clause is "in Toronto or Kingston."

Dr. MOORHOUSE—That word " or " has no business there.

Dr. SANGSTER—But, it is there.

Dr. MOORHOUSE—It is only an interpolation. It was "and." There are corruptions even in Holy Writ, and if such is the case, how much more is it likely to creep into this Act.

Dr. BARRICK—We just see where we are drifting to ; we drift down to Kingston, then we drift up to London, and the more we cultivate that sectional weakness the worse it will be for this Council, and the worse it will be for the profession of this Province. No matter what was in the Act, we are here to-day to deal with the Act as it is ; and while the Act is as it is and these examinations are to be held in Toronto or Kingston, I say, consid-ering the finances of this College and the desire there is on the part of the profession at large that the expenses should be reduced so that we can show a balance on the right side, I maintain that the members of this Council are recreant to their duty if they do not, by all the means that lies in their power, endeavor in every way to curtail the expenses of this Council. Of course, every one has seen during this session and during former sessions, that every attempt that has been made to reduce the expenses of this Council has been objected to, and objections have been thrown in the way, and it will always be so, but we will have to keep hammering away at this until we gradually get the affairs of this Council down to a proper business basis. With this in view, gentlemen, I must strongly support the clause to have the examinations held in Toronto, because, as Dr. Moorhouse has stated, he is in favor of consolidating the examinations ; but if Kingston has an examination, then he claims, and has good ground for claiming, that there shall be an examination at London; and when Hamilton rises to the point of having a medical school, Hamilton will want an examination, and so we will go on with our examinations all over the country, frittering away our revenue and getting deeper and deeper into debt. I can quite understand the men from the east wishing to have the examination held at Kingston, and I can understand the men from the west wishing to have an examination at London. We have this trouble in every municipality, and especially in the wards of cities, and we must in this Council endeavor to rise above that. We have taken the ground in dealing with the applications of the candidates which came before us to-day that we should rise above anything of a personal nature ; that we should, in deciding, take a higher ground and not legislate for individuals nor for sections, but adopt that legislation which is best for the whole Council, best for the whole profession. Of course, if you have an examination in Kingston instead of Toronto, the men in Kingston will save their fees coming up here, but the men in the west and in the centre will have imposed upon them extra fees to go to Kingston. But, if you consider all the grievances of students in this matter, you will have an endless amount of trouble. We must adopt that course which is the best for the welfare of this Council, and especially for the welfare of the financial side of it. Our finances are going behind, I believe, every year, and if nothing is done in a vigorous way to stem that tide, to stem the heaping up of that deficiency, we will, after awhile, come to a point that we will not be able to hold examinations anywhere.

Dr. CAMPBELL—I believe that it would be an expedient thing to have the examinations all held in Toronto, and I believe it would be in the interests of economy to have them held in Toronto. But there is something better than expediency, there is something nobler and grander and more desirable than economy, and that is that justice should be done and that faith should be kept (hear, hear) ; the whole foundations of society rest upon this, that men keep faith with one another, and majorities have no right in after days to break compacts that have been solemnly entered into in earlier days, simply because they have the strength to do it. If it be true, and I believe it is not questioned by anyone, that one of the conditions of the compromise necessary to the formation of this Council originally, was that the examinations should be held in Toronto and Kingston, either alternately or simultaneously, I do not care whether it is expressed in the Act or not, I maintain it is the duty of this Council and the Council is in honor bound, even though the expenses were much greater than they are, to carry out positively the compact into which it entered. The interests of the Council, and those interests are the interests of the profession, depend upon honor and good faith being kept in all sections of the profession, with all branches of the profession, with all institutions in any way connected with the profession, and it is an unwise thing, an unsafe thing, a dangerous thing for us to break any compacts that may have been entered into, even though we have the legal power to do it.

Dr. BRAY—Mr. Chairman, I was a member of the Finance Committee ; this question has come up on three or four different occasions during the past ten or fifteen years, and while I am in favor of economy just as much as anybody else, I quite agree with Dr. Campbell. I had some notes here on some points on which I intended to speak, but Dr. Campbell has covered the ground, so that I will not repeat what he has said ; he has put them before you a great deal better than I could do. There is just this about it, students should be considered to a certain extent. Our government considers the students. Why is it they have examinations held at every collegiate institute and high school in every county in this Province ? Why not bring them down to Toronto University and make them pass their examinations there, if they have not some consideration for the students ? I think it is a matter of justice. I cannot express myself, as I said before, in the eminent manner in which Dr. Campbell has expressed himself, but I say we should do justice to the weak. I don't think it is the intention of any gentleman here, I don't think it is the object of any gentleman here to build up Toronto schools at the expense of London or Kingston, and that is just what it will do if you take the examinations away from Kingston. London is a little differently situated. I would be quite glad, indeed, for the members in the west, if it were in our power, to grant the holding of examinations in London, but there is nothing in the Act to that effect, so that there is no use talking about it. Kingston is differently situated ; there is a large tract of the Province of Ontario east of Kingston, and there is a very small tract of the Province west of London. However, that is beside the question. Since we have had examinations at all, since this Council commenced to hold examinations, Kingston has been recognized, and I cannot see why we should take that privilege away to-day. In the original Act, which I have seen, the word "and" is used ; in the present Act the word "or" replaces it, how it got there I cannot say.

Dr. SANGSTER—I think the gentleman is wrong. Dr. Fowler will bear me out in saying that it is claimed the change was made in the Act before it was finally issued from the Legislature.

Dr. BRAY—I think in the first Register of this Province you will find the Act printed there, and the word "and" in it.

Dr. MOORE—You will.

Dr. BRAY—I have seen it; I do not think it was the intention of the Legislature to change this purposely. Often words are put in and often words are left out, and sometimes whole sentences, inadvertently. I think that must have been so in this case. I will ask Dr. Sangster, if he can possibly get hold of the original Register, to look it up.

Dr. SANGSTER—I will do so gladly, because it strengthens my view infinitely to say that the change was made by the Legislature, and that the word "and" was changed to "or," that is to me a most emphatic proof that it was done designedly by the Legislature. The Legislature does not allow any clerical errors in its Acts.

Dr. BRAY—I do not wish to detain the Council any longer but to express my hope that no change will be made, and that no injustice will be done to Kingston. I speak warmly and feelingly on this subject. I am a western member, representing a constituency on the border, but at the same time I have feelings, as we all must have, for my *Alma Mater*; Kingston is mine, and I have strong love for my *Alma Mater*, and, if for nothing else, I would like to see no injustice done, but there are higher reasons for not doing an injustice than even that.

Dr. GEIKIE—As an old member of the Council I would like to say a few words. Dr. Barrick has spoken about us being very emphatic in regard to economy, but I do not think we have striven very hard to instil economy. I am extremely anxious to have our business carried on, and everything done in the direction of economy. As a Toronto school man or a college man, whichever you like, I repudiate the idea of desiring to build up the colleges in Toronto at the expense of our sister colleges elsewhere. While I would like to see our Kingston friends feel that there would be no great injury, perhaps no injury at all, by having the examinations all held in Toronto, still Dr. Fowler has stated with great earnestness, and I am long enough in this Council and old enough to remember, that there was a compact; and I quite agree with Dr. Campbell when he says that if we are to economize and wish to economize, we must economize in such a way that it will not be at the expense of good faith; and I feel it would be a breach of faith. Dr. Fowler is true; he is a most straightforward man, and he would not speak with the earnestness with which he has spoken unless he felt deeply the truth of what he was saying, and in the face of that I could not vote for the clause, as against that agreement, in the very teeth of it, I could not. With regard to holding examinations at London, that is a different thing; the Council is not committed to that, and while I wish luck to our sister in London, I would just say to Dr. Moorhouse, send the students down to Toronto, at all events, and save a new expense being incurred.

Dr. THORBURN—I have a recollection of the formation of this Council, and took an active part in it, and we had a great deal of difficulty in reconciling the different faculties and schools, and it was only by the promise that we established the Council; one of the conditions was that the examinations should be held alternately in Toronto and Kingston, and I think it would be a very great breach of truthfulness and honesty to depart from that without sufficient cause. I am just as anxious as anybody that we should economize in every way that is compatible with truth and honor, but I must oppose any motion that would deprive Kingston of its rights.

Dr. WILLIAMS—I have listened with a good deal of interest to the discussion on this subject; we have heard the strongest points raised upon both sides of the case. I think that there are other points in addition to expediency and in addition to the financial point. Dr. Barrick has dwelt with a good deal of force on the financial side of the case, and undoubtedly there is a certain loss to the Council by having the examinations at Kingston. The question of expediency is not exactly so easily settled; it is true it might be convenient for the Council at present to hold the examinations all in Toronto, but the point has been raised that by so doing you would disaffect not simply the case of the University, but you would disaffect the entire alumni of Kingston. We might just stop and enquire what would be the effect of that. I admit, in all frankness, if I could have exactly my own way, if I had a clean sheet of paper to start the scheme upon, I would unquestionably have one certain building and have all the examinations in that place. But, is that the position we occupy? I think not. We occupy the position that, having had a diversity of interests, we are trying to concentrate those interests as much as possible; but in concentrating those it must not be by breach of compacts, it must not be by the strong adopting a measure that will make the weak feel disaffected; but we must adopt such a course as will bring, as nearly as possible, the whole united interests of the profession into harmony. If we make those in Kingston, and the alumni of that institution feel that because we have got strength we are going to take advantage of them, and take away from them what they believe, whether we do or not, is their right under the original compact, I submit we are not working in the interests of the Council, and the small amount of money that we save will be more than lost by the diversity of interests that we cause. There is another point to be borne in mind, and it is this, there are people at the end of the College at Kingston—I do not need to tell you that there are strong men there, with strong influence, and just impress upon them that they are being treated unjustly by this Council, and they will bring the influence they have got to bear upon the members of the Government, and they will bring it to bear in such a way that they will make this Council regret having taken the step. I do not exaggerate the matter when I tell you that Kingston has strong power and strong men, and they can bring that power to bear. Does it not stand us in hand to walk carefully and do exactly what is fair and just to all parties? Otherwise, we will be brought to grief more suddenly perhaps than we think of. The financial part is not the only part we have to consider in Council matters; there is the general good and harmony of the united profession. I believe the time will come when all examinations will be held in the City of Toronto, that there will be one central place. I do not believe Dr. Moorhouse will ever see examinations held in London. There may be a possibility of such things occurring, but it will be when there are more inhabitants in the Province of Ontario than Dr. Moorhouse will ever live to see; it will be a long day before that come to pass. I believe it will be in this country as it is in England, that there will be concentration; the students have to come from all over the world to one city in England if they wish to obtain a certain degree. I believe it will be so in the Province of Ontario, when, if a man wishes to be registered in Ontario, he will have to come to the centre of medical education, and that will be in the city of Toronto. While that would be what I would like to see, that is not the practical way to get at our condition to-day; we have not that clean sheet, but we have a diversity of interests which we have got to bring together, and we have got to adopt the best means we can to make that a progressive and united interest; and when the time comes, as I believe it will come, sometime in the future, probably not in my day, it will be a united interest centred in Toronto, and then it will be to the interests of the profession to have the examinations in Toronto; but that will not be, if we take what Kingston believes, and what its alumni believe, to be their just and honest right from them by force, when it was an original compact made with them.

Dr. Brock—As the President of this Council, and the old members have declared it was a solemn compact, just as solemn as was made with the Homoeopaths and with the Eclectics, I certainly think that as this Council is acting on the policy of harmony and good-will I, for my part, will withdraw my support from the motion to adopt that clause of the report.

Dr. Logan—Something over twenty years ago this matter was discussed by us in the Council, privately and otherwise; I can recollect very well having a discussion, and asking my friend, Dr. Fowler, if he was not willing that the examinations should be conducted entirely in Toronto; and he said, "Certainly not." I said, "Why?" He said, "Because we had an understanding with a certain number of men, and it was a matter of honor between us that this be the case in the future." When I discovered that, I at once abandoned my objections. I was very much in favor of lessening the expenses by not going to Kingston. I thought it was a very unwise thing to be expending money in this way, and it was for that reason I endeavored to find out the exact nature of the arrangement; and from the moment I was convinced of the exact nature of the arrangement until now, I consider that I am in honor bound to adhere to that arrangement. Many of the members here are new men, and they are not acquainted with this arrangement, they probably have no knowledge of it, but when we inform them that such was the case, I cannot see how any honorable man can do otherwise than agree with those who have this knowledge in their possession. Now, it has been said this Council is expending enormous sums of money, and we must really adopt some method of lessening this expenditure. I say, if you are going to economize and cut down the expenditure of this Council at the expense of the honor of the men who endeavored to establish it, I feel sorry for you.

The Chairman put the motion to have Clause 2 of the report struck out, which, on a vote being taken, was declared carried; seventeen voting for, and eight against, the motion.

Dr. Henderson read Clause 3 of the report, and moved its adoption.

Dr. Williams—What difference will that make in the present arrangement.

Dr. Henderson—It will make a difference of one hour.

Dr. Pyne—They have five hours now, and that will make it six—three hours in the morning and three in the afternoon. I may say this was suggested to me by the examiners themselves.

On motion, Clause 3 of the report was adopted.

Dr. Henderson read Clause 4 of the report.

Dr. Moorhouse—I may state as far as I understand this retainer of $20.00, when the examiner goes down he gets $20.00 whether he has anything to do or not. Is that not it, Dr. Pyne?

Dr. PYNE—Yes. $20.00 was paid to every examiner, but there are two examiners on the Board who do not read any papers. That $20.00 provided for in the by-law is, as it were, a retainer for reading the first fifty papers. The assistant examiners in medicine and surgery do nothing for that $20.00, and it is suggested to cut that allowance off. The others will get their $20.00 the same as usual.

On motion, Clause 4 of the report was adopted.

Dr. HENDERSON read Clause 5 of the report.

Dr. MOORHOUSE—I think they have been in the habit of giving fifteen minutes to each student for his oral examination. I think that any examiner would be able to learn what a student knows in ten minutes.

Dr. McLAUGALIN—That reflects greatly on the lecturer.

Dr. MOORHOUSE—I think the examiner could tell. We might cut off that five minutes. `

Dr. EMORY—I desire to call the attention of the Council to the fact that last year you appointed a special committee to take into consideration the examinations, with a view to seeing what could be done in the way of making a more able test of the candidates' acquirements. I think Dr. Moorhouse was a member of that Committee.

Dr. MOORHOUSE—But I didn't assent to that.

Dr. EMORY—That was adopted by the Council without a dissenting voice, and I have heard that a large percentage of the students regarded that as a decided advance.

Dr. ARMOUR —What was adopted?

Dr. EMORY—The lengthening of the time to fifteen minutes. I have had a student come to me with his knees knocking together, and, at first it would take two or three minutes before he could answer what was asked him. I claim that ten minutes is not sufficient. Let us not have the examination a farce. I hope the Council will not stultify its action of last year by shortening the time when it has only been one year in exercise, and I think that on the question of an examination, and making it a thoroughly genuine test of the attainments of the candidate, is the last place to begin to economize.

Dr. DOUGLAS—I am in harmony with the views of Dr. Emory. Five minutes is a short time enough for a student who comes in a little bit excited and nervous, in which to express his knowledge as to what is attempted to be drawn from him by the examiner. He comes in, and he is a little excited, and if he knows he has only ten minutes to spare, and a minute or two has already gone by, in his nervous, excited condition the result will be that he becomes more excited still, and he has only eight minutes left. I can speak within a comparatively recent time with regard to the time that is allowed on oral examinations in the old country. I did not take my examinations in the old country until after I had been in practice for several years. They do not think there of giving you anything less than fifteen minutes, and occasionally you will find an examiner who is decidedly considerate. I know a friend of mine who went over there, and who was in the room undergoing his oral examination at the same time I was. When the examiner saw he was excited, he simply sat down and chatted with him until the gentleman felt at home, then he went on and passed a splendid examination. I was a little surprised to listen to the remarks of Dr. Moorhouse, who is an old teacher. Ten minutes is a brief time ; I do not think you can do justice to a student in less time then fifteen minutes.

Dr. MOORHOUSE—I was opposed to the fifteen minutes last year, and I am still opposed to it.

Dr. EMORY—I sat beside the examiner in Pathology a year or two ago, and candidates came up, and he started on Pathology, and the bell rang before he got to Therapeutics ; and when he started on Therapeutics the bell rang before he got to Pathology, and the student practically got nothing. There is but one exception in which on an examination a man does not have two subjects, and that is Anatomy. And I think fifteen minutes is not too long to find out what a man knows about Medical and Surgical Anatomy.

Dr. MOORHOUSE—If each examiner has two subjects I certainly think fifteen minutes is not too long.

Dr. EMORY—There is Medical Jurisprudence and Sanitary Science, Therapeutics and Pathology, Operative and Non-operative Midwifery, and Operative and Non-operative Surgery.

Dr. MOORHOUSE—I move that the clause be struck out.

On motion, Clause 5 of the report was struck out.

Dr. HENDERSON read Clause 6 of the report.

Dr. MOORHOUSE—There is no expense in keeping those wet specimens.

Dr. PYNE—Of course, it is a human body kept in alcohol. I think it was thought $50 was an excessive allowance for each examination ; there being two in the year, it is $100 a year.

Dr. WILLIAMS—I admit to having felt a very great deal of surprise to learn that the same subject was being used for the last five years. I supposed when we paid $100.00 a year for those specimens that we were paying for having fresh subjects prepared each year. I have the greatest objection to having poor specimens used. I think we should have the very best, and we are paying a good price to get the best. If we are not getting the best, then I think we should reduce the price. I admit that my preference would be, if that specimen that has been preserved for five years is not a first-class article, it should be set aside and new ones had each individual year.

Dr. GEIKIE—We have methods of preservation now that we knew nothing of years ago, but I am perfectly sure they are exceedingly careful to have them renewed as often as there is the least necessity.

Dr. DICKSON—Has there been any complaint on the part of the students ?

Dr. GEIKIE—I have not heard of any.

Dr. MOORHOUSE—The glycerine preparations will keep for fifty years. Are you quite sure, Dr. Pyne, that they are preserved in alcohol ?

Dr. Pyne.—Yes, I am sure it is alcohol ?

Dr. WILLIAMS—I admit I am not very familiar with the modern methods of preserving specimens, and if it is possible to have them kept in good condition I have no objection, but I have very serious objection to imperfect specimens being used. If they are at all imperfect, I think the examiners should be condemned, and condemned strongly.

The CHAIRMAN—That difficulty can be gotten over in this way, that when it is understood a new one is supplied he will get his $100.00. As I understand the clause, it so puts it.

Dr. ROGERS—Will you read the clause.

Dr. HENDERSON re-read the clause.

Dr. HENDERSON—We thought when we did not get a fresh specimen each year we should not pay this sum.

Dr. WILLIAMS—If the specimen is good and fit to be used, I think $25.00 is quite sufficient.

Dr. MOORHOUSE—I do not think Dr. Grasett would foist a bad specimen on us.

Dr. GEIKIE—I know Dr. Grasett very well ; he is one of the most difficult gentlemen to please, and if we tried to force him to use old specimens I am sure he would object just as hard as anyone ; he is a conscientious and faithful examiner. His attention only requires to be drawn to the fact to, I think, bring from him an emphatic contradiction. Nobody would sanction anything of that kind.

Dr. ARMOUR—I have no doubt that this specimen that has been used five years is quite up to the mark and is all that is desired in the way of a specimen, from what I have heard regarding it. In the first place the specimen, I believe, was valued by the Council at $50.00 and then for each examination $50.00 was paid every time the specimen was used. Now, it has been used five years. Of course, it is worth something to keep that specimen. I suppose it is kept at Dr. Grasett's. He was getting $50.00 and we thought that was rather too much under those circumstances and that $25.00 would be a liberal allowance for its use.

Dr. MOORHOUSE—I suppose the original idea was he had to get a fresh one for every examination.

Dr. ROGERS—Is it a full body dissected ?

Dr. PYNE—Yes.

Dr. ROGERS—Where is it kept ?

Dr. PYNE—Dr. Grasett keeps it himself. Probably he keeps it at Trinity College.

Dr. ROGERS—Does he allow Trinity students to see that specimen, too ?

Dr. PYNE—No, he is not that sort of man.

Dr. ROGERS—It is not kept in this Council building, where it ought to be kept.

Dr. PYNE—No.

Dr. ROGERS—It ought to be kept here.

Dr. PYNE—We have no vat.

Dr. ROGERS—We ought to have a vat ; it could be had at a very small expense. I would move that this Council purchase a vat.

Dr. SHAW—It has occurred to me that we should have a new specimen each year; the question of expense is not the only one to be considered, but also the question of whether the subject is not one that would become familiar to the students year after year. I do not for a moment suppose that the examiner in Anatomy will allow the specimen to be kept in any place where it would be open to students studying medicine ; I do not think he would do that, but it occurred to me, before Dr. Rogers made any remark, that it would be a very easy thing for the students who attend one year to familiarize the students of the next year, to some extent, with what the subject was like.

Dr. ROGERS—What would it cost to have a new specimen every year ?

Dr. PYNE—I do not know, I am sure.

Dr. MOORHOUSE—It would cost $25.00 for the body, to be ginwith, then something to dissect it.

Dr. CAMPBELL—In the meantime, this clause of the Committee's report say that as long as an old specimen is used every year $25.00 is enough.

On motion of Dr Henderson, clause 6 of the report was adopted.

Dr. HENDERSON read clause 7 of the report, and moved its adoption.

Dr. ARMOUR—I move that clause 7, as read, be erased and the following substituted therefor : "We recommend that the offices of Registrar and Treasurer remain separate, as at present, and that the Registrar shall receive a salary of $1,500.00 and the Treasurer a salary of $400.00." It has been said that it is outside of our power to amalgamate these two offices. I do not think it is. However, for my part, I would not approve of such an amalgamation ; I think it is very much better to have the two officers than one. I have had some experience regarding this in municipal matters, and I know it has generally not been at all so satisfactory to have them amalgamated in one as to have the offices separate. With regard to the salaries, we had this up a year or two ago ; I made some recommendations then regarding it, and just for your information I will read what I said then, and I may say that this proposition, if it is received, will reduce the Registrar's salary about $3 0.00. My own opinion is that since Dr. Pyne has a fairly lucrative practice of medicine probably by receiving $1,50).00 for his services here he will be well paid.

Dr. ROGERS—Will Dr. Henderson kindly read that clause again.

The CHAIRMAN—It has been moved that that clause be struck out, and that upon which Dr. Armour is speaking is a motion to amend the clause.

Dr. WILLIAMS—I would suggest before that matter is taken up that you separate the two offices.

The CHAIRMAN—That might be done by striking out the the the reference to the Treasurer; it would then read as follows : "We recommend that the offices of Registrar and Treasurer remain separate, as at present, and that the Registrar shall receive a salary of $1,500.00."

Dr. HEDERSON—Take the Treasurer's salary first, because we have another clause in regard to the Registrar's salary.

Dr. ARMOUR—I think I am in order. As I stated, I will read from page 169 of the Announcement of 1895-96 : "For the first ten years, up to 1876, the Registrar's salary was either $400.00 a year, or an unknown amount, paid from office receipts ; for the five years, from 1877 to 1881, inclusive, it was $750.00 ; for the three years, 1882, 1883 and 1884, it was $1,000.00 ; for the six years from 1885 to 1890 inclusive, it was $1,200.00 ; and since that time it has been $1,800.00 with some pickings." My opinion is that we might well reduce this under our present financial circumstances, and I think the Registrar would still be very well paid if we reduce it to $1,500.00 a year. I do not know whether it will be out of order for me to refer to a subsequent clause of this report, perhaps there would be no harm in doing so as it is connected with this, which recommends that commissions on the rents collected should not be allowed the Registrar, but that the Council allow him a stenographer instead. I know there was a feeling that the Treasurer's salary should be reduced, and some held the view that it might be reduced very materially. I disagree with this altogether, I have only proposed here a reduction of $100.00. It is a position of very considerable responsibility, the handling of the funds of this Council a large amount of money goes through the Treasurer's hands during the year, and I think that he should receive a fair compensation, and, in my opinion $400.00 is not at all too much. During the past year we have paid, perhaps under exceptional circumstances, $500.00 ; it is proposed now to reduce it to $400.00. If my amendment to that clause is carried we will save $600.00 in salaries, taking into consideration the question of the commission on rents. It seems to me that no one would have any just cause of complaint if this was done.

Dr. CAMPBELL—The succeeding clause in the Committee's report was read to us when the report was submitted and Dr. Armour has already referred to it. By that it seems the Committee propose to reduce the Registrar's emolument by cutting off the commission he has hitherto been in the habit of recieving for collecting rents. If that is done, I think that is about all the reduction that would be expedient and wise and fair in the case of the Registrar. I should be opposed to reducing the salary he is now receiving. The proposition to give the Treasurer $400.00 I have no objection to. I move to amend the amendment of Dr. Armour by striking out the portion that refers to the salary of the Registrar.

Dr. ROOME—If it is as Dr. Armour has read it, it is not an amendment at all.

Dr. ARMOUR—I moved that Clause 7 be erased and the other substituted for it.

Dr. ROOME—That does not refer to the same subject at all, therefore, you cannot put a substitutionary clause in.

Dr. ARMOUR—Clause 7 says : "The reduction of the Treasurer's salary or the amalgamation of the offices of Registrar and Treasurer."

Dr. ROGERS—I think we can ask for the Chairman's ruling as to whether this is an amendment to Clause 7 ; it is a substitution, but not an amendment.

The CHAIRMAN—It is not an amendment even from Dr. Armour's own point of view, because he starts out by directing that this clause (7) be erased ; consequently a clause that is erased cannot be amended.

Dr. ROGERS—And he substitutes something entirely different to the clause in the report.

Dr. ARMOUR—I can get at it in another way, but it takes some time to do it. I think you fully understand what I mean by that amendment, whether it is in order or not. It is only in Committee of the Whole, and it can finally be revised again when it comes before the Council. There can be no injurious result following the irregularity, if there is one.

The CHAIRMAN—You might get over it in this way, by directing that the clause be erased, and the matter fixing the Registrar's salary will come up later.

Dr. ARMOUR—We can move that the clause be erased and I will keep this clause which I have read and add it to the report subsequently.

Dr. ROGERS—The clause does not mean anything.

Dr. HENDERSON—The clause certainly contains merely a recommendation.

Dr. HENRY—I cannot vote for that.

Dr. WILLIAMS—This is a matter which is going to come up again before we are through with this report ; we do not need to split hairs as to whether it is exactly in order in that form. These two points are coming up, and we might just as well deal with them now as at any time. We are only wasting time in endeavoring to put them off to some future time. I think you might just as well let Dr. Armour state his motion and let it be dealt with at once.

Dr. ROGERS—The next clause of the report makes it clear as to what they wish done with regard to the Registrar's salary. This is not the proper clause to bring that amendment in on. I think the next one would be.

Dr. CAMPBELL—The next clause refers simply to the reduction of the Registrar's receipts by cutting off his commission. It strikes me that, while the point of order is literally correct, after all, you must remember that an amendment simply means that you strike out certain words and insert others. It would simplify matters perhaps to take Dr. Armour's amendment, and then take my amendment to his amendment, that the words " $1,500.00 " be stricken out and the words "$1,800.00" inserted ; that will fix the Treasurer's and Registrar's salaries, and then when the next clause comes up you can cut off the commission given to Dr. Pyne for collecting the rents.

Dr. ROOME—We might not be in favor of cutting off the commission. I do not want to raise any objection, I do not want to quibble about it, but I want to be in a position that I can vote conscientiously.

Dr. ARMOUR—No one has objected so far to the item with regard to the Treasurer ; and there is an opportunity now to vote whether the Registrar's salary shall be $1,500 or $1,800. I really cannot see the difficulty any member can have in voting on the question that is before the chair now.

The CHAIRMAN—I can put the motion as it is, and if any member desires to move an amendment it can be done.

Dr. DOUGLAS—Before that is put I rise for a little information. I am one of the junior members at this session, and I have had but little opportunity of learning the extent of the duties of the Registrar. I know something of what his duties are, but I do not know as to the extent of them, or what portion of his time is consumed in looking after matters in connection with this College. I would like to give an intelligent vote, but if the other members of this Council are cognizant of these facts I will not trouble any member of the College to give me the information that I ask now, but will simply ask that I be excused from voting, for without that information I am not in a position to give an intelligent vote, and I do not care to vote to reduce that salary if the work is worth the money. I infer from some of the remarks that have fallen from some of the senior members of this Council that they believe that the Registrar is not being paid too much, or if too much a very trifling sum in excess.

Dr. WILLIAMS—I think the President is in the room, and I have no doubt that he is as familiar with the work of the Registrar as any person else, and probably would state briefly whether or not there is an abundance of work for the pay received.

Dr. THORBURN—I do know something about the work and worth of the Registrar. During certain periods of the year, during the sitting of the Council and during the examinations, his work at this building commences at nine or ten o'clock in the morning and continues very often until after midnight. I am not prepared to say how many weeks in the year this is the case. At other times he is in the office a certain number of hours every day, but that does not answer the question altogether. He is constantly receiving letters and communications at all hours of the day and sometimes at night. Even when not here he is occupied, and as for his practice outside I am very sorry to say it is not very extensive, nor can it be extensive. It is understood he is doing the work of the College, and his time is to a very great extent occupied by it, but he seems to me to be a man of exceptional knowledge ; you can hardly refer to anything relating to the Council or profession that he

8

does not know ; and, what is more, he takes great pleasure in giving you information. He is a man of wonderful tact and good address. I never saw him lose his temper for one moment, and he certainly has very great provocation at times. He is ever ready to listen to the profession and to the students, and if he can give them any advice he is only too happy to do so, and I do not know of a more efficient officer in any office, or any institution, financial or otherwise, that is more efficiently served than this Council is by the present Registrar, and I maintain the salary of $1,800.00 is rather low, if anything. I would quite agree with taking away his commission, but in lieu of that I think we should supply him with a stenographer.

Dr. DOUGLAS—This $1,800.00 does not represent to him $1,800.00.

Dr. THORBURN—It is less than that. He pays a great deal of money for the services of a stenographer.

Dr. SANGSTER—There is no doubt about Dr. Pyne's efficiency. What are the hours set down ?

Dr. THORBURN—The hours are from two to four o'clock, but I say that does not represent the time. I come here frequently after five and six o'clock, and he is still here.   And oftentimes in the morning I communicate with him, and I am only one of a thousand people ; and he is asked all kinds of questions ; he frequently writes at home far more than he does here. He goes home and makes up his reports.

Dr. SANGSTER—Your proposition is to make no change ?

Dr. THORBURN—I would make no change in the $1,800.00, but I would take away his commission.

Dr. SANGSTER—You would give him a stenographer?

Dr. MOORHOUSE—What would a stenographer be worth ?

Dr. ARMOUR—In 1889 it was found that Dr. Pyne had been furnished with a stenographer at a cost to the Council of $120.00 a year. We struck that out ; we did not allow him that during the session of 1895 and he has paid for his own stenographer ; it was the understanding with the Council that he should pay his own stenograhper since that time.

Dr. MOORE—I might say for Dr. Douglas' information that Dr. Pyne receives and answers over thirty letters in a day, and his postage account is over $700.00 ; that will give some idea of what the Registrar's work is.

Dr. MACHELL—While the office hours of the Registrar are from two to four o'clock, he is practically here all afternoon.

Dr. SHAW—If anybody wishes to see him he is here, but he wishes to have the other hours free so that he can leave if he is called away in an emergency.

Dr. THORBURN—He does more in his own house than he does here.

Dr. MACHELL—Another reason why it is advisable to have the office hours from two to four is that he may be free to do a certain amount of office work, and be free from outsiders coming in.

Dr. THORNTON—As a member of the Council I am in favor of every possible economy, but in carrying out that idea we are placing ourselves in a very peculiar position. Last year a motion was brought before this Council to reduce the sessional indemnity of the members ; but the members wouldn't stand it at all, and until we are prepared to be in with ourselves I am not prepared to make any very radical changes in the salaries of the working officers of this Council. I think on principle the commissions in connection with the revenue derived from this building should under no circumstances be allowed to Dr. Pyne ; and taking that view of the matter I would be inclined to support Dr. Campbell's amendment. The idea of placing ourselves in the position of being masters of the situation and positively refusing to reduce our own indemnity, and robbing the officers of the Council in this direction, I consider is inconsistent.

Dr. BROCK—In bringing in this report to the Council I believe the members of this Committee were to a great extent agreed that if we took away Dr. Pyne's commissions which he received, and which we thought we ought to take away from him, we would not touch his salary ; and I for one would not support the cutting down of the salary after taking away that sum of money from him. I would support the motion that the Treasurer receive the sum of $300.00, which I thought at the time was fair and sufficient. Old Dr. Aikins did that work for nothing for years. I think $300.00 would be sufficient.

Dr. THORNTON—I am prepared to materially reduce the sessional indemnity to the members of this Council, and I would have endeavored to reduce it long ago if I had thought I could have accomplished it.

Dr. HENDERSON— It was not the intention of the majority of the Committee to reduce Dr. Pyne's salary. As you will see from the next clause, they merely intended he should not receive the commissions from the rents, but that he should have the same salary.

The CHAIRMAN stated Dr. Campbell's amendment that the words " $1,500.00 " in Dr. Armour's amendment be erased and the words " $1,800.00 " inserted in lieu thereof, which a vote having been taken was declared carried

The CHAIRMAN stated Dr. Armour's amendment as amended as follows : "That clause 7 of the report be erased, and the following substituted therefor, 'We recommend that the offices of Registrar and Treasurer remain separate, as at present, and that the Registrar receive a salary of $1,800.00 and the Treasurer a salary of $400.00.'"

Dr. HENRY—What is the security we demand from the Treasurer in the performance of his duties to the Council ? If it is $10,000.00 it will take all his salary to pay the per centage to get that security.

Dr. ARMOUR—The question has been put.

Dr. WILLIAMS—Dr. Henry has raised the question as to the amount of security required by this Council from the Treasurer.

The CHAIRMAN—I think he was told by somebody $10,000.00.

Dr. WILLIAMS—If the Treasurer has to give $10,000.00 security it will take his whole salary.

Dr. THORBURN— I may say that in other institutions the institution pays half and the official half.

Dr. ARMOUR—My own opinion is we should have a bond for from seven to ten thousand dollars,

DR. WILLIAMS—Can the Treasurer draw the money which he deposits out of the bank without having the cheque for it countersigned ? If it has to be countersigned, then there is no object in demanding such large security from the Treasurer.

Dr. ARMOUR—He cannot draw it out of the bank without the cheque being counter-signed, but at times Dr. Aikins during last year has deposited at one time upwards of $7,000.00.

Dr. WILLIAMS—That would show that at some time he had $7,000.00 in his hands.

Dr. ARMOUR—He deposits what he receives during the month.

Dr. WILLIAMS—Under those circumstances it would seem that $10,000.00 security is not too large.

Dr. CAMPBELL—And under those circumstances the salary of the Treasurer would really be about $300.00, if it was made $400.00.

Dr. SHAW—I have just learned from the Treasurer that there are no bonds.

Dr. ARMOUR—Last year it was $4,000.00. The Treasurer in $2,000.00 and two securities of $1,000.00 each.

Dr. THORBURN—I am informed by the Treasurer that he makes a bank deposit every day. He does not wait till the end of the month.

Dr. SANGSTER—How large would be his largest deposit.

Dr. THORBURN—I don't know.

Dr. SANGSTER—Not probably more than $500.00 or $1,000.00.

Dr. THORBURN—No, not as much. You can see in the bank book what his daily deposits were.

Dr. SANGSTER—It was incidentally mentioned here just now that the securities that were ordered by the Council last year were never executed. I would like to know if that is the case ?

Dr. SHAW—I believe that is the case. I believe they were not executed. The member of the Council who was here last year, who is not present this year, failed to have them executed.

Dr. DICKSON—Under what circumstances ?

DR. SHAW—I do not know that.

Dr. ROGERS—I think that is a painful thing to talk about. We cannot speak of a thing which occurs on the part of a member who is not with us now. It is something which happened, which is an oversight to a large extent.

Dr. SANGSTER—In a matter of such importance as that, that this Council gravely orders and decides that it is necessary that bonds should be executed on the part of one of its executive officers I claim this Council is entitled to the fullest information.

Dr. MOORE—You cannot get it from the dead.

Dr. ROOME—(Referring to bank deposit book) The most that has ever been deposited at one time was $1,270.00. Last year at one time there was deposited $2,900.00, he having held it over Saturday, and Monday being a holiday, but the most at any other time since was $1,200.00.

Dr. ARMOUR—There is nothing to hinder the Treasurer from keeping the money as long as he chooses.

Dr. ROGERS—I think he ought to give a small bond of two or three thousand dollars.

Dr. CAMPBELL—The question of the Treasurer's bond hardly comes in here now ; I think we should settle the question of the Treasurer's salary.

Dr. WILLIAMS—I think the question of the bonds only comes in incidentally to get at what salary he will have left when he pays for the bonds. I myself think the bonds ought to be somewhere in the neighborhood of $5,000.00. I do not think $5,000.00 would be an unreasonable amount to ask him to put up, then there would be the cost of obtaining that amount. I think I heard some gentleman say about $15.00 a thousand ; if that is what the Guarantee Companies ask, that would be in the neighborhood of about $75.00 ; so that if he got a salary of $400.00 there would be about $325.00 left.

Dr. BROCK—When this Council accepts its auditor's report the Guarantee Company is released. That holds good with regard to a public corporation.

Dr. LUTON—I would like to enquire as to the average amount of money that remains in the bank from one end of the year to the other to the credit of this institution, and whether such balance draws any interest or not, and if it does, who gets it ?

Dr. ROOME—There is no direct interest given for it, but there is a note, and as soon as a certain sum comes in the bank allows him to take so much off the note, which is practically the same thing as interest ; the Council gets the benefit of it.

The CHAIRMAN stated Dr. Armour's motion as amended which, on a vote being taken, was declared carried.

Dr. HENDERSON read Clause 8 of the report, and moved its adoption.

Dr. ROOME—I do not see that we are going to make any particular saving by that clause. If we take away the commission we have to supply him with a stenographer, and if we allow him the commission he has to engage his own stenographer, which will cost him about $130.00 a year. It is a question whether it would not be an inducement to allow him the commission. If he can raise a larger sum by inducing tenants to remain, and get new tenants to come in, he will strive harder to do so if he gets a commisssion on what he collects. It is saving we are after, and if we cannot make a saving by taking away this commission, I do not think we ought to interfere.

Dr. ARMOUR—I would move that that clause be amended in this way, that the clause in connection with Clause 8, which reads as follows, be erased : "If this clause meets with your approval, we recommend that the Council pay the Registrar's stenographer." I think that the Registrar will be pretty well paid with the $1,800.00 that we have assigned him now, and that he should pay his own stenographer, and perhaps if he paid his own stenographer the work would be just as well done.

Dr. HENRY—What would it cost yearly for a stenographer ?

Dr. ARMOUR—It was $120.00 in 1895.

Dr. PYNE—I don't think it will cost that much now under the arrangement I have, because I just pay per folio ; some months it is more and some months less. I don't think it will go over that amount at any rate.

Dr. WILLIAMS—I think the question raised by Dr. Roome is worthy of consideration. He throws out the idea that the Registrar is a piece of ordinary human nature. We were inclined to think sometimes that he was a little more than that, a little higher, and that possibly he hadn't the appreciation of the dollars and cents that possibly the rest of us have. If what Dr. Roome says is true, that he is actuated by the same motives as the rest of us, there is no question that if we were doing the business we would look after renting the building with a good deal more energy if the pay was a little better. If, on the other hand, you took from us the compensation, I just question whether the rest of us would feel the same zeal—if it were a patient, in running after a patient that paid us nothing as in running after a patient that paid us something. If Dr. Pyne is of the same human nature as the rest of us, that which will put most zeal into his work is to allow him for the work done. If we take that matter home to ourselves, what would we do ? Would you feel the same zeal in hitching up your horse and going out in the storm and attending a patient where you knew you would never get a cent as you would where there was a hope of reward ? The hope of reward has a great deal to do with the speed with which we get to patients, although we may go as a matter of duty to attend patients. I recollect hearing of an English physician who, when he examined even one of his own, took a guinea out of one pocket and put it into the pocket where he put the fees which he received, in order to make himself believe that he was being paid. I think that the rest of us are just about made up in that way, that we would display a great deal more zeal in doing work, and look after it with the proper energy if we were to be compensated in some way for it. You take the commission away, and there is no special reason why Dr. Pyne should make any special effort in regard to the matter, only in so far as he is not given to neglecting any of his duties. We would hope that he would not neglect that, but while that is true in an honorable man, it is the other side of human nature that requires taking care of sometimes, and I believe that we must remember the human nature while we are dealing with the Registrar as well as with ourselves. I think the better way is to let him pay his own stenographer and we pay him a reasonable commission on the work done in connection with the building. If that commission is too large, reduce it to a smaller amount ; but certainly the best way, in my mind, is to pay the commission for the work done.

Dr. BARRICK—There is no doubt that the amount of work that is done by the Registrar is very great ; it is well done, it is cheerfully done, it is done early, it is done late, and I would prefer paying him a straight salary, whether it is $1,800.00 or $1,900.00, without a commission. If the argument adduced by Dr. Williams is the correct one, then perhaps if we were to pay him a commission upon the collection of the annual fee we might perhaps get more money in, but I do not for a moment think that Dr. Pyne would be influenced in that way. I think we should pay him a good salary and have him do all the work and employ what help he requires, but let it be a straight salary apart from any commissions. When the question of paying him $1,800.00 was up, it was with the understanding that the commissions were to be struck off. Whether it be more, or whether it be less, let it be a straight salary without any commissions, without paying any typewriters or anything else. I think that would be far preferable. I think Dr. Pyne will take just as much interest in renting the rooms and in collecting the rents as he will if we paid him a salary and a commission, like a commercial traveller who goes out and is paid so much salary and so much commission.

Dr. MOORHOUSE—I quite agree with Dr. Barrick that when that $1,800.00 was decided upon as the salary of the Registrar, it was with the distinct understanding that that was to be all he should receive, and we would be breaking faith with the former vote if we allowed him more now. I have every confidence that our Registrar will do just as well and will exert himself with as great zeal as he would if he got ten per cent. where he only gets five now ; and I would cast all thoughts of anything about human nature aside entirely, I would not think of that for a second, and I think as the vote originally was for $1,800.00 we have no right to interfere with that now. He was to do the work of collecting the rents, and the understanding was that we, as a Council, were to pay his stenographer.

Dr. ARMOUR—I didn't understand it that way. The understanding was that the $1,800.00 should go without commissions. However, supposing we leave it just as it is now, if the amendment I moved does not carry it will not affect the cost at all materially ; if the stenographer costs $120.00 a year and the Registrar's commissions from rents amount to about $200.00 a year, there will only be a difference of about $75.00

Dr. ROOME—At that time the other resolution had not come up; and here we find that we are going to pay for a stenographer $120.00 a year, and the Registrar only got $150.00 in commissions the year before last and this last year something over $200.00 and we have no guarantee, owing to a building that is being built alongside of us, whether he will get $120.00 for commissions during the coming year. If we cannot benefit ourselves is it not better to leave it in his own hands to engage his stenographer and pay her what he likes and allow this commission to remain as it is? If we were going to save $200.00 by it I would say save it.

Dr. THORNTON—When I voted a few minutes ago it was with the distinct understanding that when we paid $1,800.00 we were done paying. Ever since I have been in this Council we have continually got the cart before the horse, and we have been mixed up in that way year after year. In voting we have voted that a certain sum be given Dr. Pyne and I think that should be the end of it—that is a business view of it—otherwise, a man does not know what he is doing. I generally agree with a great deal of what Dr. Williams says, but from my acquaintance with Dr. Pyne I have not the least misgiving whatever in connection with the way he will do the work. I admit Dr. Williams has known Dr. Pyne longer than I have, but I am not prejudiced, in Dr. Pyne's case, on that account at all. (Laughter.)

Dr. WILLIAMS—I presume the assumption is that Dr. Pyne is made of somewhat better clay than the rest of us. I gathered from what Dr. Roome and some others said that he was of the same kind of human nature. I know, speaking for the rest of us, that it would make a difference where there was a hope of reward ; that with Dr. Pyne it will not do so shows that he is made of better clay than the rest of us.

The CHAIRMAN—The clause in connection with Clause 8 reads as follows : "If this clause meets with your approval we recommend that the Council pay the Registrar's stenographer."

Dr. MOORHOUSE—We voted the $1,800.00 on the understanding that we pay for the stenographer.

Dr. ROGERS—That is right.

The CHAIRMAN stated Dr. Armour's motion that the clause in connection with Clause 8. which reads as follows, be erased. "If this clause meets with your approval we recommend that the Council pay the Registrar's stenographer."

Dr. ROGERS—That erases both the commission and the stenographer. .

The CHAIRMAN—It does not refer to the commission here. This is all Dr. Armour proposes to erase : "If this clause meets with your approval we recommend that the Council pay the Registrar's stenographer," and that the balance of Clause 8 should remain.

Dr. ROGERS—What is the balance of the clause ?

Dr. ARMOUR—The balance of the clause strikes out the commission, but the balance of the clause has not yet been passed upon. We have to pass on this motion first, and then the balance of the clause afterwards.

Dr. WILLIAMS—If I get a proper understanding of it, one part strikes out the commission and the other part strikes out the stenographer.

Dr. Armour—We are only striking out the part with regard to the stenographer now. If we vote this motion down then the Registrar gets the stenographer and the commission too.

Dr. Moore—If this motion of Dr. Armour's is voted down the stenographer stands, and then we can vote the commission away from the Registrar.

The Chairman—Quite so. This clause clearly does away with the intention of the Council to pay the stenographer.

Dr. Williams—The only part that is carried so far is changing the Registrar's salary back to $1,800.00 ?

The Chairman—Yes.

Dr. Williams—Then we come to this clause, and we have carried nothing with reference to the commissions ?

The Chairman—No.

Dr. Williams—Then we are dealing with the three items?

The Chairman—Two. You dealt with the salary in the former clause. The clause you are dealing with now is as to the stenographer and the commission.

Dr. Sangster—It is all to me just as clear as mud, and it is made considerably clearer by the consciousness that the Council pays for no stenographer, and therefore I cannot understand a reference to it in that connection at all.

The Chairman—In this clause it was proposed that the Council should pay for a stenographer.

Dr. Brock—As I understand it, we give Dr. Pyne $1,800.00 a year, and he does our work for us. This building belongs to the College, and he will collect the rents as a part of his business and he will also do the work, as we expect him to do, as Registrar.

Dr. Moorhouse—And that we furnish him a stenographer.

Dr. Sangster—Although I did not intend to speak upon the question, of the two I would infinitely prefer to leave things as they are. First, because I think there is a good deal in what Dr. Williams argued, that it would be a spur, even to Dr. Pyne, to obtain tenants for unoccupied rooms, to feel that there was not only the approbation of this Council behind him, but there was a certain anticipatory jingle in his pockets connected therewith. In the second place, when the Registrar pays the stenographer he is apt to be a little more economical in regard to the stenographer's services than if the Council pays the stenographer. I think he would be more or less than human if it did not make a difference.

The Chairman stated Dr. Armour's motion.

Dr. Sangster—If that clause is erased, it then leaves it open to the Council to continue the arrangement that exists at present ; that is, to vote a commission to the Registrar ?

The Chairman—In order to do so it will be necessary to carry the clause as amended by this motion.

Dr. Rogers—I move in amendment that the clause be erased.

Dr. Shaw—I second that.

Dr. Sangster—I would move that the Council discontinue its discussion, and rise and report progress, and that the Council be a deputation to wait upon the official solicitor to get that motion put in shape. (Laughter.)

Dr. Henderson read Clause 8.

Dr. Rogers—I move that the whole clause be struck out.

Dr. Campbell—You have got to dispose of the amendment.

The Chairman puts Dr. Armour's motion, that the clause in connection with Clause 8, which reads as follows, be erased : " If this clause meets with your approval we recommend that the Council pay the Registrar's stenographer," which, on a vote having been taken, was declared lost.

Dr. Dickson put Dr. Rogers' motion, seconded by Dr. Shaw, that Clause 8 of the report be struck out, which, on a vote having been taken, was declared carried.

Dr. Henderson read Clause 9 of the report and moved its adoption, which, on a vote having been taken, was declared carried.

Dr. Henderson read Clause 10 of the report and moved its adoption.

Dr. Sangster—I do not propose to avail myself of this clause to make any remarks, because I am assured the subject can come up again afterwards, and I merely wish to give notice that it will come up afterwards, because we will have to substitute a motion going over the ground of the daily indemnity to members. I have been told that the adoption of that report does not prevent us bringing up that or any other subject we may choose to bring up in the Council.

Dr. Roome—I must take exception to that, because we will be here all summer. (Laughter.)

Dr. Sangster—In the earlier part of this discussion I rose and asked the question, whether an erasure from that report would commit this Council to silence in the future sessions of the present term of this Council, and I was told, No. Dr. Campbell and others got up and told me that this was merely an expression of opinion and was not the regular report of the Finance Committee, and it was open to us to reconsider any item that was there discussed and dealt with. I shall consider that I have been the victim of a gross breach of faith if there is any attempt on the part of this Council to close my mouth on that or the subjects connected with that in the remaining sessions of this Council.

Dr. CAMPBELL—I did say that as to a number of clauses that were then under discussion, but with regard to this clause, I think there is a recommendation that we adopt a certain thing, and I think if we pass that we are committed.

Dr. SANGSTER—It will meet my view to bring the subject up in the Council at a future session, and obtain an expression of opinion from it to that effect, because I can ask for the yeas and nays on that point equally as well as upon the point of reducing the indemnity paid to the members of this Council.

Dr. WILLIAMS—There is one legitimate way by which Dr. Sangster can attain his object, and that is this, this report is simply passed through Committee of the Whole ; when this Committee rises it is necessary that the report shall be adopted in the Council ; when a motion is made to adopt that report, Dr. Sangster has it open to him to move an amendment that it be not adopted, but be referred to the Committee of the Whole. That is Dr. Sangster's only method of getting it before the Council this year.

Dr. SANGSTER—I am perfectly prepared to go on ; I can stay here as long as others can, and talk as long as others can. I want to understand whether I am at liberty to continue the discussion to-night, or whether, in order that we may close at a decent hour, I shall be at liberty to take up this matter again ? If that is so, I would move that the Committee rise and report progress.

Dr. WILLIAMS—The Committee simply requires to rise ; by rising they do not adopt the report in the Council, The Committee can rise now, then you can move to adjourn without a motion to adopt the report in Council.

Dr. SANGSTER—All I want is to be treated in good faith, so as not to have my mouth closed. I am prepared to go on to-night if you decide to do so, but I would prefer its being ̇eft over until to-morrow morning ; but it is for the Council to decide what shall be done.

Dr. HENDERON again read Clause 10 of the report, which, on a vote having been taken, was declared carried.

Dr. HENDERSON moved that the Committee rise and report, which, on a vote having been taken, was declared carried.

The Committee rose, the President in the chair.

On motion of Dr. CAMPBELL, seconded by Dr. ROGERS, the Council adjourned, to meet at ten o'clock a.m., Friday, July 9th, 1897.

FOURTH DAY.

FRIDAY, July 9th, 1897.

The Council met at ten o'clock a.m., in accordance for motion for adjournment.

The PRESIDENT (Dr. Thorburn) in the chair.

The REGISTRAR called the roll, and the following members answered to their names :—
Drs. Armour, Bray, Brock, Campbell, Dickson, Douglas, Geikie, Graham, Griffin, Hanly, Henderson, Henry, Logan, Luton, Machell, Moorhouse, McLaughlin, Reddick, Rogers, Roome, Sangster, Thorburn, Thornton, Williams.·

The minutes of the previons meeting were read by the Registrar, confirmed and signed by the President.

NOTICES OF MOTION.

Dr. ARMOUR—To introduce a by-law to fix the salary of the Treasurer.

Dr. ROGERS—To appoint a Legislative Committee.

COMMUNICATIONS, PETITIONS, ETC.

None.

Dr. BRAY—I was sorry I was not in the room yesterday when you made your motion, Dr. Sangster, in reference to the commutation of fees ; if I had been here I would have asked you to refer that to the Finance Committee, who have dealt with that kind of thing before. I think you can get the information you want from them and I would move, with your consent, that that be referred to the Finance Committee.

Dr. SANGSTER—To report when ?

Dr. BRAY—As soon as possible this session.

Dr. SANGSTER—I have no objection to that.

Dr. BRAY moved, seconded by Dr. MOORHOUSE, that, with the consent of the Council, Dr. Sangster's motion introduced in reference to the commutation of fees be referred to the Finance Committee, which, on a vote having been taken, was declared carried.

Dr. ARMOUR—I understood the first order of business to-day was to be the consideration of the report we left off yesterday evening.

The PRESIDENT—Yes, we are ready for it.

Dr. CAMPBELL—I do not know that there was a special order fixed. I think that is unfinished business.

Dr. ROOME—To-day being Friday, I think it would be well for this Council to adjourn to allow the committees to do their work so that they can report this afternoon ; I think it is very important to do this if we expect to get the work done this week. I would move, seconded by Dr. Campbell, that the Council do now rise and adjourn until 2 o'clock p.m., for the purpose of allowing the Committees to meet and prepare their reports.

Dr. SANGSTER—We did that the day before yesterday and we practically lost the whole of the evening session, and we certainly have no time to lose; but if the Council is clearly of the opinion that that would expedite matters, I would say adopt that course.

Dr. BRITTON—Do I understand the resolution correctly ? I think it was stated by. Dr. Roome that it was desirable to adjourn now and meet at 2 o'clock this afternoon.

The PRESIDENT—That is what I understand.

Dr. BRITTON—I might say that the Education Committee has yet some very important matters to consider, and I think it would take all our time between now and two o'clock to get matters in complete shape for presentation this afternoon.

The PRESIDENT—Is it your pleasure that the Council do now stand adjourned until two o'clock ?

Dr. THORNTON—Would it not be well before we adjourn, if there are any reports, to have them read now ?

The PRESIDENT—That will rest entirely with the Council.

Dr. ARMOUR—Mr. President, the Finance Committee have a great deal of work to do yet. We have been so constantly in the Council that we have not been able to get on as we desired. This report that was left over last night will only take a few minutes to complete it ; there are a few votes I would like to have on it and then we would know how to proceed with our estimate in the Finance Committee ; if that were disposed of I would have no objection to the adjournment.

Dr. BRAY—I think the motion of Dr. Roome is a very proper one. Dr. Armour knows well enough we have got a good deal to do in the Finance Committee and we have a lot to do in the Education Committee, and I think it will expedite matters to adjourn. The trouble has been in the past that the reports of these committees are rushed through at the very last moment, and some things slip in that would not be there, and other things are omitted that should be there. I think we should give due consideration to these committees so that they may be in a position to give satisfactory reports. (Cries of " Question, question.")

Dr. MACHELL—Before adjourning I would like to move the reception of the report of the Property Committee.

The PRESIDENT—Has that been read and discussed ? (Cries of "question, question."

Dr HENRY—We ought to finish that report we were discussing last night so late ; it was understood that we would.

The PRESIDENT stated the motion.

Dr. SANGSTER—I claim that that would be a distinct breach of faith. It was distinctly understood that the first order of busines—

The PRESIDENT—It will rest with the Council.

The PRESIDENT put the motion for adjournment which, on a vote having been taken, was declared carried.

The Council adjourned to meet at two o'clock p.m.

AFTERNOON SESSION.

The Council met at two o'clock p.m. in accordance with motion for adjournment.

The PRESIDENT (Dr. Thorburn) in the chair.

The REGISTRAR called the roll, and the following members answered to their names : Drs. Armour, Bray, Britton, Brock, Campbell, Dickson, Douglas, Emory, Fowler, Graham, Griffin, Hanley, Henderson, Henry, Logan, Luton, Moore, McLaughlin, Reddick, Rogers, Roome, Sangster, Thorburn, Thornton, Williams. The minutes of the previous meeting were read by the Registrar, and confirmed, and signed by the President.

Dr. BRAY—In accordance with a notice of motion which I gave on the first day of meeting, I now move that the Council go into Committee of the whole to consider the report of the Discipline Committee *re* one Charles John Parsons. The notice of motion I gave was that this should be the first order of business at two o'clock to-day.

The PRESIDENT—That is so. This morning we had a similar case, and we did not go on with it.

Dr. BRAY—This is a different thing. I move that this matter be taken up now, and then I will read the report the first time.

The PRESIDENT—This is a special thing which Dr. Bray gave notice of the first day of the Council meeting.

Dr. BRAY—This is a very particular report, and it has to go through in a legal way. The reason I gave notice of motion so early was, we had a meeting of our committee on Monday last to fix on a time when this report should come before this Council and send a notice to that effect to be served on the defendant in this case and on his solicitor, this notice has been sent, and we have the affidavit back showing that the notice has been served according to law, and I think this should be gone into at once.

The PRESIDENT—The Council agreed to this notice of motion at the time.

Dr. McLAUGHLIN—A notice of motion is not sufficient to do this.

Dr. BRAY—I now move that.

Dr. McLAUGHLIN—Was a motion carried that this should have precedence ?

Dr. BRITTON—It was carried.

Dr. BRAY read the report of the Discipline Committee *re* Charles John Parsons as follows :

To the President and Members of the Council of the College of Physicians and Surgeons of Ontario:

Your Committee on Discipline beg to report that during the past year they have had before them the case of Charles John Parsons, and have held an investigation thereon, particulars of which are appended to the end of this report, together with the findings of your Committee thereon. There is also appended a copy of the evidence submitted and the proceedings taken before your Committee. All of which is respectfully submitted.

JOHN L. BRAY, Chairman.

To the President and Members of the Council of the College of Physicians and Surgeons of Ontario :

Your Committee appointed to enquire into the facts beg leave to report as follows : *Re* Charles John Parsons, M.D. For erasure from the Register as a member and registered practitioner of the College of Physicians and Surgeons of Ontario. Your Committee duly met, after notice of the charges in the subject matter of the enquiry to be conducted had been given to the said Charles John Parsons, who did not appear personally but was represented by Counsel, on the 28th day of October, 1896, at the City of Belleville, in the County of Hastings, when witnesses were examined in support of the petition and when the letter hereto annexed dated the said 28th day of October, 1896, from the said Charles John Parsons to your Committee was read ; and after hearing the evidence, a transcript of which accompanies this report, your Committee arrived at the following conclusions :

CHARGE NO. 1.—That the said Charles John Parsons has been guilty of infamous or disgraceful conduct in a professional respect, the particulars of which are as follows : That the said Charles John Parsons did in or about the month of October, 1894, extort money from one A. E. Finley of the township of Calendar in the County of Lennox and Addington, by means of threats that he would cause the said Finley to be prosecuted under the provisions of the Ontario Medical Act, for practising medicine, not being a registered medical practitioner. Your Committee report that this charge is proven.

CHARGE NO. 2.—That the said Charles John Parsons has been guilty of infamous or disgraceful conduct in a professional respect, the particulars of which are as follows : That the said Charles John Parsons did in or about the month of October, 1894, extort money from one J. R. A. Caldwell, of the Township of Caledar in the County of Lennox and Addington, by means of threats that he would cause the said Caldwell to be prosecuted under the provisions of the Ontario Medical Act, for practising medicine, not being a registered medical practitioner. Your Committee find that this charge is proven.

CHARGE NO. 3.—That the said Charles John Parsons has been guilty of infamous or disgraceful conduct in a professional respect, the particulars of which are as follows : That the said Charles John Parsons did in or about the month of October, 1894, enter into an agreement with A. E. Finley and J. R. A. Caldwell of the Township of Caledar in the County of Lennox and Addington well knowing that they were not registered medical practitioners, whereby said Parsons in consideration of a sum of money, agreed not to prosecute, disturb, hinder or inform upon the said Finley and Caldwell in the unlawful practice of medicine contrary to the provisions of the Ontario Medical Act ; and further in that the said Charles John Parsons having received the money agreed to be paid as aforesaid, nevertheless caused the said Finley and Caldwell to be prosecuted and fined for unlawfully practising medicine contrary to the provisions of the said Act. Your Committee find that this charge is proven.

CHARGE No. 4.—That the said Charles John Parsons has been guilty of infamous or disgraceful conduct in a professional respect, the particulars of which are as follows : That the said Charles John Parsons extorted money from one J. R. Helms, residing near Arden Post Office, in the County of Lennox and Addington, under threats of prosecuting the said Helms for violation of the Ontario Medical Act, and well knowing that the said Helms was not a registered medical practitioner, entered into an agreement with him that in consideration of payment of a certain sum of money he would not prosecute, disturb, hinder or inform upon the said Helms in the illegal practice of medicine, and further that he the said Parsons, having entered into the said agreement with the said Helms and received the money in pursuance thereof, nevertheless informed against the said Helms and caused him to be prosecuted and fined for practising medicine contrary to the said Act. Your Committee find that this charge is not proven.

CHARGE No. 5.—That the said Charles John Parsons has been guilty of infamous or disgraceful conduct in a professional respect, the particulars of which are as follows : That the said Charles John Parsons attempted to extort money or other valuable consideration from one George Shaw, of the village of Queensborough, in the County of Hastings, by threats of informing against the said George Shaw and causing him to be prosecuted for violation of the Ontario Medical Act. Your Committee find that on this charge no evidence was submitted.

CHARGE No. 6.—That the said Charles John Parsons has been guilty of infamous or disgraceful conduct in a professional respect, the particulars of which are as follows : That the said Charles John Parsons at various times between December 1st, 1894, and May 1st, 1895, attempted to extort money or other valuable consideration from one Boothby, of the village of of Coe Hill, in the County of Hastings, by threats of prosecution under the Ontario Medical Act and the Ontario Pharmacy Act, and for selling liquor without a license. Your Committee find that this charge is proven.

CHARGE No. 7.—That the said Charles John Parsons has been guilty of infamous or disgraceful conduct in a professional respect, the particulars of which are as follows : That the said Charles John Parsons attempted to extort money or other valuable consideration from one J. R. Harding, of the village of Coe Hill, in the County of Hastings, by threats of prosecution for practising medicine contrary to the Ontario Medical Act. Your Committee find that this charge is proven.

CHARGE No. 8.—That the said Charles John Parsons has been guilty of infamous or disgraceful conduct in a professional respect, the particulars of which are as follows : That the said Charles John Parsons attempted to extort money or other valuable consideration from one R. Robinson, of the village of Maynooth, in the County of Hastings, by threats of prosecution for practising medicine contrary to the provisions of the Ontario Medical Act, and afterwards for valuable consideration aided the said Robinson to escape the consequences of his said act. Your Committee report that no evidence was submitted on this charge.

CHARGE No. 9.—That the said Charles John Parsons has been guilty of infamous or disgraceful conduct in a professional respect, the particulars of which are as follows : That the said Charles John Parsons travelled about from place to place in the more northern and sparsely populated parts of Ontario, and having ascertained the names of a large number of persons including those above mentioned, who were practising medicine illegally, not being registered medical practitioners, approached such persons with a fraudulent and dishonest scheme to extort money from them by threats of prosecution, pretending that he, the said Parsons, desired to settle in the neighborhood, and would compel them to cease practising unless they paid him a certain sum of money by way of blackmail. Your Committee find that this charge was proven.

Your Committee also beg to state that the Registrar has notified the said Charles John Parsons to appear before this Council on Friday, 9th inst., at two o'clock.

Appended to this report is a copy of the evidence submitted, the proceedings taken before your Committee, copies of certain exhibits produced on the before mentioned investigation, together with a copy of the admissions made by Mr. E. G. Porter, solicitor for Dr. Parsons, on his behalf.

All of which is respectfully submitted.

Dated the 9th day of July, 1897. Signed on behalf of the Committee.

JOHN L. BRAY, Chairman.

APPENDIX TO REPORT OF DISCIPLINE COMMITTEE.

The following is a copy of the Exhibits referred to at the close of the report of the Discipline Committee, *re* Charles John Parsons.

Letter marked " Exhibit 5," reads as follows :

ORMSBY, 9th Dec., 1894.

"WITHOUT PREJUDICE."

Mr. Boothby, Coe Hill.

SIR,—A friend informed me of Coe Hill as a good place for a medical man ; he told me of the existence of three unlicensed practitioners and of a good drug store. As the profession is so overcrowded in the front and being fond of sport, I concluded that I would do fairly well where three already existed, and a place that would keep a drug store would surely keep a doctor. At a very considerable loss and expense I came to Coe Hill, and was much disappointed. However, I resolved to give the country a trial. I wrote to Mr. Harding, and informed him of my arrival, and requested both Mr. Harper and himself to cease practice. I did not serve you with a similar notice because I did not then know but what you had a perfect right to keep a drug store. I now find that you have no such right and that you are liable at any time to arrest. That is my information from headquarters. Now, I have received a very liberal offer from a gentleman at Coe Hill of a house, garden, wood, pasture, etc., etc. If I accept it, which I am inclined to do, it puts you in a rather awkward position, and to be plain I will explain that position. Mr. Harding will have to cease practice, and you will have to stop the sale of drugs, and as there has been misrepresentations made to the neighborhood that the former was a qualified English doctor, and that you were a qualified English druggist, I shall be compelled to take warrants against both of you and prove to all what claims you really have. The place of trial would depend on my solicitor's advice. This is what I am empowered to do, but it is not how I am inclined to act, and simply out of regard for you, though I have never met you. You are already in possession, and to save a considerable amount of money, etc., etc., for both of us, I will tell you what I will do. You know the value of your business to you and whether it will be to your interests to give it up and be fined. You and Mr. Harding give me a reasonable amount to cover my expenses, and I will leave the neighborhood. This may seem at first sight a little hard on you, but still you have had a good thing for some years, and you have had it illegally. You cannot expect me to let you rob me of what I am licensed to do and protected by the law to do, and that is just what you have done for two months. To-day is Saturday ; I expect to hear from you by Monday's mail ; after that I shall act as it suits me. I want you to distinctly to understand that there is no atttempt at blackmail, and that this offer is made without prejudice, and I believe I am acting against my own interests, as I have been offered a lucrative partnership in Coe Hill. You had better see Dr. Harding, if it interests you.

I am, etc.,

(Signed.) C. PARSONS.

Certificate marked "Exhibit 9 " reads as follows :

COE HILL, May 27th, 1895.

This is to certify that in the matter of the Ontario College of Pharmacy against H. A. Boothby, I had no hand. Had I wished him proceeded against I would have acted myself. I consider his establishment a boon to the district, and more than a convenience to the general public. Mr. Boothby has had great experience in his business and seems a skilful and clever dispenser altogether well up. I think the justice of the case would be well met if only the costs were inflicted, as Mr. Boothby has interfered with no one's rights but my own, and I am perfectly willing to lay aside mine for the general welfare. And I sincerely hope that no magistrate will think me presuming too far when I say that in giving sentence Mr. Boothby's long and valuable services should be remembered.

(Signed.) C. J. PARSONS, M.D.

Letter marked " Exhibit 10," reads as follows :

COE HILL, April 9th, 1895.

To Mr. Boothby, Coe Hill :

SIR,—Some scoundrel or scoundrels sent me by mail the enclosed, but I dare say as it is written in your interests that you are quite aware of its contents. Of course you are aware *that the sending of that letter to me is a Penitentiary* affair, so I keep the original as I am quite an expert at comparison of hand-writings, and I may ferret the writer out yet. *Greater seeming impossibilities have happened. As the writer was too great a coward to put his name to this and as you are doubtless aware of his identity,* I beg to inform you most respectfully, but at the same *time definitely, that I shall not leave Coe Hill till it suits me to do so.* The threat of the white caps only makes my resolution so much the stronger. You have for a number of years conducted an " *illegal* " business and *I have written to my solicitors* for advice as to the method of procedure best to follow *for successfully stopping the dispensing and prescribing business followed in your establishment and against the law.* When I get their reply I *shall act accordingly,* and I am doing you no injustice because you have no right whatever to the business, every bottle of medicine you make and sell *you break the law.* I called in your office or store yesterday, and asked you in a most civil manner to confine yourself to the *legitimate business of a druggist,* and as I was giving you such a chance I wished you not to dispense Mr. Harding's prescriptions except for his own personal family, etc. You refused this, because you said that if you gave up such dispensing and prescribing you would lose money. Just put yourself in my place, what else is there for me to do but act as I do ? It is my right and everyone's that is on the Register to practise in this Province. I have no wish to injure you at all, you cannot say but that I have shown great forbearance. It is my present intention to open a drugstore myself if my negotiations with you fail. It is a matter of perfect indifference to me whether the threat in that notice is genuine or not ; it will not affect me in the slightest, but I wish you to understand that if you have anyone so foolish as to act in the manner threatened among your friends, to please remember that the law is on my side, and I shall not allow any person or persons to lay a hand on me *with impunity.* Of course, if they attack me they will do so unawares, *and if they do not disable me I shall kill a man or two and the law cannot touch me.* When Mr. Harding was fined similar threats were made ; a friend told me at the time, and I do not think I showed any cowardice. I came to Coe Hill every time I was sent for. You must remember I have *two very strong colleges* behind my back ; they have been at my call before, and suppose *I send for a detective* and search up a lot of evidence through the country. The magistrate that hears the case will hardly favor you *when I produce the threat sent me to-day, and my college refuses to accept anything less than the penalty in each case. It will be rather heavy, $25 at least for each offence.* Mr. Harding was let off lightly on the distinct understanding that he would not practise. Has he *kept his word given in honor ?* It is time for me to leave Coe Hill when another man comes in, of course, I mean a properly qualified medical man. We do not happen to live in Michigan, but in a country under British law and rule. I belong to a family who would spend a trifle to ferret the mystery out if anything happened to me. Moreover, I treat the whole affair with contempt. *I have an inkling now as to who wrote the notice.* In less than three hours, with the assistance of a competent magistrate, I could get to the bottom of the whole affair. *To-morrow morning I may send for one of our detectives to ferret the whole business out ;* we keep three, and it would not cost me a cent, but I will sleep on it and think it over. It is something new to get such a notice as that with its threats, when most illegal " quacks " are caught, they are glad to get off with a fine. It is useless to lengthen this long letter more, but let me tell you in conclusion that *to-morrow I shall communicate with the college and insist upon the penalty* being collected for each offence according to the statute, that I have no intention of leaving Coe Hill, and that as the people have been accustomed to a drug store in the place I will open one. If the people will not patronize me, then it is time for me to leave Coe Hill, *but rest assured they will not employ you and your friend without you qualify or you give your service for nothing,* and I do not think that is likely. I am not afraid to put my name.

(Signed.)   C. J. PARSONS.

Letter marked " Exhibit 11," reads as follows:

(Copy of letter addressed to Dr. Parsons, of Coe Hill).

DR. PARSONS,—You have played this bluff game the second time with quiet and respectable citizens, and you are requested by the people of this vicinity to vacate the town at once, or we will have to take the necessary steps to kick or hoist you out in Michigan style.

(Signed.)   By Order of Committee of White Caps.

N.B.—I corrected the spelling.   (Signed.)   C. P.

The following is an extract from the evidence of Henry Boothby submitted on the investigation before your Committee :

41 Q.—You thought this (Exhibit 9) was soft soap and this (Exhibit 10) was blackmail ? A.—Yes, I did most decidedly.

42. Q.—Do you think you would deserve that recommendation from an honest man if all these statements in Exhibit 10 were true ? A.—I certainly think he had no right to write it at all. (Refers to Exhibit 9).

43. Q.—You have not been given an opportunity of saying whether or not you are a White Cap, you may have that opportunity if you wish. A.—I most emphatically deny that *in toto.* I had nothing to do with it, I had no part in it.

(Admissions made by Mr. E. G. Porter, on behalf of the said Charles John Parsons).

Mr. PORTER addressed the Committee as follows :

Mr. CHAIRMAN,—I desire to say on behalf of my client, Dr. Parsons, that after having heard the evidence adduced against him before the Committee to-day I have advised, and I think it would be in the proper performance of my duty to say to the Council that I think it is needless to proceed further with the investigation of the case by taking additional evidence. I may say that Dr. Parsons has instructed me that he feels very keenly the position that he has been placed in by the evidence that has been given of his conduct before the Committee to-day. The explanation for his absence from the meeting of the Committee is the sense of shame he feels for the conduct he has been guilty of and that has been complained of in this matter. Dr. Parsons is, as you know, a duly licensed practitioner, and is entitled to every consideration at the hands of the Committee, more especially as those who are accusing him are admitted upon the evidence to be persons who are themselves violating the law ; the wrongful acts complained of have been committed against people of that character, and I ask that the Committee do not visit his wrong-doing with the same punishment they would if the circumstances were otherwise. On behalf of Dr. Parsons I wish to make the further admission that he is guilty of the offences charged against him, and very much regrets having been guilty of that conduct ; and undertakes now with this Committee and the Medical Council not to offend in that respect, or in any other respect again ; and he offers now his sincere apology to the Committee, to the Council and to the medical profession at large, and I ask the Committee on his behalf to deal as leniently as possible with the case. As counsel for Dr. Parsons I now sign this understanding in the following words :

To the Discipline Committee and the Medical Council of the College Physicians and Surgeons of Ontario :

I submit myself to the action of the Council in the premises, and admit that I am liable on the evidence to have my name erased from the Medical Register of Ontario. I undertake and agree not further to offend in the premises, and ask the Committee to suspend action on the report of the Committee so long as I in good faith comply with the above undertaking.

(Signed.) { C. J. PARSONS.
{ E. GUS PORTER, his Solicitor.

Witness,
ALEX. DOWNEY.

BELLEVILLE, Ont., Oct. 28th, 1896.

Dr. SANGSTER—I beg to call attention to the fact that this work was deputed to the Discipline Committee, and it certainly cannot be necessary, unless some question arises and calls for it, to go into it in detail.

Dr. BRAY—I thought not, but there are some gentlemen who want to hear something about it, and that being the case, I move, seconded by Dr. ROGERS, that the Council go into Committee of the Whole.

The PRESIDENT put the motion, which, on a vote having been taken, was declared carried.

Council in Committee of the Whole.

Dr. DOUGLAS in the chair.

Dr. BRAY read statutory declaration of service of John C. McNair, letter from Mr. E. Gus Porter and letter from Dr. Parsons, respectively, as follows :

DOMINION OF CANADA } In the matter of
PROVINCE OF ONTARIO } THE COLLEGE OF PHYSICIANS AND SURGEONS OF ONTARIO
To Wit. } and
DR. CHARLES JOHN PARSONS.

I, John C. McNair, of the City of Belleville in the County of Hastings, do solemnly declare that I did on Wednesday, July 7th, A.D. 1897, leave a copy of the hereunto annexed notice with Wm. Farnham in the office of Mr. E. Gus Porter, in the City of Belleville.

And I make this solemn declaration conscientiously believing the same to be true and by virtue of the Act respecting extra-judicial oaths.

Declared before me at Belleville, in the County of Hastings, this 7th day of July, A.D. 1897.

P. J. M. ANDERSON, a Commissioner, etc. J. C. McNAIR.

"*Re* Dr. C. J. Parsons.

"*R. A. Pyne, Esq., Registrar College Physicians and Surgeons, Toronto.*

"Dear Sir,—I have to-day been served with a notice to show cause in the above matter. I beg hereby to give you notice that I was only engaged by Dr. Parsons to appear for him at the investigation, and at that time ceased to have any connection with the case and am not now his solicitor and have no authority to accept service of any papers for him or act for him in any manner, besides, I have not his address, so cannot send the notice you have served on me to him. "Yours truly,

"(Signed.) E. Guss Porter."

"Belleville, Ont., July 7th, 1897.

"*R. A. Pyne, Esq., Toronto,*

"Sir,—You spoke in your last letter to me of an opportunity that would be given me to appear before the Council personally.

"I beg to say that I shall be unable to appear there or anywhere until my affairs in England are settled, as I have done nothing for two years and my attempt to practise at Arden was a failure owing to Finlay & Helms practising presumably with the Council's permission, at least they represent it so, and the magistrates supporting them.

"I have given my version, and I mean no disrespect to the Council. When I once pointed out to Finlay the falseness of his testimony, he as much as told me that he would swear anything to injure me. He appeared at the enquiry drunk, and with a black eye that he received in a drunken brawl at Tweed on the way to Belleville.

"Kindly excuse this, as I am writing with a broken hand.

"I am, yours truly,

"(Signed.) C. Parsons."

"Lavant P.O., July 6th, 1897.

Dr. Bray—Is it your pleasure we shall take this report up clause by clause or take it as a whole?

Dr. McLaughlin—Has this been submitted to our solicitor to see whether we are on clear ground and that we can erase the name.

Dr. Bray—This is following exactly the course given by the solicitor in other cases, and the form is exactly the same as that drawn out by our solicitor, excepting the charges are put in here as they occur. I think we are following out the same practice we have done before in similar cases.

Dr. McLaughlin—The Committee will notice that the ground upon which we are asked to erase this name is that of blackmailing. We are agreed it was damnable conduct that this man was guilty of, but the question in my mind is, are we at liberty, or have we authority to erase the name of a man who blackmails or does a thing of that kind. The Act says, "an offence which, if committed in Canada, would be a felony or misdemeanor, or been guilty of any infamous or disgraceful conduct in a professional respect." This is not in connection with his profession, because any man, non-professional, could do that sort of work. I do not want to overstrain this Act, but at the same time I want to feel we are on sure foundation before we erase this name and get into a lawsuit for damages. From the reading of this section it would seem to me we have jurisdiction with a man, in so far as his disgraceful conduct is connected with his profession; for instance, if we knew a man was an abortionist, if it was proven before our Committee, then he would be guilty of disgraceful conduct in a professional respect, and we would have a ground upon which we might erase his name; but here is a crime that is outside of our profession. Any member of the profession can commit it, but will we be safe if we go on and erase that man's name because he has been guilty of blackmailing?

Dr, Bray—To a certain extent I agree with what you say. I may differ as to whether you can call this "in a professional respect" or not; he is a professional man, but, as you say, you draw the distinction as to whether it is a disgracful conduct in a professional respect. But there is another thing, we have not the affidavit that this man has been served, and I think perhaps the best way to dispose of this case, taking this man'a admissions, and on account of the points that Dr. McLaughlin has raised, would be for this Council to suspend sentence on this man; it will have just the same effect, and he will not transgress any more. He asks for that, and by his solicitor he admits he is liable to have his name erased.

Dr. McLaughlin—I do not think that makes any difference.

Dr. Bray—I do not think it does either, from a legal point of view, but having made these admissions, if the Council sees fit we may suspend him and notify him that as long as he does not again offend he shall not be stricken off. I think to settle this matter it would be better if some gentleman would move that this man be allowed to go on suspended sentence. That is my view as a member of that Committee.

Dr. WILLIAMS—What has been the effect on those who have gone on suspended sentence before.

Dr. BRAY—Dr. McCully is out of the country, Dr. Washington is out of the country ; I do not think there is anybody now practising.

Dr. McLAUGHLIN—Dr. McCullough is out of the country.

Dr. BRAY—He was erased ; and we erased Dr. Lemon's name, but I do not think there is a man who has been before the Discipline Committee who is practising in Canada to my knowledge.

Dr. PYNE—I think Dr. Anderson is out of the country, too.

Dr. WILLIAMS—He is not out of the country ; he is keeping a drug store.

Dr. BRAY—As far as I know, it has had a very wholesome effect, and there is nobody now practising medicine who has been before this Committee. Those who have been struck off have gone ; and those that have been allowed to go on suspended sentence have left the country, so far as I am aware.

Dr. SANGSTER—I stated last year, when referring to the case of Dr. McCully, who was allowed to go on suspended sentence that he had left the country and was carrying on in the United States a system of the most disgraceful knavery and advertising himself as a member of the College of Physicians and Surgeons of Ontario and parading the fact that he had not been disqualified by the Medical Council of Ontario, and I stated that fact should have the effect on this Council of declining to allow other men to go on suspended sentence. If a man is guilty of disgraceful conduct in a professional respect, he is worthy of having his name erased from the register, and the erasure of his name exercises a strong deterrent effect upon all others who are inclined to travel the same road. I think the penalty imposed by this Council should be erasure of the name from the register, or nothing.

Dr. ROGERS—I just want to call your attention to this. Dr. McLaughlin read part of section 34, subsection 1 of the Act amending the Ontario Medical Act, if he will be kind enough to read subsection 2, it is as follows : "(2) The Council may, and upon the application of any four registered medical practitioners, shall cause enquiry to be made into the case of a person alleged to be liable to have his name erased under this section, and on proof of such conviction or of such infamous or disgraceful conduct, shall cause the name of such person to be erased from the register." It does not say "in a professional respect."

Dr. McLAUGHLIN—That refers back.

Dr. ROGERS—I hold myself this is quite as much in a professional respect as anything possibly could be. I feel inclined, as a rule, to be lenient towards a man who has committed a first offence, but as I understand this case, this man is rather an old offender, and I do not know of any form of crime that could be much worse than that of a legalized medical practitioner attempting to, in a sense, give a license to an unregistered medical practitioner. This man went through the country and wherever he heard of a person practising who was not registered, he immediately saw him and said, unless you do so and so—give me money—I will have you prosecuted. In that sense he meant to say, if you do give me money I will let you go on. I think that is a very serious crime to attempt to register or give a permit to people of that kind to practise medicine.

Dr. McLAUGHLIN—Pardon me, have these men, who are represented as practising, the Council's permit to practise ?

Dr. ROGERS—No. This Council has no power to give a permit and never gave a permit. But this man went through the country giving permits or making agreements, which was practically the same thing. I think it is, in a professional respect, a crime.

Dr. SANGSTER—If you really decapitate a man for a breach of the law in that respect the penalty is a severe one and it is one that exercises a wholesome terror upon other would-be delinquents. If you suspend them, or suspend occasionally, the natural argument is : "I will make a poor mouth to the Council, and some good natured fellow will get up and recommend that I be kept on and I will be a good boy in the future." And that individual may be, but a dozen others will offend the same way. These trials cost this Council a very large sum of money ; they are about the most expensive element we have in our management. I have a perfect confidence in the justice and good sense of leniency as far as it can be extended by the Discipline Committee ; and when they state that a man has been guilty of disgraceful conduct in a professional sense, then I claim that the full penalty of that offence should be administered.

Dr. BRAY—I agree exactly with Dr. Sangster. This man has done more than Dr. Rogers has intimated ; he has not only pretended to issue a permit to those men and taken their money, the inference of which was that that would be the end of it, but he prosecuted them as well ; and I think that it is "infamous and disgraceful conduct." But inasmuch as this man has not been served, I do not know that it would be legal for us to strike his name off the register to-day. We attempted to serve him ; we served what was supposed to be his solicitor and we sent a notice to be served on himself, but we had not the affidavit back. Do you think, Dr. Pyne, you will get that affidavit back?

Dr. PYNE—I am afraid not.

Dr. SANGSTER—Would not it be better to suspend action upon it until you have further time to have him served ?

Dr. BRAY—Not taking action now does not prohibit the Committee investigating further if they choose, or anything of the kind if anything comes up that will make the case stronger the Committee can go on and investigate, but I think myself it would be just as well, as this man is not served, to take no action at the present time.

Dr. SANGSTER—I will agree to that.

Dr. CAMPBELL—Where in the Act does it require that he shall be notified to appear before the Council ? He has got to be notified to appear before the Committee.

Dr. McLAUGHLIN—I think the principle involved there is that no man shall receive sentence without being present.

Dr. CAMPBELL—The Committee is really the court where he has to get his sentence.

Dr. McLAUGHLIN—Here is where the verdict is given.

Dr. CAMPBELL—I do not think there is anything in the Act which requires it.

Dr. BRAY—At any rate it has always been the practice.

Dr. EMORY—Dr. Carter wasn't present the other day when his name was erased. (Laughter.)

Dr. CAMPBELL—I think this man's conduct was disgraceful in a professional respect. His conduct was not the conduct, could not have been the conduct, of some other man not a physician, his offence is that he blackmailed as a physician. He went as a physician to these men, and as a physician he blackmailed them ; as a registered practitioner claiming the right to practise there he blackmailed those men ; it seems to me that would bring it clearly within the sphere of disgraceful conduct in a professional respect. Had he not been a registered practitioner the effect of his conduct would not have been the same. As far as that goes, I think we would be safe. The only point is whether we have gone as far as we ought to go in notifying him to be here.

Dr. PYNE—Subsection 5 of Section 35 of the Act amending the Ontario Medical Act covers the point

Dr. BRAY read the section referred to as follows :

" 5. At least two weeks before the first meeting of the Committee to be held for taking the evidence or otherwise ascertaining the facts, a notice shall be served upon the person whose conduct is the subject of enquiry, and such notice shall embody a copy of the charges made against him, or a statement of the subject-matter of the enquiry, and shall also specify the time and place of such meeting, etc."

Dr. BRAY—That has been complied with. He was served and he appeared, not personally, but by counsel.

Dr. ROGERS—So far as you know, he has not notified this lawyer who has written here to-day, nor notified this Council, nor notified you as Chairman of the Committee, nor notified the Registrar of any other counsel representing him. So far as you know the gentleman you notified was his solicitor.

Dr. BRAY—Yes.

Dr. ROGERS—If that gentleman appeared as his solicitor, and Dr. Parsons never notified you that he had another solicitor, you had a right to presume he was still his solicitor, and in serving him.

Dr. BROCK—Is there any record of conviction against this man in the Courts of Justice?

Dr. BRAY—Not that I am aware of.

Dr. BROCK—None of these men whom he tried to blackmail attempted to prosecute him.

Dr. BRAY—No ; they couldn't.

Dr. BROCK—Does he not by the letter acknowledge notice and refuse to appear ?

Dr. BRAY—No, he does not. That letter is dated the 6th of July, 1897. What date was the notice sent ?

Dr. PYNE—This is a letter from the bailiff at Sharbot Lake who endeavored to serve him, he says : " I have found that C. J. Parsons is out north in the county ; he left by train at Donaldson's Mills, and went on foot into the country. He was supposed to have gone east. If I had had the papers a week earlier I would likely have got him at Orton or Wright. Will find out his whereabouts if I can, and advise you, if this will be of any use to you, as I did not get him on the writ that you sent."

Dr. BRAY—I think that letter throws a little light on it ; I think this man is trying to evade service, and I have very grave doubts whether or not he did not receive the notice from this Council.

Dr. ROGERS—I think your position is very strong. If he has never notified you of a change of solicitors, you have a right to assume that the gentleman who appeared before the Committee as his solicitor is the solicitor still.

Dr. BRAY—This is an important matter, and we do not want to do anything that would be invalid or illegal, and if it is allowed to stand over, there may be a chance of serving him. It is a question as to what is best to do with this man ; I think we are convinced from the evidence that his conduct was infamous and disgraceful. Can anybody here satisfy the Council that it is not necessary to serve him personally to appear here and show cause why his name should not be erased ?

Dr. McLAUGHLIN—It seems to me that there are legal technicalities that render it unsafe for us to go on and erase the name. I am pretty clear that this man should be notified to appear before the Council, because the Council is a continuation of the court that began wherever the investigation began. If that court adjourned it was simply a matter of common law that he should be notified of the adjournment of that court and when and where it was to meet again ; if that has not been served upon him I am doubtful. Has the Executive Committee power to erase a name ?

Dr. BRAY—No.

Dr. McLAUGHLIN—I would like to see his name out as quickly as possible.

Dr. ROGERS—I would suggest, in order to save time, that we rise, and that the Solicitor, Mr. Osler, or his assistant be asked to advise us either this afternoon or to-morrow morning.

Dr. THORNTON—I think the matter should be clear to us as to his conduct being disgraceful in a professional respect. If I understand the letters read here, one addressed to a druggist, and one to Harding of Coe Hill, he undertakes to extract money from those men, not as a citizen, or a subject, or an ordinary individual, but from the position he occupies as a professional man ; he says he intends to come there to practise and that he does not intend to be interfered with by quacks, and on that ground he offers to take a certain amount of remuneration and give up the job. I think that this is disgraceful conduct in a professional respect as clearly as anything can be, and as far as that goes I would not hesitate a moment in dealing with his case. I think it should be dealt with. It happened in my own division, and I heard a good deal about it, and I think the charges here proven are only a few of the acts which he undertook, whether he succeeded in them or not. This was brought to my notice almost daily during the time it was going on.

Dr. MOORE—So far as offending from a professional standpoint is concerned, I think there is no doubt about it at all, because he levied the kind of blackmail that could only be levied by a licensed medical practitioner ; it could not be levied by any ordinary citizen. If he had not been a licensed medical practitioner he would not have driven those men out nor could he have levied the blackmail. His conduct is most disgraceful from more standpoints than one ; you have not heard a half or a quarter of the despicable tricks this fellow played ; he did it not only with one, but with five or six people ; he apparently is a bad man from every standpoint.

Dr. WILLIAMS—It is not clear to me that the Executive Committee have not power under certain circumstances to strike the name off, but the authority would have to be delegated by the Council. On page xvi., Section xiv. of the Register it says, " The Council shall appoint annually from among its members an Executive Committee to take cognizance of and action upon all such matters as may be delegated to it by the Council, or such as may require immediate interference or attention between the adjournment of the Council and its next meeting ; and all such acts shall be valid only till the next ensuing meeting of the Council ; but such Committee shall have no power to alter, repeal or suspend any by-law of the Council." I think under that if the Council decide they want that name struck off, on condition that it is in harmony with Mr. Osler's opinion, they can give that authority to the Executive Committee and that Committee can strike the name off.

Dr. GEIKIE—While Dr. Williams was speaking I was just thinking that it would be well to have a consultation with our Solicitor, and have his opinion as the ground of our action in this particular case ; and if the Solicitor's opinion be such as will warrant the erasure of this name, that the Council clothe the Executive Committee with authority to act, and in that way the name may be erased ; that is, on the supposition that the Solicitor's views shall be such as to make it clear to the Committee that there is no legal difficulty in the way of the erasure.

Dr. BRAY—In a very few minutes we can telephone Mr. Osler's office and ask him if it is necessary that this man should appear here, or should be notified, or served to appear here before we erase his name.

Dr. McLAUGHLIN—It will take some time to do that.

Dr. BROCK—I am informed that Mr. Osler is not in the city.

Dr. McLAUGHLIN—I think our course is to move that the matter be handed over to the Executive Committee, and that if Mr. Osler is of the opinion that we have power to erase his name, that the Committee be instructed to erase it.

Dr. ROGERS—I think the best thing would be for the Committee to rise and sit again when we have Mr. Osler with us. I do not think we ought to have any opinion over the telephone ; he ought to be here.

9

Dr. BRAY—It will have to be done either to-day or to-morrow.

Dr. ROGERS—I would move that this Committee rise, and go into Committee of the Whole again as soon as Mr. Osler is here.

The CHAIRMAN put the motion, which, on a vote being taken, was declared carried.

The Committee rose. The PRESIDENT in the chair.

Dr. BRAY—Will it not be well to instruct the Registrar or somebody to have Mr. Osler present this evening in conformity with the resolution passed in Committee of the Whole. I would move that Mr. Osler, or his representative, if he is out of the city, be asked to attend here this evening at 8 o'clock and advise the Council on this matter.

Dr. SANGSTER—I heard somebody say that Mr. Osler was out of town.

Dr. BRAY—Some member of his firm will act for him. I might say it has been the custom when these reports have been gone into and the members who have been complained against have been present with their legal counsel, and have been heard before this body, Mr. Osler has been present to advise the Council. I think perhaps when this report of the Discipline Committee goes back into Committee of the Whole it will be a great deal better to have Mr. Osler here personally.

Dr. ROOME—If the party were here with counsel he could reply to Mr. Osler, but as he is not present I think it is better to have the opinion in writing.

Dr. SANGSTER—In all these cases I think the Solicitor's opinion should be in writing ; and I think it should be the opinion of the Solicitor and not somebody else's opinion about that. I think we might have the utmost confidence in the opinion of Mr. B. B. Osler, and very little confidence in the opinion of the man who acts for him.

Dr. MCLAUGHLIN—Everything that is submitted to our solicitor should be submitted in writing. The only thing we want to know now is whether the Executive Committee have power to deal with this matter if we delegate that power to them. Mr. Osler cannot come here to-night and give an opinion without carefully going over all of these documents and carefully looking up the law ; he will not venture to do it. A message could be sent to him asking " Has the Council power to delegate to the Executive Committee authority to erase a man's name ?" And if the Council has that power, I think we had better dismiss the case and allow the Executive Committee to deal with it.

Dr. ROOME—Could we not ask him the question as to whether we can act without having the man present ? Couldn't we submit the questions in writing and send them to him ?

Dr. MCLAUGHLIN—That does not relieve me of all my difficulty, because if we had power to go on the question might arise, have we the power to go on the premises.

Dr. MOORE—I do not think there is any doubt about it.

The PRESIDENT—I think it would be well if you would put that question in writing, and we will send it over to Mr. Osler's office and get his opinion on it.

Dr. MCLAUGHLIN—Allow me to read what I propose submitting to Mr. Osler : " Has the Council power to delegate to the Executive Committee authority to erase from the register the name of an offender convicted of ' disgraceful conduct ? ' "

Dr. WILLIAMS—That covers the case I think.

Dr. MCLAUGHLIN—The second question is, " Is it necessary for the Council seized of the evidence of disgraceful conduct on the part of registered practitioner before proceeding to authorize the Registrar to erase such practitioner's name from the register to have proof that such practitioner has been notified to appear before the Council ? "

Dr. BRAY—I would just addd to that, " After having already appeared before the Discipline Committee."

Dr. MCLAUGHLIN—I will add that. Then I say, " Does the conduct of which Charles John Parsons was found guilty, come within the meaning of Section 34 of the Ontario Medical Act ? "

Dr. THORNTON—Is the first question complete ; should it not be " infamous and disgraceful conduct ?' Is being convicted of " disgraceful conduct " sufficient, should it not be in a " professional respect " ?

Dr. MCLAUGHLIN—That is covered in the last question.

Dr. DICKSON—Could not the opinion asked for on the questions submitted in Dr. Armour's motion, which was lost, and which I gave notice of motion to have reconsidered, be submitted to Mr. Osler at the same time.

Dr. BRAY—I have been thinking over the matter of Dr. Dickson's motion, and I think perhaps it would be more satisfactory to a large number of the members of this Council that that opinion should be obtained. I was opposed to it yesterday, but I am quite agreeable if, without any discussion at all, this motion of Dr. Dickson's to reconsider Dr. Armour's motion, together with Dr. Armour's motion, can be carried, and these questions submitted to Mr. Osler, that it should be done.

NOTICES OF MOTION.

1. Dr. DOUGLAS—To introduce a by-law to fix the times, manner and places for holding the next examinations.

2. Dr. ROGERS—To pass a resolution confirming the action of the Executive Committee *re* the continuation of the time on the mortgage on the College building.

Dr. ARMOUR—Has the Executive Committee reported ?

The PRESIDENT—No.

Dr. ARMOUR—I think the Executive should bring in a report before we pass upon this.

Dr. ROGERS—It is only a notice of motion.

COMMUNICATIONS, PETITIONS, ETC.

The REGISTRAR read communications, which were referred to the respective committees.

MOTIONS OF WHICH NOTICE HAS BEEN GIVEN AT A PREVIOUS MEETING.

Dr. WILLIAMS moved, seconded by Dr. Shaw, and resolved, that the mover have leave to introduce a by-law for the purpose of levying the annual fee, that the by-law be now read a first time.

The PRESIDENT put the motion which, on a vote having been taken, was declared carried.

Dr. WILLIAMS read the by-law entitled, " A by-law to levy the annual fee, as follows : Whereas it is necessary and expedient that an annual fee be paid by each member of the College of Physicians and Surgeons of Ontario towards the general expenses of the College, and whereas the Council is authorized by Statute to pass by-laws for this purpose ; Now, therefore, the College of Physicians and Surgeons of Ontario enacts as follows : That each member of the College shall pay to the Registrar towards the general expenses of the College for the current year, an annual fee of the amount of two dollars ($2.00) pursuant to the provisions of Section 27 of the Ontario Medical Act."

Dr. ARMOUR—I think it will be in order now to discuss that.

The PRESIDENT—You had better discuss it in the second reading.

Dr. ARMOUR—We have not an opportunity to discuss it then.

Dr. ROGERS—It should be discussed on the second reading.

Dr. ARMOUR—I would prefer to discuss it now.

Dr. WILLIAMS—I would just explain that it is not my intention to carry this by-law through to its third reading until completion. I wish it got it to the stage in Committee of the Whole, when it may be discussed.

DR. ARMOUR—I have no objection.

Dr. WILLIAMS—Moved, seconded by Dr. Shaw, that the Council do now go into Committee of the Whole to read the second time the by-law entitled, " A by-law to levy the annual fee."

The PRESIDENT put the motion which, on a vote having been taken, was declared carried.

Council in Committee of the Whole.

Dr. GEIKIE in the chair.

Dr. WILLIAMS—I move that the by-law be now read in Committee of the Whole. Carried.

The by-law received its second reading.

Dr. WILLIAMS—In bringing this matter before the Committee, perhaps a little explanation may be wise. There is no question about the correctness, so far as the by-law is concerned, under the law ; we have the right to impose that fee and pass that kind of a by-law. There is a question however that naturally crops up, and that is as to whether or not Section 41*a*, which was put in force by a by-law last year, continues in force until repealed by the Council, or whether it continues in force by Statute, and that the Council have no power to repeal it after it is once put in force ; also whether Section 41*a*, requires to be inserted in the by-law in each individual year. In order to make this perfectly satisfactory and to know exactly the course we are in, I intended, when we got into Committee of the Whole, proposing that a subcommittee should be appointed consisting of Drs. Dickson, McLaughlin and myself, to submit the question to Mr. Osler and have his official opinion upon the matter, which will settle the question for all time, and an opinion on the other questions which have been brought up can be obtained by the same Committee. Dr. McLaughlin having in charge the obtaining of Mr. Osler's opinion upon the questions which he has written out, the whole matter can be done at the same time, and if it is your pleasure to adopt this suggestion, I move that a subcommittee of the Committee of the Whole, consisting of Drs. McLaughlin, Dickson and myself, be appointed to wait upon Mr, Osler, to obtain his opinion upon the points mentioned.

The CHAIRMAN put the motion which, on a vote being taken, was declared carried.

Dr. ROGERS moved that the Committee rise and report progress and ask leave to sit again, which, on a vote having been taken, was declared carried.

The Committee rose, the President in the chair.

Dr. WILLIAMS—I think steps should be taken to obtain Mr. Osler's opinion upon these matters at as early a period as possible, as it is necessary that the work of the Council be proceeded with. I do not know whether the best method would be to telephone to the office and ascertain whether Mr, Osler is in, and ask him to be prepared for a meeting right away, or not ; probably the Registrar can tell us.

Dr. PYNE—I will go and telephone now, and see what arrangements can be made.

Dr. SANGSTER—Wouldn't it be better to have Mr. Osler come here ?

Dr. WILLIAMS—We will allow Dr. Pyne to make the arrangements.

Dr. DICKSON moved, seconded by Dr. ARMOUR, that Dr. Armour's motion, relative to obtaining the opinion of Mr. B. B. Osler, Q.C., be reconsidered, and that the Registrar do now read the said motion.

Dr. ARMOUR—I desire to read the motion again.

The Council consented to Dr. Armour re-reading the motion.

Dr. ARMOUR—"I move, seconded by Dr. McLaughlin, that the advice of Mr. B. B. Osler be had on the following : 1st. Had the Medical Council at the annual session of 1895 a legal right to assess an annual tax on the medical profession for the years 1893 and 1894, as enacted in Clause 3 of by-law No. 69 ? 2nd. To what part of the arrearages of the annual tax which are outstanding at various dates, from 1874 to the present time, can Section 41a of the Medical Act, passed in 1891, be legally applied for their collection ?" There is a subsequent clause here which I ask to have erased, "also that the President, Vice-President and the mover be a delegation to wait on Mr. Osler to secure the above advice."

Dr. ROGERS—That has already been before the Council.

Dr. ARMOUR—But as we are referring it to this Committee, I want to erase that provision for a special committee, and leave it to the subcommittee of the Committee of the Whole now appointed.

Dr. ROGERS—There is no reason for that.

Dr. ARMOUR—We will leave it as it is.

Dr. WILLIAMS—I do not see any reason why Dr. Armour should not strike his pen through the part referring to a special committee, and then hand it over to the other Committee.

Dr. ROGERS—Certainly, to save time.

Dr. ROOME—This has got to have a two-thirds vote ; what is the object of it ? What do you want a second committee or second resolution for ?

The PRESIDENT—It is only by the permission of the Council that he is allowed to do this.

Dr. ARMOUR—I desire to state to Dr. Roome that we have already had the unanimous understanding of the Council to reintroduce this resolution.

Dr. ROGERS—There never was a unanimous resolution.

The PRESIDENT—I think not. Dr. Bray is the only one that spoke of it. You will have to follow the rules.

Dr. McLAUGHLIN—Do you declare it carried or not ?

The PRESIDENT—No. The only thing that was stated was by Dr. Bray, who said he wished to withdraw his opposition to it.

Dr. DICKSON—There is nothing at stake that warrants losing five minutes ; I think, if the members of the Council want to act honorably with each other, they should allow that clause of Dr. Armour's motion to be erased, and allow the special committee to submit it to Mr. Osler.

Dr. BRAY—At that time Dr. Williams had made a motion to go into Committee of the Whole, but I did not know that ; I thought there was nothing before the Chair, and I wished to expedite matters by asking the Council to take up Dr. Dickson's motion to reconsider this question, but I was called to order by Dr. Williams, who said there was a motion before the House. I would be very happy to support Dr. Dickson's motion ; I think, after due consideration, it would give a great deal of satisfaction to a large number of the members of this chamber if Mr. Osler's opinion could be obtained. I am prepared to support that motion whenever it comes up.

Dr. ROGERS—I think there is no objection to Dr. Dickson setting an opinion on any point not covered by Dr. Williams' motion.

Dr. WILLIAMS—As a matter of fact, my resolution covers a part of what was in the resolution moved by Dr. Dickson ; we thought by handing it all over to the same Committee they would get all the information on the two points at the same time.

The PRESIDENT put Dr. Armour's motion to refer it to the subcommittee of the Committee of the Whole, which, on a vote having been taken, was declared carried.

Dr. ROGERS moved, seconded by Dr. WILLIAMS, that the by-law to appoint a Discipline Committee be read a first time.

The PRESIDENT put the motion, which, on a vote having been taken, was declared carried.

Dr. ROGERS read the by-law, as follows :

"BY-LAW NO. 78.

"Under and by virtue of the powers and directions given by subsection 2 of Section 36 of the Ontario Medical Act, Revised Statutes of Ontario, 1887, Chapter 148, the Council of the College of Physicians and Surgeons of Ontario enacts as follows :

"1. The Committee appointed under the provisions and for the purpose of the said subsection shall consist of three members, three of whom shall form a quorum for the transaction of business.

"2. The said Committee shall hold office for one year, and until their successors are appointed, *provided* that any member of such Committee appointed in any year shall continue to be a member of such Committee, notwithstanding anything to the contrary herein, until all business brought before them during the year of office has been reported upon to the Council.

"3. The Committee under said section shall be known as the Committee on Discipline."

Dr. ROGERS moved, seconded by Dr. WILLIAMS, that the by-law to appoint a Discipline Committee be referred to the Committee of the Whole and read a second time.

The PRESIDENT put the motion, which, on a vote having been taken, was declared carried.

COUNCIL IN COMMITTEE OF THE WHOLE.

Dr. GRIFFIN in the chair.

On motion the first three sections of the by-law were adopted as read.

Dr. ROGERS—I move that the first blank in Section 4 be filled by inserting the name, Dr. Bray, Chatham. Carried.

Dr. ROGERS—I move that the second blank be filled by inserting the name, Dr. Logan, Ottawa. Carried.

Dr. ROGERS—I move that the third blank be filled by inserting the name, Dr. Moore, Brockville. Carried.

Dr. ROGERS—I move that the whole by-law as read, be received and adopted in Committee of the Whole. Carried.

Dr. ROGERS—I move that the Committee rise and report. Carried.

The Committee rose, the President in the Chair.

Dr. ROGERS moved, seconded by Dr. WILLIAMS, that the by-law be read a third time, passed, numbered, signed by the President, and sealed with the seal of the College of Physicians and Surgeons of Ontario.

Dr. SANGSTER—I wish to place myself on record as objecting to the name of one member on that Committee ; I have done so each year since I have been here ; I do it on principle, I do it from no personal reason ; I think the Discipline Committee appointed to try the delinquencies of members of the profession should consist exclusively of men who are here as members of the profession, and it is on that ground that I object to the name of an appointee of the educational bodies being on that Committee ; I know it is only a formal protest, but I could not help but make it.

The PRESIDENT put the motion, which, on a vote having been taken, was declared carried.

Dr. ROGERS—Mr. Osler writes Dr. Pyne that as a matter of form the Council should pass a resolution confirming the action of the Executive Committee in getting an extension of time on the mortgage on this building.

Dr. SANGSTER—I understand that that committee has not reported yet.

The PRESIDENT—We have not had the report yet.

REPORTS OF SPECIAL AND STANDING COMMITTEES.

Dr. ROGERS as chairman read the report of the Board of Examiners as follows :

To the President and Members of the Council of the College of Physicians and Surgeons of Ontario :

GENTLEMEN :—I beg leave to report that as President of the Medical Council and Chairman of the Board of Examiners I inspected the schedules of the Examiners and Registrar, and therefore report on the result of the Professional Examinations held in Toronto, in September, 1896 and in Toronto and Kingston, in May, 1897.

For the Primary Examination in September, 1896, thirty-one candidates presented themselves, of whom eleven passed and twenty failed, thirty-five per cent. passing. For the Final examination in September, 1896, thirty-two candidates presented themselves, of whom twenty-two passed and ten failed, sixty-eight per cent. passing.

In May, 1897, one hundred and fifteen candidate presented themselves for the Primary Examination of whom sixty-nine passed and forty-six failed, sixty per cent. passing. For the Intermediate Examination forty candidates presented themselves, thirty-three of whom passed and and seven failed, eighty-two per cent. passing. For the Final Examination forty-eight candidates presented themselves, of which number thirty-four passed and fourteen failed, seventy-two per cent. passing.

The number of each candidate with the number of marks obtained on each subject, both written and oral, will be found in the schedule of the Registrar, the number of marks in each case being taken from the schedules of the Examiners.

The schedule of the Registrar, so prepared, has been inspected by me and certified correct.

The examinations were as practical as possible.

In Anatomy, wet and dry specimens were used of the whole human body, viscera, bones and models.

In Histology, Pathologoy and Therapeutics, microscopic and gross specimens were used; while in Chemistry practical work was required in the laboratory.

In Medicine and Surgery, clinical examinations were held in the General Hospitals in Toronto and Kingston.

In Midwifery, Medical and Surgical Anatomy subjects, models and intruments were used.

The members of the Board of Examiners have been requested to submit any recommendations or suggestions they might be disposed to make in connection with the examinations, and any made are appended hereto.

It is suggested that candidates taking the Primary and Intermediate or Primary and Final at one time shall be obliged to pass in Anatomy and Physiology of the Primary to be allowed any subjects in the Intermediate and Final.

All of which is respectfully submitted.

(Signed)   A. F. ROGERS.

TORONTO, June 24th, 1897.

Dr. ROGERS—In explanation of the last section of the report, I might state that there were several cases where candidates applied for permission to take the Primary and Intermediate Examinations together and they failed in their Primary and it seemed to be an absurdity to allow a man to get through with his Final Examination and be plucked in his Primary, and my recommendation is that where a man fails in Anatomy and Physiology he should not get any reward or value for anything else. I do not think it is necessary to go into Committee of Whole on this report, it is so late, and I will move, seconded by Dr. Henderson, that the report be adopted.

Dr. WILLIAMS—There is a recommendation in the latter part of it which is practically taking out of the hands of the Educational Committee a part of their functlon. I submit that you should pass that recommendation over to them; if it is passed in the Council now it ties the hands of the Educational Committee, and they are dealing with that very subject; that ought not to be adopted here, but should be passed over to that Committee to be taken into consideration in the curriculum which they are now preparing.

Dr. ROGERS—Is it possible to pass a report of that kind over to a committee?

Dr. WILLIAMS—I think you can hand the report over for consideration.

The PRESIDENT—The whole thing?

Dr. WILLIAMS—The whole thing. If you cannot, I will have to move that that portion of the report be struck out.

Dr. McLAUGHLIN—Ultimately the Education Committee may see fit to make an alteration in that. My impression is that the better way would be to strike out the last section of that report, and then it can be handed over to the Committee on Education.

Dr. GEIKIE—I think Dr. McLaughlin's suggestion is perfectly correct.

Dr. WILLIAMS—If Dr. Rogers consents to withdraw that part of the report, or hand that part over to the Education Committee—

Dr. ROGERS—I do not think the report is worth anything if you cut that out.

Dr. McLAUGHLIN—I move that the last section of the report be struck out, and that it be handed over to the Educational Committee.

Dr. SHAW—I think that is an important matter, and I feel very strongly on the question, and I would second Dr. McLaughlin's motion.

Dr. ROGERS—I think you are taking a very serious step. In the first place, there is not a university of any standing in Canada that allows a candidate coming up for both the

Primary and Final, if he does not pass his Primary, to get credit for anything. You cannot find a university in the civilized world that has not the regulation that where a student fails in his Primary he gets nothing.

The PRESIDENT—If that is the case, the Educational Committee will soon rectify the matter.

Dr. ROGERS—That is not the motion before this House ; the motion is to erase it. I am going to defend this, and I am going to state my reasons. I know of three different students to-day who have been plucked in their primary before this Council, plucked twice, but who have passed their final. It seems perfectly absurd for us to allow a man who does not know enough about Anatomy, Physiology and Materia Medica to pass our primary examination to give him credit for having passed in Surgery, Medicine, and all the other final subjects. I made enquiry, and I found that the Royal College of Surgeons in London, England, would not do it—

Dr. WILLIAMS—I would like to rise to a point of order. The motion is not whether that shall or shall not be allowed, the question is whether or not it shall be adopted by the Council while the subject of the curriculum is in the hands of the Educational Committee and while they are dealing with it.

Dr. ROGERS—We are discussing the question as to whether this section of the report should be erased.

Dr. McLAUGHLIN—I move, seconded by Dr. SHAW, that the last clause of the report be struck out, and that it be handed to the Educational Committee for consideration.

Dr. ROGERS—You moved to have it erased before.

The PRESIDENT read the motion.

Dr. ROGERS—I will consent to that.

Dr. DICKSON—Anyone reading that motion would not know whether it was meant that the Clause should be struck out or that it should be handed over.

The PRESIDENT again read the motion, and, on a vote having been taken, declared it carried.

Dr. BRITTON presented and read the report of the Committee on Legislation.

Dr. BRITTON—I beg to move, seconded by Dr. BARRICK, that the report of the Committee on Legislation be received and adopted.

Dr. SANGSTER—I cannot agree to the adoption of that report ; it is not correct. When the Legislative Committee met on that occasion, I did not agree to clauses 1, 2, 3 and 4 ; on the contrary, I expressly stated my determination that if those clauses were discussed before the Government, I would take the liberty of expressing my views to the contrary. I am sure there was a distinct agreement arrived at that no details should be given, that it should merely be presented. The President of the Council broke that agreement by going into the matter in detail, and I feel constrained to express the views of myself and friends on the other side of the question. I protest against being placed in the position of adding an assent to the first four clauses of that petition.

Dr. ROGERS—I, as President of the Council, am the person referred to by Dr. Sangster, and as possibly it might be a question of veracity between Dr. Sangster and me, must simply leave it to the word of those who were present.

Dr. SANGSTER—That is right.

Dr. ROGERS—I must say for myself that I am entirely in accord with the report made by Dr. Britton. I, as President, advocated the presentation of this petition to the Legislature as well as the Government, and because Dr. Sangster objected to that course, Dr. Britton, in order to bring us all into harmony suggested, or some one suggested, and he acquiesced in it, that we only present present the petition at the present time to the Government.

Dr. SANGSTER—Without detail.

Dr. ROGERS—I beg to deny for myself ; and I hope for others, that there was any such an arrangement. I cannot conceive anything more futile than for a body of men to say they will take a petition to the Government and not present it ; they could not present it unless they read and explained it ; it would be about as impossible to present that petition to the Government unless they read it and explained it as it would to present it to the Czar of Russia. We agreed unanimously. I am not going to accuse Dr. Sangster of wilfully misunderstanding it. If Dr. Sangster did not understand that agreement which we all understood that is another thing, but for him to say that we all agreed not to present the petition in detail, what does that mean ? I, as President, simply spoke on the petition before the Government, which my report will show. I simply read the four points of the prayer in that petition, and in doing so I supposed, and I think the others supposed, we were carrying out the agreement, the agreement being we should not present the petition to the Legislature nor ask for legislation at that time, but that we present the petition to the Government and Premier. That was the agreement.

Dr. SANGSTER —Is it not an extraordinary thing that a report of a committee can be prepared—cooked, if I may use that expression, or if it is not proper I withdraw it.

Dr. BRITTON—I would certainly object to the word "cooked," because that would be equivalent to saying that I was not a gentleman.

Dr. SANGSTER—I withdraw it. Is it not an extraordinary thing that a report of a formal body can be prepared and presented to the Council without the members of the Committee ever having seen one line of the report or acquiescing in it. With regard to the question of veracity, I am quite content that the gentlemen who were on that Committee should testify. Before I rose to my feet in the Chamber where the members of the Government were, I turned around to Dr. Barrick, who was sitting behind me, and I said, is that not a distinct breach of that agreement; and I understood him to agree with me. There were other gentlemen there and it need not be a question of construction between Dr. Rogers and myself. I would like to know the feeling of all the gentlemen who were in that room. I think Dr. Machell will bear me out that it was a distinct understanding before we went there that details were not to be entered into.

Dr. BRITTON—In preparing this report of the Committee on Legislation, I found it to be not a very simple task ; there was a good deal of work in connection with it, and having prepared it exactly in accordance with the facts that had occurred, there are no opinions expressed, there is simply a narrative of the facts ; I did not think there was any urgent necessity for submitting the report to the different members of the Committee for their consideration before it was presented to you. If there are any omissions in the report, if there is anything introduced that should not be there, if there is anything there that is correct but which is not in proper form, I am quite ready to have the Committee set me right, quite ready to have this report amended to make it right. I am satisfied it is correct from the first word to the last. I must give you in as few words as I can what actually occurred. As it is stated in the report I was appointed as chairman; a few minutes after we started discussing the petition, and Dr. Rogers spoke on this bill which had been prepared, I did not know until then that it had been drawn up. It was then stated by some members of the Committee, I think first by Dr. Williams, that they had been given to understand by certain members of the Local Legislature that the present time, perhaps owing to the peculiar construction of the Legislative Assembly, was not considered to be opportune for medical legislation, therefore that it would not, perhaps, be a wise thing to introduce this bill or ask for its introduction. Then, came up the matter of the petition. I do not know that Dr. Sangster was the first to speak, but I shall refer to him only at present, because it is he who is challenging the correctness of this report. Dr. Sangster rose to his feet and said—I cannot reproduce his words, but I shall give them in substance—"Mr. Chairman, I must take certain exceptions to this report, and I want you and the other members of the Committee to understand that if we go to the Legislature or to the Government, that I shall feel free to critize this petition as I think best." Then he went on to speak of the heading of the petition, and so on and so on, until he came down to the prayer of the petition, and I might be allowed to read the first clause of this prayer : "Therefore your petitioner humbly prays : 1 That your Honorable Body will extend to the medical profession of this Province the courtesy of not changing or amending the Ontario Medical Act until any proposed change or amendment has been placed before the Ontario Medical Council for consideration." When he said, "Mr. Chairman, I submit that this petition is not prepared in accordance with the original resolution, which does not read in that way at all ; it read as follows : ' That Your Honourable Body will extend to the medical profession of the Province the courtesy of not changing or amending the Ontario Medical Act until any such change or amendment be asked for by the Medical Council of Ontario.'" On the back of the circular which was sent out to the profession you will find printed a resolution moved by Dr. Bray, and seconded by Dr. Dickson, which probably you have all seen. Dr. Bray's resolution is exactly in accordance with the petition ; it directs that this first clause be inserted. There is quite a difference between the two ; we asked the Local Legislature in accordance with the resolution passed by this Council, not to introduce any new legislation without first consulting us. Dr. Sangster contended that the original resolution was that we should ask that they would not amend or change the Medical Act unless they are asked to do so by us. There is all the difference in the world. We sat there for a few minutes, and finally I asked Dr. Pyne for the original resolution in Dr. Bray's handwriting. All of these motions are kept on file. Dr. Pyne produced it, and handed it to me, when I found the transcript of it, which you will find on the back of the circular, identical with the resolution, and that this first clause of the prayer was framed perfectly in accordance with the order of the Council. You may think I am a little prolific in dwelling on these particulars, but later on you may see the importance of it. Dr. Sangster contended that this petition was not framed in accordance with the original resolution, but that the original resolution had been materially changed ; or, in other words, the petition was quite outside of what was intended. There were some who felt that, perhaps, inasmuch as we might not be wise in seeking for immediate legislation, we might as well allow the petition to remain, and to present it at some future time when we required the legislation. Dr. Williams, I think, was of that opinion, or slightly so at any rate. But, however, the matter was discussed for some little time, and finally Dr. Rogers made the remark that inasmuch as the petition had been framed and signed, that it must and would be presented, and I made use of this remark, "Gentlemen, I do not know how we can afford to break faith with 1,821 medical practitioners of Ontario who have signed this petition ; to ask for the signing of a petition is equivalent to a solemn agreement on our part to present it, and although we may not seek for immediate legislation, although the time appears to be inopportune for that, still the sooner our necessities are brought before the Government the sooner our redress will be granted. If they know what we require it will be one step towards securing legislation." There was some further discussion, and finally one member of the Committee appealed to me, I think it was Dr. Williams ; he said, "Mr. Chairman. can you suggest what course should be followed ?" My reply was this—Dr. Sangster still contending against the petition,—"Gentlemen, it would be worse than useless for us as a divided body to go before the Premier and the Government of Ontario, to ask for any redress of our grievances unless we go there unanimously. We cannot afford to go there and let there be one dissenting voice, because we will not only secure nothing, but it would be manifest to the Government that we are not united amongst ourselves about the very thing we are requiring." I said, "Gentlemen, what I propose is this ; I will, as fairly as I can, enunciate the principle underlying each clause of this petition, and at the same time I ask you as to whether or not you are satisfied that that clause be laid before the Government." I took clause one, as stated in this report of the Committee which has been presented, and before asking the question I said, "Now, gentlemen, I want you to understand,"—and I repeated it three times so that there could be no mistake, so that every man after having committed himself, could not go back on his track—I said, "gentlemen, I want you to understand that I shall ask the question, and if there is no dissenting voice, we will understand we are all agreed." That, as I said before, was repeated again and again. I went over clause 1, and I made some remarks upon it, and said, "Is there any dissension or do all agree? Are you all agreed?" There was no dissenting voice. Clause 2, the same ; clause 3, the same ; clause 4, the same. Now, I said, "Gentlemen, I shall ask you individually as to the whole prayer, clauses 1, 2, 3 and 4," and I turned first to my left, "Are you agreed?" and finally I came down to Dr. Sangster who sat on my right ; I did not name the others, but when I came to him I said, "Are you agreed, Dr. Sangster?" He did not say "yes," he did not say "no," he bowed his head in acquiescence.

Dr. McLAUGHLIN—I must rise to a point of order. I would like to know, if this is the report of the Legislative Committee; if that Committee has been properly brought together to consider that report ; and whether that is the report of that Committee that is before us or is it Dr. Britton's report? I would like to have this point settled before we go any further. If it is possible for a Committee to report without some of the members of that Committee being called together in order to consider whether the report is correct or not it is an extraordinary state of affairs and I would like the ruling of the chair as to whether that is correct or not. I submit that no report can be presented without calling the Committee together.

Dr. BRITTON—Whether that is regular or not does not concern the matter about which I am speaking and which is before the chair at present.

Dr. McLAUGHLIN—It does concern us here, because we have a difference of opinion and a wrangle which is being fought out in the whole Council that should have been fought out in the Committee.

Dr. ROGERS—It was fought out in the Committee.

Dr. BRAY—The Council have already accepted and received that report, therefore, it is before the Council.

Dr. McLAUGHLIN—No, it is not.

Dr. BRAY—It is before the Council, whether it is right or wrong.

The PRESIDENT—It was received by the Council.

Dr. ARMOUR—What is the motion before the chair?

Dr. BRITTON—I moved that it be adopted.

Dr. McLAUGHLIN—I still say it is not the report of the Committee.

Dr. BRITTON—It was received as the report of the Committee and we have to discuss it now.

Dr. McLAUGHLIN—Did you call the Committee together in order to consider that report?

Dr. BRITTON—I did not, and I gave my reasons why I did not, some time ago. After this occurrence, after all had acquiesced and after Dr. Sangster acquiesced in the way I have said, the motion was carried that we should then—

Dr. McLAUGHLIN—On that point of order I desire to read from Dr. BOURINOT : "The report of every committee must be signed by the chairman and be the report of the majority."

The PRESIDENT—I think that report is signed by the chairman.

Dr. BRITTON—Am I to proceed?

The PRESIDENT—I think so. That is my ruling.

Dr. BRITTON—In accordance with the motion made by someone, seconded by Dr. Barrick, we adjourned at that time with the intention of interviewing the Government at two o'clock in the afternoon, which we did, and we brought with us the petition. This petition was presented by the President, Dr. Rogers. He addressed the Premier and members of the Government on the lines of the petition, and I might say that his address was confined almost exclusively to an enunciation of the principle of each of these clauses of the prayer and to an emphasizing of these. After he sat down, the gentleman who has called in question the veracity of this report I have prepared, rose to his feet, and I think perhaps I can best convey to you the course that he took by reproducing, as far as my memory will let me, the speech that he made on that occasion ; I cannot give it verbatim. He said, "Mr. Premier, as the time is short I do not wish to take up any more of the time of the members of the Government than will be absolutely necessary and I shall try to be very brief." He took the petition in his hand and said, ". first of all I take exception to the heading of this petition. What does it say Mr. Premier ? 'To the Honourable the Premier, Honourable Members of the Government and Honourable Members of the Legislative Assembly of Ontario.' Who, Mr. Premier, ever heard of any such thing as a petition being directed to two or three or more different bodies," when he was interrupted by the Honourable A. S. Hardy, who said, "Oh, yes, a petition might be directed to any number of bodies that is desired. Of course if this is to be subsequently laid before the Legislative Assembly some little change in the heading might be thought necessary, but that is all." Dr. Sangster continued, "I might say, I think Mr. Premier, that the first clause is utterly incorrect, that it is not at all in accordance with the resolution as passed in the Council ;" then we took the Announcement of 1896-97 and referred to page 83. I shall read the resolution as it appears in the Announcement. I might say to you that, it appears in the Announcement at page 83 as originally moved by Dr. Bray before Dr. Dickson's suggestion was made, but the original resolution as amended, which had been filed away, had been read and submitted in Committee. I submitted it to Dr. Sangster ; at any rate, I read it in the Committe and showed it to him to prove that he was erroneous in his criticism. Dr. Bray framed the resolution, and the words found on page 83 are, "That a form of petition be framed and sent to every medical man in the Province by the Registrar for signatures, praying that the Government and Legislature of Ontario will not alter or amend the Medical Act, or introduce or carry through any new medical legislation, unless such legislation, or new Medical Acts, be asked for by the College of Physicians and Surgeons directly, or through their Legislative Committee." I proved conclusively to Dr. Sangster in the Committee, and every other member on that Committee will bear me out, that he must have known that that part of the petition is framed in accordance with the resolution. Dr. Dickson, the seconder, in looking over this resolution at the time it was moved in Council, said, "I would prefer that it be arranged a little differently, that it shall not emanate from us that it is new legislation, but that the Government will confer with us before enacting any new legislation." The reply of Dr. Bray near the bottom of the page in the Announcement is, "As long as I can attain my object, I am not very particular as to the wording of the resolution." As appears on page 84, he consented to his resolution being amended in accordance with Dr. Dickson's suggestion, and that one is the one that was printed on the back of the circular and Dr. Sangster knew that in the Committee. I made it as plain to him as I have made it to you now. I think everybody here understands it. When Dr. Sangster arrived at that part, he said to the Government, "the petition is not framed on the ground of the original resolution," the original resolution was as I have read from the Announcement, "unless such legislation or new Medical Acts be asked for by the Legislative Committee of the Council or by the Council itself." He went on to argue on that line ; he said it would be an outrageous thing that any legislation which might be beneficial to the profession could be precluded from introduction into the House unless asked for by the governing body. And, going on to illustrate, he said, supposing that any member of the Council, or supposing that I were derelict in the discharge of my duty, supposing I were high-handed, or that I ignored the wishes of my constituents or any other part of the profession, what a great injustice would be done, if this Legislature should enact that any person who was injured by the course I pursued, or took other exception to my conduct in the matter, be debarred from the introduction of new legislation or from coming here to seek for redress for the wrong done ; and as an analogy he took the cases of such bodies as the United Order of Workmen and so on. I do not know what you, gentlemen, think of his conduct in that matter, but I had no intention of saying a word concerning his conduct until he stood up and challenged the truthfulness of the report made by me ; I thought then it was about time that I should protect myself and show that I had done what was right, show that I had reported what was true ; and I must leave the corroboration or denunciation of what I say to the members of the Committee. Then he went on with clause 2 of the prayer. If you, gentlemen, do not wish to hear it all tell me and I shall not keep you waiting. (Cries of "Go on," "Go on.") The doctor continuing, said : Clause 2, in brief, is asking the Legislature to allow this Council the full control of the standard of pre-medical education. Dr. Sangster took the same course as I would have taken in that case ; he urged the necessity of restoring our privileges in that direction. He said, "By an Act passed some time ago one of our functions was virtually annihilated : we had only two of any consequence, first, to control the standard of pre-medical education, and, secondly, to see that the medical or professional training was up to the proper standard for the protection of the public." He came to Clause 3, and he made no reference as to how it had originated. Of course we know how it came into existence. It was through the resolution of Dr. Henry that it was necessary for us to adopt a medical tariff. You know upon what grounds we had a medical tariff ; the different constituencies had the opportunity of framing their own tariff and submitting it to this Council for endorsation and then it became a rule for the guidance of a judge in assessing in courts of law. Not very long ago, through the influence brought to bear by a certain section of the Legislature of Ontario, we all know what that section is, because it is always opposed to any profession, and it is especially opposed to the medical profession—it seemed to the Government absolutely necessary that something should be done. I am speaking from a political standpoint. Perhaps, had I been a legislator, from a political standpoint I might have felt forced to do the same thing as such a legislator did because legislation has to be effected for the body politic, not for individuals ; but we had that tariff blotted out of existence. I do not know whether or not this Council or its Committee on Legislation had been apprised of the fact ; I do not think I knew of it until all at once it fell like a bomb-shell on me that the legislation was completed, that a bill had been introduced and passed through its several readings, and we no longer had a tariff. That is one of our functions of which we have been deprived. Dr. Sangster said, "Mr. Premier, a very large number"—I want to be discreet in the words I use ; I am inclined to think he said, "The largest proportion of my constituents," but I want to be careful that I do not go beyond the lines of absolute truth ; it is a little difficult to reproduce everything at so late a date, but he said at least this much, "A very large number of my constituents have no special desire for a tariff ; indeed, they think they are just as well without one." There may be some gentlemen present who think they will be just as well without a tariff. Dr. Sangster should have borne in mind that 1,821 men in Ontario wanted a tariff. But supposing a tariff had been of no particular use the very fact that the Legislature thought it expedient to step in and deprive us of a certain function which we had was sufficient to make us, as liberty-loving men, go there and demand that that privilege be granted to us again. There was no earthly reason, so far as justice is concerned, why that power should be taken away. I call your attention to another point. Remember what Dr. Sangster said, that a very large number of men in his constituency had stated to him that they were not fond of or anxious for a tariff. I have gone over that petition, I have taken the three counties, York, Ontario and Victoria, and I found that in our last election 126 persons cast their vote in Dr. Sangster's constituency, and ninety-eight cast their votes for Dr. Sangster himself.

Dr. McLAUGHLIN—This is not connected with the question before us. Dr. Britton seems to have set himself to make an attack upon Dr. Sangster, and he is going in all· directions to do it. Dr. Britton has already occupied twice his time.

Dr. BRITTON—I ask the voice of this Council as to whether or not I must quit ; whether I am to be choked off now.

The PRESIDENT—I think Dr. Britton is entitled to speak. A grave accusation is made against his character.

Dr. BRITTON—As I said before, 126 persons voted in our last general election in Dr. Sangster's constituency, 98 voting for Dr. Sangster and 38 voted for his competitor ; in that constituency there are somewhere between 140 and 150 members, out of which 124 signed that petition ; in other words, 124 virtually said to Dr. Sangster we would like you, being on this Committee on Legislation, to assist us in having that petition granted, in having a tariff enacted again, or rather the privilege granted to our representative of re-enacting a tariff. I shall not say a word more upon this ; a good many may have said to Dr. Sangster that they did not care whether they had a tariff or not. That may be perfectly true ; I am not accusing him of uttering a falsenood, but at the same time he should have been aware of how many of his constituents wanted that tariff re-enacted, but if he was aware and took the course which he followed it was equivalent to saying, "My constituents do not know what they need ; they are a lot of country bumpkins ; I do not represent a city ; I just represent country places like Lindsay "—

The PRESIDENT—I must call you to order Dr. Britton ; you are going a little far.

Dr. BRITTON—He further said, "Mr. Premier and gentlemen, these last clauses were added on as a bribe to secure the signature to the petition of those who would not have signed it had these clauses not been there." That is enough for me to say regarding that. I have told you the course he took in the Legislature ; I have told you the course we all agreed upon unanimously before we went there ; I have told you that he turned on his tracks when he got there ; I have told you that we, figuratively speaking, as soldiers, went to face the enemy ; I have told you that one of our company who had stood shoulder to shoulder with us and said, " Yes, we will all fight together," threw down his arms and turned the muzzle of his rifle on his companions when he met the enemy. It is quite open for anybody to speak ; I am ready to leave my case as to my honesty in preparing this report in the hands of the members of this Committee. (Applause).

Dr. SANGSTER—Mr. President and Gentlemen, I am a little taken by surprise ; as I told you I had no idea that report-had been prepared, and I had seen nothing of it until the attack made by the gentleman in the room this afternoon. I attack his veracity so far as saying that when he declares the first four clauses of that petition were indorsed unanimously by the Legislative Committee, he was saying what was not true. He says that he is very anxious to keep within the regions of truth, and I can only say for a gentleman who professes to be anxious to keep within the regions of truth that he has wandered very far indeed. His statement contains some truth and some error that, I think, perhaps, may have been unintentional, and some error that I can only think was intentional and premeditated. It has been my misfortune this morning to oppose a pet scheme of Dr. Britton's to eliminate the fifth year from the medical curriculun—

Dr. BRITTON—I object to that. That comes within the report of the Committee on Education, and I say that a man who comes forward here and imputes motives in that way is far outside the limit of parliamentary procedure.

The PRESIDENT—I think it should be withdrawn.

Dr. SANGSTER—I am stating it was my misfortune or my fortune to strongly oppose a pet scheme of Dr. Britton's to eliminate the clinical year from the medical course.

Dr. BRITTON—I say that Dr. Sangster must withdraw every word of that because I have not the opportunity of stating the circumstances on which I suggested that the fifth year be withdrawn.

The PRESIDENT—Under the consideration of the educational report you will have an opportunity.

Dr. BITTON—This is done for the purpose of making it appear that I was making an effort to reduce the standard of the medical profession. He must withdraw it.

Dr. SANGSTER—The effort is to show the animus of the attack this afternoon.

Dr. BRITTON—That is imputing a motive. If Dr. Sangster does not withdraw it I shall ask the Council to order him to withdraw it.

The PRESIDENT—Do you ask that I shall insist on that at present ?

Dr. SANGSTER—I do not want to put the Council in any unpleasant position, therefore, I will withdraw it. I will proceed. Some of the things that Dr. Britton has stated correctly represent me in my position before the Government last spring and before the Legislative Committee ; others grossly misrepresent me. I state that the move freely, as you Mr. President were present, and I am prepared to submit myself very largely to your own sense of honor and justice in the matter ; you were present on that occasion and heard the entire discussion. I objected to the course taken by the Executive Committee in regard to the petition, and I objected to these clauses from the very outset and I objected to the course of the Executive Committee because they founded their petition upon a motion of Dr. Bray's which, as I stated frankly before the Legislative Committee, had been discussed ; that Dr. Dickson had proposed an amendment to it, and that that amendment had been formally put, so that when the motion was put to the Council last year it was put and passed as the motion of Dr. Bray's and not as the amended motion by Dr. Dickson. This was in the Council building, not before the Legislative Assembly. The Announcement was turned up and the paragraph referring to the discussion supported my contention in that matter. Then the Registrar was asked whether Dr. Bray's motion was not the one put to the Council ; he stated that it was. The minute-book was produced, it was looked over and the resolution was found and the Registrar declared it was in the handwriting of Dr. Bray, and I remarked, you cannot expect the profession to attach much importance to your Announcement if such gross errors as that can creep into it, that an important resolution of that kind can be omitted. Then, I objected to the action of the Executive Committee because they embraced in their petition a matter that had never been mooted in the Council at all. the seeking to attain from the Legislature increased powers of punishment for that class of persons that we term "quacks." I stated that could only have been thrown into the petition as a sop to induce medical practitioners to attach their signatures thereto. I stated with regard to the petition for a tariff that when it was explained to the medical men that the tariff we were seeking was not a tariff to produce a uniform system of fees, but merely a tariff that should be a criterion to judges in courts of law as to what might be adjudged as reasonable charges, not many practitioners cared about such a tariff as that. I objected to the mixing up of these three things together. Then, the Executive Committee, without one word of concurrence or authority from this Council, had not only decided to issue that petition in its three-fold form and to obtain signatures to it, but they had proceeded upon the strength of that to get Mr. Osler to prepare a draft of the bill to be introduced into the

Legislature and to be introduced, you understand, Mr. President and gentlemen, without any reference to this Council, to be introduced then and there into the Legislature. They had consulted some of the medical members in the House who strongly opposed the introduction of the bill at the time for these purposes, saying the time was inopportune and that it would be fatal to make any attempt in that direction. Then the question of going before the Government came up, the clauses were read one by one and I dissented from each one of the four clauses. I declare that I dissented from each one of the four clauses, and finally I agreed to one, on which the Committee unanimously agreed they could go to the House on, that was the one seeking the right to determine our own matriculation and curriculum requirements. Dr. Williams took strong ground against attempting to force any legislation at that time. Dr. Machell and Dr. Williams both spoke about attempting to present the petition to the Legislature at that time. We then proceeded to the House with the distinct understanding on my part, and I am sure there are gentlemen in the room who will bear me out in saying, that while that petition might be shown to the Government and its general purport might be named—(the President meanwhile insisting that he had been instructed by the Executive Committee to carry that petition to the Government, and that he must do his duty)—the understanding was that it should be presented there, and its general character explained but no details entered into. We met in the House, and as I say, Dr. Barrick sat behind me. To my surprise the President got up and presented the petition and entered into it clause after clause explaining it, explaining the one with reference to the "quacks," the one with reference to the tariff as well as the one referring to the proposed legislation. I remarked to Dr. Barrick at the time, "that is a distinct breach of our agreement." And I got up and objected to the petition. I objected to the petition as Dr. Britton says ; I objected to it on its introductory form, I objected to it because it was not the petition authorized by resolution of the Council, I objected to it because I thought that to seek legislation or to present a petition to the Government or to the Legislature at the present juncture, seeking increased power to impose higher penalties upon quacks. and seeking a tariff of fees which I claim was not required, and not asked for by the profession when they understood in what limited acceptance the tariff of fees was proposed. I stated that those two clauses could only serve to further antagonize the Legislature to the profession ; and upon the whole I objected to the petition being presented to the Government. I stated what Dr. Britton says, only he states it in a somewhat incorrect form, that I did not think anybody should be permitted to stand between the Government and the Legislature on the one hand and the people or profession on the other ; that I was like other people, I was human, liable to err and that I would not place my own constituents in the position of having a body, of which I was a member, standing between them and the freest possible access to the Legislature and to the Government in case they thought they were in any way wronged or treated with injustice. I stated that I could not conceive that the Government would give or could give this Council the power proposed, because if they proceeded to do so they would have to promise to Workmen's Associations and to other incorporated associations . that no legislation should be intoduced into parliament that was opposed to their interests, unless it first emanated from themselves. I have stated, as far as I can remember, but I would not undertake, as Dr. Britton has undertaken, to repeat a man's words that were uttered six or nine months ago ; and although I claim to have a very retentive memory, I do not profess that I could repeat my own words or any other gentleman's words at that distance of time. Dr. Britton claims he repeats the *ipsissima verba.*

Dr. BRITTON—Excuse me, I said I thought I could repeat some of the words, that I could in any case give the substance of what was said, and you are now reproducing very well indeed what you said on that occasion, and it only confirms what I, a short time ago, narrated.

Dr. SANGSTER—That is a matter for the gentlemen in this room to determine. Dr. Britton has made his statement and I claim he has wandered very far from the true and exact statement of the case as it occurred. I have made my rebuttal. I have tried not to use hard terms ; I have been prompted to say things that are severe, and I think the members of this Council know that if I give way to the impulse that is in me I can, at times, say things that are very severe, but I have restrained myself from doing so ; I have tried to give you a plain, true and unvarnished statement of the things that occurred on that occasion and I can only now leave myself in your hands, and in the hands of the other gentlemen that were there, to say whether my statement or Dr. Britton's is the more correct or the more honest explanation of what occurred on that occasion.

The PRESIDENT—Since you have asked the different members of the Committee to express their recollection of what occurred, I think it is only right that they should give expression to it. I would ask Dr. Machell what he recollects about it.

Dr. REDDICK—Couldn't we be spared any more of this kind of thing ?

Dr. SANGSTER—The matter has assumed a very serious form. Here are two gentlemen who have risen in this room and who have spoken upon matters attacking my veracity, and I ask the fullest examination into the facts of the case by this Council ; I think less than that would be less than what is due.

Dr. BRITTON—I am very anxious for the members of the Committee to tell us what their recollections of this occasion are.

The PRESIDENT—I will ask Dr. Machell to narrate what he remembers of it.

Dr. MACHELL—I am afraid I cannot throw very much light on this subject, but I will tell you my connection with it at that meeting. Dr. Sangster certainly was very much opposed to the proposition.

Dr. SANGSTER—Do you mean in the committee room before we went to the Government ?

Dr. MACHELL—Yes. Dr. Sangster was very much opposed, but after a good deal of discussion by nearly everybody, my understanding was that Dr. Sangster agreed practically with all the points, and agreed that it should be presented to the Legislature   What Dr. Sangster said at the meeting in the Legislative building I do not know.   I arrived too late to hear what was said by anybody ; the meeting was just breaking up when I arrived.

Dr. ROGERS—Your recollection was that we agreed to have the petition put before the Government.

Dr. MACHELL—Certainly.

Dr. BARRICK--As the seconder of the resolution to adopt this report, and as a member of the Legislative Committee, I will as briefly as possible, state my recollection of the facts. I may state first that when Dr. Brittton read his report I listened to him very carefully and my own conviction was, as he went on from clause to clause, that it was a correct interpretation of what took place. Now, we had nothing at all to do with the rightness or wrongness of the Executive Committee in ordering any work ; we had nothing to do with regard to discussing whether the questions there were right or wrong, we were met there as the Legislative Committee to deal with a petition signed, as it was stated, by some 1,821 medical men.   Now, Mr. Chairman, supposing I had disagreed with every part of that petition, my duty was to present that petition—(hear, hear)—and if every member of that committee individually opposed every clause in it, as the Legislative Committee, .were bound to present the petition coming to us signed by 1,821 medical men ; that was clearly our duty. Now, you all know that some people are very anxious tò make speeches and there was an uneasiness manifested at this committee meeting to get away to the Legislature, and I stated most emphatically then, gentlemen, what discussions you have, what differences you have, let them be settled right here ; do not let us go to the Government divided.   I was very emphatic upon that.   There is just a little difference of opinion here, but when things are explained I think you will find there is not such a great difference after all. Dr. Sangster clearly did state there that he did not approve of certain things, but so far as my recollection goes we settled upon this : we will present the petition just as it is without any comments. That was our duty, gentlemen.   We were not going there to defend the revisions of that, we were going there simply to present the petition to the Government, and, so far as I know, that was the distinct understanding ; and Dr. Sangster, I think agreed to that, namely, the simple presentation of the petition.

Dr. SANGSTER—May I ask, as important in connection with that, whether Dr. Barrick does or does not remember I stated if details were entered into by the others that I would reply ?

Dr. BARRICK—That is right.

Dr. BRITTON—I would like to ask another question of Dr. Barrick. Was or was it not the case that Dr. Sangster made that statement long before the general discussion took place and long before the unanimous conclusion was arrived at that we should go to the Government to present the petition ?   In my report I have stated that early in the discussion, Dr. Sangster announced he was to be left free to criticize the petition if it went before the Government.

Dr. BARRICK—If the petition was discussed before the Government then he would hold a free-hand, but if the petition was presented and no discussion, that he was perfectly satisfied.   That is as far as I recollect.

Dr. SANGSTER—That is correct.

Dr. BARRICK—That was my·understanding. I fully understood when we went to the Legislature that we went there to present the petition, that we did not go there to discuss that petition, because had that been the case, I would have said, gentlemen, discuss this petition right here and settle what you are going to do.   We went to the Legislature and the petition was presented and the prayer of the petition was read and I thought that was the end of the matter and I must say that I was greatly surprised when the President, who is always full of debate as you all know, was so boiling over that he had to discuss it. I thought it was a very uncalled for thing ; I thought it was a breach of faith in connection with that Committee. I went there for the purpose of simply presenting that petition, as it was our bounden duty to do, but I did not go there to discuss it because I knew if we did we would have the same differences before the Government as we had had in our committee meeting, and that was to be deplored ; and I felt very anxious as Dr. Rogers went on discussing this, because it was certain if it was discussed that Dr. Sangster would reply. What I understood to be our duty in going to the Legislature was just merely to present the petition ; that is one thing I am very clear on because I am sure every member of that Committee must remember I said most emphatically, let us not go to the Legislature divided. If we can unite upon presenting the petition, let us go and present the petition ; if we are going to discuss the matter let us discuss it and settle it in this room here and become unanimous upon something.

Dr. ROGERS—Allow me to ask the speaker a question ; he has brought my name into prominence. How could the petition be presented unless it was read or something in some way said explaining it to the Government ?

Dr. BARRICK—I might just answer that the petition explains itself. There was the petition and Dr. Rogers read the prayer of the petition, which it was our duty to present, and that spoke for itself.

Dr. BRITTON—Would I be allowed to ask Dr. Barrick a question. What was your interpretation of the meaning of my question when I asked the individual members of that Committee did they agree ? What was your interpretation of the meaning of my question when I asked you individually whether or not you dissented from my statement regarding each clause and the necessity for its recitation ?

Dr. SANGSTER—The gentleman asked no question individually ; he took the clauses up *seriatim* and asked me : "Could you agree to that, Dr. Sangster ?" and I said, "no," to the first four of them, and I agreed with the one referring to the curriculum.

Dr. BRITTON—Is that correct, that he said "no" to each of the four ?

Dr. BARRICK—There were so many "no's."

Dr. BRITTON—Did he answer ?

Dr. BARRICK—Dr. Sangster said "no" to so many of them that I do not know—.

The PRESIDENT—That is not the question asked by Dr. Britton ; he asks whether he turned to each and every one of the members of the Committee and said, do you dissent or will you remain' quiet.

Dr. MCLAUGHLIN—I submit that that question should not be put.

Dr. ROGERS—That is a most absurd thing.

Dr. BARRICK—So far as I can recollect, the only thing we agreed unanimously upon was the presenting of that petition as it was.

Dr. MCLAUGHLIN—Hear, hear.

Dr. RGOERS—Did Dr. Sangster oppose the petition after—

Dr. BARRICK—I thought you both went a little too far.

Dr. WILLIAMS—I was present at the meeting of the Committee in the building ; our opinions were asked with reference to the petition, and I believe that I was the first to speak on the subject, and I expressed my opposition to presenting the petition to the Legislature in pretty strong terms. While I did that, I said that I was but one, and if the majority decided that it was the right thing to do to present it, my opinion should be waived and I would act on the voice of the majority. Dr. Sangster subsequently expressed himself about in the same terms that I had, with the exception that he did not consent to waive his opinions subsequently ; but, he said that if the petition was discussed before the Government, he reserved to himself the right to criticize it or to express the other side. We then talked over the matter for some time. The importance was presented by Dr. Barrick and some others that we should not go unless we went as a united Committee ; there should be no division before the Government. Upon that promise it was understood that there should be no discussion, only in general terms ; that there should be no details gone into. That was my understanding. When that was arrived at, Dr. Britton put the question to all the parties present and severally they promised, as I·understood, to abstain from any discussion, providing it was only presented in general terms, and Dr. Sangster's assent was given, as Dr. Britton says, by a distinct bow. It was my conviction that Dr. Rogers had kept pretty well within what our understanding was on the general terms. That was what I thought, and I was a good deal surprised when Dr. Sangster got up to discuss the other side. I admit that I came away believing that Dr. Sangster had committed a breach of faith with the Committee in that matter. That was the impression left on my mind. I will go into no details further.

The PRESIDENT—I will ask Dr. Emory to give us his recollections.

Dr. EMORY—I was fortunately sick in bed.

Dr. ROGERS—I have a report in which the matter can be brought up again.

Dr. BRITTON—You were present, Mr. President, I ask you to give your impression.

The President—I think it is an understood thing that the President is not required to enter into discussions, but if it is wished by both yourself and Dr. Sangster I will be very glad to say what I recollect of the meeting.

Dr. Sangster—I would like you to do so.

The President—I have not a very retentive memory.

Dr. Sangster—I am so conscious that I was honest to the best of my intention that if one hundred were there I would like them individually to give evidence. Dr. McLaughlin also was there and I have no doubt he has a distinct recollection of the circumstances.

The President—As a member of the Committee I may say we met in the College building and the petition already referred to was read and discussed ; Dr. Sangster took strong opposition to it on the lines that have already been indicated. Some of the members, myself amongst others, were averse to presenting the petition to the Legislature, because we had been informed by leading men in the Legislature that it was an inopportune time and it would probably be thrown out and do us more harm than good. There was further discussion and we thought an expression coming from so many members of the profession could not be ig-nored, therefore it was agreed that we should call upon the Government, but not on the Legislature, and read the petition to them, point out its salient points and leave it for future consideration. I recollect the action in the room, already referred to. Dr. Sangster was strongly opposed to it, and moreover said he reserved to himself the right of discussing the matter if it were made the subject of discussion. However, afterwards, the clauses were taken up and Dr. Britton asked us severally and conjointly if we were agreeable to allowing them to go as they were, that was asked two or three times, "Do you agree to it ?" That was the distinct understanding. When the petition was presented to the Government I thought that Dr. Rogers, our then President, was exceedingly fair and kept to the lines very closely ; he read the prayer of the petition and merely explained it ; did not go into any discussion of the different points ; and I congratulated myself upon his success, as I thought, at the time. After that I must say I was rather surprised to hear Dr. Sangster get up and oppose the resolutions as he had formerly done when we first met in committee. That is my recollection. He has already stated what he said to the Government and, so far as I can remember, what he has said is exactly correct. There might have been a misunderstanding on his part with regard to the discussion ; that is a part that is open to discussion.

Dr. Rogers—He opposed the prayer of the petition.

The President—He opposed it, and opposed it in the committee room, too.

Dr. Rogers—And before the Government.

The President—Yes, he opposed it there and he said it was a breach of faith.

Dr. McLaughlin—I regret exceedingly the bitterness that has been brought into this debate by Dr. Britton.

Dr. Britton—You should withdrew that ; I have not brought any bitterness into it,

Dr. McLaughlin—I withdraw the word because I do not know the meaning of it. If there has not been acrimony on the part of our friend Dr. Britton I have never seen any. I I think Dr. Sangster, for him, was exceedingly calm ; he has exercised a degree of calmness.—

The President—That you did not anticipate.

Dr. McLaughlin—That everyone in this room might well emulate and particularly, I might venture to say again without being offensive, Dr. Britton. The whole of this trouble has arisen because Dr. Britton has irregularly brought in a report of Dr. Britton alone. I have not yet been able to find one single member of that Committee who was called on to consider that report before it was presented to the Council to-day, and that is practically the report of Dr. Britton and not the report of the Committee. If Dr. Britton had done his duty and called that Committee together.

Dr. Emory—Is Dr. McLaughlin discussing the whole question or stating his recollection of the facts ?

Dr. McLaughlin—The whole question is before the chair.

The President—I would rather you would give your recollection of the facts first and then go on.

Dr. McLaughlin—My recollection is this, I was summoned to the city to attend a meeting of the Property Committee and having nothing to do at the time that the Legislative Committee was in session I went into the room and listened to the discussion and I heard Dr. Sangster vigorously oppose every prayer of that petition but one—most vigorously. The agreement was finally made, as Dr. Barrick has stated, that this petition should be presented to the Government without comment, and all the members of that Committee agreed if that petition was handed into the Government, without comment, they would not discuss it. People who present petitions to the Government do not necessarily go themselves ; at the same time, petitions are sometimes brought and people speak upon them. I submit that instead of this being a mere presentation of the petition, Dr. Rogers went into a minute and detailed statement of everything. I think I can call to the recollection of the Committee one thing that occurred that will corroborate my statement. Dr. Rogers spoke pretty extensively upon this "That your Honorable Body will extend to the medical profession of this Province the courtesy of not changing or amending the Ontario Medical Act until any proposed change or amendment has been placed before the Ontario Medical Council for consideration." He urged that before the Government, and if he will recollect, I recollect and I presume that some other members of that Committee will recollect, the Attorney-General said, "Oh, that is something that we cannot grant, but if your Bill, or any other Bill, comes in it will be referred to a committee and then you will be heard before the committee." That passed, showing the minuteness with which Dr. Rogers went into the details of that petition. There is not a clause in the prayer of that petition that the gentleman did not discuss and I venture to say he spent not less than half an hour in discussing the various prayers of the petition. I understood at once and I felt the very moment he began to discuss that first clause that Dr. Sangster was free to go on and discuss that upon the other side. As said by Dr. Barrick, I thought it was unfortunate, but that was my impression and I thought Dr. Sangster was perfectly keeping the agreement he made in that room when he commenced to discuss that upon the other side. Dr. Rogers presented the idea, "Now here is an important matter, you ought not to allow a Bill to come into this Legislature without first submitting it to the Medical Council." That was the whole bone of contention. Dr. Sangster, I think, properly took the ground that it was a retrograde movement and, as I told you, the Attorney-General said, "No, we cannot grant you that prayer." It is the most absurd prayer that was ever put into a petition because if the Medical Council has a right to say the Government shall not introduce a Bill until we consider it then the Oddfellows have the same right, the Church Courts have the same rights, the Templars have the same right, and the manufacturers and every other body of men in this country have just as much right to make that prayer as we have and if you do that the whole wheels of legislation are stopped. I mention that to corroborate my memory of what took place and I do not think it is necessary to discuss that any further. I thought Dr. Sangster was perfectly within his agreement which he made in the committee room when he began to discuss that question. I want to say a word or two about the petition, I want to tell you that that petition was not presented to the Government in the proper sense of presenting a petition, because you never present a petition to the Government and then lug it away home with you. The great big volume was brought up there and laid on the table and not one Minister of the Crown, except one, opened that book to look at the petition and he simply looked at it and shut it up without reading one sentence. The petition was not presented to the Government, it was simply carried up there as an exhibit and laid upon the table for a few minutes and then taken away home and now it is in the archives of this Council.

Dr. ROGERS—A few minutes ago I thought you said, "half an hour;" now you say, "a few minutes."

Dr. McLAUGHLIN—Your "few minutes" up there are just what they are like here. I regret exceedingly that this discussion has come on, and I would like to see this whole matter settled up peaceably and amicably yet. I understood Dr. Britton to say that every member of the Committee that was present there agreed to every item in that petition. I cannot understand how he came to that conclusion. I am not saying but what he came to it honestly. We know in this Council that Dr. Sangster, along with myself, fought that resolution when it was brought in by Dr. Bray, we fought it as hard as we could fight it. How is it possible for Dr. Britton, knowing all of these things, to say that he questioned Dr. Sangster in regard to that petition, and that he said he agreed to it ? I do not believe that Dr. Britton wilfully put that in there knowing it to be anything else but correct, and my friend Dr. Sangster did not question his veracity as a gentleman when he put it there, but 'the further the debate went on it seemed to get the more bitter, and language was used that I regret was used. The whole thing was a misunderstanding. Dr. Britton, no doubt, understood what he thought, others understood otherwise, as I did, as Dr. Williams did, and as Dr. Barrick did, that the agreement was that the petition should be taken up there, that it was not presented in the way a petition should be presented, because if it had been it should have remained there, but it was to be taken up for the Government to look at.

Dr. BRITTON—Without discussing any details ?

Dr. McLAUGHLIN—Without discussing any details, and it was discussed.

Dr. BRITTON—The President says not.

Dr. McLAUGHLIN—I say so and Dr. Sangster says so, and I have told you the answer the Honorable Mr. Hardy gave.

The PRESIDENT—Part of your statement in regard to the Attorney-General is correct, but you have not told the whole truth. He said he could not promise that sort of thing, but it was an Act that was always granted, it was granted the Law Society, but we couldn't expect the Government to undertake a thing of that kind.

Dr. McLAUGHLIN—Quite so ; I quite agree with that. If this Council agrees to bring in a bill, and there is no doubt about it that bill can be taken up to the Government and you can privately discuss it with the Attorney-General. To ask the Government to bring in no

10

law amending the Medical Act without first submitting it to this Council was not spoken of by Mr. Hardy. The other statement you made was, if we want to bring in a bill amending the Ontario Medical Act let us frame it, let us take it to the Government, let them give their opinion upon it, and let us modify it according to their opinion in order that we pass it through the House ; but to ask members of Parliament not to introduce a bill without the permission of the Council, or to ask the Government to do it is a thing unprecedented in the history of legislation.

Dr. BRAY—I think there is a misunderstanding as to the resolution. I was not a member of the Committee, and I do not desire to say anything about the Committee, but when I brought in that resolution I read it in the first place as it appears in this Announcement, and Dr. Dickson, as seconder of that resolution, suggested that it was pretty strong and that some words which he suggested should be put in the place of some words I had used ; I accepted that suggestion, and there was no amendment made to that. It has been stated here there was an amendment. It was never put. There was only one resolution brought in by me ; there was no amendment ever proposed. There were some words suggested by Dr. Dickson, and I accepted them and put them in my original resolution as they are, in my own handwriting.

Dr. ROGERS—As probably this is a matter involving some little interest to a few of us I am glad indeed to have listened to the eloquent remarks of Dr. McLaughlin. I do not know, and I would not like to insinuate, that Dr. McLaughlin happened in there in order to support his friend Dr. Sangster before the Government in case a discussion of that kind arose, but he really did happen to be there although he was not a member of the Legislative Committee. He has given a statement here to-day in one way, Dr. Sangster in another, and Dr. Barrick's somewhat in their favor ; as against that there is yourself, Mr. President, Dr. Britton, Dr. Williams, Dr. Machell, and myself, who agree with the statement as made by Dr. Britton. There are one or two important items which may be considered; in the first place, you will have to consider this petition which was before the Government ; it had been sanctioned by the great majority, it had been signed by 1,821 medical practitioners, or the great majority of the medical men of this Province, it had been signed by 124 members of Dr. Sangster's own division, it had been signed by a majority in Dr. McLaughlin's division.

Dr. McLAUGHLIN—I beg your pardon.

Dr. ROGERS—It had been signed by a majority in Dr. Sangster's division, and I believe by a majority in every division in Ontario—the vast majority. Dr. Sangster took it upon himself not only, I believe, to break a contract entered into with us as a Legislative Committee, but he went before the Government and opposed the petition signed by the majority of his own members—the majority of the members who sent him here—whose representative he is, whom it is supposed he stands here to represent. He went before the Government with this petition, and although 124 members of his own constituents had signed it he opposed it before the Government and denounced it in the strongest possible language.

Dr. SANGSTER—I am willing to leave myself in the hands of my constituents on that question, and if they condemn me, I think I would be as unfortunate as my friend, Dr. Rogers.

Dr. ROGERS—Perhaps that is so, but time will tell. In regard to the statement of my friend, Dr. Barrick, I am sorry he has found that I was so given to debate in this Council, and it may be that at some future time he will learn a little better. I do not think I ever debate a subject unless I have good reason to. However, in making this statement before the Government with regard to the petition I carried out exactly, as clearly as a man could, the agreement entered into. I laid the petition before the Government ; I read the petition and I simply, and nothing more, explained it. I think I was not more than five or six minutes explaining the whole matter. Then we had the exhibition of seven or eight medical men of this Council going before the Government, and one medical man getting up and denouncing what the others had asked for. We had the exhibition of a medical profession, of a body claiming to say by their petition that they were a united body, and one man getting up and saying, we are not united. This was done, for Mr. Harcourt said, only seven and one of you opposes the rest.

Dr. SANGSTER—We had the exhibition of one man purporting to be President of an important public body in this country daring to deliberately break faith with his colleagues, and after going to that House with the understanding that his mouth was shut, venturing to enter into details upon that which he had promised not to touch upon.

Dr. ROGERS—I have the floor. I have not any fear of answering you either here or elsewhere ; you need not worry at all.

Dr. SANGSTER—In the back yard.

Dr. ROGERS—Well, I am not of the same character of blackguard which perhaps you belong to.

Dr. McLaughlin—I ask for your ruling, Mr. President. Dr. Sangster has simply referred to Dr. Rogers asking Dr. Armour into the back yard a few years ago.

Dr. Rogers—He attempts to say, he wants to maintain, that in his exhibition before the Government he was doing nothing extraordinary in exhibiting the medical profession as a most un-united body, as a body that was not worthy of the consideration of the Government, and as such the Government should not grant their prayer. I maintain in thus denouncing the petition which the majority of his constituents had signed, and which 1,821 medical men had signed, that he has not only broken faith with the Council and broken faith with the profession in his division, but with the whole profession in Ontario.

Dr. Henry—I move that we adjourn.

Dr. Brock—I second that.

Dr. Britton—Notwithstanding that motion, I would personally like to see this matter come to an end. I still feel that I took the proper course in justifying myself, and that I acted the part of a gentleman, and when I was accused of an act of untruthfulness I could do nothing less than take the course that any one of Her Majesty's British subjects feels he is called upon to take, that is, to vindicate himself. I have been accused of using rather extreme language ; I cannot recollect a solitary word I used that I now think was extreme. I think this discussion should go no further.

The President—I agree with you.

Dr. Britton—I am satisfied, and I move the adoption of this report.

Dr. Bray—Before that motion is put, I would like to say a few words.

Dr. Henry—Isn't there a motion that we adjourn ?

The President—From what I can infer from Dr. Britton, and I think from Dr. Sangster too, there is no desire on the part of anybody—

Dr. Britton—No, I propose that it come to an end.

Dr. Rogers—I have a report that covers part of the same ground.

Dr. Sangster—I would be satisfied that the thing should end here.

Dr. Bray—I regret exceedingly that this trouble has taken on such a bitter form, and I hope that we will not see any such proceedings here in the future. I am glad Dr. Britton is satisfied, and Dr. Sangster is satisfied, to have this discussion dropped, and now let it drop and be dead and buried forever.

Dr. Britton—I move, seconded by Dr. Barrick, that this report be adopted.

Dr. McLaughlin—I do not like that report to go as it is because it does not seem to be right. I would suggest that the report should go back to the Committee and that they reconsider it, and I am satisfied if that is done, it will be so altered that we will be able to rush it through without any discussion. I would move that it be referred back to the Committee for amendment.

The President—I would be afraid that that would open up the thing again.

Dr. Sangster—I do not think the Legislative Committee, as a committee, has any desire to do any injustice, and I am quite satisfied it should be referred to it. This is not the report of the Legislative Committee, it is the report of Dr. Britton.

Dr. Britton—I have not the slightest objection to it going to the Legislative Committee.

Dr. McLaughlin moved, seconded by Dr. Douglas, that the report of the Legislative Committee be referred back to the Committee for reconsideration.

The President put the motion, which, on a vote having been taken, was declared carried.

On motion of Dr. Roome, seconded by Dr. Moore, the Council adjourned to meet at eight o'clock, p.m.

EVENING SESSION.

The Council met at eight o'clock p.m., in accordance with the motion for adjournment.

The President, Dr. Thorburn, in the chair called the Council to order.

The Registrar called the roll, and the following members answered to their names : Drs. Armour, Barrick, Bray, Britton, Brock, Dickson, Douglas, Emory, Fowler, Geikie, Graham, Griffin, Hanly, Henderson, Henry, Logan, Luton, Machell, Moore, McLaughlin, Reddick, Rogers, Sangster, Shaw, Thorburn, Williams.

The Registrar read the minutes of the last meeting.

Dr. Armour—There was a motion on which, with the approval of the Council, I was allowed to reintroduce ; it was the one with regard to which Dr. Dickson gave notice of motion to reconsider. It is not shewn on the minutes.

Dr. Pyne—The reason for that probably is that I did not get it, because it was put in the hands of the special committee appointed to interview the solicitor.

Pending the return of this resolution the minutes were allowed to stand without signature.

NOTICES OF MOTION.

Dr. ROOME—For a special committee to be appointed to secure tenders of offers for the purchase of the College Building, the same to be reported to the next meeting of the Council for consideration as to whether the property shall be sold or not. •

COMMUNICATIONS, PETITIONS, ETC.

None.

MOTIONS OF WHICH NOTICE HAS BEEN GIVEN AT A PREVIOUS MEETING.

Dr. HENRY—I gave notice that I would introduce a by-law to amend by-law No. 70. I move now that leave be granted to introduce a by-law to amend by-law No. 70, and that it be read a first time. The only amendment I propose is to alter the sum that was granted for the per diem allowance from $12.50 to $10.00. I find there is a disposition on the part of the Council to exercise a good deal of economy, and I believe we could not commence at a better place than amongst ourselves. We have shown a disposition to cut down the expenses of some of our officials, one in particular, and I believe it is a move in the right direction; but we should commence with ourselves.

Dr. BRAY—Before that by-law is read I would say to Dr. Henry that the Finance Committee has a report bearing on it, and if he will leave that over until the Finance Committee's report is presented it will be much better; we are working at it as hard as we can.

Dr. HENRY—I was waiting for it to come up, because I know there is a clause in it with regard to this matter. However, that ought not to debar me from bringing this by-law up.

Dr. BRAY—I do not wish to debar you.

The PRESIDENT—It will have to be discussed subsequently. As I understand, you are willing to allow this by-law to stand over until the report of the Finance Committe comes in.

Dr. HENRY—Yes, if it comes in.

The PRESIDENT—It will come in.

Dr. HENRY—I move, seconded by Dr. SHAW, that by-law No. 70 be received and read a first time.

The PRESIDENT put the motion which, on a vote having been taken, was declared carried.

Dr. HENRY read the by-law.

ENQUIRIES.

None.

REPORTS OF STANDING AND SPECIAL COMMITTEES.

Dr. ROGERS presented and read the report of the Executive Committee.

Dr. ROGERS moved that the report of the Executive Committee be received, which, on a vote having been taken, was declared carried.

Dr. FOWLER presented and read the report of the Committee on Registration.

Dr. FOWLER moved that the report of the Committee on Registration be received, which, on a vote having been taken, was declared carried.

Dr. HANLY presented and read the report of the Committee on Rules and Regulations, appended to which is the opinion of Mr. B. B. Osler.

Dr. HANLY moved that the report of the Committee on Rules and Regulations be received, which, on a vote having been taken, was declared carried.

Dr. SANGSTER—When is the proper time to ask that typewritten copies of that report be supplied to members of the Council? It is an important report. It does not touch, in some cases, the points raised, because, for instance, in the matter of the Prosecutor's salary, no one raised the point as to the ability of the Council to settle the remuneration of the Prosecutor. It was as to the mode by which it was to be settled; the contention was that the Council could only settle that by a by-law. Mr. Osler appears to have overlooked that.

Dr. HANLY—I think the Solicitor refers to that, and refers to Section 58 of the Ontario Medical Act as the authority.

The PRESIDENT—When would you like to have these reports?

Dr. SANGSTER—As soon as they can be furnished.

The PRESIDENT—I think in revising the by-laws it would be well to include the solicitor's opinion.

Dr. SANGSTER—It is too late. We asked certain questions from the solicitor for our guidance, and his answer does not guide us in the least, because he does not touch upon the points raised in several instances.

The PRESIDENT—The stenographer thinks that we might get typewritten copies of this report to-morrow morning.

Dr. MACHELL presented and read the report of the Property Committee.

Dr. MACHELL moved that the report be received which, on a vote having been taken, was declared carried.

CONSIDERATION OF REPORTS.

Dr. ROGERS moved, seconded by Dr. LOGAN, that the report of the Executive Committee be adopted.

Dr. ARMOUR—I think it would be better to go into Committee of the Whole on that report; there are some objectionable features in connection with that report that will have to be considered.

Dr. ROGERS moved, seconded by Dr. LOGAN, that the Council do now go into Committee of the Whole to consider the report of the Executive Committee which, on a vote having been taken, was declared carried.

COUNCIL IN COMMITTEE OF THE WHOLE,

Dr. GRAHAM in the chair.

Dr. ROGERS—I have already read the report. Do you wish me to take it up clause by clause, or do you wish me to read it over?

Dr. SANGSTER—Read it clause by clause.

Dr. ROGERS read Clause 1 of the report which, on motion, was adopted.

Dr. ROGERS read Clause 2 of the report which, on motion, was adopted.

Dr. ROGERS read Clause 3 of the report.

Dr. ROOME—Who authorized the Committee to frame an Act and apply to the Government?

Dr. ROGERS—It was on motion of Dr. Bray.

Dr. ROOME—There is nothing in the proceedings showing that there was power placed in the hands of that Committee to do that.

Dr. ROGERS—I think so.

Dr. ARMOUR—I think Dr. Bray's and Dr. Dickson's resolution did not give any authority to any committee from the Council to seek legislation in any way.

Dr. SANGSTER—If there is one thing clear in the records of this Council it is that the Executive Committee had not one particle of right to apply to the Legislature, or to take the first step to apply to the Legislature, to obtain amendments to the Medical Act. I will defy the members of that Committee to find the first line of authority in the proceedings of the Council. I say it would be a most dangerous precedent to establish to place in the hands of the Executive Committee or the Legislative Committee, or even both combined, the power of going over the heads of the Council and, without consulting the Council, obtaining or seeking to obtain an amendment to the Medical Act. That has been the main gist of complaint against the Executive Committee; it was upon that point I have somewhat pointedly attacked that Committee. During the past few months I felt it my duty to the fellow-members of this Council to utter my protest in no uncertain terms against the usurpation of power on their part which belongs to the Medical Council as a whole. I doubt whether the gentlemen in this Council will allow any committee to go over their heads, to transcend their power by usurping power that does not and cannot by any possibility be regarded as belonging to them.

Dr. ROGERS—This is the motion on the back of the circular which was sent to the profession in connection with the petition : " Moved by Dr. Bray, seconded by Dr. Dickson, That a form of petition be framed, and sent to every medical man in the Province by the Registrar for signatures, praying that the Government and Legislature of Ontario will not alter nor amend the Medical Act, nor introduce, nor carry through any new medical legislation, unless such amendments, or new Medical Act, or Acts, be first submitted to the Council of the College of Physicians and Surgeons of Ontario, directly or through the Legislative Committee."

Dr. ROOME—Was there not another motion in reference to it ?

Dr. ROGERS—There is the other motion which is printed on the back of the circular : "Moved by Dr. Henry, seconded by Dr. Dickson, and resolved : That in the opinion of the Medical Council there should be established a Medical Tariff for the Province of Ontario, in order that the reasonable charges, or fees, of the registered medical practitioners, may have a legal status in all courts of law in this Province ; that such Medical Tariff should be framed and sanctioned by this Council, but it should only come into legal force when it has received the sanction and approval of three judges of the Supreme Court of Judicature of Ontario ; that such Medical Tariff, when it comes into legal force as aforesaid, may be

printed, and copies of which shall be distributed to the registered medical practitioners of
Ontario, and each copy, bearing the seal of the College, and the signature of the Registrar
attached thereto, shall be received in all courts in lieu of the original tariff; that such
copies of the said Medical Tariff shall be a scale of reasonable charges within the meaning of
Seeton 39 of the Medical Act." We have here a direction to get a petition. We could not
have the power to have a tariff without going to the Legislature, it was impossible. I did
not want to go to the Legislature, none of us wanted to, but here are two directions and we
could not help ourselves.

Dr. SANGSTER—When that matter was up for discussion last year and it was objected
to by myself and others, we were distinctly told by Dr. Bray and others that the intention
was merely to have that petition signed to use it if we needed to.

Dr. ROGERS—I have nothing to do with that. As far as we could understand it was a
direct direction on the part of the Council to the Executive Committee to get a petition first
and also to get power to have a Medical Tariff.

Dr. REDDICK—It was distinctly understood that this petition was simply and purely for
the purpose of furnishing information to the members of this Council, to get the feeling of
the members of the profession throughout the Province. There was no talk of going to the
Legislature, in fact the opposite was talked of. It was thought unwise, but it was thought
that we should get the feeling of the members on this particular subject.

Dr. GEIKIE—I had no idea of such a thing; if I had had the least idea I would have
spoken to some of the members of the Executive Committee and warned them it was a pretty
ticklish time to approach the Legislature. I am surprised.

Dr. CAMPBELL—I do not think there was any intention on the part of the Executive Committee to exceed its powers or go beyond the direction of the Council. The Registrar, I think,
was instructed to prepare the petition. It was thought advisable, as it was an important
matter, that the Executive Committee should oversee its preparation and distribution. The
Executive Committee, at least, I for one, and I think speaking generally for the other
members of the Committee too, was by no means anxious to go to the Legislature for any
legislation whatever. More than that, I think it is perfectly safe to say that the Executive
Committee would not have gone of its own accord to any Legislature unless with the full
approval of the Legislative Committee of this Council which has been formed for the purpose
of watching and overseeing legislation. But, we went this far, we were perfectly justified I
think in making all the necessary preparation and in making all the necessary enquiry and
that was all we did. In order to meet the views of the members of the Council who wanted
a tariff bill we had a form of bill drawn up so that the Legislative Committee, when they met,
could see it. In order that we might know what the conditions were in the Legislature the
Legislative Committee went and consulted the medical men in the House to know what
the feeling was. That I think was all legitimate; we were seeing and looking after the
situation and making enquiry and making preparation. The Executive Committee, so far as
I know, would never have undertaken to go to the Legislature without a direct vote of this
body in so many words saying you must go, but we did consider it was our duty to make all
necessary enquiry and then to have things in shape for the Legislative Committee, which we
did, on the day of the final meeting of the Executive Committee that they might consider
and discuss the matter and see what had better be done. That is as far as the Executive
Committee went and as far as they had any intention of going. I believe they were within
the limits of their duty in so doing.

Dr. SHAW—I understand from Dr. Campbell that there was an Act drawn up by the
Solicitor to submit to the Legislature if it was thought best.

Dr. CAMPBELL—It was drawn up for submission to the Legislative Committee, so that
they might consider and see what had better be done. We wanted to have everything in
shape, so that when the Legislative Committee met they would have all the information
before them.

Dr. SHAW—What became of it?

Dr. ROGERS—A copy of it is in the Committee's report.

Dr. ROOME—The reason I asked the question I did, was that I had read the proceedings
through and I could not find anything. The resolution moved by Dr. Bray was one that I
could not say I approved of very much. If I had been a member of the Local Legislature,
I would not have wanted any petition like that presented to me. I think that a man who
is elected to that position goes untrammeled by any party. Still, at the same time, I am
not going to take any exception to it now, as I was not here at the time the resolution was
passed. In reference to the resolution moved by Dr. Henry, I think that does not very
clearly authorize this Committee to take the action they did. I am not disapproving of it,
no harm is being done and perhaps sometimes we are a little thick-headed. I am not
trying to raise any ill-feeling, I simply wanted a little information for myself, so that if I
was asked the question, I could answer it.

Dr. SHAW—I think the Council only authorized the Committee to take up two questions, the question of the tariff and the question of the petition to the Profession. There were two other clauses added to that, and I do not remember that the Council gave instructions to that effect, and I for one was somewhat surprised when I received the petition asking the medical profession to authorize and endorse the change in the curriculum, giving the Council complete power as indicated in that petition. The fourth clause was in regard to prosecutions, or something of that kind. I would like to know why the Committee added these two clauses in addition to the instructions given by the Council.

Dr. ROGERS—If you remember, the year before last the Discipline Committee was instructed to get certain information, and in giving that information, one member, Dr. Moore, made use of the following words, which are shown at page 58 of the Announcement of 1896-97, which were taken universally by the members as an authority : "We know that if a man sells liquor without a license, he may be fined $50.00 for the first offence, with the addition of a month or two months in jail ; on the next conviction there is no option of a fine, he has to go to jail for three months, and if he is found guilty a third time, he has to go to jail for four months without the option of a fine; so that you see in this case the punishment is progressive. But the punishment is not progressive under our Act, and really a designing man with a little capital could put this Council to a very great deal of expense. If we can only obtain from the Legislature the same law as that which applies to liquor sellers, we then would be enabled to put the unlicensed practitioners and quacks to flight to a moral certainty. We spoke to Mr. Cartwright, the Deputy Attorney-General, on this subject, and Mr. Cartwright thought as we had a precedent in the license law, we might safely go to the Legislature and probably get an amendment to our Act." I might say that this was talked over by the members of the Council, and it was felt at the time without any specific, pointed, positive resolution that if we were going to have a change in the Medical Act—

Dr. ARMOUR—Without any resolution at all. There was no resolution endorsing—

Dr. ROGERS rose as if to speak.

Dr. SANGSTER—I object, Mr. Chairman, the gentleman who is on his defence must not be interfered with. Dr. Rogers has taken the casual remarks of the members of the Council as authority for approaching the Legislature for a new enactment.

Dr. ROGERS—No ; but Dr. Sangster is censured in this report, and I am very glad to have my intentions, my thoughts and words so well understood and so well interpreted by Dr. Sangster.

Dr. SANGSTER—It is sometimes necessary, too.

Dr. ROGERS—I hope it never will be necessary to interpret your acts. Your record is so bright and clear and clean that it has never been necessary, in the world. That was a specific statement by the Discipline Committee after having received instructions from this Council to ascertain certain ways of improving the Medical Act, and that was one of the answers given. In consideration of the fact that we were getting up a petition, it was thought advisable by the Council and by all parties concerned, and I may say we consulted almost all the medical men we come in contact with in Toronto who were members of this body, and we all came to the conclusion that it would be wise to add this to it. Although it was not, as I said before, a pointed resolution, it was accepted by the Council in the same way as a resolution. That is the reason I am asked by Dr. Shaw—

Dr. SHAW—How about Clause 2 ?

Dr. ROGERS—Clause 2 of what ?

Dr. SHAW—Clause 2 of the petition. I mention this because I was spoken to by one of my constituents. There was considerable surprise amongst the members of my constituency that we were approaching the Legislature again, particularly when the last efforts in that direction had met with so small success with the members of the Government. I understood there were just two recommendations by the Council.

Dr. ROGERS—What would that formal petition be ? What was the petition for ? Dr. Bray moved a resolution to have a petition, and what was it for ?

Dr. SHAW—Dr. Bray can tell you that. I do not attempt to explain Dr. Bray's resolution.

Dr. ROGERS—The reason of Dr. Bray's resolution is well understood in this Council. Every member of the Council ought to know we were taken by the throat, figuratively speaking, by the Minister of Education—

Dr. SHAW—That is just the admission I wanted.

Dr. ROGERS—This resolution was put there so as to get the Legislature and the Minister of Education to allow us to have control of the matriculation again. That was the full reason for the motion to have a petition. That was not mentioned there because it would be impossible to mention every detail in a resolution.

Dr. CAMPBELL—The points that we authorized in the preparation of that petition were all matters that, to the best of our knowledge and belief, were either ordered by the Council directly, or approved of by the Council, if not by a direct vote, then by consent. We thought it advisable that all these points should be included in the one petition.   If that was an error of judgment, it was certainly done with the best intention to present the views of the Council. I am not prepared to say it was an error.   I did not suppose that that form of criticism would have been brought up or I would have taken the trouble to have looked up the debates in the Council for the last two or three years ; I think every one of those four points in the petition will be found clearly expressed by the members of the Council as things necessary to have and, therefore, although the particular resolution which Dr. Bray introduced did not say we must specify in that petition every one of those separate things, we assumed—I think we were not assuming too much—that we were to express the views of the Council on all those disputed points ; they were all matters on which the Council had clearly expressed its opinion.

Dr. SANGSTER—I contend on the contrary that the only authority to be found within the covers of the two last Announcements—I can go no further back than that, the life of this Council extends no further back than that—are, the authorization of the petition touching the manner in which medical legislation might be introduced into the House, which we were assured by those who had charge of it when it was challenged was merely intended to be kept in reserve for future use, if necessary ; secondly, a resolution approving of the adoption of a provincial tariff, without one line of instruction to the Executive Committee or the Legislative Committee, or to both combined, or to any other body of men, to take the first step towards securing legislation thereon; and thirdly, the casual remarks made by Dr. Moore, which have been read to you.   I defy the last speaker, after spending two weeks in going over the entire proceedings of this Council, to find one tittle of authority beyond that.   I repeat it would be a most dangerous precedent to establish to allow the Executive Committee or the Legislative Committee, because I think the Legislative Committee have no more power than the Executive Committee, to usurp and act upon one of the most cherished functions of this Council as a whole ; if the Medical Act is to be taken and tinkered with by sub-committees of the Council without the sanction and authority of the Council as a whole, I ask what is your Medical Act likely to become in the course of a few years ?

Dr. CAMPBELL—Is it disputed that those points in the petition are the opinions of the majority of this Council ?

Dr. SANGSTER—There are no opinions from the majority of the Council.

Dr. CAMPBELL—Opinions are often expressed in debate without being formulated in a resolution.   Those opinions have been repeatedly expressed, and I for one had no idea there was any serious objection to any one of them.

Dr. HENRY—So far as that is concerned, for years past I have wished that we might get legislation in connection with that question.   I certainly thought and expected when that resolution was moved here last session, that if the Committee approached the Legislature for any legislation they would take that matter up and try to bring it to a successful issue.   I was not surprised at it ; I supposed they would take up the question of the tariff if they approached the Legislature on other matters.

Dr. McLAUGHLIN—There is not a shadow of a doubt that the only authority given to the Executive Committee by the Council last year was to circulate the petition, the idea of which was moved by Dr. Bray, and seconded and carried in the Council ; beyond that there was no authority whatever delegated to the Executive Committee ; on the contrary, when the motion by Dr. Henry was discussed in Council, it was mentioned by different persons that it was unadvisable under the present temper of the House to go near it for legislation of any kind or description.   As said, I think either by Dr. Campbell or Dr. Williams, the temper of the House is such now that you may go there for something and you will go away with something very different from what you expected to get.   There was a faction in that House that was wielding an influence to some little extent ; although small in numbers, they held a sort of balance of power, and we knew they were hostile to us ; and the general opinion of this Council was, I think I can safely say, that it was not wise to approach the Legislature for any legislation.   I know this personally, I was their friend for many years when I was in the Legislature, and having a knowledge of their thoughts, I thought it would be better for the Medical Council not to go near the House at the present time, otherwise they would get into a difficulty they knew not of.   I agree with the motion of Dr. Henry, although I voted against it at the time.   I do agree that when the proper time comes we may approach the Legislature for legislation along that line, but at the present time I think nothing could be more injudicious than to go there.   In regard to all the other items in that petition, there was no authorization for putting them in.   I have already expressed my views in regard to the part that was authorized, and it is not necessary I should characterize it again.   But I do regret that a learned body, such as this Council, should go to the Legislature with a bungled-up petition that was neither regular nor anything else, and that it has become, as I know—

Dr. ROGERS—Excuse me, I want to ask the gentleman speaking if we went to the Legislature ?

Dr. McLAUGHLIN—The petition was got up to go.

Dr. ROGERS—We did not go yet.

Dr. McLAUGHLIN—Try to compose yourself, listen to what I have to say, and do not jump before necessity arises. That petition was got up to go to the Legislature and to go to the Government. Here was a petition addressed to the Premier of Ontario and the Government and addressed also to the Legislature. Such a petition was never heard of before. If you desired to address both parties you should have had two petitions. I say that these gentlemen rushing before the Legislature without knowing what they were doing were doing a very unadvisable thing; and I go still further and say that the members' of that Legislature and Government, who have seen the heading of that petition, laughed at the irregular manner in which that petition was got up. I think it is to be regretted that that petition was got up at all; it has cost this Council I presume $200, I do not think it can be less; perhaps it is not that much, and it is not worth that much, and I do hope that the Council will dig a grave fathoms deep and bury it never to be seen again. I was not in the chamber when something like a censure was read out.

Dr. SHAW—That is not before us now.

Dr. McLAUGHLIN—I regret that this Committee went beyond its powers. I am not going to accuse them of any ill-disposition or any evil design or anything of that kind, but I think it was unwise. Had that bill gone before the Legislature no man in this Council can possibly tell the damage it would have done us, because the temper of that House was such that we would have come away with a maimed bill. When I raised the question I was not satisfied with the authority for going, but Dr. Campbell explained it, and I take no objection, but in future I do not think any committee should attempt, in any legislation of any kind, to go without the direct vote of this Council. I feel, as a member of this Council, I would be held responsible in the country if any mishap should occur. I do not think the Committee went with any intention of doing the Council any harm, and at the same time this was a simple thing but a serious thing might have happened.

Dr. ROGERS—It was a very big vote. I look upon a vote of 1,821 medical men as being a large vote.

Dr. ROOME—They did not vote to go to the Legislature.

Dr. ROGERS—Yes they did, the petition was to that effect.

On motion, Clause 3 of the report was adopted.

Dr. ROGERS read Clause 4 of the report, which on motion was adopted.

Dr. ROGERS read Clause 5 of the report, and moved its adoption.

Dr. REDDICK—I move in amendment that that clause be stricken out of the report. I do this because possibly it will bring in a repetition of what we had this afternoon; it is the very same thing coming from another committee, in fact from a committee that we might reasonably infer had nothing to do with it. It is the report of the Executive Committee, and it is dealing with something that took place in the Legislative Committee.

Dr. ROGERS—No.

Dr. REDDICK—This particular clause refers to something that took place when the Legislative Committee went before the Government.

Dr. ROGERS—And the Executive Committee together.

Dr. REDDICK—This report is calculated to create just what the majority of the members are endeavoring to get rid of. Here, again, it comes up stronger than ever from another committee, and I think it is an uncalled-for addition to the report, and something that I believe the members of the Council, in the interests of what is right, should set their foot on.

Dr. McLAUGHLIN—Is it possible that a member of a committee cannot express his views upon that committee without another committee taking hold of him by the ears and lugging him before the Council and lecturing him for what he did on another committee? Have we come to a time in this Council when liberty of opinion and speech can have no avail? The Executive Committee was not present in the Legislature. The President, who was a member of that committee, was present, and there may have been two members of that committee present, but the committee that went before the Legislature was the Legislative Committee and no other committee, and I say that no committee has a right to take into its hands to give a report of what transpired in connection with another committee. We have a committee which arrogantly takes to itself the power to declare its opinion of what transpired in the Legislature, and that committee was not there to know what transpired. Now, Mr. Chairman, this is a most extraordinary report, and I do hope that this Council will at once frown down everything of this kind. I know what that is brought into that report for. It is evident upon the face of it they want to get a hit at a certain gentleman; I say, if that is so, and it looks very much like it, that it is unmanly. I do hope that this Council will at once assert its dignity and declare to the committee that they will not allow one committee to transgress and go over the fence into the region of another committee and report a censure to the members of that committee.

Dr. ARMOUR—I just desire to say that I think this is a most unusual proceeding. I have had considerable experience in reports of committees, but I never heard before of a committee censuring a member of that committee in a report brought in in this way or in any other way. I never heard a precedent of that kind. I think there are none existing amongst any civilized organizations, and I am very sorry that any committee of this Council would stoop to such work. Of course, the majority of committees can do what they like, they can present what report they choose, but I think it could not be shown that a majority of any other committee in this Province has ever made a report on the lines that this report is based on with regard to this clause. While it would be deplorable that such a recommendation of censure of one member of a committee should come from any committee it is still more deplorable it should come from the chief committee of this Council.

Dr. CAMPBELL—I suppose in this hot weather it would be pardonable to restrain from violent exertion, and I do not think it is at all necessary that any member of this Council should get excited unduly. I assume when a committee is reporting it not only reports the facts that it knows, and its recommendations to us in that report, but it may express its opinions. The Executive Committee were appointed to look after the affairs of the Council in the interim, and it was the duty of the Executive Committee to see that this petition was regularly presented to the Government. The Committee did so. I admit, sir, that I was not there. I had been in the city at the meeting of the committee the day before, but the Committee waited for the Legislative Committee, and when this petition was presented I was not able to be present and did not have any personal knowledge of the dispute that may have arisen on that day. When I was informed by the majority of the committee who were there that when the petition ordered by this Council, as I supposed, signed by the members of the College in good faith, as I presumed, was being presented to the Government in accordance with what I understood to be the instructions of the Council, a representative of the Council opposed the action of the Council there I did feel regret, and I had no hesitation in signing the report expressing regret that any member of the Council had undertaken to oppose the action of the Council, decided on by the Council. Now, no one questions the right of every member of this body or any other body to dispute the will of the body in the body ; no one questions the right of any member of a committee to express his opinions in that committee, and to oppose with all his force the opinions of the majority of the committee, if he wishes to ; but when a committee is carrying out a delegated work then I say that committee is bound to do the work it is ordered to do, and any member who cannot conscientiously do it should retire from it. (Hear, hear.) The Committee were simply presenting to the Government the petition which they understood was drawn up by the authority of the Council. No member of that Committee, I maintain, had any right to oppose it there. He might have objected to it in the Council, but even if he did not favor or approve of everything that was in it he was acting, when before the Legislature, in a delegated capacity and not as an individual, and he was carrying out, or ought to have been carrying out the will of the body that was sending him there. For that reason I felt regret that there should have been any dispute before the Government when the matter was presented there. I did not have any feeling of regret that there should have been disputes in the Legislative Committee because the members had a perfect right to dispute it there if they chose to do so, but it did seem to me there should not have been any dispute before the Legislature. It has been stated to-day that the dispute was a breach of faith, and each party blames the other. Now, I am willing to assume that there was reasonable ground therefore for the difference of opinion, and that there might have been a discussion of this matter before the Government through a misunderstanding ; I am willing to assume the most favorable view and to assume that that was the case, and I therefore bring no charge against any member of this body of having broken faith or anything else. I have no personal knowledge of the matter, but I did feel regret when a committee of this Council was going to the Government that any person there should have created a disturbance and made the Council and profession appear before the Government as a disunited body. For that reason I had no hesitation in signing my name expressing my regret. I do not think the Executive Committee, in expressing the regret that they feel, are exceeding their powers. If we feel regret surely we may express our regret. It would be a very unheard-of thing that a committee could not express their feelings on a matter. If they are sent to carry out a work and something has deterred them surely they may express their regret that such a thing has happened. The Executive Committee, in connection with the Legislative Committee in presenting the petition to the Government, felt that there was opposition there and they have expressed their regret. It seemed to me they have not done anything that was not right. We only express our regret that a certain occurrence took place, and I think everybody nearly will feel that it is reasonable, no matter who the author of the disturbance may have been. It is a cause of regret that anything of that kind took place.

Dr. McLAUGHLIN—I think, on a moment's reflection, Dr. Campbell will see the complete fallacy of his argument. His argument is that the place to fight out differences of opinion is in the committee. Why, sir, we violate that every hour in this chamber. You go to your Committee of Finance or any other committee, they fight out their differences in the committee, and the men who are in the minority come right here to this Council and express their views. You go to the Legislature ; they have their differences there, they fight and fight by the hour over railway bills and everything else ; they come to a decision, and the report of the majority is presented to the Legislature, then the men who are opposed to any of these bills exercise their undoubted prerogative of expressing their views. I say the right of the minority is always in existence. Dr. Campbell is arguing directly contrary to his own proceedings in this chamber from time immemorial, unless he has always been with the majority. I say it is fallacious to say that unless a man differs from the report of the committee in the committee he is ever after condemned to silence.

Dr. CAMPBELL—Does Dr. McLaughlin really misunderstand me, or was I so utterly unable to express myself ? I am inclined to think that must be the case. I never for a moment said that when you disagreed with a report in the committee that when you come back to report to the body, if you are in the minority, that you cannot there express your opinion. I stated the general principle that when a committee is going from a body in a delegated capacity to carry out a certain work for that body, outside of that body, then loyalty to the body that has formed that committee and given them a work to do is required of every member. While I do not suppose Dr. McLaughlin has a very high opinion of me—

Dr. McLAUGHLIN—I have, sir.

Dr. CAMPBELL—He certainly has a very low opinion of me to think I would give expression to such an opinion as that which he has just now stated.

Dr. McLAUGHLIN—I have a very high opinion of Dr. Campbell ; he is one of the ablest men in the Council. When he made his statement before he made the general statement as I understood it and stated it. However, I will take him on his own ground. I say if a Legislative Committee is appointed by this body to present a certain matter to the Legislature, and if a majority of that body say we agree we will present it this way, that does not rob the minority of its responsibility to the Council and to its constituents of presenting its views before that body. I say that is true in regard to all legislation and all petitions. I can give you a recent illustration : There was a large army of temperance people who went to the Government and asked for certain legislation ; they went on certain general principles, so that the principles were presented, but there were others who went there, differing from the views of the majority, who expressed their views. I challenge Dr. Campbell to find a single law, a single precedent, where men differing from the majority have retired and would not come forward and present their views ; I say it would be cowardly for them to do so. It is the duty of a minority on important matters, such as is involved in this case, to express their views. Dr. Campbell loses sight of one point which has been clearly proven on the floor of this chamber here to-day, namely, that there was, to say the very least of it, a very grave misunderstanding between the gentleman who reported on that committee and Dr. Sangster. There were gentlemen who corroborated the position of Dr. Sangster ; there were others that seemed to give it a different coloring, so that, as far as Dr. Sangster was concerned, there was no breach of faith ; we have no evidence that there was. There is evidence there was a breach of faith upon the part of the gentleman who presented that petition. Some of us think so. I do not say that is the opinion of the whole Council, but there evidently was a grave suspicion that there was a breach of faith on his part, and Dr. Sangster was then set free, set at liberty, and he simply carried out before the Government exactly what he told the committee he would carry out if the details were gone into, and for this manly act a committee that was not seized of the case at all ventures to step in and censure him.

Dr. ROGERS—I move the adoption of the clause.

Dr. McLAUGHLIN—The motion was that that clause be struck out.

The CHAIRMAN—Do you withdraw your motion, Dr. Reddick ?

Dr. REDDICK—No. I do not think that clause has any business in this report.

Dr. ROGERS—I have no hesitation, gentlemen, in saying I never felt more pain in giving an expression on any matter in my life than I did on this. I will leave the matter in the hands of the Council.

The CHAIRMAN put Dr. Reddick's motion that Clause 5 be struck out, which, on a vote having been taken, was declared lost.

The CHAIRMAN put the motion that Clause 5 be adopted, which on a vote having been taken, was declared carried.

Dr. ROGERS read Clause 6 of the report and moved its adoption. Carried.

Dr. ROGERS read Clause 7 of the report.

The CHAIRMAN—I think inasmuch as we are not going to get legislation now that that line recommending the adoption of the bill, especially as it is one the Council has not seen, had better be stricken out.

Dr. ROGERS—But in case you did—

Dr. CAMPBELL—If we were going to ask for legislation at any time it would have to be considered afresh.

Dr. ROGERS—I thought it was wise to have it adopted, because I thought we might perhaps be called upon to act hurriedly. I move the adoption of Clause 7 of the report with the erasure of the words "and we recommend the adoption by the Council of this bill."

Dr. GRAHAM put the motion which, on a vote having been taken, was declared carried.

Dr. ROGERS read Clause 8 of the report, and moved its adoption. Carried.

Dr. ROGERS read Clause 9 of the report and moved its adoption, Carried.

Dr. ROGERS read Clause 10 of the report and moved its adoption. Carried.

Dr. ROGERS moved that the Committee rise and report. Carried.

The Committee rose. The President in the chair.

Dr. ROGERS moved, seconded by Dr. MOORE, that the report of the Executive Committee be adopted as amended.

Dr. REDDICK moved in amendment, seconded by Dr. ARMOUR, that the report of the Executive Committee be not adopted but be referred back to the Committee to strike out Clause 5.

The PRESIDENT put the amendment which, on a vote having been taken, was declared lost.

Dr. ARMOUR—I ask that the yeas and nays be taken.

Dr. SANGSTER— I ask the permission of the Council not to vote.

The PRESIDENT—Will the Council grant Dr. Sangster his request?

Dr. MCLAUGHLIN—It is not a matter for the Council to decide at all, the rule is that where it is a personal question involving a member he shall be excused.

The PRESIDENT instructed the Registrar to take the yeas and nays.

The REGISTRAR took the yeas and nays as follows :

Yeas—Drs. Armour, Barrick, Hanly, Henry, McLaughlin, Reddick and Shaw.—7.

Nays—Drs. Bray, Britton, Brock, Campbell, Dickson, Douglas, Emory, Fowler, Griffin, Henderson, Logan, Luton, Machell, Moore, Rogers, Roome and Thorburn. —17.

The PRESIDENT put the main motion which, on a vote having been taken, was declared carried and the report adopted as amended as follows :

To the President and Members of the Medical Council of the College of Physicians and Surgeons of Ontario.

GENTLEMEN,—1. The Executive Committee met on the 10th of December, 1896, by instruction of the President, for the purpose of considering a letter which you will find attached to this report, from S. Alfred Jones, asking for the registration of one Jacob Zielinski. It was moved by Dr. Campbell, seconded by Dr. Thorburn, that the communication of S. Alfred Jones *re* the registration of Mr. Zielinski has been duly submitted to the Executive Committee, and as his application for registration has been considered on former occasions by the Medical Council of Ontario, the Committee suggest that Mr. Jones present any evidence of claim he has on behalf of Mr. Zielinski to the Medical Council at the Annual Meeting in the summer of 1897, when the application can be fully considered.

2. The resolution which was passed by the Council at the session in 1896, directing that a petition be sent to each registered medical practitioner for signature was considered and a form of petition was drawn up and adopted, together with an explanatory circular. A copy of the petition and circular are enclosed with this report.

3. These were sent to each member of the College of Physicians and Surgeons of Ontario, enclosed with stamped envelopes for return to the Registrar, Dr. Pyne. As a result, 1,820 members responded and returned their copies of the petition signed. Your Committee then placed the matter of securing an amendment to the Medical Act before the medical members of the Legislative Assembly, and they stated that inasmuch as there was an element in the Assembly antagonistic to the medical profession it would be better not to seek an amendment to the Medical Act until after a new election of the Local Legislature, when it is hoped the element indicated would not be returned. Your Committee deemed it wise to accept the advice of the medical members, and decided not to present the petition at present to the Legislature.

4. Your Committee decided, however, to lay the petition before the Premier and the members of the Government, and your Committee with the Legislative Committee met the Premier and Government by appointment. Your Committee beg to report that the Minister of Education answered on behalf of the Government that his proposed Act of 1896 in regard to matriculation was only intended to "clean the slate," and he would not interfere with the Council's matriculation again, and that the Council might now adopt whatever standard of matriculation they thought best.

5. Your Committee deems it only right to report to the Council that we deeply regret that one of the members of the Council, who was present as a member of the Legislative Com-

mittee, should have felt himself called upon to denounce the petition before the Premier and Government, notwithstanding that an agreement had been entered into beforehand that the Committee and Legislative Committee should be unanimous in their presentation. Your Committee expresses their sincere regret that the denunciation by the member of the Council present had the effect of showing a divided Council and took away from the petition to some extent the good which it would undoubtedly have produced.

6. Your Committee nevertheless feel assured that the petition presented during last session of the Legislative Assembly prevented any attempt to tamper with the Ontario Medical Act, and further, it secured for the Council complete control once more of the standard of matriculation. Your Committee, however, urge upon the Council the importance, should it be deemed best to raise the standard of matriculation again, to do so not on the grounds of checking the overcrowding of the profession inasmuch as the Premier plainly made it clear to us that such a public impression had been the main factor in compelling the Government to interfere with us in 1896.

7. Your Committee enclose with this report a copy of the proposed Bill to amend the Ontario Medical Act, which was prepared by our solicitor, Mr. B. B. Osler, Q.C., and which is drawn out in accordance with the terms of the petition.

8. March 2nd, 1897. Committee met. Members present. Drs. Rogers, Campbell and Thorburn. It was moved by Dr. Campbell, seconded by Dr. Thorburn, that this Committee, having read the proposition made by the Canada Life Insurance Company to Mr. B. B. Osler, Q.C., wherein said Company offers to continue the loan on the building of the College of Physicians and Surgeons of Ontario, at the rate of three and a half per cent. per annum for three years, and also that insurance on said building may be reduced to twenty-five thousand dollars ($25,000), it is therefore resolved that said offer be approved, and it is directed further that in case the Property Committee of the Ontario Medical Council accept the said offer from the said Company, the President and Registrar are hereby empowered to sign said renewal of mortgage. Carried.

9. It was moved by Dr. Campbell, seconded by Dr. Thorburn, that the communication of Dr. Carruthers, of Little Current, Ontario, be replied to by the Registrar, to the effect that the Council has no power to interfere in a matter of the kind referred to in his letter.

10. The Registrar then read a letter from the Hon. Mr. Ross, which he was instructed to acknowledge and reply to in accordance with the regulations agreed upon in 1896. The communication of Joseph Boyle, B.A., M.A., was then considered, and the Registrar was instructed to reply as follows : That upon his presenting a certificate of one year's clinical work subsequent to his three years' medical course and receipt of M.D. degree from Queen's University, he be allowed to take his Primary, Intermediate and Final Examinations in May, 1897. It was moved by Dr. Campbell, seconded by Dr. Thorburn, that the petition of F. E. I. Johnston, a British Licentiate, having been considered by the Committee, the Registrar be instructed to say that the request cannot be granted, and that the Registrar be further instructed to inform Mr. Johnston that he can send a petition to the Council in 1897 should he so desire.

All of which is respectfully submitted.

A. F. ROGERS,
J. THORBURN,
CL. T. CAMPBELL.

COLLEGE OF PHYSICIANS AND SURGEONS OF ONTARIO,

TORONTO, 11th January, 1897.

DEAR DOCTOR,—You will find herein, in a stamped envelope for return, a petition to the Legislature which has been sent to every member of the College of Physicians and Surgeons of Ontario. Will you be good enough to sign the petition and post it as soon as you conveniently can, as I have to get the copies put together and bound for presentation to the Legislature, and the time is short before the House meets. By doing this you will greatly oblige,

Yours faithfully,

R. A. PYNE, Registrar.

THE COLLEGE OF PHYSICIANS AND SURGEONS OF ONTARIO.

CIRCULAR TO MEMBERS.

TORONTO, January 11th, 1897.

DEAR DOCTOR,—By direction of the Ontario Medical Council, as shown by the two resolutions printed on the back of this circular, the enclosed Petition to the Legislature of Ontario is sent to you for signature. We respectfully ask you to carefully read the Petition, and, in the interests of the Medical Profession, to sign and post the same with as little delay as possible. The Petition has been sent to each member of our Profession residing in Ontario, enclosed in a stamped envelope for return ; and when we receive the copies back they will be classified in Counties, and joined together as one Petition to our Legislative Assembly. In this way the united strength of the Medical Profession will be demonstrated, the object being to endeavor to check the increasing tendency to radically alter the Ontario Medical Act. Every member of our Profession is vitally interested in having our Medical Act maintained in an unbroken continuity, with the exception of such changes as receive the consent of a majority of the registered practitioners of the Province, or the Medical Council, and which are recognized as just and equitable towards all classes. And yet the events of the last two or three years have shown that there is a very serious and alarming danger of the Medical Act being, if not destroyed, altered and changed to such an extent as to render it all but useless. Let us remind you of a few of the changes and proposed changes of the past two years :

FIRST.—In 1895 a Bill was introduced into the Legislature by Mr. Haycock, for the purpose of changing or really nullifying the Medical Act. You will find a copy of that Bill on page 77 of the Proceedings of the Ontario Medical Council, as published in the Announcement for 1895-96. Had that Bill become law, the condition of the Medical Profession would have been put back to where it was thirty years ago. The practice of Obstetrics would have been placed largely in the hands of uneducated midwives, quackery would have become rampant in Ontario, the status of the Medical Profession would have been reduced, and the rights of the physicians which they gained in passing the Examination of the Medical Council would have been taken away. The proposed Act was revolutionary and destructive. True, it was defeated in the House by a large majority, but the mere introduction of such a radical measure should warn the members of the College of Physicians and Surgeons of Ontario that if they wish to preserve their corporate rights, they must abandon all sectional and petty differences, and unite in upholding the honor and dignity of our profession.

SECOND.—During the session of the Legislature in 1895, the Medical Act was changed by repealing Section Sixteen, and thereby all Tariffs of Fees in the Province were cancelled.

This Section Sixteen gave each Division Association the power of adopting a Tariff of Fees, which, after sanction by the Medical Council, became a scale of reasonable charges before all Courts of law. If a Physician had to sue to recover his fees the Judge was compelled to accept the Tariff, and render judgment in accordance with its provisions. The repealing of Section Sixteen of the Medical Act took this right away. To-day we have no Tariff, no authorized scale of charges as a guide for a Judge, who is thus empowered to absolutely decide what shall be a reasonable charge in any given case, and the opinion of the Medical Profession as to what does constitute a reasonable charge is thereby ignored. It was unfair and unjust to cancel Section Sixteen of the Ontario Medical Act without the slightest regard for the opinions of the Profession, or their representatives in the Medical Council. We were simply ignored, and the right of having a Tariff of Fees was taken away without even the ordinary courtesy having been extended to the Profession, through the Medical Council, of consideration before this radical change was made. If the Legislature is prepared to mutilate the Medical Act in that way, one may well ask, what change will come next ? It is safe to assume that no further change will be made by the Legislature if the Medical Profession unite in a Petition, such as is enclosed for your signature, without at least giving you, through the Medical Council, an opportunity of considering any proposed alteration. As you will notice, we propose now to have one Tariff of Fees for the whole Province of Ontario, and before it comes into force it must be accepted by three Judges of the Supreme Court of Ontario, which in itself will give it a legal status, and render it more acceptable to County and Division Court Judges. The intention is to frame the Tariff more in detail, so that the Medical Practitioner will receive fees for whatever his work may be, and he will be guided in making charges : but in case he is forced to sue in any Court of law the Judge will be compelled to give judgment according to the Tariff. In a word, such a Tariff will give a legal status to the physician's fees, and it will have a moral influence with clients, and thus largely prevent litigation in collecting our reasonable charges.

THIRD.—While the session of 1895 saw the Medical Act attacked and changed, the session of 1896 brought several Bills proposing to alter the Act. The first was the one proposed by Mr. German, and you will find a copy of this Bill on page 53 of the Announcement for this year. This Bill proposed to compel the Medical Council to register any British Licentiate upon passing only our present Final or Clinical Examination. The result of this would have been that he would have escaped our Matriculation, Primary and Intermediate (or old Final) Examinations. This Bill was withdrawn, but had it become law it would have been almost a fatal blow to the College of Physicians and Surgeons of Ontario, and vividly portrays to the members of the College how lightly certain members of the

Legislature consider the interests of our profession when Bills of that kind can be seriously introduced.

FOURTH.—In 1896 Mr. Haycock again struck at the Medical Act. He introduced a Bill restraining the Medical Council from charging any student more than Fifty Dollars for all his Examinations and Membership Diploma. How we were to carry on the Examinations no one could tell, but the result would have been, if the Bill had become law, that the College would have been closed for want of funds. When we consider that the Law Society charges law students nearly double the fees which the Medical Council charges medical students we are forced to conclude that there must be some reason why Mr. Haycock attacks the Medical Profession and leaves the Legal Profession severely alone. Is it because the Legal Profession is a strongly united body of men, alive to their interests, and loyal to their calling? Mr. Haycock's Bill was defeated, largely owing to the splendid speech of the Hon. G. W. Ross, who championed the Medical Profession in terms both enthusiastic and brilliant, but nevertheless every member of our profession must realize that this itching desire on the part of some members of the Legislature to tamper with the Ontario Medical Act must end, sooner or later, in the Act being mutilated unless we arouse to the danger of the situation and show by a united front that we are alive to our interests and prepared to maintain them.

FIFTH.—During the session of 1896 the autonomy of the Medical Profession received the most serious blow which was ever given since our Incorporation in 1879. If the College of Physicians and Surgeons are not permitted to govern their own affairs in all things then we must conclude that the Government and Legislature assume that, as a Profession, we are composed of incapables, totaly unfit to govern ourselves and unworthy of confidence. The Bill of the Hon. Mr. Ross, printed on page 53 of the Announcement, 1896-97, and entitled "An Act Respecting Matriculation in Medicine," is the strongest kind of evidence that the Legislature considers the Medical Profession in Ontario is an apathetic and disunited body, devoid of union and strength, and emphasizes the necessity for the enclosed Petition, and for each Physician taking a keener interest in the welfare of the Corporate Rights of his Profession. The Bill of the Hon. Mr. Ross simply meant that the right of regulating the standard of pre-medical education should be taken away from the Medical Profession; that hereafter we should be compelled to accept the standard of matriculation which he, in that Bill, had arranged for us; that, in other words, the Legislature knew better than we did what grade of preliminary education should be attained by a student before he begins the study of Medicine. The Bill was only withdrawn by the Executive Committee of the Medical Council agreeing to adopt the terms of the proposed measure. If, however, all the physicians in Ontario sign the Petition, sent herein, then the Medical Council will doubtless be permitted to resume full control of the grade of pre-medical education. The standard of preliminary education, which the Medical Council has now maintained for many years, is the Junior Matriculation in Arts of the Department of Education, and during the session of the Council in 1895 we slightly increased this by requiring that the student in passing this Examination should take Second Class Honors in four subjects. The standard, thus increased, did not by any means equal the Senior Matriculation in Arts of Toronto University, and the Examination was not nearly so high as the Matriculation adopted by the College of Physicians and Surgeons of the Province of Quebec. If the Medical Council are to be deprived of the right of specifying the grade of pre-medical education then it is useless for us to ever hope to bring the education of the Medical Profession in Ontario to anything like an equality with that in European countries. With an extremely overcrowded profession, with double the number of physicians which the requirements of the population demand, the Medical Council should be allowed to gradually improve the educational requirements of our calling, or at least keep pace with those in sister Provinces.

Having noticed a few of the many changes and proposed changes of the Medical Act which have been brought before the Ontario Legislature during the past two sessions, is it likely the session in 1897 will pass without another attempt, and perhaps several attempts, being made to change the Ontario Medical Act? Already the Executive Committee of the Medical Council have received notice of one Medical Bill.

PROPOSED PRIVATE ACT TO REGISTER MR. ZIELINSKI.

For some years a person styling himself Dr. Zielinski has been applying to the Medical Council for registration without examination, and while his case has been carefully considered, he did not by any means demonstrate either that he has passed examinations in Medicine or that he had sufficient knowledge of Medicine to warrant us in registering him, and he was informed that he must comply with the law and pass the Examinations of the Medical Council if he wished to practise in Ontario. Within the past few weeks Mr. S. A. Jones, Solicitor for

Mr. Zielinski, has written a letter to Dr. Pyne wherein he states that it is his intention to have an Act passed at the next meeting of the Legislature compelling the Medical Council to register Mr. Zielinski without examination.   We feel assured, however, if the Petition enclosed herein is signed by a majority of the physicians residing in Ontario, that no more Medical Amendment Acts will be introduced unless sanctioned by at least a portion of the profession, and the Private Bill to register Mr. Zielinski will never materialize.

APPEAL TO THE PROFESSION.

We have thus reviewed the many attempts to tamper with the Medical Act during the past two sessions, and we sincerely record the fact that if our Act has not been grossly mutilated it was on account of the loyal support given us by the Government of Sir Oliver Mowat, and indeed the brilliant speeches of Sir Oliver and Mr. Whitney when the Haycock Bill was before the House in 1895 were the chief means whereby that notorious Bill was defeated. Similarly during last session the Hon. Mr. Ross's clever speech in opposition to Mr. Haycock's Bill was laden with pleasing and complimentary statements with reference to the Medical Council and the Medical Profession of Ontario.   We are also deeply indebted to our *confreres* who are members of the Legislative Assembly, viz., Doctors A. McKay, Baxter, John McKay, Ryerson, Willoughby, Meacham and Preston.   These medical members have zealously striven to guard the interests of the profession and save the Medical Act from ruthless alteration, and their efforts have been aided by many other members on both sides of the House. Nevertheless, what must be the inevitable result if each succeeding session of the Legislature finds two or three Bills to alter the Medical Act without the slightest reference to the opinions of the Medical Council or the members of the profession ?   A loyally united profession, as evidenced by the united Petition, will tend in no ordinary degree to avert this danger.   Whatever differences of opinion we may have regarding various questions of Medical politics, we should all stand shoulder to shoulder in maintaining the Medical Act and preventing its reckless and unconsidered alteration.   Let anyone recall what the Medical Council has accomplished in ridding the Province of quacks, in disciplining such men as Washington, Lemon, Rose, McCully, and others, in elevating the standard of medical education in Ontario, and then say that we have not in our Medical `Act a boon well worthy the cordial support of our profession.   The Medical Council is composed of thirty members, and of these the general medical practitioners elect seventeen territorial representatives, or a majority of the whole body, and the Homœopathic practitioners elect five, so that twenty-two are elected every four years by the profession.   Therefore the practitioners have absolute control of the Medical Council, which ensures that the wishes of the profession will always be carried out. We now ask every member of the College of Physicians and Surgeons resident in Ontario to sign the enclosed Petition and thus strengthen the hands of the Medical Council in protecting and maintaining the Medical Act.   We ask you to sign the Petition, and we also ask you to use your influence with the Member representing your County in the Local Legislature. There is no man in any locality who has the political influence which the medical practitioner has ; his influence is far-reaching and widespread ; he is respected and looked up to by every class in the community, and no aspirant for political honour is so foolhardy as to wilfully incur the enmity of an indignant medical profession in the field whence he desires to be returned to the Legislature.   It will only cost you a few minutes' time to write to your Member for the Local Parliament and protest against the Medical Act being changed unless the proposed alteration has been first placed before the Medical Council for consideration or has received the sanction of a large section of the Profession.   Request your Member to support the terms of the enclosed Petition and to vote against Mr. Zielinski or any one else being registered in Ontario without complying with the requirements of the Medical Act.   The mere fact of your writing to your Member of the Legislature supporting the Petition will have a splendid effect in checking the present tendency to mutilate the Medical Act.   In conclusion, kindly forward the Petition without delay, and then write a letter to your Member for the Legislative Assembly on the lines indicated.

A. F. ROGERS, President of Council.

CL. T. CAMPBELL,

JAS. THORBURN,

Members of Executive Committee.

R. A. PYNE, Registrar C.P. & S. of Ont.

At the Annual Meeting of the Ontario Medical Council held in June, 1896, the following resolutions were adopted :

Moved by Dr. BRAY, seconded by Dr. DICKSON,—

"That a form of petition be framed, and sent to every medical man in the Province by the Registrar for signatures, praying that the Government and Legislature of Ontario will not alter nor amend the Medical Act, nor introduce, nor carry through any new medical legisla-tion, unless such amendments, or new Medical Act, or Acts, be first submittted to the Council of the College of Physicians and Surgeons of Ontario, directly or through its Legislative Committee." Carried.

A. F. Rogers, President.

Moved by Dr. Henry, seconded by Dr. Dickson, and resolved,—

"That in the opinion of the Medical Council there should be established a Medical Tariff for the Province of Ontario, in order that the reasonable charges, or fees, of the registered medical practitioners may have a legal status in all courts of law in this Province ; that such Medical Tariff should be framed and sanctioned by this Council, but it should only come into legal force when it has received the sanction and approval of three Judges of the Supreme Court of Judicature of Ontario ; that such Medical Tariff, when it comes into legal force as aforesaid, may be printed, copies of which shall be distributed to the registered medical practitioners of Ontario, and each copy, bearing the seal of the College, and the signature of the Registrar attached thereto, shall be received in all courts of law in lieu of the original tariff; that such copies of the said Medical Tariff shall be a scale of reasonable charges within the meaning of Section 39, of the Medical Act." Carried.

A. F. Rogers, President.

Certified true copy, R. A. Pyne, Registrar.

June, 1896.

PETITION.

To the Honorable The Premier, Honorable Members of the Government and Honorable Members of the Legislative Assembly of Ontario.

The Prayer and Petition of the Undersigned being a resident and ratepayer of the Province of Ontario, and a duly qualified and registered medical practitioner of this Province, humbly showeth :

1. That the medical practitioners of this Province have complied with the terms of the Medical Act thereof, have passed a thorough examination in all branches of their profession before the Examiners of the Ontario Medical Council, and they have also paid the fees necessary for medical registration in this Province ; that having thus complied with the terms of the said Medical Act their interests and rights will be injured if the said Medical Act should at any time be changed or altered in such a way as to interfere with its practical operation by the Medical Council.

2. That in the year 1895 an attempt was made to change the Ontario Medical Act, which, had it succeeded, would have destroyed the existence of the Ontario Medical Council, and abrogated the rights of the medical practitioners by lowering the status of medical education and registration in this Province, but thanks to the Government and the good sense of the majority of the House, the attempt was frustrated.

3. That in the year 1895 the Ontario Medical Act was altered by an Act which repealed Section Sixteen of the said Medical Act, and took away from the medical practitioners of this Province the right of having a Tariff of Fees. That Section Sixteen of the Medical Act was repealed without consulting the Medical Council, and without the members of the Medical profession being in any way notified of such a proposed change. That a Tariff of Fees is necessary to give a legal status to the reasonable charges of the medical practitioners of this Province, and this right of having a Tariff formed part of the conditions under which the physicians of this Province paid their fees and became registered medical practitioners of Ontario.

4. That in the year 1896 a Bill was proposed which, had it become law, would have taken away from the Medical Council the right of regulating the standard of preliminary education for the medical profession. That the effect of this proposed change in the Medical Act was to force the Medical Council to lower the standard of pre-medical education in this Province to a considerable degree.

5. That in the year 1896 a Bill was introduced into the Legislature which aimed at allowing even the lowest grade of physicians in England to become registered in Ontario by passing a very easy and meagre examination, to the detriment of students in Ontario who have to pass the entire examinations of the Medical Council before they can register as medical practitioners in this Province.

6. That the Medical Act has been administered by the Ontario Medical Council, and a fair but thorough examination on all branches of the medical profession has been held twice each year, and the people of this Province have been guaranteed that only properly educated

and thoroughly competent medical practitioners shall be allowed to practise medicine in Ontario. That the Medical Council has, also, at great expense disciplined dishonorable medical practitioners, and thereby has protected the public against imposition and fraud. That the Medical Council has, at a heavy expense, guarded the people of this Province against quacks and mountebanks. That having faithfully fulfilled the duties and responsibilities as enacted by the Medical Act, without any expense or cost to the people of the Province, the Medical Council, as the Executive of the Medical Profession, has earned the confidence of Your Honorable body in Ontario, as well as that of the people of this Province.

7. That the Ontario Medical Council is composed of thirty members, twenty-two of whom are elected by ballot every four years by the registered practitioners of Ontario. That the said Medical Council is directly responsible to the said medical practitioners for its conduct, and therefore is the only body in Ontario authorized to speak in behalf of the members of the medical profession.

8. That in England, while the British Medical Council is not as a body responsible to the medical profession, having only five elective members, yet the British Parliament, since the British Medical Act was passed in 1858, has never allowed any change in the said Act without first having placed the proposed change before the Medical Council for the opinion of that body, and this courtesy has produced a feeling of security and stability in the minds of the profession in the Mother Country, whereas changes in the Medical Act of Ontario have caused a feeling of insecurity in the minds of the medical profession of this Province.

THEREFORE YOUR PETITIONER HUMBLY PRAYS :

1. That Your Honorable Body will extend to the medical profession of this Province the courtesy of not changing or amending the Ontario Medical Act until any proposed change or amendment has been placed before the Ontario Medical Council for consideration.

2. That the Medical Council may be allowed full control of the standard of pre-medical education. The great advances in medical science at the present time demand that the medical student shall be thoroughly educated before he begins the study of medicine, and in order that the Ontario Medical Council can guarantee to the people that medical education here shall keep pace with that of European countries, it is essentially necessary that the student shall be fully equipped before entering upon his professional studies. And this is not unreasonable, for the educational facilities of the Ontario School System are such as to place this equipment within the reach of everyone whether rich or poor.

3. That Section Sixteen of the Medical Act which has been repealed may be replaced by a new Section empowering the Medical Council to formulate a Medical Tariff applicable to the whole Province. That such Medical Tariff shall only come into force when it has received the sanction and approval of three Judges of the Supreme Court of Judicature of Ontario, such Judges to be nominated for this purpose by the Lieutenant-Governor in Council, and that certified copies of the said Tariff of Fees may be issued by the Medical Council.

4. That in order to aid the Medical Council in protecting the people of this Province against unqualified medical practitioners and charlatans, and against the shameful fraud perpetrated by travelling Medicine Companies, that Section Forty-five of the Medical Act may be amended by rendering the penalty more severe for violation of the said Medical Act.

AND YOUR PETITIONER WILL EVER PRAY.

Name...

Residence................................

County...................

Date...............

Dr. BRAY—We are now ready to proceed with the further consideration of the report of the Discipline Committee re Dr. Parsons.

The PRESIDENT—Would you like to have the report read again ?

Dr. McLAUGHLIN—No.

Dr. BRAY—I have enquired of the Solicitor with regard to the points raised by Dr. McLaughlin and others as to the conduct of Dr. Parsons being "infamous and disgraceful in a professional respect," and the Solicitor says that it is, decidedly ; and he says more than that, it is criminal and it is not necessary to be unprofessional conduct in that respect as long as it is criminal. He has also drawn out a form of resolution in the event of this Council striking out the name of Dr. Parsons, and I would move the adoption of the report of the Discipline Committee *re* Charles John Parsons.

Dr. MOORE—I second that.

The PRESIDENT put the motion, which, on a vote having been taken, was declared carried and the report adopted.

Dr. BRAY—This matter is now before the Council to deal with it.

Dr. McLAUGHLIN—This resolution has been written out by the Solicitor in order that we may have it carefully worded, and to guard the Council against any future trouble :

Moved by Dr. McLAUGHLIN, seconded by Dr. DICKSON : Whereas the Council caused inquiry to be made into the case of Charles John Parsons, a registered medical practitioner, alleged to have been guilty of infamous or disgraceful conduct in a professional respect, and to be liable to have his name erased from the register ; and whereas the Council has duly ascertained the facts of the case of the said charges against the said Charles John Parsons by the Discipline Commitee of the Council, duly appointed under the provisions of the Ontario Medical Act ; and whereas the said Committee has reported that the said charges are proven and the report of the said Committee and the evidence adduced before them are now before the Council, and the Council has determined to act thereon—Be it resolved, that the said report of the Discipline Committee be adopted, and that the name of the said Charles John Parsons be erased from the register, and that the Registrar be and is hereby directed to erase from the register kept by him, pursuant to the provisions of the Ontario Medical Act, the name of the said C. J. Parsons, and it is hereby further directed, under the provisions of the Ontario Medical Act, Section 38*b*, that the costs of and incidental to such erasure be paid by the said Charles John Parsons to the College of Physicians and Surgeons of Ontario forthwith after taxation by one of the taxing officers of the High Court of Justice for Ontario. And the Registrar is directed, after such taxation, to obtain the issue of such costs by the said College.

The PRESIDENT put the motion which, on a vote having been taken, was declared carried.

Dr. BRAY—I would ask the Registrar to take the yeas and nays according to the legal form.

The PRESIDENT directed the Registrar to take the yeas and nays.

The REGISTRAR took the yeas and nays as follows ;

Yeas—Drs. Armour, Barrick, Bray, Britton, Brock, Dickson, Douglas, Emory, Fowler, Graham, Griffin, Hanly, Henderson, Henry, Luton, Machell, Moore, McLaughlin, Reddick, Rogers, Sangster, Shaw, Thorburn, Williams.

Absent—Drs. Campbell, Geikie, Logan, Moorhouse, Roome and Thornton.

The PRESIDENT declared the motion carried unanimously.

REGISTRATION COMMITTEE'S REPORT.

Dr. FOWLER read Clauses 1, 2 and 3 of the report which, on motion, were adopted as read.

Dr. FOWLER read Clause 4 of the report.

Dr. CAMPBELL—Mr. Zielinski claims in his petition that there were certain rules and regulations of the Council some years ago, which rules and regulations he had not been able to find, under which any one who was practising under the Eclectic system between 1865 and 1874 would be entitled to registration. I informed his counsel such was not the case ; his counsel then admitted that Mr. Zielinski's legal claims were not very strong, but on account of his being an old man he thought it would only be an act of fairness on the part of the Council to allow him to practise ; and he stated that in his interview with the Commissioner of Crown Lands, Mr. Gibson, that gentleman had informed him he thought it was a case of hardship in which the Council might grant his petition by allowing him to practise.

The PRESIDENT—This party has been before the Council on several occasions, and every indulgence and every patience has been exercised towards him, and he has had every opportunity to produce certificates. There is no evidence that he ever studied at all.

On motion Clause 4 of the report was adopted as read.

Dr. FOWLER read Clauses 5 and 6 of the report which, on motion, were adopted as read.

Dr. FOWLER moved, seconded by Dr. BARRICK, that the report of the Registration Committee be adopted as a whole, which, on a vote having been taken, was declared carried, and the report was adopted as follows :

The Committee on Registration submit the following report on the various matters referred within the accompanying recommendations :

1. Application of Dr. Henry Cooper asking to be allowed to practise pending the Examinations, he having been unable to attend the Spring Examinations on account of ill health. The Council cannot waive its rules in this case.

2. Application on behalf of Mrs. Susan Plunkett, asking permission to practise as a midwife. The Council has no power to grant her registration for such purpose.

3. Application of Dr. Arthur J. Rayson, of Neebish, Michigan, asking for an interchange of authority to practise in Michigan and Ontario for Physicians registered in either. country and practising near the border. The Ontario Medical Act makes no provision for any such interchange.

4. Application of Jacob Zielinski asking to be registered, he having been a practitioner of the Eclectic System prior to 1870. The Medical Act requires that to secure registration under such circumstances the applicant produce a certificate from the Eclectic Medical Board. The petitioner presenting no evidence of having this qualification, his petition cannot be granted.

5. We have examined the report of the Registrar on persons matriculating and passing the Primary, Intermediate and Final Examinations for the year ending June 1st, 1897, and believe the same to be correct. There were Matriculates, 57 ; those passing Primary, 80 ; passing Intermediate, 35 ; passing Final, 56.

Resolved that the above report be adopted.

(Signed,)   FIFE FOWLER, Chairman.

Dr. HENDERSON—Mr. President, the Special Report of the Committee on Finance was considered and amended last night in Committee of the Whole, and I now move, seconded by Dr. ROGERS, that the report be adopted as amended.

Dr. ARMOUR—We undertook to make some reduction in our expenditure and we made some recommendations in this report which, if adopted, would make a reduction of about $2,000.00 ; after it got through the Committee of the Whole, the reductions were reduced to $185.00. Now, we have had a good deal of talk about economy· and the necessity for the reduction of expenses for some years. There appear to be a good many members of the Council who favor economy, but the result of the deliberations of the Committee of the Whole would not indicate that there was a very great demand for economy. However, I would like to give the members an opportunity to place themselves on record with regard to several of those items of expenditure which we desire to cut down, which are mentioned in that report. I would move, seconded by Dr. SANGSTER, that the report be referred back to the Committee of the Whole with instructions to amend Clause 8 of the report, by substituting $1,500.00 as the salary of the Registrar for the $1,800.00 contained therein.

The PRESIDENT put the amendment which, on a vote having been taken, was declared lost.

Dr. ARMOUR—I ask for the yeas and nays.

The PRESIDENT instructed the Registrar to take the yeas and nays.

The REGISTRAR took the yeas and nays as follows :

Yeas—Dr. Armour and Sangster—2.

Nays—Drs. Barrick, Bray, Britton, Brock, Campbell, Douglas, Emory, Fowler, Graham, Griffin, Henderson, Henry, Logan, Luton, Machell, Moore, Rogers, Roome and Thorburn—19.

Dr. SANGSTER—I have another amendment to make, but I do not want to make any lengthened remarks. The members of the Council are on record, or at least a large number of them, by their speeches last evening in connection with the report of the Finance Committee. For some years past this Council has been expressing some anxiety to retrench ; that anxiety hitherto has gone no further than words, and the impression is very generally prevailing and the profession have a desire to know where these efforts at reform are dropped in this Council, and it is in order to place the names on record so that the profession may know just where the pinch comes that I am moving these resolutions. I move, seconded by Dr. Armour, that the report be not now adopted, but be referred back to the Committee of the Whole with instructions to restore Clause No. 1, which recommended that only one examination·be held each year, and thus provided for an annual saving of $600.00.

The PRESIDENT read the amendment.

Dr. SANGSTER—I have stated there that that proposed reduction in the expenses of the College is set down at $600.00 ; that it does not, in my opinion, correctly designate the amount of saving that one examination would cause, but as I make the difference between the profits to this Council in the spring and fall examinations to be fifty-six per cent. of the sum paid in, and fifty-six per cent. of $1,600.00, the sum paid in within the last year for fall examinations, would be $900.00, a sum saved by having only one examination a year. The average sum saved by having only one examination during all the years past in which you would have two would be $700.00 annually. Now, $900.00 or $700.00 or even $600.00

is a very serious sum, a seriously large sum, for this Council to throw away upon what I maintain is a mere expensive piece of sentimentality. It was stated here last night that this Council had a duty to perform to the students. Now, the duty to the medical students who are in connection with the College, or those who expect to graduate here, is certainly no more a paternal matter than it is the duty of the Government of Canada to think of the country generally or the Educational Department to those who are attending the schools of the country. The Educational Department takes no such position in this respect as the Council takes. The Educational Department holds one examination a year, and only one, and if the young man or young woman who may have spent all their money and exhausted the resources of their friends, fail in a single subject and only by a slight mark, the Department has so little consideration, so little paternal anxiety for him or her that they most unhesitatingly refuse to give a standing and the student is sent back, and the next year has to go through the examination from the beginning ; and if the proposition were to be made to the Ontario Government or the Educational Department that two examinations a year should be established to allow those who fail at the first to get through without having to endure another year's siege of study they would simply not listen to the proposition at all ; their reply would be, the country is not suffering for want of teachers or for the want of students entering into our universities. It would be an impolity on the part of the Department of Education to multiply their examinations so as to facilitate the admission either into the teaching profession or into the universities. I claim that is the proper way in which this Council should look at the matter. The country is not suffering for need of doctors ; if there were a dearth of medical men, it might be quite right and would be quite right for the Council to make provisions to facilitate the entrance of young men and young women into the profession, but the country is not in any sense suffering, and the expenses to the College and to the Council for holding a supplementary or fall examination is a greater expense than the Council ought to be asked to bear, and it is certainly a greater expense than the profession as a whole is prepared to condone. It is on those grounds that I am moving that resolution, and merely that the members may be able to place themselves on record by their votes as to the position they occupy thereupon.

Dr. REDDICK—I must entirely differ from the arguments used by Dr. Sangster. He points out it will be a saving of six or seven hundred dollars by having only one examination a year. He makes a comparison with the pupils attending our public schools ; he says that if they fail to pass they are sent back for another year. That may be right. In this case we have an instance before us of a young man who, no doubt, has limited means, who nearly succeeded in passing. He passed the examination of the College where he had studied well, and he fails in our examination by one mark and a half on a very unimportant subject, a subject that has no particular effect upon the practitioner in this country, namely, sanitary science. Is it right to say to that man who is willing to pay for an examination to have the chance in six months of passing in order that he may go to the country and earn his livelihood, " No, you failed by one mark and a half and we will send you back to labor of the same kind again "?—and he has to wait patiently for a year before he gets his license. In a college it would be different if he failed, but in this case he has practically passed and he is only asking for a license that he may practise his profession and make his livelihood. In such a case it is pretty hard to say to this man, "You shall not again have an opportunity to pass." I say it is very unjust to be unfair for the sake of saving a few paltry dollars. In the report it was stated that there were $1,600.00 paid by pupils and it only cost in the neighborhood of $800.00 for those examinations. It is not our money we are using, it is their money. It would be unfair and unjust to this Council that we should take that stand for the sake of saving five or six hundred dollars ; it would be better for us to knock two or three or four dollars a day off our sessional indemnity and allow the students to have an opportunity.

The PRESIDENT—These arguments you have just heard were very fully ventilated yesterday, and I hope any gentleman who is going to speak will bear that in mind.

Dr. McLAUGHLIN—I simply want to utter a sentence or two. This Council, we all know, is passing through a wave of very great depression financially, and it becomes us to adopt every means to tide us over that wave and then probably we will be able to go it once more with flying colors, financially. But, if we could curtail expenses it would be advisable. Two examinations in one year is a modern invention. In my day, as you know, Mr. President, if we did not get through in one year we had to wait until the next year. For the sake of economy I think we ought to try to economise for a time until we get into clear sailing. I think we ought to pinch ourselves in every direction in order to accomplish that end.

Dr. BROCK—The arguments that were advanced last night upon every one of these points have been sufficient to educate me to vote to-night, and I think we had better take a vote at once.

The PRESIDENT put the amendment which, on a vote being taken, was declared lost.

Dr. SANGSTER—I ask that the yeas and nays be taken.

The PRESIDENT instructed the Registrar to take the yeas and nays.

The REGISTRAR took the yeas and nays as follows :

Yeas—Drs. Armour, Barrick, Brock, Dickson, Graham, Henderson, Henry, Machell, McLaughlin and Sangster—10.

Nays—Drs. Britton, Campbell, Emory, Fowler, Griffin, Logan, Luton, Moore, Rogers, Roome, Shaw, Thorburn and Williams—13.

Dr. SANGSTER moved, seconded by Dr. ARMOUR, that the report be not now adopted, but that it be referred back to Committee of the Whole with instructions to strike out Clause 10 and to substitute therefor a recommendation to the effect that the daily allowance paid to members of the Council be commuted into an annual sessional indemnity of $50.00, which would reduce the yearly cost of Council meetings by some four or five hundred dollars or more.

The PRESIDENT read the motion.

Dr. SANGSTER—I think that the members of the Council should show a desire to begin their efforts at economising, if they ever do begin them, at home—begin with their own allowance. I do not at all insinuate that the members of this Council are receiving more than their services are worth ; on the contrary, I know they are not receiving as large a payment as their services justly require, but I think they are receiving a larger allowance than the finances of this Council warrant, and there ought to be therefore a reduction. I have put it in the form of an annual sessional indemnity for the reason I have already stated on more than one occasion to this Council, namely, when we have a sessional indemnity of $50.00 we know the maximum cost of the meeting of the Council. If we have a per diem allowance the session of the Council may run over five days, it may run a good deal more than that, and the expenses of the Council may become very great. Where there is a per diem allowance there is always an effort made in connection with that, or arising from that, to curtail the full discussion of business and towards the end of the discussion to rush matters through at such a rate that the regularity, order and legality of our proceedings is very materially a matter of suffering. I won't take up any more of your time. This motion is made merely to put on record the votes of the members of the Council.

Dr. EMORY—In the event of this amendment of Dr. Sangster's prevailing will it have the effect of fixing this annual sessional indemnity for all time, or will it only fix it for this year ? If it would only fix it for this year I would feel like supporting it.

Dr. SANGSTER—That is only a recommendation on which, if it is sustained, a by-law will follow.

Dr. DOUGLAS—Before this motion is put I rise for a little information. I think I have noticed in the Announcement for the last two years that the question of the sessional indemnity has been up before this Council and pretty extensively discussed, and that a year or two years ago a committee was appointed to take into consideration the whole question, that they discussed this matter and arrived at what they believed was a fair conclusion. I ask for information as to whether that is correct.

The PRESIDENT—I believe such is the case.

Dr. DOUGLAS—If that is correct, and a committee composed of members of this Council have taken time to go into this question to ascertain the facts regarding it, I think it is unfair, it is most vexatious, that year after year the same question should come up and be a cause of discord in the Council, after the trouble the members of the committee have taken in order to settle it, and apparently settle it somewhat permanently. I rise to set myself straight because this is my first session and I would like to vote intelligently and fairly, and I think, drawing the conclusion from the report of that committee, when they reported as they did, I feel like sustaining the action of that committee a year or two ago. (Hear, hear.)

Dr. BRAY—Mr. President, I did not intend to say anything upon this question, but the remarks of Dr. Douglas have brought me to my feet. This question was discussed by the committee. I was not one of that committee, but I read the report. Dr. Sangster was on that committee. That committee brought in a unanimous report that it should be $12.50 a day, and now one member of that committee gets up and wants to undo what was done two years ago. The same thing was tried last year and I think it is just wasting time to keep bringing this matter up. If the majority of this Council and the whole of that committee were unanimous two years ago that it should be $12.50, and if our finances are no worse now than then—on the contrary they are better to-day than they were two years ago—there is no reason for making this change and I would oppose it.

Dr. MCLAUGHLIN—I did not intend to say anything, and I would not now except to correct some statements that were made. The report that was brought in was unanimous, but it was brought in as a compromise. The report did not represent the views of Dr. Sangster and myself on the question of a sessional indemnity.

Dr. WILLIAMS—I happened to be the Chairman of that committee and the matter came up in the Council, and was in Committee of the Whole, and a subcommittee was appointed to deal with that subject. I cannot at present name all the members who were on that committee ; I recollect Dr. Roome, Dr. McLaughlin and Dr. Sangster, the others I have forgotten for the moment. When the matter came up the sessional indemnity was spoken of and was proposed by Dr. Roome ; it was considered for some time and finally dropped. The committee were not individually of the same opinion when they came together, but the collective opinion when they came away was the same. They agreed to make a certain report and all stand by that report. They took the report into Committee of the Whole, the Committee of the Whole adopted it, and the Council subsequently adopted it on receiving it from the Committee of the Whole. I believe those are the facts as they occurred.

Dr. SHAW—-Before that is voted upon, to make myself consistent I will have to speak a word. It is well known I am in favor of reducing the amount paid to the members. As I understand the proposition, it is an indemnity of $50.00 each session to each member of the Council, and therefore it is manifestly unfair if there are no travelling expenses allowed—

Dr. McLAUGHLIN—Oh, yes. It is only the per diem allowance which is changed. The travelling expenses remain the same.

Dr. BRAY—It does not say so.

Dr. McLAUGHLIN—It does not deal with it at all.

Dr. SANGSTER—That was the intention. I moved that resolution merely to open up the way for the introduction of a by-law afterwards if the contention in the resolution was sustained. The adoption of the special report of the Committee on Finance, I was told, would shut off all further attempt at changing the sessional indemnity this year. My impression of that conference is not exactly the same as my friend Dr. Williams' ; it slightly differs. I do not think the question of a sessional indemnity was mooted in that committee meeting ; it was afterwards mooted when we returned to the Council by Dr. Barrick and Dr. Brock. I would not say positively that it was not spoken of in the committee room, but that is my recollection. I had not felt at liberty to make the explanation I am going to make now because I felt that my lips were sealed by the agreement we came to there, but I will say now that the proposition made by myself and Dr. McLaughlin, when we went into the committee room, was that the daily allowance should be $10.00, when I recollect there was a demand made on the part of Dr. Campbell that the allowance should be $14.00 ; there we hung for a little while, Dr. McLaughlin and myself on the one side and four or five gentlemen of the committee remaining on the other side.

Dr. WILLIAMS—Do you say four on the other side ?

Dr. SANGSTER—I do not know that I do. I believe you were in the chair.

Dr. WILLIAMS—Do you mean to say that all the others expressed themselves with regard to the $14.00 ?

Dr. SANGSTER—I am not quite sure, but that is my impression.

The PRESIDENT—If I am not mistaken there is too much discussion on this question ; we are not in Committee of the Whole.

Dr. SANGSTER—I merely wanted to make the explanation.

Dr. WILLIAMS—I wish to ask Dr. Roome to state whether or not, before we went into the committee at all, he had not brought up the question of sessional indemnity, and whether or not he did not bring it up when we were in committee.

Dr. ROOME—I might say I did ; I advocated it very strongly. The argument used against it was that it would not be fair to those living at a distance from the city. I approved of a sessional allowance, and to get over the difficulty I made a proposition that we pay the members so much a mile over and above their railway fare. But the members of the committee disagreed on that ; some were favorable to the $10.00 allowance and some to the $14.00. We all agreed we would report at $10.00 a day, and an additional four cents a mile for those who took a Pullman, would make it up over and above what it cost them by taking a return ticket. I was proposing five cents a mile, which would leave those coming a distance of two or three or four hundred miles, enough to pay them what they spent in going and coming, but that was not adopted and we agreed on the other. (Cries of "Question, question.")

Dr. CAMPBELL—I think the matter has been discussed enough. I move that the main motion and all amendments be now put.

The PRESIDENT—Shall the main motion be now put ? (Cries of "Carried, carried.")

Dr. ARMOUR—I rise to a point of order. I say after an amendment is moved you cannot put the previous question until the amendment is withdrawn or disposed of.

Dr. CAMPBELL—I moved that the main motion and all amendments thereto be put. I understand that the house proceeds at once to vote on whatever propositions are before the body.

The PRESIDENT—This has been carried, therefore I really think it is quite in order, and it is the law laid down in our regulations which say, " The chairman shall put the previous question in this form, 'Shall the main question be now put ?' And its adoption shall end all debate."

The PRESIDENT put the main motion that the report be adopted, which, on a vote having been taken, was declared carried, and the report adopted as follows :

MEDICAL COUNCIL CHAMBER, July 7th, 1897.

Mr. President and Gentlemen :

In compliance with a resolution of last meeting of the Council regarding retrenchment, the Finance Committee met and have considered the matter, and report for your consideration :

There are several sources of expenditure in which a reduction might be made, if, after your deliberation thereon, they would be considered in the interests of the Council.

1st. One examination each year would save, we are informed by the Registrar, about $600.00.

2nd. If the examinations were held in one place it would be a further saving of $400.00.

3rd. If the time of oral examinations were increased from five to six hours each day—say three hours in the forenoon and three in the afternoon, which could not be considered excessive labor—there would be also a saving of $200.00.

4th. Regarding the examinations, we are also informed that by the withholding of the retainer of $20.00, now paid the Examiners who conduct no written examinations, a saving of $40.00 would be effected.

5th. If ten minutes' oral examination were considered sufficient instead of fifteen as now required, a saving of $200.00 would be thereby effected.

6th. We have also been informed that the Examiner on Anatomy has been using for five years the same wet specimens continuously, and for which he has been allowed $100.00 per year. Your Committee consider $25.00 to be sufficient when the same specimens are used.

7th. The reduction of Treasurer's salary or the amalgamation of the offices of Registrar and Treasurer.

8th. As regards the maintenance of the building, the expense might possibly be somewhat lessened by making it a part of the Registrar's work to let the apartments and collect the rents without being allowed a commission thereon, as has been the custom in the past. We consider, however, now that it is the most cheaply managed building in the city of Toronto. There has been an annual saving of $983.00 effected on the carrying of the building by the reduction of interest and amount of insurance carried, which will be referred to by the Property Committee in their report, and on temporary loans interest reduced from 7 per cent. to 6 per cent.

If this clause meets with your approval we recommend that the Council pay the Registrar's stenographer.

9th. The reduction of interest and amount of insurance carried was largely brought about by the efforts of your Registrar.

10th. The reduction of expenses connected with the annual meeting of the Council. With regard to the indemnity of members, we do not consider it judicious to open up á fresh discussion of this matter again, as the by-law fixing the sessional allowance has been thoroughly considered at previous sessions and no change is recommended.

11th. Discussion might at times be shortened and expenditure lessened in this way.

All of which is respectfully submitted.

(Signed,)   G. HENDERSON, Chairman.

Dr. SANGSTER—I call for the yeas and nays.

The PRESIDENT instructed the Registrar to take the yeas and nays.

The REGISTRAR took the yeas and nays as follows :

Yeas—Drs. Bray, Britton, Brock, Campbell, Dickson, Douglas, Emory, Fowler, Graham, Griffin, Hanly, Henderson, Logan, Luton, Moore, Reddick, Rogers, Roome, Shaw, Thorburn and Williams—21.

Nays—Drs. Armour, Barrick, Henry, McLaughlin and Sangster—5.

On motion of Dr. ROOME, seconded by Dr. ROGERS, the Council adjourned to meet at eleven o'clock a.m., Saturday, July 10th, 1897.

FIFTH DAY.

SATURDAY, July 10th, 1897.

The Medical Council met at eleven o'clock a.m., in accordance with motion for adjournment.

The PRESIDENT, Dr. Thorburn, in the chair, called the Council to order.

The REGISTRAR called the roll and the following members answered to their names : Drs. Armour, Bray, Brock, Campbell, Dickson, Fowler, Geikie, Graham, Griffin, Hanly, Logan, Luton, Moorhouse, McLaughlin, Reddick, Roome, Shaw and Thorburn.

NOTICES OF MOTION.

Dr. ARMOUR—To introduce a by-law to fix the salary of the Prosecutor.

Dr. McLAUGHLIN—To introduce a by-law for the purpose of appointing an Auditor and fixing his salary or fees, and giving instructions in regard to certain duties.

Dr. SANGSTER—That the Solicitor's opinion be obtained in writing on the question of whether any and which of the educational bodies now sending representatives to this Council have ceased to have the legal right to do so.

COMMUNICATIONS, PETITIONS, ETC.

The REGISTRAR read a communication re Geo. B. Gray, of Aurora.

Dr. McLAUGHLIN moved, seconded by Dr. ARMOUR, that the complaint against Geo. B. Gray be referred to the Discipline Committee to investigate, which, on a vote having been taken, was declared carried.

MOTIONS OF WHICH NOTICE HAS BEEN GIVEN AT A PREVIOUS MEETING.

Dr. ARMOUR moved, seconded by Dr. REDDICK, that a by-law entitled " A by-law to fix the Treasurer's salary " be now read a first time.

The PRESIDENT put the motion, which, on a vote having been taken, was declared carried.

Dr. ARMOUR read the by-law as follows :

" BY-LAW No. —.

"A BY-LAW TO FIX THE TREASURER'S SALARY.

"WHEREAS power has been granted to the Medical Council of the College of Physicians and Surgeons of Ontario under Section 13 of the Ontario Medical Act to make by-laws to fix the salaries of officers (R.S.O. 1887, C. 142) ; Be it therefore enacted as follows :

"1. That the salary of the Treasurer of this Council be and is hereby fixed at $.... per annum to be paid monthly."

Dr. ARMOUR moved, seconded by Dr. REDDICK, that the by-law just read a first time entitled " A by-law to fix the Treasurer's salary " be now referred to Committee of the Whole for a second reading, which, on a vote having been taken, was declared carried.

Council in Committee of the Whole. Dr. HANLY in the chair.

Dr. ARMOUR—I would now move that we proceed to the consideration of the single clause of the by-law. I would move that the sum of $400.00 be inserted after the sign $.... in the second line of Clause 1.

The CHAIRMAN put the motion which, on a vote having been taken, was declared carried.

Dr. ARMOUR moved the adoption of the clause, which, on a vote having been taken, was declared carried.

Dr. ARMOUR moved the adoption of the preamble, which, on a vote having been taken, was declared carried.

Dr. ARMOUR moved that the title be adopted, which, on a vote having been taken, was declared carried.

Dr. ARMOUR moved that the by-law as passed clause by clause in Committee of the Whole be now adopted as a whole, which, on a vote having been taken, was declared carried.

Dr. ARMOUR moved that the Committee rise and report, which, on a vote having been taken, was declared carried.

The Committee rose. The PRESIDENT in the chair.

Dr. ARMOUR moved, seconded by Dr. REDDICK, that the by-law just read a second time in Committee of the Whole, entitled " A by-law to fix the Treasurer's salary," be now read a third time and that the same be passed, sealed with the seal of the College and signed by the President and Registrar.

The PRESIDENT put the motion, which, on a vote having been taken, was declared carried.

Dr. ARMOUR—In accordance with a notice of motion in the hands of the Council, I beg leave to move, seconded by Dr. McLAUGHLIN, that leave be given to introduce a by-law entitled "A by-law to amend by-law No. 69 and by-law No. 75 by placing in suspension Sec. 41a of the Medical Act commonly known as the Penal Clause," and that the same be now read a first time. Mr. President, I have introduced this by-law with the hope and expectation that it may receive a majority of the votes of the members of this Council entitled to vote on it. It will be remembered that two years ago this by-law was introduced unconditionally and at that time it was supported by five of the territorial members, and again last year, in 1896, it was introduced unconditionally and at that time it received the votes of seven out of the seventeen territorial members. As the Homœopathic representatives of the Council are, as I understand, pledged to support this by-law, and if it meets with the approval of a majority of the territorial members, and from the promise made by certain members here last year I believe that it is probable, we have just cause for the assurance that we may now secure the requisite number of votes to place it again in suspension. The territorial members I believe have come to know, and have become very much better acquainted with the nature of this enactment and of the abhorrence with which it is held by a large portion of the members of the profession ; and it is just possible that it will receive a very large majority of the votes. Mr. President, it is probable and I think quite possible had it not been for the influence exercised by certain appointed members who do not represent the profession and who have no vote in the matter, but who have exercised their voices very fluently in favor of this penal enactment, that it would not have been removed last year from the suspension it received in 1893 from the Legislature.

The PRESIDENT—Am I to understand that those who represented the schools voted on this question ?

Dr. ARMOUR—No, but they spoke in favor of it, and I take exception to that, and I think I am within my privilege to do so. There is no question but that the territorial members who represent the profession in the Council now come here as far as I know, free to exercise their judgment with regard to the assessment of a tax, but with one exception there was no territorial member elected at the last general election who pledged himself in favor of reinstituting Section 41a ; and I might add that the very territorial members who now favor Section 41a owe their elections to their opponents having taken that stand. The members of this Council must know how unanimously the profession are against the necessity of practising their profession from year to year on an annual certificate ; and if a goodly number have submitted to it during the past year, they have unwillingly done so. However, they have done so. With regard to the payment, a good many have paid ; of course, they have not had the annual certificate without they have paid, and a small portion, over half of the profession, have contributed their fees and taken out the annual certificate. But a good many of these men have stated to me that they had hopes when the next election came around that they would be able to place men here who would not require the necessity of an annual certificate to practise their profession. While a goodly number have paid, I think it must not be taken for granted that they have paid on account of this threat of penal coercion. I would be very sorry to learn that a single member of my profession should yield to such threats, but I think it is more probable that they have paid on the ground that it was represented to them that this Council was in need of funds to carry on its affairs, and I think it was on account of that appeal and not the threat of coercion that a large number paid ; and it is quite probable that if they had been appealed to in that way only there would now be few in arrears. Even if this Council was unanimous in this matter, it seems to me it would be quite impossible in this free country to enforce this clause against a rebellious profession ; the Legislature that gave this undue power, as I believe it to be, would repeal it before harm was done anyone. I think, Mr. President, the results of it already show that it was a very unsafe power to entrust this Council with ; the way it has been used I think has shown that it was a very unwise power to place in the hands of this Council, however eminent the members may be that compose it. As you will remember, in 1895 an assessment of $6.00 was made by this Council, clearly, as I felt, without any warrant ; the Council is only entitled to assess $2.00 in any one year. But this Council assessed $6.00—

Dr. ROGERS—When was that ?

Dr. ARMOUR—In 1895.

The PRESIDENT—But not for one year.

Dr. ARMOUR—They assessed it in one year ; I did not say for one year.

The PRESIDENT—The impression to be gathered from your remarks would be that it was for one year.

Dr. ARMOUR—I said in one year an assessment was made of $6.00 while the statute says that this Council has only power to assess $2.00 in one year. I think that should be clear enough to anyone.

The PRESIDENT—It is ; it will pass.

Dr. ARMOUR—There is no doubt we will hear from Dr. Britton on this matter as we have on a former occasion. He is not now in the room. He desires to justify his interference with the financial affairs of the Council on the ground that the fees paid by students are paid on behalf of the medical schools.

Dr. WILLIAMS—May we have that resolution read till we know what is being discussed ?

The PRESIDENT read the resolution.

Dr. ARMOUR—I was saying, Mr. President, when interrupted, that Dr. Britton had claimed or attempted to justify his interference with the financial affairs of the Council by the assumption that the fees paid by the students were paid on behalf of the medical schools or universities, one of which he represents. I have had that experience of fee paying myself. I have paid my fees to this Council when I came in many years ago and it never occurred to me when I paid such fees that I paid them on behalf of anyone but myself. How different with Dr. Britton when he paid his fees. I suppose we have a right to assume from the stand he took last year that when he contributed his money and paid his fees to the Council it was not on his own behalf but on behalf of the medical school at which he pursued his studies. This is loyalty to the medical schools ! Well, perhaps, it is calculated to win confidence. But the fact is, that the Council have the power to receive the fees from the students and they are not under obligation to the medical schools or any other corporate bodies. Now, however the territorial representatives may be influenced in the matter, I trust they will not be influenced by the representations of the irresponsible members of the Council—

Dr. BRITTON—Mr. President, I do not think that such a term as irresponsible—

Dr. ARMOUR—Irresponsible with regard to this matter. I think, Mr. President—

Dr. BRITTON—Would you kindly explain why I am irresponsible ?

Dr. ARMOUR—You are not responsible to the medical profession for the assessment of a fee.

Dr. BRITTON—Am I not responsible to the medical profession as to how that fee shall be disposed of ?

Dr. ARMOUR—Unfortunately you are not responsible to the medical profession in a representative capacity.

Dr. BRITTON—Am I not responsible to the medical profession personally as to how that fee shall be disposed of ?

Dr. ARMOUR—I don't think so.

Dr. BRITTON—You don't think so ?

Dr. ARMOUR—I don't think they have any power to call you to account if you squandered all the funds of this Council, but they have power with regard to a territorial member.

Dr. BRITTON—I would ask one question in a quiet fashion, and I would desire it to be answered in a deliberate way, too. Have you arrived at a conclusion that satisfies yourself as to the method that was adopted for the purpose of making me and all other school and university representatives "irresponsible" as you call it ? Is it right in accordance with your own convictions of justice ?

Dr. ARMOUR—I am quite competent to answer that question, but that question is not before us now. Bring it up in the right way and I am quite willing to answer it.

Dr. BRITTON—I do not intend to enter into the discussion of it.

Dr. ARMOUR—It is altogether out of order.

The PRESIDENT—I don't think it is altogether out of order. You make a suggestion that a member is irresponsible.

Dr. GEIKIE—There is one thing that I would like to notice with regard to the matter Dr. Armour spoke of ; he was speaking of loyalty and of the fees these students paid, and that they were of no consequence to the colleges. I would like to know what the Council would do if there were no colleges ?

Dr. BRAY—I don't like any interruptions.

Dr. ARMOUR—I seem to have said something that has hurt Dr. Geikie's feelings in the matter with regard to the fees of students. Although he didn't say so, he left the impression that he still has the idea that the Council is indebted to the colleges for students. Perhaps sometimes they do receive a—

Dr. BRAY—I rise to a point of order. I think that has got nothing to do with the question before us.

Dr. ARMOUR—What is your point of order ?

Dr. BRAY—The fees of the students have got nothing to do with the by-law.

Dr. ARMOUR—It has been used in justification of appointed members using their influence here to assess a tax on the profession and to collect it by penal enforcement.

Dr. DICKSON—I do not think the speaker should be interrupted, and it is very undesirable that the speaker should make remarks that should call for an interruption. I claim his remarks with regard to the fees of students are quite out of order.

Dr. ARMOUR—Mr. President, it will be remembered last year how Dr. Britton deplored the fact that the Legislature—

The PRESIDENT—You are speaking to the Council.

Dr. ARMOUR—I am speaking to you.

The PRESIDENT—Dr. Britton is not on his trial.

Dr. ARMOUR—He is, I think.

Dr. BRITTON—I am perfectly willing to allow the gentleman to make any reference he likes to me, because I suppose later on I will have the privilege—

Dr. ARMOUR—One interruption begets another, and that is the way the business of the Council moves on. Dr. Britton deplored the fact that the Legislature had paralyzed his arm in this matter by depriving him of his vote. I think we can safely assure Dr. Britton that there is not the least probability of his recovering from that disability. But the members will remember that before Dr. Britton's arm was paralyzed in this matter he refused to vote for penal coercion. Now he puts himself in the position of recommending members to commit themselves in a way that when he had the power he refused to commit himself. Well, gentlemen, I trust that none of these intrusions from the appointed members will influence the votes of the territorial members. I do not think it will when their attention is properly called to it. It is quite possible when these speeches were made last session and the session before that the territorial members didn't know whether those individuals had a vote or not. I therefore leave the matter with you and trust that this by-law may receive a majority of the votes.

Dr. BRITTON—Mr. President, I am compelled to say a few words. I shall make the sentences as short as I possibly can, and there will not be many of them. The gentleman who has just spoken has made special reference to me, but I speak not simply on behalf of myself but on behalf of a principle. It is quite true that I made the statement on a former occasion that it was an unjust matter, it was a very unwise act on the part of the Legislature to deprive representatives of universities and medical colleges of this Province of certain of their privileges and to limit their functions ; in other words, to make a discrimination between the different classes of members of this Council. I claim this, so long as I am qualified by Act of Parliament to represent the University of Toronto and sit in this chamber I should have the privilege of exercising every function that belongs to any member of this chamber; there should be no distinction drawn. I come, I think, representing just as respectable a body of men as the constituents of the gentleman who has spoken, and I think that they have just as much interest in the educational progress of this country. The University of Toronto and other universities have done more than any class of men in the interests of medical education ; they took the initiative, and they have been in the front ever since, and still I perceive a man will get up and call me "irresponsible." He, forsooth, would make me appear as a sort of a half nonentity ; I have sense enough, or possibly he may concede that much, to express an opinion upon other matters, and I think I have judgment enough to know whether to keep my hand down or raise it when certain questions are put before this assembly. But the position that I have no right on earth to say whether or not my fellow-practitioner shall pay a paltry fee of $2.00 per annum is ridiculous. Well, gentlemen, that is the position I am placed in. I will have to repeat a few words of what I said last year ; it is for the purpose of letting you see that the contention I made is correct that I should still have every power I originally had ; that there should be no restriction, and I make this claim at the outset that the amendment to the Medical Act, which prevented the appointed members, as termed by a certain gentleman here, the representatives of the teaching bodies and of the universities, from voting or taking any part in connection with the levying of the annual assessment was brought about by false representation, was the result of what I might call fraud. That is a strong expression—

Dr. ARMOUR—I rise to a point of order. What Dr. Britton says is not true. I think it is hardly in order to specify the result of the deliberation of the Legislature, which was the enactment, as being brought about by fraud.

The PRESIDENT—I don't think he accuses anyone of being parties to that.

Dr. BRITTON—I intend to connect it with a certain class of men.

The PRESIDENT—You can class, but you cannot name.

Dr. BRITTON—I am not going to name. I do not mean to say there was any such thing as false representation in our Legislature, far from it. I have been a supporter of the present Liberal Government ever since it was a Liberal Government, and it would be the last thing in the world that would be expected of me to say that the members of our Government act fraudulently, or that any member of the Government, by false representations, brought about such and such acts ; no such thing was the case, but there was misrepresentation. I shall give you a short history of it. There was a certain agitation throughout the country concerning this very question of levying an annual fee. I may repeat what perhaps nearly all of us already know, but I have been placed in the position that I must do so. The Council informally knew of this agitation, they knew of it through letters that appeared in the public press. They thought it wise some years ago, I think it was in 1892, to pass an order or resolution in this Council to the effect that the so-called Defence Association be requested to appoint a committee to confer with a committee from this Council to discuss matters concerning which there were differences of opinion. At the appointed time both committees met ; discussion took place for some time, and finally one gentleman, a member of the committee from this Council, suggested that those who took opposite views to some that were taken by the Council should formulate what might be called a bill of rights, or practically express on paper what their desires were in order that they might be submitted to the committee and settled by the Council. This was done. I need go no further, so far as that is concerned ; but I might say that in that discussion the statement was made by a certain gentleman who is here to-day, and endorsed by another, that " we will continue to agitate as we have done through the public press, we will use our best efforts to secure the private ear of this, that and the other member of the Local Legislature. We have influenced a great many in that way, and we intend to pursue the same course." I have no right to say, I have no right to suggest even, what these individual gentlemen whispered into the ears of the Local Legislature, but I think I have a fair right to infer what they said. It will be remembered by all of you that on a certain occasion, I cannot give you the exact date, I think it was within a few months of that time, a circular appeared, and I think a copy of this circular was sent to every member of this profession in the country ; this was what we might call in a certain sense, perhaps, the "prospectus" of the Medical Defence Association. I will use the term "manifesto," perhaps that will answer if they object to the term "prospectus." One clause in that was to this effect : The influence of the appointed members of the Council is such that the Council proceedings are influenced, are affected by them to such a degree as to be inimical to the interests of the profession. They have the Homœopaths in line, they have managed to put a string on each of a certain number of the territorial representatives so that by means of these two classes they manage to control the Council. They have no right, therefore, to have anything to do with the levying of an assessment. Now, I challenge any member of this so-called Defence Association to stand up and say that that argument was never used ; and, if he does so, then later on I shall adduce the proof in black and white that what I have said is perfectly correct. I have given you reasons why I have believed all along, and I know to-day as a matter of fact that the University of Toronto, or any other university in this country, Queen's or Trinity, cannot be ignored to any great extent ; still, we representatives have been to a certain extent restricted in this Council by legislative enactment, and that was brought about the way I have indicated. The universities of Toronto, Queen's College, Western Ontario and Trinity University are bodies of a fair degree of importance. Their influence is felt by all, from the highest in the land down to almost the lowest and the poorest ; their names are household words, and amongst them they have a grand body of superior and bright-minded clever men ; their alumni are, I might say, the large majority of the medical profession of this country, a very large number of the legal fraternity, and amongst them are, perhaps, the best of the clerical profession. I am not going to either of these to ask for their favors, I think we are able to look after ourselves ; but I can tell you, Mr. President, that it would be just as well that no further threats of the same kind be made as were made in the circular formerly. I mean to say that should any further threats be made by any body of men that further legislation would be sought for to reduce still further our usefulness in this Council, it is barely possible that the grand educational institutions of this country will arise in their might and will bring such a power of influence to bear upon the Government that the Defence Association will feel as though a bombshell had burst in its midst. I have nothing more to say.

Dr. WILLIAMS—I would like to make a suggestion. This question is dealing with Section 41a. We appointed a subcommittee of the Committee of the Whole the other day to obtain the Solicitor's opinion upon that question. We will have that whole matter before the Committee of the Whole again. I suggest that if that is allowed now to have its first reading, and then is referred to the Committee of the Whole, we can have the whole matter discussed at one time and it will shorten the matter up at least one-half. If the Council would just consent to this by-law getting its first reading now and then read it a second time and refer it to the Committee that will not hinder the debate a particle. We have the other all ready to go into Committee of the Whole, and the two can be discussed at the same time, if the Council will agree to that.

Dr. BRAY—I was going to rise to make a suggestion somewhat upon the lines that Dr. Williams has. Not that we go into Committee of the Whole, but that Dr. Armour withdraw this by-law for the present until the opinion from Mr. Osler has been brought in by the committee.

Dr. WILLIAMS—I do not care which way it is done.

Dr. BRAY—I want to reply to one remark that Dr. Armour has made, and in doing so I am speaking to the motion which is before the house. I say that Dr. Armour made a reflection, not only on the territorial members, but on the constituents who sent them here, when he said they were so ignorant as not to be able to understand the reading of that by-law, just two clauses of which I will read : "The fees to be paid by the members of the college towards the expenses of the college, and the means of collecting and enforcing the same are to be in the discretion of the elected members of the Council." The latter portion of the clause reads, "But the only members of the Council entitled to vote on any by-law under this section shall be the elected members of the Council, nine of whom must be present at the passing of the by-law." If we are so ignorant that we cannot read that in English, then I say it is time that we got instructions from somebody.

Dr. ARMOUR—I didn't use the word "ignorant" in my speech. I think I am correct in saying that.

Dr. BRAY—You said that a majority of the members "did not know," and what is the difference between "did not know" and being "ignorant"?

The PRESIDENT—I think we will stop this discussion, and either decide to go into Committee of the Whole or suspend this notice of motion until we have the Solicitor's opinion.

Dr. ARMOUR—I object to suspending the notice.

Dr. WILLIAMS—There is certainly another way, and that is a motion to read the by-law the first time. The reading of it a first time is a formal matter that does not hurt anybody. After the first reading the second motion refers it to the Committee of the Whole, then when the Committee meets all that there is to be done is to make a motion that the Committee rise, and then the two can come in together and the discussion can take place.

Dr. McLAUGHLIN—If the Council will grant that we get a straight vote of yea or nay upon this by-law proposed by Dr. Armour, we will accede to that.

Dr. BROCK—I ask to have a straight vote taken now.

Dr. ROGERS—You can have a straight vote now on this motion, but we are not going to allow, in order to satisfy any good-natured member who wishes to accede in a pleasant way to the advancement of such a thing, a by-law of that kind to have even a first reading. We propose, if possible, to not allow it to have one reading. I characterize it as an outrage on this Council to bring it forward after what has been said during the past two or three years.

Dr. ARMOUR—Is Dr. Rogers speaking to the motion?

Dr. McLAUGHLIN—I rise to a point of order. For Dr. Rogers to say what Dr. Armour has done is an outrage is entirely out of order, and I hope the members of the profession will place themselves on their dignity.

Dr. ROGERS—I say we must either have that motion withdrawn or else it must not get its first reading. We will never let the defence men go to this country and say their by-law got a first reading.

The PRESIDENT—If you insist upon it, I must put the motion. I think it would be a very good way indeed to settle it with this vote.

Dr. WILLIAMS—If you propose taking a vote on it now there is no alternative but to discuss the question in full. It is not fair to the new members to ask them to vote on a question like that without it being discussed. I will move, seconded by Dr. BROCK, that the Council do now adjourn until two o'clock.

The PRESIDENT put the motion, which, on a vote having been taken, was declared carried.

The Council met at two o'clock p.m. in accordance with the motion for adjournment.

The PRESIDENT, Dr. Thorburn, in the chair called the Council to order.

The REGISTRAR called the roll and the following members answered to their names : Drs. Armour, Barrick, Bray, Britton, Brock, Campbell, Dickson, Douglas, Emory, Geikie, Graham, Griffin, Henderson, Logan, Moore, Moorhouse, McLaughlin, Reddick, Rogers, Sangster, Thorburn and Williams.

NOTICES OF MOTION.

None.

COMMUNICATIONS, PETITIONS, ETC.

None.

MOTIONS OF WHICH NOTICE HAS BEEN GIVEN AT A PREVIOUS MEETING.

Moved by Dr. ROGERS, seconded by Dr. LOGAN, and resolved, that the action of the Executive Committee of 1896-97 in re extension of time of the mortgage on the College building, be and is hereby confirmed by this Council.

Dr. McLaughlin—When the Property Committee met and a proposition was before us, you will remember that I took the ground that I thought it was better not to enter into an agreement with the Canada Life for three years, but only for one year, until the matter of the building should be entirely and fully laid before the Council and the views of the Council taken upon it. I thought that was a wise thing then, and I think so still. I will not raise any objection to the passage of this resolution just now, but I wish to have it understood that I was not in harmony with making an arrangement for three years, but only for one year, and then submitting the whole matter to the Council.

The President put the motion, which, on a vote having been taken, was declared carried.

Moved by Dr. Rogers, seconded by Dr. Logan and resolved, that the following gentlemen constitute the Legislative Committee, viz.: Drs. Britton, Emory, Machell, Campbell, Williams and the mover.

The President put the motion, which, on a vote having been taken, was declared carried.

Moved by Dr. Rogers, seconded by Dr. Britton, and resolved, that Dr. Thorburn, Dr. Henry and Dr. Campbell constitute the Executive Committee of the Council for the ensuing year.

Moved by Dr. Sangster, in amendment, seconded by Dr. Armour, that Drs. McLaughlin, Barrick and Emory be the Executive Committee for the ensuing year.

Dr. Geikie—Isn't there some regulation that says that two of the three members shall be the President and the Vice-President?

Dr. Sangster—No, sir; the regulation bearing upon that is by-law 39, which declares the number of which each committee shall consist, and the President and the Vice-President shall be *ex-officio* members of the standing committees, and the Executive Committee is one of the standing committees. I do not intend to enter at large into discussion of this resolution, I think it must be unnecessary, because we have spent a good deal of time in other years over the appointment of that committee. I would not have moved the amendment at all were I not strongly of the opinion that there is a principle involved, and that the rights of the medical electorate and the safety of the College funds is concerned in the appointment of that Executive Committee. There is no doubt that in accordance with the provisions of the Legislature giving the medical electorate a representation of three-fifths of the membership of this Council, that the membership ratio should be respected in the formation of all standing committees of this Council, and it should be especially respected in the formation of the Executive Committee, which is the governing committee of the Council, and to which the interests of the College are largely entrusted during a very large portion of the year. We have had reason, Mr. President, to complain, and to complain strongly of the manner in which that Committee has been constituted in the past year and in previous years. I have shown, and if I am requested to do so, and given time to do so, I can again show that that Committee has transcended its powers by seeking legislation on behalf of the College without being authorized to do so, by inserting in the petition that was circulated amongst the profession last year's provisions, the insertion of which was not authorized by the Council, and the insertion of which was calculated to bring the medical profession into direct conflict with the Legislature, and more especially with that element of the Legislature known as the Patrons. I claim it is largely owing to the distribution of the Executive Committee, that it was upon the authority of the Executive Committee that the fall examinations of the last two years have been held. It has been denied, but if it was not on the authority of the Executive Committee the only other authority that is open to the suspicion of ordering them is the Registrar, because certainly the Council has never ordered, and there is certainly no provision in the Council regulations that authorizes or suggests a fall examination. There is no doubt that the fall examination has been a source of great and unnecessary expense to this College. I have satisfactorily shown, not only to my own satisfaction, but to the satisfaction of the electorate at large, that an average loss of $700.00 per year has been involved in holding those fall examinations; that last year the actual loss was 56 per cent of $1,600.00, or, in other words, $900.00; and I again claim that is too much to pay for a piece of sentimentalism, and I can use no better term with regard to it. I have shown that that Committee has at times refused to permit members of this Council to obtain a simple return that involved no expenditure; and on behalf of the electorate, of which I am a representative, I have claimed in the past, and I now again claim, that the by-law of the Council shall be respected in the formation of that Committee, and that five members shall constitute that Committee, namely, three elected and two *ex-officio*. I do not think that is asking too much, nor do I think it is asking too much that we should receive the common British justice of having one of our representatives, one of our members, upon that important Committee. I am quite sure the continued refusal of this Council to allow a member of what is known as the Opposition in this Council a seat upon that Committee will be regarded by the profession as an indication that there is something in the acts of that Committee that should not be freely open to the investigation of the Council and of the profession. I say it challenges that construction, and I say that on the part of simple British justice the Opposition, representing over a third and nearly a half of the medical electorate of this Province, should be recognized by the admission of one member thereof into this important Committee. It has been claimed that the committee of five would be too expensive ; it has been pointed out in opposition to that, that the expense of this Committee in the past has not arisen from the number that were appointed on it but from its holding frequent meetings. During the last ten years the only expense involved by a committee of three was an expense of some $78.00 last year or the year before. If for nine out of ten years a committee of three can conduct the business of the Council without any expenditure at all, at the same rate a committee of five would conduct it without any expenditure at all. On the other hand, it has been shown that a small committee of three has involved an expenditure of over $300.00, while again, a large committee of ten or thirteen I think has, on two occasions, involved no expenditure at all. The only proper way to reduce the cost of the Committee is to debar them from holding meetings for the discussion of business ; or, in other words, make them conduct their business by means of epistolary correspondence ; or otherwise cutting off all expenditure for attendance on that important Committee. I do not intend to occupy your time more largely, I merely restate what I have said before in order to place the Council on record as to the principle involved in the appointment of this Committee. With regard to the *personnel* of that Committee I have proposed three gentlemen living either in Toronto or next to Toronto. Dr. Barrick and Dr. Emory are both residents of Toronto, and Dr. McLaughlin is perhaps the nearest to Toronto of any of our outside men ; and the President and Vice-President are *ex-officio* members. I have no special objection to Dr. Campbell being on that Committee, except that he has been on that Committee for so many years that it begins to look as though he had a peremptory right to a place on that Committee. I do not think any member should be permitted to occupy such a position.

Dr. GEIKIE—I ask that there be brevity in the speeches ; it is all very nice to talk about economy, but this talking cost this Council $4,526.00 in 1895. All this talking is ridiculous, and I hope the members will proceed with the business of the Council and not waste any more time.

Dr. WILLIAMS—Sometimes we are surprised at the course our members take. If it were not that I think the last speaker, Dr. Sangster, wants to justify himself in the course he has taken in the past I would be surprised. Dr. Sangster has previously taken very strong grounds with reference to this Executive Committee and he has ventured to make some very strong charges ; these charges have, in the main, been brought home and established to be founded not upon facts. He has made the statement in the past, if not to-day, that this was an irresponsible Committee of three, and he has taken the ground that it was elected unconstitutionally. Now, sir, I do not need to discuss this, and I am somewhat surprised that Dr. Sangster should discuss it when here lying upon his desk, upon my desk and upon the desk of every member of this Council is the opinion of our Solicitor that that Committee was appointed last year in the regular and legitimate way. I am surprised that a man with the astuteness of Dr. Sangster should have the hardihood to undertake to take up the time of the Council here with a statement of that kind with the opinion of the Solicitor right before him. I do not need to characterize that kind of conduct ; we will just let it pass. The Committee is appointed according to the constitution and there is the Solicitor's opinion ; we need nothing more. Another question has been raised and that is that the Executive Committee exceeded their powers. I am not prepared to say they have not, sometimes ; in fact, I go further and I say that they undoubtedly have. But, gentlemen, we are not here to-day to discuss past committees ; we are here to appoint a new committee and we have nothing to do with the committees that have exceeded their powers. When they transacted their business and put in their report, if they exceeded their powers, it was the business of the Council then to have censured them and to have brought them to task for having done so. That has gone by ; now we are to appoint a new committee and the committee proposed is not responsible for the acts of past committees. Now, sir, the question is whether or not the course that has been pursued by the Council of late years in appointing the President and Vice-President and one member of the Council on that Committee is a reasonable and legitimate course, and we have the Solicitor's opinion that it is in accordance with the law. With reference to the statement as to cost, I submit that any member who will take the cost of the Committee from the time the Council was established, up to the present time, and will follow that down year after year and year after year, he will find when the Committee got down to three and continued with three for the last number of years, that that was the time the cost of the Committee got down to a low figure. If he will take the years just immediately preceding that, when there was a large Committee, that is the time when he will find a large cost, running up to four or five or six hundred dollars a year ; and I claim that that is an ample consideration for the Council to reduce the Committee to a small number. And there is still more good reason, when they have reduced it, to keep it down to the lowest figure that they can. It is all very well to come here and preach economy, but it is still more important to do your work in such a way that it will result in economy ; and that I claim is one of the results in bringing that Committee down to the smallest number possible, and three is the least number that will fill the legal requirements of the Act. Under these circumstances I am surprised that the matter should be raised again and the time of the Council taken up in discussing it. I have nothing to say against the personnel of the men who are proposed by Dr. Sangster, nor do I think anything can be said against the men who were proposed in the first place, and under these circumstances, having heard the two sides, I trust the Council will come to a vote upon the question without wasting the whole afternoon over it.

Dr. SANGSTER—I believe I have a right to reply, if this ends the discussion; if it does not and further discussion ensues, I of course reserve for myself the right to reply.

The PRESIDENT—You have a right to reply once.

Dr. SANGSTER—I will not occupy much of your time, I merely wanted to point out my reading of the Solicitor's opinion, and I think perhaps it may have escaped Dr. Williams' notice. The Solicitor's opinion is that the Executive Committee, as constituted last year, was legally constituted and at the close of the clause in which he states that he says : "I understand that the provision that the President and Vice-President should be ex-officio members of the Committee is re-enacted each year." That has never been re-enacted in any year since I have been in the Council. It is stated in your by-law, No. 39, that they are ex-officio members of all committees. In each year I have been in the Council, the President and Vice-President of the Council have been not ex-officio but appointed members of that Committee. I claim that the Solicitor's opinion is in accordance with my views, and not in accordance with the views of the majority of this Council.

Dr. ROGERS—The main motion is that Dr. Thorburn, Dr. Henry and Dr. Campbell shall form the Executive Committee for the ensuing year. That means a committee of three. Dr. Sangster's amendment is that Dr. Barrick, Dr. McLaughlin and Dr. Emory be the committee. That means, of course, under our by-laws that not only three but that five should be appointed. We all know one of the strongest contentions made by Dr. Sangster and his two friends in this Council, because I think this large body which Dr. Sangster represents here consists of three, is economy ; their strongest contention is economy. Yet, after all, when he has one opportunity of practising economy by keeping down the size of that Committee he always takes exception to it. There are some things he has said which I think are rather hard on the honesty and integrity of the members of this Council. He says the principle involved in this motion is the safety of the college funds ; in other words, a committee of three members of this Council are not as safe to trust with the funds. of this Council as five ; that is his contention. Or, in other words, you Mr. President, Dr. Henry and Dr. Campbell are hardly as responsible as Dr. Barrick, Dr. McLaughlin, Dr. Emory, Dr. Henry and yourself. I think that is rather unfair, to put it mildly ; it is unjust to accuse any three members, I do not care what three, of not being honest enough to manage the funds of this Council as well as five. Surely this Council is not going to endorse such a thing as that. That is what is stated. Now, he says that last year the Committee transcended its power ; that, Mr. President, was up before the Council last evening and I think it was thoroughly threshed out ; at least, Dr. Sangster and his friends had every opportunity of threshing it out, and as far as my recollection serves me they took every advantage of that opportunity. Now, having threshed it out, Dr. Sangster still comes back and reiterates a statement which presses somewhat severely on the honor and integrity of the Committee of last year. I say it is unjust to reiterate a statement which he was unable to carry in this Council last evening. He also says that it was on the authority of this Committee that the fall examination has been held. We all know that that is something which is contained in our regulations; it is printed and published to all concerned ; it is passed every year by the Educational Committee's report ; every year that Committee's report brings in the curriculum and in that is a statement that the fall examination shall be held. Now, whatever may be doubted in regard to the hair-splitting legality of that position, mind, it is a fact well known to Dr. Sangster, well known to the triarchy which he is the supreme head of in this Council, that the Executive Committee had nothing whatever to do with arranging the fall examination ; that has been arranged for by the Council in regulations that have been passed year after year, and therefore why should any man be, I will say unkind enough, if you like to put it that way—if I made the statement which Dr. Sangster has made I would say "dishonest enough"—to state we, the Executive Committee, exceeded our powers in adopting a date for the fall examination? Another thing he says, and he has repeated this not only to-day but time and time again, until, like many of his statements, to me they become rather nauseous, that the Executive Committee refused a member of this Council information. That statement has been made time and time again and denied ; still, Dr. Sangster reiterates the statement. It is a question who is to be believed, the Executive Committee or Dr. Sangster.   Still he goes on, not only in this Council but in print and in every way reiterating a statement which I will characterize to-day as not being true.   The Executive Committee never objected or refused to give him information which was properly asked for.   He also mentioned the very brilliant would-be triarchy which he has the honor to be the head of, or at least I suppose he is, and he characterized them in this Council as the opposition ; he puts them on a somewhat high pedestal—

DR. SANGSTER—I rise to a point of order.   I don't think the member has any right to characterize me as the head of a triarchy ; I have never called him the tail of any element in this Council.

Dr. ROGERS—Perhaps not.   I would rather be the tail of any element in this Council than the head of his.

The PRESIDENT—Dr. Sangster himself has made the public declaration that he is leader of the opposition.

Dr. SANGSTER—I have denied that.   No, sir, I am too modest a man—

The PRESIDENT—I will call it to your memory.   In the meeting we had last year some-one asked you if you were the leader of the opposition and you said you had the honor to be.

Dr. SANGSTER—I claim that your memory is at fault.   I assure you, much as I should like to have the honor of being the head, I have never assumed to be in that position.   I very much regret it is not in my power to claim that position as I should really feel it just as much an honor as my friend Dr. Rogers would feel it an honor to be the tail of any other part of this Council.

Dr. BRITTON—Mr. President, I might simply corroborate what you stated.   Dr. Sangster was asked whether he was the leader of the opposition and he said, "I am the leader of a certain sect in the Council."

Dr. ROGERS—Without dwelling too much, Mr. President, on Dr. Sangster's assumption that he and his two friends constitute the opposition in this Council, I am quite satisfied to leave him in that position ; I am quite satisfied for three men to constitute themselves into what they call the opposition, but it remains for the profession to say whether they like the acts of the opposition.   I seriously object to a number of men coming here and constituting themselves into an opposition, what for?   To preach economy and by their practice to not only produce the greatest extravagance, but, I say, Mr. President, their conduct in this Council has brought expenditure on us and on the profession which more than balances, which doubles, the amount which would have been saved had all their requests been acceded to.   Now, I have no intention, I have no desire, Mr. President, to even utter a word on behalf of my friend Dr. Campbell ; I do not think I am capable of defending him half as well as he is capable of defending himself, but I must enter a protest against the assertion on the part of Dr. Sangster that Dr. Campbell must assume by this time a peremptory right to be a member of the Executive Committee.   Dr. Campbell, by his appointment on that Committee, shows he has the confidence and the entire confidence of this Council, and therefore, it is unkind, to say the least, to even mention a thing like that.   Again, Dr. Sangster mentions the fact that the Executive Committee is an irresponsible triarchy ; if that is true, then the whole Council is an irresponsible triarchy, because the Executive Committee are drawn from the Council and they have to report to the Council, and therefore their acts are always open to be investigated, to be talked over and in every way cut to pieces, if necessary, by the Council.   But that was done last night and still we find the report of the Executive Committee adopted exactly as it was brought before the Council.   This being the case it seems to me hardly just or kind of any man to state that that Committee is an irresponsible triarchy.   I feel that such a state-ment going out to the profession is not just to the profession and it is not just to the public.   I say statements of this kind, gratuitous statements—I cannot help but say that if I stated them I would consider them as untrue statements—going to the Legislature, to the country, has injured the Council in the eyes of the Legislature and profession of this Province.

Dr. BARRICK—I do not intend to discuss anything but just the facts.   We have a legal opinion upon the constitution of this Committee and I will guarantee that if you ask a boy in the first division of the Collegiate Institute how many members should be on the Executive Committee he would answer differently from the solicitor and I will tell you why.   It says that the Registration Committee shall consist of seven members, and everybody knows that it consists of nine members ; because the President and Vice-President are members.   The Education Committee consists of nine members, everybody knows it consists of eleven members, because the President and Vice-President are members.   The Rules and Regulations Committee consists of five members but the same school boy would know that it consists of seven members, because the President and Vice-President are ex-officio members.   The Print-ing Committee consists of five members ; that boy would know, as every member in this Council would know, it consists of seven members, because the President and Vice-President are ex-officio members.   The Complaints Committee the same.   The Executive Committee consists of three members.   Why, anyone would know that that committee consists of five members, because the President and Vice-President are ex-officio members.   This is one of the bones of contention that is being brought up here every year and I do hope that the committee that is appointed to revise the by-laws will see that this is made plain. If you are going to have three members on that Committee, then you must put in one member. That shows the ridiculous position of the matter. The Executive Committee consists of three members, and if it is to be three members then you must put in the by-law "one member ; " because the President and Vice-President are *ex-officio* members.

Dr. ROGERS—What about the Discipline Committee ?

Dr. BARRICK—The Discipline Committee consists of three or five members, and if the President or Vice-President are *ex-officio* members of that Committee then it will be five or seven members.

The PRESIDENT—I beg to say that these are very good suggestions of yours, Dr. Barrick, but they are more for the Committee on Revision than for this particular discussion.

Dr. SANGSTER—I rise for a moment to explain that the by-laws state that the President and Vice-President shall be *ex-officio* members of all committees except the Discipline Committee. (Cries of "Question, question.")

The PRESIDENT put the amendment, which, on a vote having been taken, was declared lost.

The PRESIDENT put the motion, which, on a vote having been taken, was declared carried.

Dr. SANGSTER—I ask that the yeas and nays be taken.

The PRESIDENT instructed the Registrar to take the yeas and nays.

The REGISTRAR took the yeas and nays as follows :

Yeas—Drs. Bray, Britton, Brock, Dickson, Douglas, Emory, Fowler, Geikie, Graham, Griffin, Henderson, Logan, Luton, Machell, Moore, Moorhouse, Rogers, Roome, Shaw, Thorburn and Williams—21.

Nays—Drs. Armour, Barrick, Hanly, McLaughlin, Reddick and Sangster—6.

Dr. McLAUGHLIN moved, seconded by Dr. HANLY, that by-law No. — for the purpose of appointing an Auditor and fixing his salary or fees be now read a first time,

The PRESIDENT put the motion, which, on a vote having been taken, was declared carried.

Dr. McLAUGHLIN read the by-law.

Dr. McLAUGHLIN moved, seconded by Dr. HANLY, that by-law No. — for the purpose of appointing an Auditor and fixing his salary or fees be referred to the Committee of the Whole and read a second time.

The PRESIDENT put the motion, which, on a vote having been taken, was declared carried.

Council in Committee of the Whole. Dr. HENDERSON in the chair.

Dr. McLAUGHLIN read the by-law a second time, and moved the adoption of the first clause of the by-law.

Dr. WILLIAMS—I think the first motion should be to fill the blank ; we cannot adopt it until that is done.

Dr. McLAUGHLIN—I am not very clearly in a position to suggest a name. I understand from the Committee who have had charge of the finances that the auditing has not been very satisfactory, and I would like to leave the filling up of the blank to the Council. If any member of the Council can suggest the name of a first class gentleman who will go through our accounts thoroughly, I would be very glad to have that blank filled.

Dr. THORBURN—I would suggest the name of Dr. Carlyle. You referred to the Committee not being satisfied when going over the accounts. There were one or two small instances where perhaps he had been rather derelict, but I do not know that it was his fault, or whose particular fault it was. We have never found any mistakes of any consequence ; in fact, no mistake of arithmetic or anything like that. One charge made against him is that he received more money for the first year's work than the by-law authorized him to get, and another one I think was that he had not looked into the mortgages to ascertain the exact legal arrangement that existed between the College and Canada Life. I claim these are not very serious, and it is a very serious matter to discharge a man holding the position he does in some of the leading financial institutions of Canada and who trust to him solely and do not insist upon having a second auditor. I think if his attention is called to the fact that he overlooked the mortgages that he will only be too glad to attend to it. I know that during this past year he has been suffering a great deal from some disease, and it is just possible in his physical condition and in his anxiety to get things right, that he might have overlooked the fact of not attending to the leases as he ought to have done. As to the $20.00, when he came to find out he had such a lot of work to do he could not accept it. I think that ought to come up under the Finance Committee's report. I should be sorry to see Dr. Carlyle thrown out on account of those two things.

The CHAIRMAN put the motion that the blank be filled by inserting the name of Dr. Carlyle and that the first clause of the by-law be adopted, which, on a vote having been taken, was declared carried.

Dr. McLAUGHLIN read the second clause of the by-law, and moved that the Auditor receive $25.00.

Dr. ARMOUR—That is not the question just now. When the Finance Committee bring in a report they will have a clause with regard to this matter, and I think the Council should be in possession of that before passing this by-law. With the permission of the Committee, I would state that there is a clause in the Finance Committee's report which says that the Auditor received $20.00 more than was authorized by the Council for the last year's audit. The circumstances are these : There was a by-law passed two years ago fixing the salary for last year at $20.00. He protested against it and asked that the Council increase that to $40.00 ; it came before the Finance Committee and they recommended that it be increased to $40.00 last year, but when the report of the Committee was considered in Council it was reduced again, and the by-law stood as it was. Perhaps I might say, the Registrar overlooked that it was erased by the Chairman of the Committee, and the report was passed. As you remember, it was passed very hurriedly and that was overlooked, though on the proceedings the resolution not allowing it is shown. I think the Auditor, if his audit is worth anything, should have known that he was only entitled to $20.00, and had made an error with regard to his own payment.

Dr. BRAY—The first part of the by-law is carried.

Dr. ARMOUR—Had I known that I would not have spoken.

Dr. WILLIAMS moved that the blank in the second clause of the by-law be filled in with the figures "$40.00," which, on a vote having been taken, was declared carried.

Dr. McLAUGHLIN—I think I will ask the permission of the Council to withdraw the third clause, because it is a serious thing to give instructions to an auditor. I think, Mr. Chairman, that this is an exceedingly important matter, and I think that the Auditor should go far beyond taking an account and seeing the amount of it and seeing that there is a cheque for that amount ; he ought to look up the by-laws and resolutions of the Council and see that there is an authority for every payment. There is no more valuable officer in the Dominion of Canada to-day than the Auditor-General, and such duties as I have stated apply to him, and he has exercised that power beneficially. I think when an account is brought to our auditor paid, as it assuredly will be, some authority should be given him, and he should be asked by this Council to make a note of it and make a report and let it be brought before the Council. But, that is not all ; there are other matters to which reference has been made. The receipts of the Council should be carefully examined by him to see that they are in harmony with the rentals in connection with this building, and in connection with other matters. I move that the third clause of the by-law be struck out.

Dr. DICKSON—I think it is important that that clause should remain in.

Dr. McLAUGHLIN—I feel that the clause instructing the auditor should be more comprehensive than this is ; the clause reads in this way, "That the Auditor be and is hereby instructed in auditing the accounts to ascertain whether or not there is proper authority for the payment of each account and make a report thereon for the use of the Council."

Dr. BRAY—The only difficulty would be to look up the authority.

Dr. MACHELL—I think it is well to leave this out for the present; it will involve a great deal more work on the part of the Auditor and on the part of the Registrar ; the Registrar will have to be in constant attendance on the Auditor, looking up authorities. It would be a matter of weeks in auditing the accounts.

Dr. McLAUGHLIN—Another important fact is, the moment we adopt the report of our Auditor every account in that report becomes binding, and if afterwards we find some person defrauding us in any amount of money we are powerless to collect it. That is a very grave matter for us to consider, and if we are to have an auditor at all and an audit of our accounts it should be as nearly perfect as we can get it. I did not know that this was the law until my friend Dr. Brock told me this morning, and I do not think this clause is sufficiently comprehensive ; I am not satisfied with it.

Dr. BRAY—I think if Dr. McLaughlin, during the interim, would suggest some scheme and bring it before the Council it would carry without a dissenting voice, because I am heartily in accord with what he says. I think we often jump into things that we would not have done if we had had more time to consider it. I quite agree with the object of that clause, but I would ask Dr. McLaughlin, as he has suggested himself, to withdraw it.

The CHAIRMAN put the motion to withdraw Clause 3, which, on a vote having been taken, was declared carried.

Dr. McLAUGHLIN moved that the Committee rise and report the by-law as amended, which, on a vote having been taken, was declared carried.

The Committee rose. The PRESIDENT in the chair.

Dr. McLAUGHLIN moved, seconded by Dr. HANLY, that by-law No. —, now passed by the Committee of the Whole, entitled "A by-law for the purpose of appointing an Auditor and fixing his salary or fees" be now read a third time, passed, numbered, signed by the President and sealed with the seal of the College of Physicians and Surgeons of Ontario.

The PRESIDENT put the motion, which, on a vote having been taken, was declared carried, and the by-law adopted as follows :

"By-law No. 80, for appointing an Auditor and fixing his salary. Whereas, power has been granted to the Medical Council of the College of Physicians and Surgeons of Ontario, under Section 13 of the Ontario Medical Act, R.S.O. 1887, Chapter 148, to make by-laws, be it therefore enacted as follows :

"1st. This Council hereby appoints Dr. James Carlyle, Toronto, as Auditor, for the purpose of auditing the accounts of the Council.

"2nd. The salary or fees to be paid to the Auditor by the Council for his services as auditor shall be and are hereby fixed at forty dollars.

"Adopted as amended.   Adopted in Council.

"G. HENDERSON, Chairman, Committee of Whole.   J. HENRY, Vice-President."

Dr. WILLIAMS moved, seconded by Dr. SHAW, and resolved, that the Council do now go into Committee of the Whole on the by-law to levy the annual fee.

The PRESIDENT put the motion, which, on a vote having been taken, was declared carried.

Council in Committee of the Whole. Dr. HENRY in the chair.

Dr. WILLIAMS—We were in Committee of the Whole on the by-law for levying the annual fee, and it was read the first time before going into Committee of the Whole. While we were in Committee of the Whole a motion was made to elect a special subcommittee of the Committee of the Whole to obtain certain opinions from Mr. Osler on questions which were placed in the hands of that Committee. The Committee interviewed Mr. Osler and laid the questions before him as carefully as they could, and are now prepared to make answer in the form of a report which I will read :

To the Committee of the Whole of the Ontario Medical Council.

GENTLEMEN,—Your subcommittee appointed to lay before Mr. Osler certain questions and to obtain his answer thereto, beg leave to report as follows :

1st. With reference to Section 41a, which was suspended by the Ontario Medical Act of 1893 : When a by-law is passed in the terms of the Statute to bring it into force, as was done by by-law No. 69 in 1895, it is in full force and virtue.   And,

2nd. It is not necessary that a by-law shall be enacted each year to continue it in force, for once brought into operation it continues until repealed.

3rd. Had the Medical Council at the annual session of 1895 a legal right to assess an annual tax on the medical profession for the years 1893 and 1894, as enacted in Clause 3 of by-law No. 69 ?   The Solicitor is of the opinion that the Council had the right to impose the fee for 1893 and 1894, as they did under by-law No. 69, and that the fee imposed under this by-law would be collectible, in that the annual certificate would be withheld until payment is made.   If an individual should think it unjust he would be obliged to take proceedings to quash the by-law, upon the validity of which there might be doubt, thereby throwing the onus of proof on the party making the appeal.   And that if he had been stricken from the register for non-payment of dues covering the period prior or subsequent to these two years during which the 41a Clause was suspended, he could not claim restoration, as invalidity for this by-law would not affect those for previous or subsequent years about which there is no doubt.

4th. To what part of the arrearages of the annual tax which are outstanding at various dates from 1874 to the present time can Section 41a of the Medical Act passed in 1891 be legally applied for their collection ?   The fees for past years are a debt to the Council and are collectible under this Act, no matter how far back they date.

5th. The Council cannot delegate to the Executive Committee the power to authorize the Registrar to erase names.

6th. When charges against a member of the College have been investigated by the Discipline Committee and the evidence has been taken, it is not necessary to notify him to appear before the Council when they are about to take action. To do so is an act of grace, and when practicable is advisable.

7th. The conduct of Charles John Parsons undoubtedly is such as may be dealt with by the Discipline Committee under this Act. It may be a charge coming under the criminal code at the same time.

8th. Your Committee understood the instructions to be that the opinions of the

Solicitor were to be obtained in writing that they might be placed on file for future reference. We were informed by him that the advice sought under these questions had previously at various dates been furnished to the Council either by direct letter or through prepared by-law, that if we wished them now put in writing from Mr. Osler's office, they could be furnished to-day. If wished with Mr. B. B. Osler's own signature it would require a week or ten days. Your Committee believe it would be very satisfactory to the profession at large were the opinions, especially bearing on the annual fee and its collection, obtained from the Solicitor under his own signature, and published in the next Annual Announcement. We therefore recommend that the Registrar be instructed to write Mr. Osler for these opinions for this special purpose.

All of which is respectfully submitted.

(Signed,)   J. ARTHUR WILLIAMS, Chairman.

Dr. SANGSTER—May I enquire from you, Mr. Chairman, or from Dr. Williams, whether I am correct in my interpretation of the opinion read from Mr. Osler. Two years ago I think an opinion was brought here from the Solicitor's office, or rather, that the by-law for the reinstitution of the clause authorizing the annual assessment and the reinstitution of Section 41a was legal and correct. I believe it was ascertained subsequently, and it is admitted now that that was not a written opinion, that it was a verbal opinion emanating from the Solicitor's office, not necessarily from Mr. B. B. Osler. I would like to know first whether this opinion is from Mr. B. B. Osler?

Dr. WILLIAMS—You say it was admitted that the opinion which you have referred to was not his opinion, but emanating from his office?

Dr. SANGSTER—Yes.

Dr. WILLIAMS—We do not admit that. The Solicitor made this statement to the Council with regard to that, and therefore it is embraced in this report : "Your Committee understood the instructions to be that the opinions of the Solicitor were to be obtained in writing, that they might be placed on file for future reference. We were informed by him that the advice sought under these questions had previously at various dates been furnished to the Council either by direct letter or through prepared by-law." So that the opinions which have been given, while perhaps not personally prepared by Mr. B. B. Osler, have been gone over and investigated by him. These opinions that we bring here are brought from a partner in his firm.

Dr. SANGSTER—I am glad to have that explanation. Now the matter I was aiming at was this : A resolution was moved here the other day by Dr. Roome, I believe, in opposition to an opinion being obtained from Mr. Osler touching the assessments for the year 1892-93 and 1893-94, because if that opinion was obtained it might lead to endless lawsuits. I thought that was a very unfortunate basis upon which to oppose the obtaining of the opinion sought, but it now appears that Mr. Osler himself practically takes the same ground. He admits that there is grave doubt about the right to press the assessment for those two years, but he claims that it was right to assess the profession, because the assessment makes each professional man in the country a debtor for that amount, and the onus of proof of the validity of the by-law rests upon the professional man who is assessed. I claim that is not the position that this reputable Medical Council of Ontario should suffer itself to be placed in. I claim this Council should know definitely and distinctly whether they have or had the legal right beyond any possibility of cavil to assess for the years 1893, '94, and if they have not a clear and indubitable right to assess in those years, they should not throw upon the members so assessed the *onus probandi*, but they should repay the professional members of the country who have been mulcted in that amount.

Dr. WILLIAMS—Mr. Osler does not go to the length of saying there is a probable doubt ; he admits that there is a possible doubt. And the entire point turns upon the legal interpretation of the word "suspension." His interpretation is that "suspend" means to hold until a certain time, which time was till an election took place, and until the new members elected had a right to say whether or not this should go into operation, and if it went into operation it started in where it was suspended. At the same time he says it could be argued in a different way, and it would be just possible the other interpretation might be taken. He thinks there would be a bare chance of that, but that the probabilities are altogether the other way. I move, seconded by Dr. MOORE, that the Committee of the Whole adopt the report of the subcommittee.

Dr. McLAUGHLIN—It is understood by that that the opinion on all points will be got from Mr. B. B. Osler?

Dr. WILLIAMS—That is the way that would read, especially the opinions bearing upon the clause as to the annual fee.

Dr. McLaughlin—That word "especially" leads to a doubt as to whether the others will be or not.

Dr. Williams—"Your Committee believe it would be very satisfactory to the profession at large were the opinions, especially bearing on the annual fee and its collection, obtained from the Solicitor under his signature and published in the next Annual Announcement. We therefore recommend that the Registrar be instructed to write Mr. Osler for these opinions for this special purpose." (See Mr. Osler's opinion at end of report of Proceedings.) There might be a question as to whether the Registrar shall take Mr. Osler's opinion on all these questions or only upon section 41a.

Dr. McLaughlin—That is the essential question.

Dr. Sangster—I think it is only on that one point.

Dr. Williams—That was my supposition.

The Chairman put the motion, which, on a vote having been taken, was declared carried.

Dr. Williams—We will now take up the by-law entitled "A by-law to levy the Annual Fee."

Dr. Williams read the by-law, and moved the adoption of clause 1.

Dr. McLaughlin—Do we not understand that the by-laws that were passed last year in regard to all these matters were permanent until repealed ?

Dr. Williams—Yes, but while Mr. Osler's opinion was that it would be legal to let it go from year to year, he, at the same time, expressed the opinion that he thought it would be judicious to pass this by-law each individual year ; he thought it would save much trouble, and possibly expense. On motion, clause 1 was adopted as read.

Dr. Williams moved that the enacting clause be adopted. Carried.

Dr. Williams moved that the preamble be adopted. Carried.

Dr. Williams moved that the title be adopted. Carried.

Dr. Williams moved, seconded by Dr. Moore, and resolved, that the Committee do now rise and report the by-law as read and passed in Committee of the Whole, which, on a vote having been taken, was declared carried.

The Committee rose. The President in the chair.

Dr. Williams moved, seconded by Dr. Moore, and resolved, that the by-law for levying the annual fee be now read a third time, and finally passed, signed, numbered, and sealed with the seal of the College of Physicians and Surgeons of Ontario.

Dr. Armour—I desire to say a few words regarding this. I have objected, under the circumstances that have existed, to making this assessment from year to year, on the ground that I thought, if proper economy was exercised, it would not be necessary, and that a great deal of friction in the profession would be avoided if we could get along without this annual fee. During the past year we have had a total net income of $20,630.17. I made a computation a few years ago, and again last year, and, speaking from memory, I believe that the necessary expense of the Council, aside from maintenance of the building, amounted to about $13,300 or $14,000, and by levying two or three thousand dollars to carry the building, aside from the annual tax, if it aggregates as much next year as it did last year, we would have an income of over $15,000, which should be ample for all expenses. However, we have not got to that point in our Finance Committee's report at the present time ; they have not yet considered the estimates, and I do not see how I, or any other member of the Council, can properly vote to assess this tax until those estimates have been presented and considered. I think no member of the Council would desire to assess this fee if it was found that there were ample funds without the assessment. So that, at the present time, I feel obliged to dissent from the preamble of the by-law which says that it will be necessary to assess the tax. I want further time for consideration, and for that reason I could not support the by-law now, and I must vote against it.

The President on request instructed the Registrar to take the yeas and nays.

The Registrar took the yeas and nays as follows :

Yeas—Drs. Barrick, Bray, Brock, Campbell, Dickson, Emory, Graham, Hanly, Henderson, Logan, Luton, Machell, Rogers, Roome, Thorburn and Williams—16.

Nays—Drs. Armour, Henry, McLaughlin, Reddick and Sangster—5.

CONSIDERATION OF REPORTS.

Dr. Machell moved, seconded by Dr. McLaughlin, that the report of the Property Committee be now considered.

The President put the motion, which, on a vote having been taken, was declared carried.

Dr. MACHELL read the report of the Property Committee, and moved its adoption, which, on a vote having been taken, was declared carried, and the report adopted as follows :

REPORT OF PROPERTY COMMITTEE.

To the President and Members of the Medical Council of the College of Physicians and Surgeons of Ontario.

GENTLEMEN,—Your Committee on Property beg leave to report that they have inspected the Building and find it in a good state of repair.

The instructions received by your Committee from the Council in June, 1896, have been carried out, and after making every possible enquiry as to the prospect of disposing of the property, your Committee found that the time was not favorable for the selling of the property, and at once gave notification to the Registrar for the carrying out of the instructions of the Council, when your Committee was empowered to rearrange the loan that fell due November 1st, 1896.

The members of your Committee resident in Toronto held a number of meetings endeavoring to secure a rearrangement of the mortgage on more favorable terms than formerly, and as soon as negotiations were sufficiently advanced, your Property Committee was called together and the loan arranged for a three years' renewal mortgage with the Canada Life at the rate of three and a half per cent. per annum from November 1st, 1896.

We also beg leave to report a substantial reduction in the insurance upon the building, the Canada Life Co. agreeing to reduce the amount heretofore carried by the College, forty-thousand dollars ($40,000), to twenty-five thousand dollars ($25,000), making an annual saving of fifty dollars ($50), on the insurance which, with the reduction of interest from five per cent. to three and a half, will make a net saving of nine hundred and fifty dollars ($950) per year in carrying the property until such time when it can be advantageously disposed of.

Your Committee also complied with your instructions in erecting the necessary closet accommodation for the building, and had the walls and ceilings of the halls cleaned and papered and the woodwork varnished after specifications had been prepared and tenders for the work received, the lowest tender being accepted. This will render further outlay in these parts unnecessary for some time.

The boilers, elevator and machinery have been inspected and found in a satisfactory condition.

Your Committee recommend that the powers entrusted to them last year in regard to the sale of the building be continued.

The revenue from the year's rents amounts to four thousand six hundred and twenty-two dollars and three cents ($4,622.03), being one thousand four hundred and six dollars and eighty-seven cents ($1,406.87) more than was received last year, eleven hundred dollars ($1,100) of which was received from the Independent Order of Foresters during the eleven months of their occupancy. This source of revenue will terminate shortly, as their own building on the opposite corner is nearing completion. This is not taking into account any allowance for our own premises occupied by the College.

Our supplies such as fuel, etc., have been purchased after receiving tenders for the same.

All of which is respectfully submitted.

(Signed,)   HENRY T. MACHELL, Chairman.

Dr. HENDERSON—The report of the Finance Committee is ready, but I have not yet submitted it to the Committee.

Dr. BROCK—I move the adjournment of this Council so that we may have this report read and submitted.

Dr. MACHELL—Before that is done may I introduce a motion ?

The Council granted leave to Dr. Machell to introduce a motion.

The PRESIDENT, Dr. Thorburn, left the chair, and the Vice-President, Dr. Henry, took the same.

Dr. MACHELL moved, seconded by Dr. DICKSON, and resolved, that having learned the details of the scheme for the founding of the Victorian Order of Nurses, the Council of the College of Physicians and Surgeons of Ontario, now in session, is of the opinion :

That the motives of the originators of the scheme should be most gratefully appreciated both by the medical profession and by the public at large, more particularly when regard is had to the exalted source from which the proposal is believed to have emanated.

The Council nevertheless believes that by virtue of our more extensive knowledge and experience of the difficulties sought to be removed, we should in the most kindly manner warn the advocates of the scheme that in actual results it must necessarily be disappointing to them, and fraught with elements of actual danger to the public, and we would respectfully suggest a very distinct modification of the scope and magnitude of the undertaking.

Dr. McLaughlin—Might not some word be used to replace the word "warned"?

Dr. Sangster—Use the word "suggest."

Dr. Dickson—Put in the word "caution."

Dr. Machell—I think myself the word "warned" is all right. There is going to be trouble if this scheme is continued.

Dr. McLaughlin—All right, I will withdraw my objection.

The Vice-President put the motion, which, on a vote having been taken, was declared carried unanimously.

Dr. Machell moved, seconded by Dr. Dickson, that the Registrar be instructed to send a copy of the above motion to the members of the Dominion and Local Houses.

The Vice-President put the motion, which, on a vote having been taken, was declared carried.

Dr. Williams—Is there no business, or can the Council adjourn?

The Vice-President called for reports of committees.

Dr. Sangster—Is there any way of knowing if we are going to get away to-night?

The Vice-President—I don't know.

Dr. Campbell—I would make a suggestion, if we want to get home early, that on matters that have been repeatedly discussed in this Council, we avoid any further discussion to-night, should any of these matters come up. We can have the votes taken on them and our names recorded, but where we have repeatedly expressed our opinions, in the interests of our own convenience and with the object of getting away early, let us dispense with further argument upon them.

Dr. Hanly—The report of the Committee on Rules and Regulations has been received and read; and I move, seconded by Dr. Campbell, that it be adopted.

The Vice-President pnt the motion, which, on a vote having been taken, was declared carried, and the report adopted as follows:

RULES AND REGULATIONS REPORT.

To the President and Members of the Council of the College of Physicians and Surgeons of Ontario.

Your Committee on Rules and Regulations beg leave to report as follows: That we recommend for your acceptance the opinion given by Mr. Osler (our solicitor) on the validity of certain acts of this Council hereto appended.

(Signed,)   JOHN HANLY, Chairman.

Moved by Dr. Sangster, seconded by Dr. McLaughlin, that the opinion of the Solicitor be obtained promptly regarding the validity of the Council's action in the following particulars: 1st, the constitution of the Executive Committee; 2nd, the payment of per diem allowances to any of the committees; 3rd, the payment of any moneys to the examiners; 4th, the payment of any salary to the Official Prosecutor; 5th, the fixing of the time of examinations; and 6th, the double examination at Kingston and Toronto.

R. A. Pyne, M.D., Medical Council Building, Toronto.

DEAR SIR,—In reply to your letter of the 11th inst., asking my opinion upon various matters therein stated, I beg to say as follows:

THE EXECUTIVE COMMITTEE.

As to the constitution of the Executive Committee, upon referring to by-law No. 39, passed at the session of June, 1896, it appears that the Executive Committee for the current year was duly constituted in accordance with Section 14 of the Ontario Medical Act, and I am of the opinion that this Committee was properly constituted by the appointment of three members, two of whom to be the President and Vice-President respectively. I understand that the provision that the President and Vice-President should be *ex-officio* members of the Committee is re-enacted each year, so that the provisions of Section 14 to the effect that the members of this Committee should be appointed annually, are complied with.

PAYMENT TO MEMBERS OF EXECUTIVE COMMITTEE.

It is possible that objection might be raised to the payment of per diem allowances to cover fees and travelling expenses of members of Executive Committee upon the ground that the Act does not specifically mention the Executive Committee in authorizing payment of fees and travelling expenses. Upon the other hand, Section 12 does not limit the right to pay fees and expenses to members of the Council for attending the general session of the Council, and Section 13 authorizes payment of salaries and fees of all officers necessary for the working of this Act. After carefully considering the matter, I am of opinion that whatever doubt there may be as to the right to pay a per diem allowance to cover fees and travelling expenses under Section 12 that members of the Executive Committee are officers of the Council necessary for the working of the Act within the meaning of Section 13, and that any reasonable allowance may therefore be paid to them in the discretion of the Council.

PAYMENT OF SALARY TO OFFICIAL PROSECUTOR.

I am of opinion that under the provisions of Section 13 of The Ontario Medical Act the Council has power to appoint an Official Prosecutor as an officer necessary for the working of the Act and to provide for payment to such Official Prosecutor of a reasonable salary out of the funds in the hands of the Treasurer in accordance with Section 58 of the Act.

EXAMINATIONS, TIME, PLACE.

I am of opinion that Section 28 of The Ontario Medical Act confers upon the Council an absolute discretion to provide for the holding of examinations at Toronto or at Kingston, or at both places, at any time or times, subject only to the provision that such examinations must be held at least once in each year.

The above are all the points that occurred to me under the headings of your letter. If there are any other questions upon which an opinion is desired I shall be pleased to consider them at your request. Yours truly,

(Signed,) B. B. OSLER.

June 23rd, 1897.

R. A. Pyne, M.D., College of Physicians and Surgeons of Ontario, Toronto.

DEAR SIR,—Your memorandum asking further explanation of some of the points considered in my opinion of June 23rd ult. has been handed to me. With regard to the payment of fees and expenses to the members of committees other than the Executive Committee, I am of opinion that members of such other committees are not officers to whom the Council can pay salaries or fees under Section 13 of the Act, and while, as pointed out in my former opinion, there would seem to be some doubt as to whether payment for attendance at committee meetings is provided for by Section 12, I am upon the whole of opinion that in so far as the work of standing committees is necessary for carrying the Act into effect the Council may in their discretion under this section provide for the payment of fees and reasonable travelling expenses to members attending such committee meetings.

The right to pay salaries and fees to the Board of Examiners is expressly provided for by Section 13 of the Act. It is expressly provided for by Section 13 of the Act that the Council must direct by by-law the time and manner of holding examinations at either Toronto or at Kingston. Yours truly,

(Signed,) B. B. OSLER.

The VICE-PRESIDENT (Dr. Henry) left the chair and the PRESIDENT (Dr. Thorburn) took the same.

Dr. BARRICK presented and read the report of the Printing Committee.

The PRESIDENT—How do the tenders compare with last year's tenders?

Dr. BARRICK—Last year it cost us $1.32 a page for the Announcement; this year it is to cost $1.78 per page.

Dr. McLAUGHLIN—I don't think that fully expresses it. Last year the publisher had the privilege of putting advertisements in at the beginning and end of the book. This year that is not involved, and any profits that may accrue from that the Council may reap them, so that you can scarcely compare the two years.

Dr. BARRICK—The Methodist Book Room people state that if we wish to insert advertisements they will print those at $2.00 per page. They do not deal in advertisements themselves. The stenographic work last year cost us ninety cents per page; for 1898, according to this tender, it is to cost us sixty cents per page. We do not know what it will cost this year, but if I remember, when it was under discussion in the session the stenographer stated he would do the work this year as cheaply as any other regularly qualified stenographer. The tenders show that Mr. Alexander Downey will do it next year for sixty cents per page. Whether Mr. Downey, the stenographer of this year, will do the work for that, of course I don't know.

Dr. LUTON—I think it was understood, although it was not mentioned there, that the Announcement was to be printed within four weeks from the time a typewritten copy was put into the possession of the publishing company. We do not want to wait, as we did last year, until November or December, before we get copies of it. I would ask Dr. Barrick if that is not there.

Dr. BARRICK—There was a delay last year in the getting out of the Announcement owing principally to the fact that a typewritten copy of the proceedings was not placed in the hands of the Registrar until about the 6th August. For the session of 1898 we have asked that a typewritten copy of the proceedings be placed in the hands of the Registrar within four weeks after the close of the session, and further with regard to the printing and binding, that copies of the Announcement shall be delivered to the Registrar within six weeks after a typewritten copy has been placed in the hands of the publishing company.

Dr. McLAUGHLIN—I suggest to Dr. Barrick that he read the letter of Mr. Alexander Downey, the stenographer, so that it may go on record, in order that the profession may see what the tender is.

Dr. BARRICK—It reads as follows : "In compliance with the circular lately issued by you calling for tenders for a verbatim report of the proceedings of the Council of the College of Physicians and Surgeons of Ontario at the session of 1898, and also for a typewritten copy of the proceedings of the Discipline Committee, I beg to submit the following : I will furnish a typewritten copy of the proceedings of the Council for the session of 1898 at the price of sixty cents for each page of the Announcement printed ; I will also furnish the four necessary typewritten copies of the proceedings of the Discipline Committee required by the Committee and by the solicitors at the rate of twenty cents per folio."

Dr. McLAUGHLIN—He does not say he will supply all that within four weeks.

Dr. BARRICK—He says, "In compliance with the circular."

Dr. BARRICK moved, seconded by Dr. McLAUGHLIN, that the report be adopted, which, on a vote having been taken, was declared carried, and the report was adopted, as follows :

Your Committee on Printing beg leave to report as follows :

1st. That in accordance with your instructions last session tenders were solicited for the printing and binding of thirty-five hundred copies of the Announcement of last year, and, after careful consideration of the same, the contract awarded to the Nesbitt Printing Co. for the sum of two hundred and seventy-four dollars and eighty cents, the lowest tender.

2nd. In accordance with the instructions of the Council, of this session, your Committee advertised for tenders for the printing and binding of thirty-five hundred copies of the Announcement of 1897, and for the stenographic work for 1898, and after carefully considering the same, makes the following recommendation : That the tender of the Methodist Book and Publishing House, of one dollar and seventy-eight cents per page for printing and binding thirty-five hundred copies of the Annual Announcement of 1897, be accepted, it being the lowest tender.

That the tender of Mr. Alexander Downey, for the stenographic work for the year 1898, at sixty cents per page of the Announcement, and twenty cents per folio of the proceedings of the Discipline Committee be accepted, it being the lowest tender.

All of which is respectfully submitted.

(Signed,)   E. BARRICK, Chairman.

Adopted in Council.

(Signed,)   JAMES THORBURN, President.

Dr. HENDERSON presented the report of the Committee on Finance.

Dr. ARMOUR—I would suggest that we take the report of the Finance Committee as read, and I would move, seconded by Dr. Henderson, that the Council do now go into Committee of the Whole to consider this report.

The PRESIDENT put the motion which, on a vote having been taken, was declared carried.

Council in Committee of the Whole. Dr. LUTON in the chair.

Dr. HENDERSON read Clauses 1, 2, 3, 4, 5 and 6 which, on motion, were adopted as read.

Dr. HENDERSON read Clause 7.

Dr. MACHELL—Dr. Phillips was in Winnipeg from 1879 to 1893 or 1894, and while he was there he paid dues to the Manitoba Council the same as he would have done if he had been here. He comes back to Ontario and he thinks it rather unjust that he should be asked to pay dues here and there also. He asks to have his dues from 1879 to 1893 or 1894, while he was in Manitoba, remitted. It seems rather a hardship that a man should pay dues in both districts ; and it seems rather unfair that a man should be compelled to stay here for another year to know in what position he is. I think we should deal with this matter now.

Dr. Armour—With regard to this matter, we found unfortunately we had no power to deal with it according to the opinion of the Solicitor. We could not remit one man his fees and not another. We may make a general recommendation with regard to it. The by-law introduced by Dr. Campbell last year provided for that from year to year, and if a remission of that kind is applied for during the year the remission will be made, but where a man comes and asks that his fees for several years be remitted, we have no power to comply with his request. I think we should acquire that power; I think we should be able to deal justly in a matter of this kind, but unfortunately we cannot do it now.

Dr. Henry—It seems to me a great injustice. I know for a fact that Dr. Phillips has been living out in Winnipeg, and after a lapse of fourteen years, having paid all the expenses and dues out there, he comes back and he asks for the remission of his fees. He is willing to pay his dues from 1893 to the present time.

Dr. McLaughlin—If we have no power to deal with it, we cannot help ourselves.

On motion, Clause 7 of the report was adopted as read.

The Chairman—It appears to be the general sense of the Council that there are a number of very great hardships, but it is not in our power to remedy these things unless it be by some special Act of the Council.

Dr. McLaughlin—I think our Solicitor has given an opinion that we have no power to make special legislation to relieve any one man.

Dr. Henderson read Clause 8.

Dr. Henderson—Mr. Boyle is here and is willing to give an explanation in regard to this matter.

The Chairman—Is it your wish to hear Mr. Boyle? I understand matters pretty well myself, but there may be members here that do not understand them and will not be in a position to vote intelligently on this clause of the report.

Dr. Campbell—If there is any member who wants an explanation, let Mr. Boyle give it.

Dr. Hanly—Some member said to me he did not understand it.

The Chairman called on Mr. Boyle to speak.

Mr. Boyle—This is a project, gentlemen, for the establishment of a square to be called "Victoria Square," right opposite to you, between your property and the City Hall. the project has been initiated by the local property owners in the vicinity of the City Hall, and in formulating their petition it occurred to them it would only be fair and equitable between themselves and the city at large that the city should control that land for all time to come without any payment of principal. There has been a negotiation going on between the owners of the property, the Knox Church people, and they have intimated their willingness to allow the corporation to have possession of that land for all time to come at a fixed annual charge to be made now; that is tantamount to a ground rent. The gross amount required for that purpose would be about $6,300 or $6,400; that amount is set out in the petition of the local property owners. The proposition is that they pay $2,000 of the amount annually with the right to commute the $2,000 if they so desire. The plan of the property, of which I enclosed a blue print to the Council yesterday, is attached to the petition. This amount is an annuity or ground rent to the church for the value of the land, and the whole amount to be paid by the local property owners would be about $6,300 or $6,400, with the right to commute the annual sum of $2,000, if it is desired.

Dr. McLaughlin—What is supposed to be the present value of the property?

Mr. Boyle—The property in that whole block is assessed to-day at about $156,000; the amount required is a little less than four per cent. on that sum, but we are fixing the price now for all time. In formulating this petition to go on to the city, it occurred to the local property owners that it would only be fair and right, in view of the advantages that would accrue directly to the property in the neighborhood in having that block of old buildings extinguished, that a portion of the annual charge should be borne by the property contiguous to the square, and the amount set out in this petition here is $2,000. That amount will be equitably distributed in proportion to the relative positions of the different properties to the square. The property on the square will pay at a ratio of three to one; the rate for the property on the square is seventy-five cents a foot; for the other property, some at sixty, some at forty, and the lowest rate is twenty-five cents a foot; that is, for property four or five hundred feet away. I will read you the petition if you like.

Dr. McLaughlin—No.

Dr. Machell—What will it cost this Council?

Mr. Boyle—It will cost this property seventy-five cents a foot, about $65.00. This proposition has been endorsed by a very influential petition from citizens at large, and that petition I may say has been signed by not only what might represent the intelligence and wealth, but the commercial and industrial activity of the city of Toronto. This matter has been lying in abeyance for the last four or five months, but by the courtesy of the Board of Control, I got the petition out so that you could attach your signatures.

Dr. McLaughlin—Do you say there will be no obligation upon this Council but the $65.00 ? Can the amount not increase ?

Mr. Boyle—No, it cannot increase ; we make that a condition of signing it.

Dr. Fowler—Supposing a man refused to join in signing this petition ?

Mr. Boyle—Although the law only specifies two-thirds, we have at the present time eighty per cent. in value and seventy-five per cent. of the number of names.

Dr. Machell—So that it is likely to be carried whether we agree to it or not ?

Mr. Boyle—I have no doubt it will be carried.

Dr. McLaughlin—If that is the case we had better do what we cannot help but do.

Mr. Boyle—It is a scheme that has been popularly approved of by the public ; and when we come down to discuss the matter from the city side, it is going to be a revenue instead of an expense. Looking at the matter from a purely selfish standpoint as to how it is going to affect your property, I do not think there can be two opinions at all but that the results will be favorable. For instance, take the appreciable rentable value of this room alone, if you were offering it for office purposes, and it would more than double the $60.00 odd that you pay annually. The room down below in the corner where Messrs. Urquhart & Urquhart, the barristers, are at present, is a room that will rent for $10.00 or $15.00 a month more than it is renting for to-day. So that if you look at it purely from a selfish point of view, taking into consideration the increased revenue you will derive from the position, you will save hundreds of dollars instead of it being a debt on your hands.

Dr. Barrick—I move that that clause be struck out. Why is this agitation ? Simply because the Church owns a lot of property, the tenants hold a perpetual lease, and they cannot get rid of the property ; the lease is renewable every twenty-one years. I believe when the lease was renewed last time there were some fourteen tenants, and the increase of the ground rent was so great that every one who wished to get rid of it had to go into bankruptcy, and only two, I believe, of the fourteen tenants are still in possession. The Church finds it can get no revenue from this property, and the beginning of this thing has been the Church trying to lease and make something out of their property, and that has been worked up persistently. The people in the neighborhood have been canvassed and bothered and pestered until the canvassers have been warned not to come near the house. I refer to the men on James Street ; they have persisted in calling, and calling, and calling, and the thing has been going on for a long time. This Council once invested in real estate and the members are not well pleased with that investment. Now, do not let us invest in anything else, do not let us pay away our money for a square. The square, so far as it is a benefit to the city at large is a question ; the idea of having a nice square here where people can go for an outing is a matter of theory. Two years ago we had the Metropolitan grounds the same way. Oh, they wanted that. We gave them that for two years, and the place of quiet where people used to go was taken possession of by the rude children in the neighborhood, so that after two years of practice they found it was no use to the citizens. However, I think you ought to consider this matter well, and if there is a doubt about it refer it to the Property Committee. If, as has been stated, they already have 75 or 80 per cent. we cannot help ourselves. I would rather have it forced upon us in that way than that we should ask for it. If we have to do it, like the paying of our taxes, we cannot get rid of it, but I should certainly ask this Council to hesitate before urging a matter of that kind, and I would suggest that they refer it to the Property Committee.

Mr. Boyle—I made the statement that this project was initiated by the property owners in the vicinity. I do not require to come here to make any statement that is not correct.

Dr. Barrick—Who initiated this undertaking ?

Mr. Boyle—I have already told you—the property owners themselves.

Dr. Barrick—Did not Knox Church people ?

Mr. Boyle—They did not. If you want to argue with me on this point—

Dr. Hanly—Haven't we had enough of this ?

The Chairman—That is a matter for the Council to say.

Mr. Boyle—I will not deal further upon the argument Dr. Barrick has raised ; I am prepared to meet him before the Board of Control and settle that part of it ; I am prepared to show the city of Toronto will have thousands of dollars of revenue out of this project, and have the square to the good. That is the position we are in, exactly. You do not understand the scheme, Dr. Barrick ; you are doing as a member of the Council did, he jumped on it before he got the evidence before him. I may tell you now that the Knox Church property is going into the market, and it is not the $3,500.00 or $3,600.00 of revenue that will be got out of it that we are wrangling over.

Dr. Hanly—That is not our business.

Mr. Boyle—No. They are wrangling over the greater revenue that will come out of the church property for commercial purposes.

Dr. Barrick—How much will they get from it ?

Mr. Boyle—$7,000.00.

Dr. Machell—I think if Mr. Boyle will give us the names of some of the property owners it will convince Dr. Barrick better than anything that can be said.

Mr. Boyle—There is Dr. Oronhyatekha, representing the Foresters' Temple; Mr. Walter S. Lee, Mr. G. W. Allan, representing the Western Canada Loan Company ; the Sproule family ; the Hon. C. A. Wood, Manager of the Freehold Loan Company—his property is around on Queen Street ; Mr. Langmuir and Mr. Meredith, for the Trusts Company—whose property is still further west on Queen Street—Mr. Geo. Gooderham and his brother ; Mr. R. Simpson, of the large departmental store ; the Jackes family, who are situated west on Queen Street ; P. Jamieson, John Ross Robertson and many others.

Dr. Barrick—Is Mr. T. Eaton's name on the petition ?

Mr. Boyle—No, sir. I can give you the reason why it is not there.

Dr. McLaughlin—The powers we have to deal with real estate are shown in Clause 2 of the Medical Act as follows : "The Medical profession of Ontario, heretofore incorporated under the name and style of 'The College of Physicians and Surgeons of Ontario,' shall be, and shall be deemed to have been from the date of its first establishment a body corporate by the name aforesaid, having perpetual succession and a common seal, with power to acquire, hold and dispose of chattel property and real estate for the purposes of this Act, and to sue and be sued in the manner usual with such corporations." The purpose of this Act is to allow us to admit matriculations, both of a literary and of a professional character, to conduct examinations and to register practitioners, and to look after them when they are registered. We have no power to deal in real estate beyond this property, and therefore I say, without any further discussion, we have no power to sign that petition to deal with the matter, and I would second Dr. Barrick's motion that the clause be struck out.

Dr. Henry—I think if all those buildings are taken away it will increase the value of this property $30,000.00.

Dr. McLaughlin—It does not matter.

Dr. Henry—If they have got a majority of the property owners along here this property will be assessed ; we cannot help ourselves.

Dr. Graham—This proposition is simply like laying asphalt on the street in front of the building, or like any other local improvement, it has nothing to do with the purchasing of real estate, as far as I can see.

Dr. McLaughlin—The law is such that if we are compelled to pay our part of that amount then we will do it, but we can take no voluntary step to help forward the proposition or deal with that property.

Dr. Campbell—Who will own this square when the project is finished ?

The Chairman—The city of Toronto.

Dr. Campbell—Then, we will not be purchasing any real estate if we agree to this thing ; we are simply consenting to an annual tax for the improvement of the property.

Dr. Machell—I think it may be the means of bringing us in an increased rental of four or five or six or ten times as much as we are paying ; I think the proper way to look at it is from an individual point of view, and if I owned this property, I would not hesitate for one single minute to commit myself to $60.00 or $65.00 a year for the purpose of having a park here. I think we could get a better class of tenants, and more tenants, and we would not be disturbed here by the smoke of factories and the noise of German bands, as we have been disturbed here every evening we have had a session ; we will also have a breathing space, and more than that it would be the means of shutting out a lot of office buildings which would certainly come into open competition with these offices we have here. (Cries of "Question, question.")

Dr. McLaughlin—Would it not be better to consult our solicitor and see whether or not we have power to do this ? I do not think we have the power at all. We have power to pay the tax if, by law, this can be forced upon us.

Dr. Machell—If we subscribe to this, we subscribe knowing distinctly that it shall be a payment of $65.00 only per year ; if we are forced to do it by the city we may have to pay $65.00 and we may have to pay $100.00, or whatever the city chooses to enact.

Dr. McLaughlin—I understood this was an equitable rate upon the frontage we have here, that it was not to be more or less, or anything else.

Mr. Boyle—We have figured it out on that basis without submitting it to the City Commissioner. If you subscribe now and make your minimum on the basis of $65.00 that settles it.

Dr. McLaughlin—Who has got the power to settle that now ?

Mr. Boyle—You have.

Dr. McLaughlin—I doubt that.

Dr. Barrick—If that square is made the property will be assessed and the amount of the assessment will, very likely, be fixed by the Assessment Commissioner. Whether you sign or not what you have to pay will be exactly the same. (Cries of "Question, question.")

Dr. ROOME—I have been advocating the disposal of this building ever since I have been in the Council ; we have been having a deficit every year. The time has been so short I have not had an opportunity to go into it. This year there is an expenditure of $2,000.00 odd over and above the revenue ; if this can be reduced, we would not have the cry coming against us that there is now. When it was costing four or five thousand dollars over and above all that was received from the building it was a great drain on the medical men who were taxed to keep it up, and with all the medical men taxed $2.00 there was very little more than enough to pay the loss on this building, and the medical profession had good grounds for complaint. If by getting that square it would increase the value of this property $1,650.00 I think it is the duty of this Council to support it.

Dr. GEIKIE—I believe it would increase it a great deal more.

The CHAIRMAN put Dr. Barrick's motion to strike out Clause 8 of the report, which, on a vote having been taken, was declared lost.

Dr. HENDERSON moved that Clause 8 be adopted, which, on a vote having been taken, was declared carried.

Dr. HENDERSON read Clauses 9 and 10, which, on motion, were adopted.

Dr. HENDERSON read Clause 11.

Dr. HENDERSON—Last year the Finance Committee recommended $40.00 to be paid to Dr. Carlyle and it was objected to, and it was carried in the Council that we introduce a new by-law to pay him $40.00. We had no power to do this.

Dr. ROOME—I understood it came before the Council, recommended by the Finance Committee, very near the end of the session, and I was under the impression that the by-law granting $40.00 was carried.

Dr. THORBURN—This proposition of $20.00 was a proposition by the Council ; it was a one-sided arrangement and when Dr. Carlyle came to get his pay he said, I can't accept that sum. I think he is entitled to the $40.00.

Dr. BARRICK—I move that Clause 11 be struck out.

Dr. MOORHOUSE—We received a letter from the auditor stating that he would not accept the $20.00, and if we wished to avail ourselves of his services we had to give him a certain amount and in order to do so, as there seemed to be such extreme satisfaction with the work of Dr. Carlyle, we voted him the $40.00.

Dr. ARMOUR—I explained this afternoon what that meant. A by-law was passed here in 1895 appointing Dr. Carlyle auditor and assigning him a salary of $20.00. He went on and did that work and when he got through with the work he thought the work was worth more than the $20.00 ; he put in a request to the Council last year asking that it be made $40.00 instead of $20.00 ; that was considered by the Finance Committee and they reported that he should have $40.00, but when it was submitted to the Council again the Council left it where it was, and said that when he accepted the duties of the office he should comply with the by-law. Notwithstanding that he has taken it upon himself, and he has been paid $40.00 against the wish or authority of this Council. I think the clause should not be struck out without something being substituted in its place.

The CHAIRMAN—Perhaps you will move an amendment.

Dr. ARMOUR—My own personal opinion is that it should remain just as it is.

Dr. BARRICK—Dr. Carlyle has been paid $40.00 for the first year and he has been paid $40.00 for the second year ; is that correct ?

Dr. ARMOUR—No, he has been paid $40.00 for the second year.

Dr. BARRICK—Dr. Carlyle was the first auditor of this Council and we did not know what his services were worth, and I presume Dr. Carlyle did not know, so the sum was fixed at $20.00. After the work was done, and after conversing with the Registrar in regard to it, I was thoroughly satisfied that Dr. Carlyle was underpaid and he ought to be paid $40.00, and I therefore move that this clause which directs him to refund $20.00 be struck out.

Dr. ARMOUR—You approve of Dr. Carlyle taking $20.00 that he was not authorized to take by the Council ? I do not think our business should be done that way.

Dr. BROCK—I think there should be an amendment stating that as a sum of $20.00 was given to Dr. Carlyle, and that as he did not understand the nature of the services required, that he now retain the $20.00 paid by the Registrar. (Cries of " Question, question.")

The CHAIRMAN put the motion to strike out Clause 11, which, on a vote having been taken, was declared carried.

Dr. HENDERSON read Clauses 12 and 13, which, on motion, were adopted.

Dr. HENDERSON moved the adoption of the report as amended in the Committee of the Whole, which, on a vote having been taken, was declared carried.

On motion of Dr. CAMPBELL the Committee rose.

The PRESIDENT in the chair.

On motion the report was adopted as amended, as follows:

July 10th, 1897.

To the President and Members of the Council of the College of Physicians and Surgeons of Ontario.

GENTLEMEN,—We beg to submit herewith the Finance Committee's report.

The Treasurer's statement, certified to by your Auditor, was placed before us on the first day of the session, thereby giving an opportunity to every member of the Council to know our present financial standing.

We have carefully examined the Registrar's books and papers referred to us, and have carefully compared them with the financial statement of the Treasurer, and we have pleasure in stating that after due consideration of the same we find them to be correct, both of your officials having discharged their duties in their usual efficient manner.

The financial state of the College is much better than last year. The annual dues are being paid much better than in former years, and the reduced rate of interest secured on mortgage on building, with a decrease in amount of insurance and lessening of interest in temporary loans, will materially add to our finances.

The petitions and accounts referred to us have been duly considered, and we report on them to you as follows :

1st. The account of B. B. Osler, Esq., our Solicitor, for services rendered to date, certified correct by the Registrar, $97.39. To be paid.

2nd. To Dr. F. Fowler, of Kingston, for acting as Deputy Registrar at the Spring Examinations, the usual fee allowed, $40.00. We recommend to be paid.

3rd. (a) Re the petition of Dr. Stalker, of Walkerton, asking receipt in full for. $10.00 for dues—he being eight years in arrears. Recommend that we have not the power to grant request.

(b) Dr. Henry Bicknell, of Camden East, to be relieved of all dues in arrears, and also in the future, he being unable to practise, being old and infirm. Request recommended not to be granted, as we have no power under by-law.

(c) Request of Dr. O. C. Edwards, of Ottawa, asking for a return of dues from 1873 to 1890. Have not power to grant request.

(d) Dr. Brunskill, of Mount Forest. Request for exemption from dues from 1880 to 1885 (while out of the country). Recommended not to be granted, as we have no power to do so.

(e) Dr. M. B. Sutton, of Cooksville, asks relief from dues. Recommended not granted.

(f) Dr. Bissonette, of Napanee, communication received. Complains of having paid dues while others have not done so. We recommend no action.

(g) Dr. G. G. Demorest, of Warkworth, asking for relief on account of age and infirmity, also exemption from dues. Can only be granted by having his name erased from the register.

(h) Dr. V. Sullivan, of Kingston, asking to be exempted from dues for years 1893, 1894, and 1895, as he was out of the country during that period. No power to grant request.

(i) Dr. Christie, of Flesherton, asks relief from assessment on account of age and infirmity. Request can only be granted by having his name erased from register.

4th. Dr. F. K. Reybold, communication offering to give lists| of graduates of the Buchanan School for ten dollars. We ask leave to refer to Discipline Committee.

5th. Dr. Sangster's request asking for information as to whom commutation fees were allowed, and by what authority. We are only aware of one instance, that of Dr. E. R. O'Reilly, of Kingston, which was ordered by the Council at its last meeting.

6th. Dr. Grey, Bruce Medical Association resolution. We acknowledge receipt of communication, and instructing Registrar to reply that their advice is being carried out as speedily as is consistent with the proper working of the Council.

7th. Petition of Dr. I. J. Phillips, of Toronto, asking exemption from dues while absent in Manitoba from 1879 to 1893. We instruct the Registrar to deal with the case according to by-law, and report at next meeting of Council.

8th. Re communication regarding Victoria Square, we recommend that the President sign it on behalf of Council, on the conditions set forth in the petition.

9th. We call attention to Miss Wasson's account of $6.25 for work ordered by President. This work we consider should have been done by Registrar. As this amount has been refunded by the Registrar to the College, we recommend that no further action be taken in the matter.

10th. We recommend the re-engagement of Mr. Wasson as Prosecutor for the ensuing year, at the salary of $600.00 per annum. But before proceeding in doubtful cases he must receive the approval of the Committee appointed for that purpose.

11th. We ascertained that Dr. Carlyle did not examine all the papers of Council, and consider that he should have done so to be able to report correctly. We therefore recommend that the Auditor be requested to examine the authority for each and every payment made by the officer appointed for that purpose by this Council, and that he also examine as far as possible into the correctness of all receipts, and all other matters connected with the finances of this College coming under the duties of that office.

We append financial statement :

Assets.

Building and site	$100,000 00
Assessment dues uncollected	8,000 00
Assessment dues for 1897	5,000 00
Council Chamber and office furniture	3,000 00
Cash in Bank	790 83
	$116,790 83

Liabilities.

Mortgage on building	$60,000 00
Notes in Bank (accommodation)	3,500 00
Estimated cost of present session	2,500 00
Accounts due and recommended to be paid	127 39
	$66,127 39
Balance in favor of College	$50,663 44

(Signed,) G. HENDERSON, Chairman.

To the Members of the Council of the College of Physicians and Surgeons of Ontario.

GENTLEMEN,—I beg to submit herewith my Financial Statement for the Council year 1896-1897 just past :

Receipts.

Balance on hand, June 3rd, 1896, at credit of College account in Imperial Bank of Canada		$45 57
Assessment Dues—Collected by Registrar	$4,184 00	
" Collected by Bank	1,757 75	
		5,941 75
Registration Fees		1,149 00

The Rebates from the Independent Order of Foresters ($31.51 and $288.00), referred to in the opposite column, are included in the office rents.

Office Rents (of rooms in College building)		4,622 03
Fines of persons practising illegally		238 49
Fees for Professional Examinations : Fall,	$1,600 00	
" " " Spring	6,910 00	
		8,510 00
City of Toronto—Settlement re injury to elevator		125 00
Refund by Dr. L. Brock, re indemnity for attendance at annual meeting		6 25
Refund by T. Wasson of amount of expenses in connection with prosecution, subsequently paid by party fined		27 50
Refund by Wm. Simpson & Co. of amount overpaid in error		10 35
Temporary loans (Imperial Bank)		44,438 91
		$65,114 85

13

Disbursements.

Council meeting, June, 1896.

Members' allowance $2,493 60
    Deducting from this sum the refund of $6.25
    appearing among the receipts, the balance,
    $2,487.35, represents the actual amount
    paid to members.
Stenographic report of proceedings, special re-
    ports typewritten, copying, etc. 189 62
                                                        2,683 22

Officers' salaries—

Registrar.................................$1,800 00
Treasurer..................................   500 00
Prosecutor.................................   600 00
                                                   2,900 00
Official prosecutor, T. Wasson, bonus voted by Council for
    1895-1896, as compensation *re* prosecutions 200 00
Official prosecutor, amount of fines collected from illegal
    practitioners—
        Paid to T. Wasson $213 49
        Paid to W. Webb 25 00
                                                238 49
Prosecutions—Legal, stenographic, and other expenses 762 71
Discipline Committee......................................   166 91
Legal services—General (ordered to be paid at last Council
    meeting) 190 05
Legal and other services, *re* College Building Loan 38 60
Executive Committee......................................   148 16
Legislation Committee 68 00
Printing diplomas, examination papers, circulars to profession,
    etc...   537 80
Printing Annual Announcement (Nesbitt Publishing Co.)....   274 80
Ontario Medical Journal Publishing Co., balance due on con-
    tract for last year 51 42

Holding Professional Examinations—

General Expenses...........................$165 15
Examiners' fees, etc., Fall Examinations.......   669 56
                                                834 71
       ' Amount of Examiners' fees, etc., for Spring Examina-
       tions not known at time of making up this State-
       ment.
Fees refunded to students................................   90 00
Audit of Registrar's and Treasurer's books, vouchers, etc....   40 00
Registrar's office supplies (including postage on circulars, etc.,
    to Profession, $505.96)...............................   676 05
Treasurer's office expenses 15 00

Interest on Mortgages to Canada Life Assurance Co.
Half year at 5% per annum..................$1,500 00
Half year at 3½% per annum................. 1,050 00
                                               2,550 00

Temporary loans repaid—

Discounts $46,312 71
Interest 587 29
                                        46,900 00
Interest on overdraft 1 40
Bank charges, *re* collection of assessment dues, costs, commis-
    sions, etc...   102 75

Building Maintenance—

Caretaker	$520	00
Elevator man	260	00
Gas	264	20

From this sum must be deducted the amount of refund from Independent Order of Foresters paid to the Registrar, $31.51, the balance, $232.69, representing the actual cost to the College of gas. Paid by Registrar to the Treasurer.

Water	765	20

Deducting the amount of rebate from I.O.F. $288.00, the balance, $477.20, represents the actual cost of water to the College. The rebate was paid to the Registrar, and by him to the Treasurer.

Carpenter's repairs	116	44
Plumbing, gas and steam fittings, etc.	201	63
Printing, glazing, paperhanging, plastering, etc.	249	95
Elevator repairs	93	93
Rubber hose	17	59
Building supplies and repairs	140	72
Miscellaneous expenditures	81	36
Commission on rent collections	231	03
Telephone for year	45	00
Insurance on building for three years....$250 00		
" elevator " " 68 00		
" boiler for one year 20 00		
	338	00
Heating	663	70
Taxes	796	80
	4,785	55
Balance on deposit in Imperial Bank	790	83
	$65,114	85

All of which is respectfully submitted.

H. WILBERFORCE AIKINS, Treasurer.

I have audited the books of the College of Physicians and Surgeons of Ontario, for the year ending May 31st, 1897. I have also compared the receipts and vouchers with the income and expenditure. I have found all correct and satisfactory. The above statement corresponds with the books.

J. CARLYLE, Auditor.

Dr. ARMOUR moved, seconded by Dr. HANLY, that leave be given to introduce a by-law entitled " A by-law to fix the salary of the Council's Prosecutor," and that the same be now read a first time.

The PRESIDENT put the motion, which, on a vote having been taken, was declared carried.

On consent of the Council, the by-law was taken as read a first time.

Dr. ARMOUR moved, seconded by Dr. HANLY, that the Council go into Committee of the Whole on the by-law entitled " A by-law to fix the salary of the Council's Prosecutor," and that the same be read a second time.

The PRESIDENT put the motion which, on a vote having been taken, was declared carried.

Council in Committee of the Whole. Dr. MACHELL in the chair.

Dr. ARMOUR moved, that the first clause of the by-law be amended by inserting the sum "600" after the dollar sign on the third line thereof, which, on a vote having been taken, was declared carried.

Dr. ARMOUR moved, that the preamble of the by-law be adopted, which, on a vote having been taken, was declared carried.

Dr. ARMOUR moved, that the title be adopted, which, on a vote having been taken, was declared carried.

Dr. ARMOUR moved, that the by-law as amended be read a second time in Committee of the Whole, which, on a vote having been taken, was declared carried.

The CHAIRMAN read the by-law.

Dr. ARMOUR moved, that the Committee rise and report, which, on a vote having been taken was declared carried.

The Committee of the Whole rose.   The PRESIDENT in the chair.

Dr. ARMOUR moved, seconded by Dr. HANLY, that the by-law entitled "A by-law to fix the salary of the Council's Prosecutor" be read a third time, passed, numbered, signed and sealed with the seal of the College of Physicians and Surgeons of Ontario.

The PRESIDENT put the motion, which, on a vote having been taken, was declared carried, and the by-law adopted as follows :

BY-LAW No. 82.

A By-law to Fix the Salary of the Council's Prosecutor.

Whereas power has been granted to the Medical Council of the College of Physicans and Surgeons of Ontario under Section 13 of the Ontario Medical Act, to make by-laws to fix the salaries of officers (R.S.O. 1887, Cap. 142).

Be it therefore enacted as follows :—

That the salary of the Prosecutor of this Council be and is hereby fixed at $600.00 per annum, to be paid monthly.

H. T. MACHELL, Chairman Com. of Whole.

Carried in Council.   J. THORBURN, President.

Dr. HANLY moved, seconded by Dr. CAMPBELL, that this Council do pass a resolution of condolence to Mr. Wasson on the occasion of the death of his wife, Mrs. Wasson, by so severe an accident on the 3rd December last, and that the Registrar be instructed to hand a copy of this resolution to Mr. Wasson.

The PRESIDENT put the motion which, on a vote having been taken, was declared carried unanimously.

It was moved by Dr. ROOME, seconded by Dr. McLAUGHLIN, that the Committee on Prosecutions, Drs. Barrick, Emory, Thorburn and Britton, be reappointed, which, on a vote having been taken, was declared carried.

It was moved by Dr. ROOME, seconded by Dr. DICKSON, that the Council extend a hearty vote of thanks to the Committee on Prosecutions for the way in which they have conducted their business during the past year.

Dr. ROOME put the motion, which, on a vote having been taken, was declared carried unanimously.

Dr. ROOME—I beg to extend to you, Dr. Thorburn, as chairman of that committee, the hearty vote of thanks just passed by this Council for the manner in which your committee have conducted the business during the past year ; it was quite satisfactory.

Dr. THORBURN—I thank you, gentlemen.

Dr. BRITTON—I think, gentlemen, the Finance Committee was called for Monday, and quite a number of the members were present at that meeting, and some come from a long distance ; I think it is only fair they should be remunerated for that.

Dr. REDDICK—Nobody is objecting to it.

Dr. BARRICK—I do not object to it ; I think they ought to be paid, but there is a clause with regard to the Committee on Prosecutions, and it was the distinct understanding, and was mentioned in the resolution, that there was to be no expense to the Council. Both of these resolutions are the same.

The PRESIDENT—I know the Committee on Prosecutions were not to accept pay because they are local men, but the members of the Finance Committee come from a long distance.

Dr. BARRICK—I am not speaking about the justice of it, but the resolution says "without any expense to the Council."

Dr. BRAY—That should never have been there.

Dr. BARRICK—It should not.

Dr. BRAY—I maintain that those gentlemen who leave home for a whole day before the Council commences, as these gentlemen on the Finance Committee have done, should be recompensed. I am in a little different position to the other members of the Committee ; we had to have a Discipline Committee meeting, and I had to attend on that Committee, and I would not charge for attending on two committees on one day. It is not on personal grounds I am speaking, but it is in justice to those who have lost money by attending here an extra day.

Dr. SANGSTER—I think when any standing committee is called to meet one or two or three days before the Council meets the members ought to be paid for it ; I do not think there can be any second opinion on it. I do not think any standing committee should receive one cent for meetings held during the session of the Council.

The PRESIDENT—I do not think there can be any opposition to it, and with your concurrence I shall rule that the members of the Finance Committee who attended here last Monday are entitled to one day's pay for that attendance.

Dr. ROGERS—I did not charge for it at all. I was here.

The PRESIDENT—But you are entitled to it ; it is only fair. You came here a day earlier.

Dr. DICKSON—The members of that committee were asked to come here in order that the work of the session might be expedited. I think they have earned it.

The PRESIDENT—I must say this, too, if you take any other body of men you will find very few who work as hard, as faithfully and as constantly as the members of this Council have done in this horrible weather which is so excessively hot. I know I have felt like dissolving and redissolving up here sometimes.

Dr. BARRICK—I hope you will not misunderstand the resolution ; it distinctly says "without any expense to the Council." If there is any way to get over that I shall move that these men be paid ; I think they ought to be paid. But still there is a distinct resolution—

Dr. GEIKIE—It was an error.

Dr. BARRICK—Is it necessary to make a formal resolution that the members of the Finance Committee should be paid for that day ?

The PRESIDENT—I don't know that it would be necessary.

Dr. BARRICK—To settle the matter, so that there may be no misunderstanding, I would move that the members of the Finance Committee who attended the meeting on Monday last are entitled to and shall receive the per diem allowance for that· day, paid to committees.

Dr. DICKSON—I second the motion.

The PRESIDENT put the motion, which, on a vote having been taken, was declared carried unanimously.

Dr. MACHELL—Mr. President, it is within half an hour of six o'clock now, and judging by the size of the report of the Committee on Education, now in Dr. Britton's hands, it will take fifteen minutes at least to read it, and I move that we adjourn until eight o'clock p.m.

Dr. SHAW—I do not know how long this report will take. I was particularly anxious to leave at 5.30 p.m., but I remained over on purpose to be present during the presentation of the report of the Committee on Education ; I hope we will be able to get through with that in an hour and a quarter.

The PRESIDENT—I think we ought to. There is no desire on the part of any gentleman here to prolong the meeting.

Dr. CAMPBELL—To expedite matters would it not be well to take the report as read and go right into Committee of the Whole upon it.

The PRESIDENT—That will shorten it.

Dr. BRITTON moved, seconded by Dr. CAMPBELL, that the report of the Committee on Education be received and referred to the Committee of the Whole for discussion.

The PRESIDENT put the motion, which, on a vote having been taken, was declared carried.

COUNCIL IN COMMITTEE OF THE WHOLE.

Dr. EMORY in the chair.

Dr. BRITTON—This, Mr. Chairman, is a supplementary report.

Dr. BRITTON read Clauses 22 and 23, which, on motion, were adopted as read.

Dr. BRITTON read Clause 24, together with Subsections 1, 2, 3, 4, 5, 6 and 7, which, on motion, were adopted as read.

Dr. BRITTON read Subsection 1 of Section 2, Medical Curriculum.

Dr. MACHELL—Do I understand that this is staved off for two years ?

Dr. BRITTON—That is the intention.

Dr. MACHELL—That is a serious thing to do. I would move in amendment that it be 1898, instead of 1899.

Dr. MOORE—This was agreed to by the Committee, and I am only speaking on it because of Dr. Machell's amendment. It was agreed by the Committee, I was going to say unanimously, that it should be put off until 1899, for, supposing we did the best we could, we would have it one year before it came into force anyway ; it does not come into force, if enacted, until twelve months from to-day. Speaking for Queen's University, we do not want to touch the eight months' course, we are not ready for it. We only ask one year longer ; and I think when the committee agreed to it, as they did, that this Council will not wish to force

Queen's University into a change she does not desire, a change she claims she is not ready for yet. We want at least a year to get ready, and if we do it within that time we think we are doing a good deal. I am satisfied that this Council will grant that.

Dr. SANGSTER—It was only last year the idea of the eight months' session was entertained at all. I do not think these changes should be sprung upon the students in institutions with too much rapidity. I think it is only reasonable to have one year more before the regulation becomes compulsory.

Dr. MACHELL—The eight months' session is not a matter of last year or the year before, it is something that has been talked of for at least three years, and I am mistaken very much in the men who compose Queen's University if they are so slow that it has taken them three years already to get the idea into their head, and that they require two years more in order to perfect it.

Dr. MOORE—We are only seeking one ; the law gives us one.

Dr. MACHELL—This matter came up last year, and would have been passed if Queen's University had not objected ; it was simply staved off to accommodate Queen's University, and to say they are not ready for the question, that they do not understand it, that they have not got their machinery in motion, makes me think they are rather slow down east. I think they are not so slow as they would like to make us believe, and there must be some other motive behind it which is their reason for wishing to stave this off year after year, year after year ; and possibly, they have the hope that it may be staved off indefinitely.

Dr. MOORE—No, it is agreed to.

Dr. MOORHOUSE—I know, as a member of the Committee, that we talked this matter over very carefully ; we went into all the various matters in connection with extending the course, and we came to the unanimous decision, not even a dissentious voice in that large Committee, but out of deference to Queen's University, which was a powerful factor amongst our educational institutions, we allowed them one year more than they could demand. Of course we could not have this law passed inside of one year anyway, and we are only allowing them one year, practically, and I know also, speaking for the west, that our own school would like two years more to make preparations for such an advanced step ; we are not quite so populous, neither are we so prepared for the later modes of teaching as the school which Dr. Machell represents.

Dr. MACHELL—I represent no school.

Dr. MOORHOUSE—Excuse me. For the schools on whose behalf he is speaking. I speak for the school on the extreme west, and Dr. Moore for the school on the extreme east, and I know that neither of these schools are in a position to undertake the eight months' session at present ; at least, I know we are not ; we wish it, but we think it ought to be brought up by degrees, it ought to be led up to. Then there was another reason that influences us somewhat. We know there is a feeling amongst the public generally that this Medical Council is trying to repress the manufacture of medical men so as to keep the preserves for themselves. We had an evidence of that a year ago last spring in the Legislature when the Patrons made an onslaught upon our Council, and we do not wish to be too abrupt in any amendment to our already existing regulations, but to spring it on by degrees and to educate the people up to it. We all know how wonderfully people can be educated up to certain ideas that at first are extremely unpleasant to them, but after mature deliberation and becoming acquainted with their various aspects, they become quite reconciled. That is one of the chief reasons on my part for not having such a thing as this sprung on us too suddenly.

Dr. GEIKIE—I do not know, as far as we are concerned, exactly what our people may say with regard to the matter. We have a note in our Announcement stating that should the Council take any definite action we were prepared to be in accord with it. We were not quite sure that it would be done and that is the way we put it. Our feeling for the last year or two has been that when the change was unanimously adopted we would go in for it and we would agree to it. (Cries of "Question, question.")

Dr. BRITTON—There has been a little discussion on this question and therefore it is my duty to say something. Gentlemen, you are quite well aware that for the last two or three years the University of Toronto has expressed its desire to this Council on different occasions to have an eight months' session compulsory, and it has given its reasons why an eight months' session is thought to be necessary. I need not go over those reasons again because you have all read them and have all heard them ; I might just state in brief that the faculty of the University felt that six months was not a sufficient period of time in which to have the work done that was necessary, and have it done in a very efficient manner, and to show that the University itself was in earnest in its request it was willing to be handicapped last session and started and completed an eight months' course of its own, and I have no reason to doubt that that University will continue to do the same thing. I am told by Dr. Machell that the Women's Medical College followed in the same line as the University of Toronto. It is a fair time to give until 1898—that gives a year. For the past years, this will be another year, and if it is deferred to the first of October,

1898, it will be about five years since the University of Toronto first raised this question ; and certainly that University is one of the representative institutions of the country, it is certainly amongst the foremost educational bodies of the country ; and I think the consideration of the Council should be given to the course the University of Toronto has taken in this matter.

Dr. WILLIAMS—In the Committee we agreed that we were making a very radical change and that it was going to involve a large amount of expense and trouble and preparation for the different schools ; and, that being the case, we thought it was only reasonable to give them one year more than the statute allowed them. The statute will allow them one year in spite of us, and generosity on our part extends it to the limit of one year. I think that it is not an unreasonable time. To insist it shall go into force just as quick as the statute will allow does not look very generous on our part, it looks as though we would force our will even though it might occasion very serious trouble and expense in making the necessary preparation. (Cries of " Question, question.")

The CHAIRMAN put the amendment, which, on a vote having been taken, was declared lost.

The CHAIRMAN put the motion that Clause 1 of Section 2 be adopted, which, on a vote having been taken, was declared carried.

Dr. BRITTON read Clause 2 of Section 2, which, on motion, was adopted.

Dr. BRITTON read Clause 3 of Section 2.

Dr. MCLAUGHLIN—Would it not be better to say 75 per cent. of the lectures involved in the course and 75 per cent. of the time ?

Dr. EMORY—75 per cent. of the eight months would be six months.

Dr. MOORHOUSE—I think Dr. McLaughlin's remarks are quite right, because some of the schools will only be teaching six months and some eight months, but by taking a percentage of the time and a percentage of the lectures it will always be applicable.

Dr. BRITTON amended the clause to read as follows : "Has attended at least 75 per cent. of the set number of lectures of each course ; and it is herein enacted that said certificate shall specifically state that such attendance extended over a period of at least 75 per cent. of the eight months' course."

On motion, Clause 3 of Section 2 was adopted as amended.

Dr. BRITTON read Clause 4 of Section 2, which, on motion, was adopted.

Dr. BRITTON read Clause 5 of Section 2.

Dr. BRITTON—It was felt by the Committee that it was necessary to make the clinical work very thorough, and I know some of the teaching bodies are doing an immense amount of clinical work, as much as it is possible to do in the time. By this clause of our report the clinical work is doubled. Originally we have not allowed any special time or ordered any special time to be devoted to Pathology.

Dr. GEIKIE—I notice with regard to that that it was pointed out that that was an innovation. If it is the case that you have had examinations this could not be considered an innovation, because if it was so considered a person might say, "Well, that is not binding upon us."

Dr. BRITTON—I might explain to Dr. Geikie and the gentlemen present that when it was spoken of as being an innovation it was meant that, notwithstanding we had been holding examinations in Pathology, we had laid down no definite course that had to be followed.

Dr. GEIKIE—It was an omission.

Dr. BRITTON—With regard to the question as to Bacteriology, I might say that that is a little like repetition, because it is like one branch of Pathology. I have consulted with some specialists—Pathologists—as to the requirements, and that is why I proposed this, and the Committee unanimously fell in line with my proposition.

Dr. GEIKIE—I should propose two six months' courses, but should Pathology really embrace Bacteriology, as it does, that is a very nice amount of Pathology to require, namely, two six months' courses ; and the twenty-five demonstrations, as a matter of fact, will come in during the six months. It seems difficult to separate Bacteriology from Pathology—it is just like separating one of the fingers of your glove from the rest.

Dr. MCLAUGHLIN—You can take two six months at Pathology and not touch Bacteriology.

. Dr. FOWLER—It does a great deal more good if Bacteriology is taught along with Pathology.

On motion, Clause 5 of Section 2 was adopted.

Dr. BRITTON read Clauses 6, 7, 8, 9, 10, 11 and 12 of Section 2, which, on motion, were adopted.

Dr. GEIKIE—In the different branches of the examination you have "Diseases of children " ; you do not require any special course upon them.

Dr. BRITTON—That was not considered.

Dr. Geikie—Is not that an omission ?

Dr. Britton—I do not think it was.

Dr. Fowler—He has part of it devoted to the diseases of children and women ; I think it would be unwise in the meantime to have separate classes of lectures for these subjects.

Dr. Geikie—I mention that because we give separate lectures.

Dr. Britton—I suppose it would be to the advantage of every institution to give separate lectures on the diseases of children.

Dr. Britton read Clauses 1, 2, 3, 4, 5, 6, 7, 8 and 9 of Section 3, re Examinations, which, on motion, were adopted.

Dr. Geikie—I was going to make a suggestion here, that where students who may have passed in their Intermediate and have gone up on one, two or three subjects of the Primary in which previously they may have failed and fail again, that in order to protect ourselves we should say that the results of the Intermediate would be withheld until all the Primary branches have been completed, that we should not publish the name of a student as having passed the Intermediate until he has made a clean slate of his Primary. The effect will be to make the man work hard to finish his Primary. This course is not open to any objection whatever, and it will save the anomaly of giving a man credit for his Intermediate examination when next year he has to go up perhaps for his Chemistry or Toxicology.

Dr. Britton—We spoke of that in the Committee, and I think our attention was diverted to something else at the time.

Dr. Geikie—I would propose that change.

Dr. Reddick—Dr. Geikie, what you propose is that if a man passes in all the subjects of his Intermediate he is not to know it in case he fails in the second Primary until he passes those subjects ?

Dr. Geikie—That is all.

Dr. McLaughlin—Can a student reach the Intermediate before he passes the Primary examination ?

Dr. Britton—I would think a student should be compelled to pass his Primary before he takes the Intermediate unless he should go up for both together.

Dr. Geikie—But that is the trouble.

Dr. Britton—I think if he has failed to pass in his Primary he should not be given credit for his Intermediate at all.

Dr. Geikie—That would be too hard. I propose simply that if he has passed in his Intermediate we should withhold the result until his Primary is completely finished ; if we do that he will work twice as hard to complete the Primary. On the other hand, if he should fail in his Primary again all he suffers is that he has to wait until he has passed the Primary before he hears the results of the Intermediate.

Dr. Williams—I think provision was made in that report for such things.

Dr. Britton—I think not.

Dr. Williams—We certainly dealt with it, and if it is not there it is an accidental omission.

Dr. Britton—I am sure nobody put it in a formal shape.

Dr. Rogers—I made that proposal before the Council, and some of the Committee thought it was not best to give a man his Final if he did not pass his Primary. I think if he fails in his Primary he ought not to get any credit for his Final.

Dr. Williams—I will put it in writing.

Dr. Britton read Clauses 10 and 11 of Section 3, which, on motion, were adopted.

Dr. Britton read Clause 12 of Section 3.

Dr. Sangster—I do not intend to take up any time in regard to this, because the mind of the Council has been expressed on two occasions, I think, with regard to it, and I think it would be only a loss of time to push the matter again. I merely wish to state that I am not personally in favor of holding fall examinations.

Dr. Douglas—Before that clause is passed I wish to state that I gave notice yesterday of a by-law that I had prepared for the purpose of fixing the times, manner and places for holding examinations.

Dr. McLaughlin—That will come up later, after the report is adopted.

The Chairman—Is your by-law in pursuance of the report or conflicting with it?

Dr. Williams—We are in harmony with the report except the date of the examination.

On motion Clause 12 of Section 3 was adopted.

Dr. Britton read Clause 13 of Section 3.

Dr. Britton—It has sometimes been complained of that unusual names are used, and that once in awhile an Examiner may take exception to a certain answer, for instance, in a clinical examination, and insist upon a certain answer because that opinion was expressed by some one who has written a work on the subject, but whose work is not mentioned in our list. We request the examiners to be very particular that they use only the ordinary names applied to diseases and confine themselves to the ordinary text-books.

Dr. McLaughlin—How are the examiners to know what are the ordinary text-books? I would suggest the use of the words "text-books authorized by the Council."

Dr. Britton—We, as a Committee, thought that it would be well to have this list revised each year, and we concluded that we would recommend that the Registrar communicate with the faculties of the different teaching bodies or universities and get from them during the year their suggestions as to text-books on different subjects, and these lists would all be laid before the Committee on Education next year, and they, in their judgment, would select the books they thought the best.

Dr. McLaughlin—Is that what "ordinary text-books" refers to?

Dr. Britton—I would say any text-book that is ordinarily used in schools.

Dr. Geikie—Or, the best standard text-books.

Dr. Sangster—I understand that Dr McLaughlin's idea is to exclude the terms that may be used in old and obsolete text-books and for that purpose he suggests the use of the words "text-books authorized by the Council."

On motion, clause 13 of section 3 was adopted.

Dr. Williams—I move, seconded by Dr. Geikie and resolved, that in case a student presents himself for both Primary and Intermediate examinations and fails to pass in all subjects in the Primary, that he be given credit for the branches in which he passed in the Intermediate, but that his standing be withheld until he has completed his Primary examination.

The Chairman put the motion, which, on a vote having been taken, was declared carried.

Dr. Reddick—I think it is a hardship for a student not to know whether he has passed.

Dr. Geikie—As an old teacher I would just say that if a student knows beforehand that that is the rule, he will work hard in order that he may not be plucked.

Dr. Williams—The intention is that he should be given credit on the books of the College for all subjects he has passed, but he cannot be given a standing on the Intermediate when he has not passed the Primary.

Dr. Britton read clauses 14 and 15 of section 3, which, on motion, were adopted.

Dr. Geikie—Are the examiners on Descriptive Anatomy expected to furnish the subjects for dissection for the examination?

Dr. Thorburn—They are not.

Dr. Brock—A letter was received here from an examiner and it was referred to the Committee on Education. May I ask what was done with that letter, and the instructions in connection with it.

Dr. Britton—I have nothing that I know of about that letter in my possession; this is the first I have heard of it.

Dr. Sangster—I remember the letter Dr. Brock speaks of and it has never made its appearance in the Education Committee.

Dr. Brock—I think it was a most important letter.

Dr. Rogers—What was it?

Dr. McLaughlin—It was a recommendation to the Board of Examiners.

Dr. Britton was here handed the letter referred to from Dr. H. Howitt, also the resolution moved by Dr. Brock, seconded by Dr. Campbell which he read.

Dr. Williams moved that the letter and resolution read be referred to the Committee on Education to be dealt with at the session of 1898.

Dr. Brock—I am satisfied with that.

The Chairman put the motion, which, on a vote having been taken, was declared carried.

Dr. Williams—The date of the fall examination was not fixed.

Dr. Britton—That was left to be arranged.

On motion the second Tuesday in October was fixed as the date for the fall examination.

Dr. Britton—That finishes the report of the Committee on Education and I move that the Committee rise and report.

The Chairman put the motion that the Committee rise and report, which, on a vote having been taken, was declared carried.

The Committee rose. The President in the chair.

Dr. Britton moved, seconded by Dr. Williams, that the report of the Education Committee be adopted as amended.

The President put the motion, which, on a vote having been taken, was declared carried, and the report was adopted as amended as follows:

SECOND REPORT OF EDUCATIONAL COMMITTEE.

Clause 22.   John McCrea.   Your Committee recommend that his request be granted.

Clause 23.   F. Thornton.   Petition as to registration as a matriculant.   Your Committee recommend that his request be granted.

Clause 24.   Your Committee recommend that Section 1, matriculation, be as follows :
Everyone desirous of being registered as a matriculated medical student in the register of this College, except as hereinafter provided, shall be required to pay a fee of twenty dollars and to conform to the following regulations :

1. Any person who presents to the Registrar of the Medical Council a certificate that he has passed the examination conducted by the Education Department on the course prescribed for matriculation in Arts, including Chemistry and Physics, and approved by the Lieutenant-Governor in Council, shall be entitled on payment of the lawful fees in that behalf, to registration as a medical student within the meaning of Section 11 of the Ontario Medical Act.

2. Any person who, before the 15th day of June, 1896, had not passed the examinations in all subjects prescribed for matriculation as aforesaid, shall be entitled to registration as a medical student on submitting to the Registrar a certificate that he has completed such examination by passing in the remaining subjects of said matriculation, including Chemistry and Physics.   Such supplemental must be passed on or before Nov. 1st, 1898.

3. Any student in medicine who submits to the Registrar certified tickets that he has attended not less than two courses of lectures at any chartered medical school or college in Canada shall be entitled on the payment of the lawful fees in that behalf, to take the primary examination, provided that the standing obtained at such examination may not be allowed until such student presents to the Registrar the matriculation certificate, but this privilege shall not be available on or after Nov. 1st, 1898.

4. A certificate from the Registrar of any chartered university conducting a full arts course in Canada that the holder thereof has passed the senior matriculation of such university or the examination conducted at the end of the first year in arts by such university shall entitle such holder to registration.   This provision shall remain in existence up to Nov. 1st, 1899.

5. Any person who, on or before the 1st day of Nov., 1895, had passed the examination of any university in Canada for matriculation in arts, or the matriculation examination conducted by the Education Department entitling to registration in arts with any university in Canada, or an examination entitling to registration with the Medical Council subsequent to July 1st, 1888, shall be entitled to registration on submitting to the Registrar a certificate to that effect, signed by the proper officer in that behalf ; but these qualifications shall cease to be recognized on and after the 1st of Nov., 1899.

6. Graduates in arts in any university in Her Majesty's Dominions are not required to pass this examination, but may register their names with the Registrar of the College upon giving satisfactory evidence of their identity, the presentation of a certificate of qualifications and the payment of the fee of $20.00.

7. Excepting as provided for in Subsection 3 of Section 1 herein, every medical student after matriculation shall be registered in the manner prescribed by the Council, and this will be held to be preliminary to his medical studies which will not be considered to begin until after the date of such registration.

SECTION 2. MEDICAL CURRICULUM.

1. Every student must spend a period of five years in actual professional studies, except as hereinafter provided, and the prescribed period of studies shall include four winter sessions of not less than eight months each ; the fifth or final year shall be devoted to clinical work, six months of which may be spent with a registered practitioner in Ontario, and at least six months must be spent at one or more public hospitals, dispensaries or laboratories devoted to physiological or pathological research, Canadian, British or foreign, approved by the Council.   The regulation relating to the eight months shall come into effect on the 1st October, 1899.

2. Graduates in arts or science of any college or university recognized by the Council, who shall have spent a year in the study of physics, chemistry and biology and shall have passed an examination in these subjects in their university course, shall be held to have completed the first of the five years of medical study, and after three years of attendance

upon medical studies shall be eligible for the intermediate examination, and must thereafter comply with the requirements for the fifth final year which is to be devoted to clinical work. Homœopathic students who attend four sessions at any medical college where nine months' sessions are taught, to be held equal to four winter sessions of this College. This shall not in any way interfere with the practical and clinical work as prescribed by the Medical Council of Ontario for the fifth year. No ticket for lectures will henceforward be accepted by the Council unless it be endorsed thereon that, as shown by teacher's roll, the pupil has attended at least seventy-five per cent. of the set number of lectures of each course ; and it is hereby enacted that said certificate shall specifically state that such attendance extended over a period of at least seventy-five per cent. of the eight months' course.

3. Application for every professional examination must be made to the Registrar of the College of Physicians and Surgeons of Ontario at least two weeks prior to examinations. No application will be received unless it is accompanied by the necessary tickets and certificates, and by the Treasurer's receipt showing that the fees have been paid.

4. Each six (or) "eight months' course,' excepting as hereinafter specified, shall consist of not less than twenty-five lectures.

5. Every student must attend the undermentioned course of lectures in a university, college or school of medicine approved of by the Council, viz. :

Two courses of not less than six or eight months each—in the different years—upon Anatomy, Practical Anatomy, Physiology (including Histology), Theoretical Chemistry, Materia Medica and Therapeutics, Principles and Practice of Medicine, Principles and Practice of Surgery, Midwifery and Diseases of Women,

Two courses of six or eight months each, consisting of not less than one hundred lectures and demonstrations in Clinical Medicine, Clinical Surgery.

One course of not less than six or eight months upon Medical Jurisprudence, Medical, Surgical and Topographical Anatomy.

Two courses of not less than three or four months, each in different years, upon Diseases of Children, Practical Chemistry (including Toxicology).

One course of three or four months upoh Sanitary Science, Practical Pharmacy. The latter to be taken prior to candidate presenting himself for examination upon Materia Médica and Pharmacy.

One course of ten lectures upon Mental Diseases.

One course of fifty demonstrations upon Physiological Histology.

Two courses of six or eight months, each consisting of fifty lectures and demonstrations in Pathology.

One course of three or four months, consisting of twenty-five lectures and demonstrations in Bacteriology.

A certificate of having attended five lectures and five demonstrations upon the use of Anæsthetics.

6. Every candidate will be required to prove that he has carefully dissected the adult human body.

7. The following are the text-books recommended by the Council in the various branches :

General Text-Books.

Anatomy—Gray, Quain, Cunningham's Practical Anatomy.

Physiology—Foster, Kirke, Yeo.

Chemistry—Roscoe, Attfield, Remsen and Jones, Richter, Simons.

Materia Medica—Ringer, Mitchell Bruce, Hare's Therapeutics, British Pharmacopœia.

Surgery—Erichsen, Treves, Mansell, Moulin, American System of Surgery.

Medicine—Hilton, Fagge, Strumpell, Osler, Roberts.

Clinical Medicine—Gibson and Russel, Vierordt.

Midwifery and Gynæcology—Lusk, Thomas, Munde, Playfair, Hart and Barber, American Text-Book Obstetrics.

Medical Jurisprudence and Toxicology—Taylor, Reese.

Pathology—Ziegler, Green, Woodhead, Coates.

Sanitary Science—Wilson, Louis C. Parke.

Diseases of Children—Eustace Smith, Ashby and Wright, Goodhart.

Homœopathic Text-Books.

Materia Medica—Hahnemann, Hering.

Medicine and Therapeutics — Goodno, Arnt, Raue's "Pathology and Diagnostics," Lilienthal.

Surgery—Fisher, Helmuth.

Midwifery—Guemsey, Ludlam.

8. Also must have attended the practice of a general hospital for twenty-four months during the first four years of study.

9. Also must have attended six cases of Midwifery.

10. Also must, before being registered as a member of the College of Physicians and Surgeons of Ontario, have passed all the examinations herein prescribed, and attained the full age of twenty-one years.

11. Graduates in Medicine from recognized Colleges outside the Dominion of Canada, who desire to qualify themselves for registration, must pass the matriculation required by the Council ; and must attend one or more full winter courses of lectures in one of the Ontario Medical Schools, and must complete fully the practical and clinical curriculum required by the Council after the fourth year, and shall pass before the Examiners appointed by the Council all the examinations hereinafter prescribed, so as to complete fully the curriculum.

12. British registered medical practitioners, on paying all fees and passing the intermediate and final examinations, shall be registered, provided that they have been domiciled in Britain for five years after having been registered therein as practitioners.

Section 3. Examinations.

1. The professional examinations are divided into three parts, "Primary," "Intermediate," and "Final."

2. The Primary Examination shall be undergone after the second winter session, and the Intermediate after the third or fourth winter session, the Final after the fifth year.

3. The following branches shall be embraced in the Primary Examination : (*a*) Anatomy. (*b*) Physiology and Histology. (*c*) Chemistry (Theoretical and Practical). (*d*) Materia Medica and Pharmacy.

4. Every candidate for the Primary Examination will be required to present, with his lecture tickets, a certificate of having undergone and passed an examination at the school he has attended at the close of his first winter session on Primary branches. Also a certificate of ability to make and mount microscopic specimens.

5. Each candidate for Final Examination must present a certificate of attendance at six post-mortem examinations, a certificate of ability to draw up a report of a post-mortem examination, a certificate of having reported satisfactorily six cases of Clinical Medicine, and six cases of Clinical Surgery, and a certificate of having passed his or her Intermediate Examination ; the certificates to be signed by the teachers referred to upon these subjects or the practitioner holding post-mortem. All candidates shall (excepting Arts graduates) present a certificate of having passed at the close of their third session in the college or school that they may have attended, an examination in such parts of Medicine, Surgery and Midwifery as may be thought advisable by the Faculties of the respective colleges or schools. This Examination is not in any way to interfere with any of the examinations of the Council.

One year's attendance after the Intermediate Examination as House Surgeon or Physician in any hospital recognized by the Council shall be held equivalent to the fulfilling of the requirements for the fifth year of clinical work.

The following branches shall be embraced in the Intermediate Examination : (*a*) Medical, Surgical and Topographical Anatomy. (*b*) Principles and Practice of Medicine. (*c*) General Pathology and Bacteriology. (*d*) Surgery other than Operative. (*e*) Surgery, Operative. (*f*) Midwifery, other than Operative. (*g*) Midwifery, Operative. (*h*) Medical Jurisprudence, including Toxicology and Mental Diseases. (*i*) Sanitary Science. (*j*) Diseases of Children. (*k*) Diseases of Women. (*l*) Therapeutics.

7. The Primary and Intermediate Examinations shall be "written" and "oral." The Final, "oral" and "clinical."

8. The following branches shall be embraced in the Final Examination: (*a*) Clinical Medicine. (*b*) Clinical Surgery. (*c*) Diseases of Women. (*d*) Diseases of Children, Medical and Surgical.

9. Candidates for the Primary who fail in all subjects save two, will be allowed these two if they have made sixty per cent. in each. Candidates for the Intermediate who fail on all subjects save three, will be allowed these three if they have made sixty per cent. in each.

10. Candidates who intend to be examined by the Homœopathic Examiner in special subjects, shall signify their intention to the Registrar at least two weeks prior to the commencement of the Examinations, in order that he may provide means of preventing their identification by the other students or by the Examiners.

11. In the event of any candidate signifying his intention to the Registrar to be examined and registered as a Homœopathic practitioner, due notice of such must be submitted to the Registrar so that the Examinations may be conducted by the parties appointed for that purpose ; prior to the acceptance of such notice from the candidate the usual fees must be paid. In the event of any candidate presenting himself for such examination, due notice must be given by the Registrar to the special Examiner.

12. It is recommended that a professional Examination be held in Toronto on the 2nd Tuesday in October, 1897 ; all candidates who have failed in a former Examination will be required to pay a feé of twenty dollars for this examination. The next professional examination thereafter, we recommend to be held at Toronto and Kingston, on the third Tuesday in May, 1898 (remainder of regulation to stand).

Your committee recommend that the Board of Examiners for 1897-98 be as follows:

Dr. F. LeM. Grasett, Toronto. . . . . *Anatomy, Descriptive.*

Dr. D. E. Mundell, Kingston . . . . . *Theory and Practice of Medicine.*

Dr. H. Howitt, Guelph. . . . . {*Midwifery, Operative and other than Operative, and Puerperal and Infantile Diseases.*

Dr. A. S. Fraser, Sarnia. . . . . *Physiology and Histology.*

Dr. A. B. Welford, Woodstock. . . . *Surgery, Operative and other than Operative.*

Dr. H. Williams, London. . . . . *Medical and Surgical Anatomy.*

Dr. G. Acheson, Galt . . . . *Chemistry, Theoretical and Practical, and Toxicology.*

Dr. H. B. Small, Ottawa. . . . . *Materia Medica and Pharmacy.*

Dr. C. V. Emory, Hamilton. . . . . . . *Medical Jurisprudence and Sanitary Science.*

Dr. C. O'Reilly, Toronto. . . . . *Assistant Examiner to the Examiner on Surgery.*

Dr. J. Third, Kingston . . . . *1st Assistant Examiner to the Examiner on Medicine.*

Dr. W. P. Caven, Toronto . . . . {*2nd Assistant to the Examiner on Medicine, Pathology and Therapeutics.*

Dr. E. J. T. Adams, Toronto. . . . . . *Homœopathic Examiner.*

13. It is recommended that the attention of the Examiners be specially directed to Clause 9 of the Rules and Regulations for the guidance of Examiners.

14. Unless otherwise stated specifically no change in the curriculum of studies fixed by the Council shall come into effect sooner than one year after such change has been made. We recommend that the Registrar be instructed to procure for Examinations as fresh dissections as possible, and that he be authorized to incur such expense as is necessary for this purpose.

(Signed,) W. BRITTON, Chairman.

Dr. ROGERS moved, seconded by Dr. MOORE, that the Rules of Order be now suspended, which, on a vote having been taken, was declared carried.

Dr. EMORY—Has the date of the next meeting of the Council been fixed ?

The PRESIDENT—I do not think it ?

Dr. EMORY—I would like to move that the time be altered, and that we meet in June as heretofore, or as soon as the Registrar says he can have the schedule ready, before the results of the examination are published ; then, if it is seen fit, the Registrar can be instructed to prepare a report of those candidates who have fallen behind in one or two subjects, and they can be taken up and passed upon and that will end all further appeals, and the Committee on Rules and Regulations can perform the functions that Dr. Sangster is so anxious the Board of Examiners should meet to perform, and it will thus save the expense of the Board of Examiners and stop all appeals ; and when the results are out everybody will know whether there has been any change made in the report of the Board of Examiners.

It was moved by Dr. Douglas, seconded by Dr. Moore, and resolved, that the mover have leave to introduce a by-law for the purpose of fixing the time, manner and place for holding examinations and for appointing examiners, and that the by-law be now read a first time.

The President put the motion, which, on a vote having been taken, was declared carried.

Moved by Dr. Douglas, seconded by Dr. Williams, and resolved, that the Council do now go into Committee of the Whole on the by-law fixing the time, manner and place for holding examinations, for the purpose of reading it a second time.

The President put the motion, which, on a vote having been taken, was declared carried.

Council in Committee of the Whole.

Dr. Moore in the chair.

Dr. Williams moved that the by-law be read clause by clause, which, on a vote having been taken, was declared carried.

Dr. Douglas read Clause 1 of the by-law, which, on motion, was adopted.

Dr. Douglas read Clause 2 of the by-law, which, on motion, was adopted.

Dr. Williams moved that the preamble be adopted, which, on a vote having been taken, was declared carried.

Dr. Williams moved that the title be adopted, which, on a vote being taken, was declared carried.

Dr. Williams moved that the Committee do now rise and report the by-law as read in Committee of the Whole, which, on a vote having been taken, was declared carried.

The Committee rose. The President in the chair.

Dr. Douglas moved, seconded by Dr. Williams, that the by-law fixing the time, manner and place of holding the examinations and appointing examiners be now read a third time, finally passed, signed, numbered and sealed with the seal of the College of Physicians and Surgeons of Ontario.

The President put the motion, which, on a vote having been taken, was declared carried, and the by-law adopted as follows :

By-law No. 83.

A BY-LAW TO FIX THE TIME, MANNER AND PLACES FOR HOLDING EXAMINATIONS AND FOR APPOINTING EXAMINERS.

Whereas power has been given to the College of Physicians and Surgeons of Ontario to make By-laws :

1. Be it therefore enacted, and it is hereby enacted, that a Fall examination be held in the College Building, in the City of Toronto, on the second Tuesday of October, 1897 ; and

2. It is further enacted that examinations be conducted in the College Building in Toronto, and in the City Hall, in the City of Kingston, on the third Tuesday of May, 1898, in the manner and form prescribed in the Annual Announcement of the College of Physicians and Surgeons of Ontario, and that the Examiners for the same be as follows :

Board of Examiners, 1897-98.

Dr. F. LeM. Grasett, Toronto, Ont. *Anatomy, Descriptive.*

Dr. D. E. Mundell, Kingston, Ont. *Theory and Practice of Medicine.*

Dr. H. Howitt, Guelph, Ont ...... *Midwifery, Operative, and other than Operative, and Puerperal and Infantile Diseases, etc.*

Dr. A. S. Fraser, Sarnia, Ont. .... *Physiology and Histology.*

Dr. A. B. Welford, Woodstock, Ont. *Surgery, Operative and other than Operative.*

Dr. H. Williams, London, Ont..... *Medical and Surgical Anatomy.*

Dr. G. Acheson, Galt, Ont......... *Chemistry, Theoretical and Practical, and Toxicology.*

Dr. H. B. Small, Ottawa, Ont. .... *Materia Medica and Pharmacy.*

Dr. C. V. Emory, Hamilton, Ont... *Medical Jurisprudence and Sanitary Science.*

Dr. C. O'Reilly, Toronto, Ont..... *Assistant Examiner to the Examiner on Surgery.*

Dr. J. Third, Kingston, Ont....... *1st Assistant Examiner to Examiner on Medicine.*

Dr. W. P. Caven, Toronto, Ont. ... *2nd Assistant to the Examiner on Medicine, Pathology and Therapeutics.*

Dr. Edward T. Adams, Toronto, Ont. *Homœopathic Examiner.*

Adopted.

JAMES THORBURN, President.

Dr. BRITTON presented and read the report of the Committee on Legislation as amended; and moved, seconded by Dr. SANGSTER, that the report be adopted.

Dr. BRITTON—As the mover of the adoption of this report may I have the opportunity of saying one word. The referring of this back to the Committee I think perhaps was, in its bearing towards any person, more important in relation to myself and another. I made certain statements in this report, I am not going to go over any of these, I do not want to take up two minutes, but you will notice in the first clause it is stated, and it is acknowledged that the discussion arose as to the proper course to follow, when presenting the petition, the final conclusion being that the conference with the Government already arranged for should take place and that the attention of the Government should be called to the nature and details of the petition. That was unanimously arrived at and there was no correction ordered to-day with regard to that, there was no dissenting voice when it was read.

Dr. SANGSTER—I dissented from the word "details" to-day. The difficulty lay in the ascription of the word "unanimously,' that the Committee unanimously decided as to the nature and necessity of it; that was not my impression and it was not the impression of several other members of the Committee. I am quite prepared to state the belief that Dr. Britton had that impression, but I had the very opposite impression. That was the whole difference of opinion there. Then at the end of the discussion there was a difference as to what might constitute the presentation of the petition by Dr. Rogers, and I thought Dr. Rogers had over-stepped the mark. It is merely a matter of impression.

Dr. McLAUGHLIN—The reading of the petition seems to me to be contrary ; in one place it mentions the word "details" and in another place it says "general terms." These two things are contrary the one to the other.

Dr. BRITTON—That is exactly as it was ordered to be presented by me now.

The PRESIDENT put the motion, which, on a vote having been taken, was declared carried, and the report adopted as amended, as follows :

To the President and Members of the Medical Council of Physicians and Surgeons of Ontario.

GENTLEMEN,—Your Committee on Legislation beg to report as follows :

On the 22nd of October, 1896, an application was made by S. Alfred Jones, barrister, Toronto, to the Hon. J. M. Gibson on behalf of one Jacob Zielinski, asking that a special Act be passed in the Ontario Legislature for the purpose of licensing said Jacob Zielinski as a member of the College of Physicians and Surgeons of Ontario. Through the courtesy of the Hon. Mr. Gibson, the Registrar of the Medical Council was communicated with and informed as to the nature of the application about to be made, the Hon. Minister intimating that he thought it proper that our Council should be represented at the interview. Hence, as there was not time to convene the General Committee, the members of the Legislative Committee resident in Toronto were asked to be present to resist this attempt to place a man on the Ontario Medical register in such an irregular way, the Committee judging it to be in the interests of the public to oppose any such proceedings.

After both sides of the question had been discussed, the Hon. Minister stated that he could not hold out any hope to the applicant that a Bill would be brought in such as he desired.

On the 13th day of November, 1896, the following letter was received from the solicitor of Jacob Zielinski, but the action threatened therein has not been taken :

Dr. Pyne, Registrar, College Physicians and Surgeons, Corner Bay and Richmond Streets.

DEAR SIR,—Since I saw you the other day I have had a consultation with my client, Dr. Zielinski, and have considered the pro's and con's of his case thoroughly, and am convinced that there is so much of equity and right in the Doctor's contentions that no Committee of the House will throw out his application for a Private Bill.

I have determined, therefore, to press the matter on, and secure this legislation for my client. I regret exceedingly that I shall have to adopt this course in opposition to the wishes of the College of Physicians and Surgeons. The fact of the Bill being passed in spite of the opposition of the College will, of course, entail a great loss of prestige to the College, and it appears to me that this was the reason which the Hon. Mr. Gibson had in mind when he suggested an amicable settlement of the matter, by the College allowing the Doctor to finish his remaining years as a duly qualified physician.

I now write to you again, before I take the formal steps for the passing of the Bill, asking the College to register the Doctor.

Whatever the views of the College may be as to the strict legal rights of the Doctor, they surely must concede that the suggestion of the Hon. Mr. Gibson that they register the Doctor, is one founded in equity, and that the refusal of the College to fall in with Mr. Gibson's suggestion will result in an Act being passed in spite of their opposition

Will you kindly lay the matter before the Governing Committee of your body, and let me have an early reply, as the House meets shortly.

Yours truly,

(Signed,)   S. ALFRED JONES.

November 13th, 1896.

Your Committee met on March 3rd, 1897, Doctors Britton, Barrick, Machell, Rogers, Sangster, Thorburn and Williams being the members present to consider the petition from the profession which had been ordered by the Council to be prepared and presented to the Government and Legislative Assembly. Dr. Britton was elected Chairman. Doctors Rogers and Britton then addressed the Committee, and the Chairman read resolutions adopted by the Council in June, 1896, as follows : At the Annual Meeting of the Ontario Medical Council held in June, 1895, the following resolutions were adopted :

Moved by Dr. HENRY, seconded by Dr. DICKSON, and resolved, "That in the opinion of the Medical Council there should be established a Medical Tariff for the Province of Ontario in order that the reasonable charges or fees of the registered medical practitioners may have a legal status in all courts of law in this Province. That such Medical Tariff should be framed and sanctioned by this Council, but it should only come into legal force when it has received the sanction and approval of three Judges of the Supreme Court of Judicature of Ontario ; that such Medical Tariff, when it comes into legal force as aforesaid, may be printed, and copies of which shall be distributed to the registered medical practitioners of Ontario, and each copy bearing the seal of the College, and the signature of the Registrar attached thereto, shall be received in all courts of law in lieu of the original tariff; that such copies of the said Medical Tariff shall be a scale of reasonable charges within the meaning of Section 39, of the Medical Act." (Carried.)

A. F. ROGERS, President.

Moved by Dr. BRAY, seconded by Dr. DICKSON, "That a form of petition be framed and sent to every medical man in the Province by the Registrar for signatures, praying that the Government and Legislature of Ontario will not alter nor amend the Medical Act, nor introduce, nor carry through any new medical legislation, unless such amendments, or new Medical Act, or Acts, be first submitted to the Council of the College of Physicians and Surgeons of Ontario, directly, or through its Legislative Committee." (Carried.)

Certified true copy.   A. F. ROGERS, President.

R. A. PYNE, Registrar, June, 1896.

Inasmuch as an opinion had been stated by a reliable member of the Legislature that the time was scarcely ripe to urge medical legislation, a discussion arose as to the proper course to follow, the final conclusion being that a conference with the Government, already arranged for, should take place, and that the attention of the Government should be called to the nature and details of the petition, after which the Committee could decide whether or not it would be wise to present the petition to the Legislative Assembly during the existing session. The following resolution was carried :

Moved by Dr. WILLIAMS, seconded by Dr. BARRICK, that the Legislative Committee meet at two o'clock and have a conference with the Government.

The Chairman then took up the petition and read the same clause, the sense of the Committee being that there was necessity for each individual clause, after which it was unanimously agreed upon that the Committee should present the petition to the Government and discuss it in general terms. After which the Committee adjourned to meet at two o'clock.

The Committee met. The Hon. Premier Hardy received the Committee, the following members of the Government being present : Honorables Ross, Dryden, Harcourt, Davis and Gibson.

The President, Dr. Rogers, now addressed the Government on the lines of the understanding arrived at in Committee. Doctors Sangster, Britton and Thorburn also addressed the Government. The petition was now inspected by the Government, the object of the petition being to show the Government that the profession in Ontario unitedly stood together for its rights, and that the principle of harmony manifestly existed in the profession, inasmuch as the petition had been signed by 1,821 members of the College of Physicians and Surgeons of Ontario out of some 2,300.

A Bill to reinstate a tariff of fees which had been framed on the lines of Clause 3 of the petition was not presented to the Assembly, as the time was looked upon as inopportune. The Bill therefore was not discussed before the Government.

This Bill and a copy of the petition are herewith appended.

We advise that the prayer of 1,821 members asking for the legislation provided for in the Bill be brought before the Government and House of Assembly at the earliest date when our medical friends in the House deem it advisable.

All of which is respectfully submitted.

(Signed,) W. BRITTON, Chairman.

AN ACT TO AMEND THE ONTARIO MEDICAL ACT.

Her Majesty, by and with the advice and consent of the Legislative Assembly of the Province of Ontario, enacts as follows :

1. This Act may be cited as the Ontario Medical Act, 1897.

2. The following section is hereby enacted as Section 16 of the Ontario Medical Act in lieu of Section 16 of the said Act heretofore repealed :

16—(1) The Council may from time to time enact, alter and amend a medical tariff, or tariffs, of professional fees, for the Province of Ontario, and such tariff being brought into force as hereinafter provided shall be held to be a scale of reasonable charges within the meaning of Section 39 of this Act.

(2) Such tariff or tariffs or any amendment thereto shall come into force if, and when, it shall receive the sanction and approval of three Judges of the Supreme Court of Judicature of Ontario who may from time to time be nominated for the purpose of revising such tariff by the Lieutenant-Governor in Council.

(3) A copy of such medical tariff, or tariffs, purporting to be the tariff in force for the time being and to have been approved by three Judges as aforesaid, and to have been printed and published by direction of the Council, and having the name of the Registrar of the Council appended thereto shall be *prima facie* evidence of the tariff of reasonable charges in force throughout the Province of Ontario under this Act.

Any person convicted of a second offence under Sections 45, 46 and 47 of the Ontario Medical Act, or any one or more of such sections, shall forfeit and pay a penalty of not less than $100.00, and for the third offence shall be imprisoned in the County jail in the County in which said third offence may be committed for a period of six months without the option of a fine.

On motion of Dr. Williams, the President left the chair and Dr. Brock took the same.

Dr. WILLIAMS—Mr. Chairman, I move that the thanks of this Council be extended to the President for the very pleasant, agreeable, dignified and impartial manner in which he has conducted the business of this Council. I will say that I have known Dr. Thorburn longer nearly than I have known any person, and that I have yet to meet the first person who would intimate in any way that he was not actuated by honesty of purpose. I believe the Council are all fully satisfied that his action in the chair during the present session has been characterized by that line of conduct, and I hope the Council will tender to him a unanimous and hearty vote of thanks.

Dr. SANGSTER—I have much pleasure in seconding that resolution. It was my duty to make some objections to Dr. Thorburn's election at the commencement; they were not objections to him personally, as I trust he knows. I wish to bear evidence to the fact that his conduct in the chair has been dignified and courteous in the extreme. I have never, since my sojourn in the Council, seen the chair as well and efficiently filled, and if it were not inconsistent with my feeling upon the subject, and if it were not against your rules of procedure, I would gladly see Dr. Thorburn remain in that chair every year he remained in the Council.

Dr. MOORE—Everything has been said that could be said. I know he is a modest man and I would not like to taffy him too much, but I must agree with what has been said, that he has filled the chair with dignity and impartiality. He has discharged his duties with dignity and honor to himself as President of this Council, as he has in every other office which he has filled. I trust the blessing of good health may be with him for many years to come.

Dr. GEIKIE—I have nothing to add except to say "amen" to what has already been said. I have not known Dr. Thorburn so long as my friend Dr. Williams because my acquaintance only commenced in the year 1849. However, he was then a kindly young fellow, and he has been a kindly old fellow and a kindly middle-aged man, and now he is a kindly gentleman up in years. I do not think we could have had a better President.

Dr. BROCK put the motion, which, on a vote having been taken, was carried unanimously amid much applause.

Dr. BROCK—Mr. President, I have much pleasure in presenting to you the resolution of thanks, moved by Dr. Williams and seconded by Dr. Sangster, and in adding my own congratulations.

The PRESIDENT—Dr. Williams and I are old friends. I think I am his senior, but I knew him very soon after his arrival in this country, and I feel this compliment coming

14

from him is one of the highest that I have ever had the pleasure of receiving.   Dr. Sangster, I am exceedingly obliged to you for your good wishes, and I have no doubt in my own mind, when you, at the beginning of our session, saw fit to make some remarks that I thought at the time not exceedingly complimentary, you did it on principle and not from any personal motive whatever.   I have tried to fill the chair as best I could, but in the first part of the session I found it pretty large and I had, therefore, at the last to move into a smaller one. (Applause.)   I have endeavored to conduct myself with proper decorum and dignity, and to be fair to all parties, and I heartily appreciate the compliments offered me.   I thank you again, gentlemen, and I hope to have the pleasure of meeting you next year.   (Applause.)

On motion, the REGISTRAR read the minutes of the final session of the Council, which were confirmed, and signed by the President.

Dr. WILLIAMS moved, seconded by Dr. BRITTON, that the Council adjourn, which, on a vote having been taken, was declared carried.

R. A. Pyne, Esq., M.D., College of Physicians and Surgeons, Toronto.

DEAR SIR,—I beg to acknowledge receipt of your letter requesting my opinion upon the questions stated bearing upon the annual fee imposed upon members of College, and the means provided by the Act for the collection thereof.   There is no doubt whatever that Section 41a of "The Ontario Medical Act," requiring payment of the fees before issue of Annual Certificate, etc., was duly brought in force by by-laws Nos. 69 and 75, and that it is not necessary to pass a by-law each year continuing this section which continues in force until repealed or modified by the Council under the authority of 56 Vic., Chap. 27, Sec. 6.

The question as to the legal right of the Council to impose an annual fee for the years 1893 and 1894, when Section 27 of the Act was suspended, presents some little difficulty, but after a careful consideration of the whole question, and having in view the fact that the suspension of Sections 27 and 41a was simply for the purpose of allowing the members to decide whether an annual fee should be paid by them or not, I am of opinion that the Council had the right to impose the fee for these years, as was done by by-law No. 69, and I think that it would have been so held by the Courts had any member of the profession taken proceedings against that by-law.   In any event, however, I am of opinion that the fees for 1893 and 1894, having been imposed by by-law of the Council, every member of the College must pay these fees before he can require the Registrar to issue his annual certificate.

I am of opinion that Section 41a of "The Ontario Medical Act," and particularly ss. 2, 3 and 4 thereof, are applicable to all arrears of the annual assessment and to any other amounts which may have been owing to the College by any practitioner, notwithstanding that some portion thereof may have been barred by the Statute of Limitations so that the College would not be able to recover the amount thereof by suit.   In other words, before a practitioner can obtain his Certificate, he must pay all fees or dues to the College whether barred by the Statute of Limitations or not.

Yours truly,

TORONTO, July 22nd, 1897.   B. B. OSLER.

Certified correct.

JAMES THORBURN, President,

Post Graduate Course

ᴣ ᴣ ᴣ McGILL UNIVERSITY

THE FACULTY OF MEDICINE of McGill University has just completed its second Post Graduate Course. This course of instruction which was given in the various departments of Medicine and Surgery is especially arranged to meet the requirements of the general practitioner who is unable to devote more than a few weeks to the task of overtaking the more recent advances in his profession. The course began May 4th, 1897, and closed June 12th. A similar course will be given in 1898, of which announcement may be obtained from Prof. Ruttan, Registrar. Detailed time-tables were issued weekly.

THE COURSE CONSISTED OF:

A. A Series of Evening Lectures on recent advances in Medicine, Surgery, Pathology, etc., four per week, and included the following among others:—

A Series of four on the "Diagnosis of Abdominal Tumors," by Prof. William Osler.
Two by Prof. James Stewart, viz: "The Hand in diseases of the Nervous System" and "Facial Expression in Nervous Diseases."
"Diagnosis and Treatment of Tuberculous Joints," by Prof. T. G. Roddick.
A series of two by Prof. Adami on "Referred Pain," "Pathology of Internal Secretion," etc.
"Surgery of the Thyroid," by Prof. F. J. Shepherd.
"Genital Tuberculosis," by Prof. William Gardner.
"The early Diagnosis and Treatment of Diphtheria," by Prof. Finley.
Two lectures on "Recent Advances in the Physiology of the Circulation and their relation to Practical Medicine and Surgery," by Prof. Wesley Mills.
"On the Diagnosis and Surgery of Appendicitis," by Prof. James Bell.
"Serum Diagnosis and Serum-therapy," by Dr. C. F. Martin.
"Modern Simple Methods of Disinfection," by Dr. Wyatt Johnston.
"Infant feeding," by Prof. A. D. Blackader.
Two lectures by Prof. Armstrong on "Gallstone Surgery and Hernia."
"Early Diagnosis and Treatment of Tuberculosis," by Prof. Lafleur.
"Climate and Disease," by Dr. Solly, of Colorado.
"The Doctor and Life Insurance," by Prof. Wilkins.

B. General Clinics.—The afternoons of each day were devoted to Clinical work in the wards of the Montreal General and Royal Victoria Hospitals. Clinics in GENERAL SURGERY were given by Profs. Shepherd and Bell. and in GENERAL MEDICINE by Profs. Jas. Stewart, Blackader, Lafleur and Finley.

These clinics were given on four days of each week, and were followed by a Special Clinic and the course in OPERATIVE SURGERY.

The afternoons of the remaining two days of each week were occupied entirely by one or more of the following Special Clinics:

C. Special Clinics.—In OPHTHALMOLOGY, including diseases of the Conjunctiva, Iris, Cornea and Retina, at the Royal Victoria Hospital, by Prof.

F. Buller, and at the Montreal General Hospital, by Dr J. J. Gardner. Special instruction in the use of the Ophthalmoscope was also given.
In GYNÆCOLOGY, at the Royal Victoria Hospital, by Prof. Wm. Gardner and Dr. J. C. Webster, and at the Montreal General Hospital, by Prof. Alloway and Dr. Lockhart.
In LARYNGOLOGY and the use of the Laryngoscope, at the Montreal General Hospital, by Prof. Birkett, and Dr. Hamilton.
In EXTERNAL PALPATION AND ASEPTIC MIDWIFERY, at the Montreal Maternity Hospital, by Prof. J. C. Cameron.
In DISEASES OF CHILDREN, at the Montreal General Hospital, by Prof. A. D. Blackader and G. G. Campbell.
In DERMATOLOGY, at the Montreal General Hospital, by Prof. Shepherd.
In DISEASES OF THE GENITO-URINARY ORGANS, at the Royal Victoria Hospital, by Prof. James Bell.
In ORTHOPÆDICS, at the Montreal General Hospital, by Dr. C. W. Wilson.
In the mornings, from nine to twelve, two or more of the following Special Demonstrations, Laboratory Courses or Laboratory Demonstrations, were given :

D. Special Demonstrations.—These were given, on SURGICAL INSTRUMENTS, by Prof. Armstrong; MENTAL DISEASES, at Verdun Asylum, by Dr. T. J. W. Burgess ; MEDICO-LEGAL AUTOPSY METHODS, by Dr. Wyatt Johnston ; OPERATIVE OBSTETRICS, by Dr. J. C. Cameron.

E. Laboratory Courses.—These were continued for varying periods, for which a small extra fee was charged, enough to cover cost of material, on OPERATIVE SURGERY, by Prof. Armstrong ; CLINICAL BACTERIOLOGY, CLINICAL MICROSCOPY of Dejecta and Blood, by Drs. Wyatt Johnston and Martin ; CLINICAL CHEMISTRY, by Prof. Ruttan, and POST-MORTEM METHODS by Dr. Wyatt Johnston.
The demonstrations in Operative Surgery, Clinical Microscopy, of Dejecta and Blood, and the Clinical Bacteriology, were given throughout the entire course, four or five times per week.

F. Laboratory Demonstrations.—On the PHYSIOLOGY OF THE CIRCULATION AND THE NERVOUS SYSTEM, by Prof. Wesley Mills ; MORBID ANATOMY, by Dr. Wyatt Johnston ; MEDICAL AND SURGICAL ANATOMY, by Drs. Elder and McCarthy ; MICROSCOPICAL METHODS, by Dr. Gunn ; URINALYSIS, by Dr. Ruttan ; SERUM THERAPY AND SERUM DIAGNOSIS OF TYPHOID, by Dr. Martin.

The courses in Dissecting and Operative Surgery, and the Demonstrations in Physiology, were given during the first week.

The fee for the whole course, including fees for both hospitals Royal Victoria and Montreal General, was fifty dollars.

Trinity Medical College

INCORPORATED BY ACT OF PARLIAMENT.

In Affiliation with

TRINITY UNIVERSITY,

UNIVERSITY OF TORONTO,

UNIVERSITY OF MANITOBA.

And specially recognized by the Royal College of Surgeons of England, the Royal College of Physicians of London, the Royal College of Physicians and Surgeons of Edinburgh, and the King's and Queen's College of Physicians of Ireland, and by the Cojoint Examining Boards of London and Edinburgh.

The Summer Session begins in April and lasts ten weeks. The Winter Session begins during the first week of October of each year, and lasts Six Months, until the Eight Months Session is generally adopted.

For Summer or Winter Session announcements and all other information in regard to LECTURES, FEES, SCHOLARSHIPS, MEDALS, ETC., apply to W. B. GEIKIE, Dean of the Medical Faculty, 52 Maitland Street, Toronto.

GUY'S CARRIAGES

MANUFACTURERS
OF

Doctors'

Carts and

Phaetons

This is a cut of solid comfort **"STANHOPE"** **WAGGON.** Fine display of Carriages of all Kinds. **PONY and PERRY CARTS** a specialty.

Matthew Guy's Carriage Works,

⚘ ⚘ ⚘ 129-131 QUEEN ST. EAST TORONTO.

LYMAN SONS & CO. ESTABLISHED IN 1800

Surgical, Dental and

Veterinary Instruments

Bacteriological Apparatus, Chemical and Hospital Glassware.

Agents for Leitz Microscopes, Arnold Sterilizers, Chloride of Silver Dry Cell Batteries and Current Controllers.

LEITZ NEW MODEL.

THE....

NEW MARSH

Stethophone

WITH

ALUMINUM DISK,
LOCALIZER,
AND DIAL

for modifying or intensifying sound. Guaranteed absolutely perfect.

SEND FOR CIRCULARS

Aluminum...

Spit Cups

Ether Cones

Tongue Depressors

Urine Test Sets

Micro Stains
"   Slides
"   Covers

AND ALL OTHER

Microscopic Accessories.

Roux's Antitoxin and Syringes

Mulford's Antitoxin and Syringes

Anti-tetanus Serum (Human and Veterinary)

SEND FOR FREE ILLUSTRATED CATALOGUE.

Lyman Sons & Co., SURGICAL SPECIALISTS AND WHOLESALE DRUGGISTS.

380-386 ST. PAUL ST., MONTREAL.

The Medical Faculty of . . . . .

Cbe Western University

Will Open its Sixteenth Session on

MONDAY, OCTOBER 4th, 1897

In their College Building, Cor. York and Waterloo Sts., London, Ont.

EACH SESSION will extend over a period of 6 months and will consist of lectures both Didactic and Clinical. Demonstrations will be given in the Dissecting Room and various Laboratories. Ample opportunities for clinical instructions are afforded in the London General Hospital and the various city charities. Every effort will be made to make each course as thorough and practical as possible.

LECTURES for final students will be so arranged that they will be completed in the forenoon, leaving the afternoon free for dispensing and hospital work.

THE MEDICAL FACULTY of the Western University is recognized by the College of Physicians and Surgeons of Ontario ; Royal College of Physicians and Surgeons, Edinburgh and Ireland, and the Faculty of Physicians and Surgeons, Glasgow.

FULL INFORMATION concerning Teachers' Fees, Medals, Scholarships, Certificates of Honor, Graduation, etc., will be given in the ANNUAL ANNOUNCEMENT, which can be obtained by addressing the Dean,

DR. MOORHOUSE, 247 Queens Ave.

Or, the Registrar, **Dr. Waugh, 537 Talbot St.** . . . LONDON

STODDART'S Patented Veneered
SURGICAL SPLINTS

These splints mark a great advance in the use of scientific appliances in surgery and fill a want long felt by every surgeon.

They consist of sixty-six pieces, each moulded to fit perfectly some part of the body and provide a splint for every kind of fracture or dislocation, thus covering the entire range of surgical fractures.

Every objection to the splints heretofore in use has been overcome by the "**Stoddart's Patented Veneered Surgical Splints,**" which are stronger, lighter and cheaper than any splints now upon the market. The "Stoddart's Patented Veneered Surgical Splints" weigh but one-half that of any others, and are equally as strong. This renders them applicable in many cases of severe sprain or dislocation, where a heavier splint could not be used or would be exceedingly uncomfortable. Their very low price allows of their being used indiscriminately by the surgeon, who formerly was obliged to make his own splints.

In the production of the "Patented Veneered Surgical Splints,' we have demonstrated that it is not necessary to weigh a patient down with heavy or cumbersome metallic, wood or felt splints, but that a light splint, equally as strong as any of these, may be used.

In placing these splints before the profession we would call particular attention to the following points of excellence: they may be cut and shaped with a pocket knife; they are pliable, and therefore require very little padding; they will not warp, are aseptic, waterproof, and, notwithstanding their lightness, meet fully all requirements as to strength.

We are satisfied that the "**Stoddart's Patented Veneered Surgical Splints**" will fill a great want in surgery, and that progressive physicians and surgeons will give them a most hearty welcome.

A. Hamilton & Co., WHOLESALE CANADIAN AGENS Hamilton, Ont.

University of Toronto

MEDICAL FACULTY

Professors, Lecturers and Demonstrators

J. H. RICHARDSON, M.D., Tor., Prof. of Anat'y.

A. PRIMROSE, M.B., C.M., Edin. Professor of Anatomy, and Director of the Anatomical Department; Secretary of the Faculty.

H. WILBERFORCE AIKINS, B.A., M.B., Tor., Associate Professor of Anatomy.

F. N. G. STARR, M.B., Tor., Lect. in Anatomy.

W. B. THISTLE, M.D., Tor.⎫
A. R. GORDON, M.R., Tor. ⎪
F. WINNETT, M.D., Tor.   ⎬ Assistant
B. E. MACKENZIE, B.A.,   ⎪ Demonstrators
 M.D. McGill.   ⎪ of Anatomy.
R. D. RUDOLF, M.B., C.M., ⎪
 Edin.   ⎪
B.C. H. HARVEY, B.A., Tor.⎭

I. H. CAMERON, M.B., Tor., Prof. of Surgery and Clinical Surgery.

G. A. PETERS, M.B., Tor., Associate Prof. of Surgery and Clinical Surgery.

A. PRIMROSE, M.B., C.M., Edin.⎫
B. SPENCER, M.D., Tor.   ⎬ Assoc. Profs.
L. M. SWEETNAM, M.B., Tor.   ⎪ of
H. A. BRUCE, M.B., Tor.   ⎭ Clin. Surg.

JOHN CAVEN, B.A., M.D., Tor., Professor of Pathology.

J. J. MACKENZIE, B.A., Tor., Lecturer on Bacteriology.

JOHN AMYOT, M.B., Tor., Demonstrator of Pathology.

J. E. GRAHAM, M.D., Tor., Professor of Medicine and Clinical Medicine.

A. McPHEDRAN, M.B., Tor., Associate Prof. of Medicine and Clinical Medicine.

W. P. CAVEN, M.B., Tor., Associate Professor of Clinical Medicine.

H. T. MACHELL, M.D., Tor.⎫ Lecturers on Dis-
W. B. THISTLE, M.B., Tor.⎬ ease in Children
                         ⎭ and Clin. Med.

R. J. DWYER, M.B., Tor.⎫ Lecturers on
G. BOYD, B.A., M.B., Tor.⎭ Clinical Medicine.

JAMES M. MCCALLUM, B.A., M.D., Tor., Prof of Pharmacology and Therapeutics.

C. F. HEEBNER, Phm. B., Tor., Associate Prof. of Pharmacology and Therapeutics.

UZZIEL OGDEN, M.D., Tor., Prof. of Gynæcology.

A. H. WRIGHT, B.A., M.D., Tor., Prof. of Obstetrics.

J. F. W. ROSS. M.B., Tor., Associate Professor of Gynæcology.

R. A. REEVE, B.A., M.D., Tor., Professor of Ophthalmology and Otology, Dean of the Faculty.

G. H. BURNHAM, M.D., Tor., Associate Prof. of Ophthalmology and Otology.

G. R. MCDONAGH, M.D., Tor., Associate Prof. of Laryngology and Rhinology.

W. OLDRIGHT, M.A., M.D., Tor., Prof. of Hyg'ne.

W. H. ELLIS, M.A., M.D., Tor., Lect. in Toxicology.

BERTRAM SPENCER, M.D., Tor., Associate Professor of Medical Jurisprudence.

Hon. DAVID MILLS, LL.B., Q.C., Legal Lecturer in Medical Jurisprudence.

DANIEL CLARK, M.D., Tor., Extra-Mural Professor of Medical Psychology.

R. RAMSAY WRIGHT, M.A., B.Sc., Edin., Professor of Biology.

A. B. MACALLUM, B.A., M.B., Tor., Ph.D., Johns Hopkins, Professor of Physiology.

R. R. BENSLEY, B.A., M.B., Tor., Assistant Demonstrator in Biology.

WM. H. PIKE, M.A., Ph.D., Prof. of Chemistry.

W. H. ELLIS, M.A., M.B., Tor. Lect. in Chem.

W. L. MILLER, B.A., Ph.D., Demonst'r of Chem.

JAMES LOUDON, M.A., Professor of Physics.

C. A. CHANT, B.A., Tor., Lecturer on Physics.

The regular course of instruction will consist of Four Sessions of six months each, commencing October 4th.

There will be a distinct and separate course for each of the four years.

The lectures and demonstrations in the subjects of the First and Second years will be given in the Biological Laboratory and the lecture-rooms of the University.

Lectures and demonstrations in the subjects of the Third and Fourth years will be given in the building of the Medical Faculty, corner of Gerrard and Sackville streets.

Clinical teaching (largely bedside) in the Toronto General Hospital, Burnside Lying-in Hospital, St. Michael's Hospital, Victoria Hospital for Sick Children, and other medical charities of Toronto.

R. A. REEVE, B.A., M.D.,
Dean.

A. PRIMROSE, M.B.,
Secretary,
Biological Department, University of Toronto.

CPSIA information can be obtained
at www.ICGtesting.com
Printed in the USA
BVHW041036210219
540828BV00009B/496/P